How the Internet
Became Commercial

KAUFFMAN FOUNDATION SERIES ON
Innovation and Entrepreneurship

How the Internet Became Commercial

Innovation, Privatization, and the Birth of a New Network

Shane Greenstein

Princeton University Press
Princeton and Oxford

Published by Princeton University Press, 41 William Street,
Princeton, New Jersey 08540
In the United Kingdom: Princeton University Press, 6 Oxford Street,
Woodstock, Oxfordshire OX20 1TW
press.princeton.edu

Jacket art © Rawpixel/Shutterstock

Library of Congress Cataloging-in-Publication Data

Greenstein, Shane M.
How the Internet became commercial : innovation, privatization, and the birth of a new
network / Shane Greenstein.
pages cm. — (The Kauffman foundation series on innovation and entrepreneurship)
Includes bibliographical references and index.
ISBN 978-0-691-16736-7 (hardcover : alk. paper) 1. Internet—Economic aspects. 2. Internet
industry—History. 3. Information technology—Economic aspects. 4. Telecommunication—
Technological innovations. 5. Entrepreneurship. I. Title.
HC79.I55G744 2015
384.3—dc23
2015016998

British Library Cataloging-in-Publication Data is available

Published in collaboration with the Ewing Marion Kauffman
Foundation and the Berkley Center for Entrepreneurial Studies,
New York University

This book has been composed in Palatino LT Std

Printed on acid-free paper. ∞

Printed in the United States of America

1 3 5 7 9 10 8 6 4 2

To Eli, Ilana, Rebecca, Noah, and Ranna.

Thank you for so much patience and love.

Contents

INTRODUCTION

1

Ubiquitous Clicks and How It All Started

I think the press has a tendency to pick a person and paint them 10 feet tall. In fact, each of us does a little piece and I've done one thing, people add on that and then another. So you get credit for doing the whole damn thing, and that's not so.
—*Paul Baran, after receiving the National Medal of Technology and Innovation*[1]

One day I watched my children use the Internet and soon found myself talking with them about the Internet in the same effusive way my immigrant grandparents talked about the wonders of electricity and the magic of transcontinental air flights. My kids just shrugged their shoulders at their father's dramatics and went back to surfing the web and playing online games.

My children cannot imagine a world without the Internet. Clicks are familiar. Hasn't it always been so?

Modern economies frequently change frontier technologies into widely used ones—from the mysterious to the unremarkable. The Internet was once exotic to all but a small set of cognoscenti, but long ago the technology spread to a majority of households and businesses. In the process of becoming ubiquitous it transformed how we work and live—changing how consumers behave, and altering how firms provide products and services.

---

[1] The quote comes from Cassidy (2011).

My children are not alone in their shrugs. Most adults today could not say where the Internet came from and how its spread caused so many transformative changes. Not only does that hold for many educated adults, it also holds for many of society's thought leaders. I have met many educated economists who know a great deal about many technologies, and yet they lack any view about the general economic lessons the Internet's spread illustrates. I have met many perceptive legal scholars and policy analysts with a similar gap in their understanding.

I have also met many who do not shrug, who are curious, especially among those too young to have lived through the relevant events. Can a knowledgeable observer explain how and why the Internet deployed as it did? To what do we attribute its impact? Can those recent events yield insights that help understand technology in the future? They do not know where to go to answer their curiosity. Many key events were genuinely complex, and, at times, involved a vast ensemble of participants with distinct motives and alternative points of view. It is not obvious where to start.

This book addresses this curiosity and points it to the deeper mystery behind the surface of events. The Internet's deployment is commonly held responsible for an economic boom. Along with that boom, and in less than one generation, the names of the leading suppliers of communications changed. So too did the predominant view for forecasting how the underlying technology in communications would evolve. To the common eye all these changes occurred in less than a decade, which is extraordinarily fast by historical standards. Any of these would be rare to see in any industry. The combination—economic boom, change in leadership, alteration of the common forecast, and rapid change—is rarer still in the history of modern capitalism. These are typically associated with only the most transformative technologies, such as the steam engine, the railroad, electricity, indoor plumbing, and the automobile. Such a combination of events merits an explanation in its own right, because the history of capitalism suggests this should not happen often, if at all.

Existing explanations leave a gap, however. While many rich and wonderful histories have been written about the invention of the Internet, most focus on just invention. That yields an answer rich in technical details and incomplete in perspective. It diminishes the role of markets and government policies for markets. Writing about policy addresses some of that gap but tends to stress legal issues, regulatory debates, and changes in court decisions. It overlooks economic incentives and the behavior policy induces from suppliers and users.

To say it broadly, comparatively less writing focuses on explaining the Internet's innovation and commercialization. Innovation is the act of turning invention into something useful, while commercialization translates innovations into valuable products and services. Innovation and commercialization must connect to each other because both involve market activities, such as building the production and distribution processes to deliver a new service to customers. That summarizes the motivation behind this book and its outlook. It is not possible to explain the deeply surprising and unique aspects of these events—economic boom, change in leadership, alteration of the common forecast, and rapid change—only with technology and policy analysis. It also requires understanding how innovation commercialized, that is, how innovations became valuable as the Internet evolved within commercial markets.

The commercialization of the Internet merits attention for a related reason—it illuminates important relationships between transformation in industrial structure and innovation. How can innovation have such a transformative role in the restructuring of industries? Specifically, replacing one economic structure with another is often called the process of "creative destruction," and a crucial question of this book might be rephrased as "What role does innovation and commercialization play in creative destruction?"

This rephrased question needs a little refining because the phrase "creative destruction" has become an overused colloquial expression. To get clear on its meaning, return to its most famous user, Joseph Schumpeter. In his 1942 book *Capitalism, Socialism, and Democracy* he describes creative destruction as an inherent property of market-based capitalist systems.

> Capitalism, then, is by nature a form or method of economic change and not only never is but never can be stationary. . . . The fundamental impulse that sets and keeps the capitalist engine in motion comes from the new consumers' goods, the new methods of production or transportation, the new markets, the new forms of industrial organization that capitalist enterprise creates. . . . This process of Creative Destruction is the essential fact about capitalism.

Schumpeter argues that little is permanent in market economies, and such impermanence serves a useful purpose in the face of large dominant firms. The market value of dominance will motivate new firms to aspire to reach a similar position, principally through creating and promulgating innovations. This activity motivates incumbent firms to fend off such entrants, also by innovating and offering those innovations in commercial markets. Altogether, says Schumpeter, more innovation results from the tournament to become a dominant monopolist, and, relatedly, from defending a lucrative monopoly position by innovating faster than those who threaten it.

Schumpeter's conceptualization directs attention at the role of contests to become monopolies in innovative activities, but it leaves open critical questions about how to best organize such a tournament in a market-based system. Many writers have considered that topic in a variety of technologies and time periods, and this book does as well, and does so in the case of the commercial Internet in the 1990s. Now a core motivation for the book can be rephrased into a seemingly simple retrospective question: What aspects of market structure played an essential role in fostering the growth and development of creative destruction during the deployment of the Internet?

The book's answer to this question focuses primarily on the experience in the United States. Why do this when the commercial Internet has reached a global scale in operation and in final service markets? In part, the US experience generates a coherent analysis and a surprising narrative. Many of the most important early innovations took place in the United States under the stewardship of the US government. The transition out of US government stewardship had a profound impact on how the Internet shaped commercial markets. The Internet also grew rapidly due to some unique structural features of the market for communications in the United States, as well as some unique environmental factors supporting entrepreneurial ventures. Many of these economic factors are not widely appreciated, and focusing on them yields novel insights.

Concentrating on the US experience also directs critical analysis and skepticism toward one the most controversial and important lessons from this experience—the role of government policy in fostering economic growth through encouraging innovation. No expert doubts that the US government played an important role in events—as buyer, lawmaker, regulator, and booster—but there is considerable debate about whether its role was salutary and purposeful. Did government policy and action nurture a positive outcome, or did the key features of the outcome arise in spite of the government role? If government actions helped, what mechanism brought about positive contributions, and why, and when can a government use such policies again? If government policy was a hindrance, what should a government avoid doing? This book aims to identify and sharpen the answers to these questions with a comprehensive examination of the experience. The focus on innovation and commercialization will lead to policy lessons that can carry over to commercialization of other technologies.

The focus on the United States also was a pragmatic choice. There were many networks around the world, and some of them, such as Minitel in France, achieved large-scale use and met some benchmarks of success. Some attempts at standardization of networking, such as the efforts put into open systems interconnection (OSI), did not realize their aspirations before folding some of their successes into the overwhelming advance of the Internet. It is certainly plausible that comparison between countries— for example, between the economic experiences within the United States, Japan, and many European countries—could identify additional factors that shaped outcomes. The required detail is simply beyond my grasp, however. Comparative questions will remain for another analyst to explore and explain.

One of the other goals of this book is to identify the grain of truth in well-known economic myths, and to dismiss the falsehoods. Economic myths are misleading economic metaphors. Usually an economic myth is based on a misreading of a short story or aphorism, and it points away from the key lessons of an event. Many economic myths purport to explain how the Internet developed in the United States, and some of them will be familiar to most readers merely from reading the news. Many economic myths about the Internet have not been confronted by scrutiny. This book must confront many of those myths and correct them.

Perhaps the most pernicious of those myths is *Internet exceptionalism.* This is the belief that the Internet followed its own unique economic rules, having little in common with other important historical episodes. This belief was common in the United States during the late 1990s, voiced with enthusiasm by participants in the dot-com boom, primarily in the entrepreneurial sector. Internet exceptionalism also can be an ideology that overly stresses the role of the unique features of Internet technology in commercial events. It misattributes most novel economic gains to technical causes, and was commonly espoused by those entrepreneurs familiar with the Internet's technical features. All flavors of Internet exceptionalism relegate economic analysis of commercial behavior and incentives to secondary status and deemphasize or overlook the influence of commercial markets in fostering or discouraging innovation. This book argues that Internet exceptionalism is just plain wrong, that it can be replaced with a coherent and sound economic explanation, and, crucially, that this explanation must serve as the foundation for understanding the broader lessons about the Internet's evolution, for explaining the innovation that took place, and for analyzing the causes behind creative destruction.

Replacing myth with sound economics faces numerous challenges when it comes to the Internet because no single participant experienced the entire event. No single story can narrate its causes. In the 1990s there was no such thing as a typical Internet company or a typical Internet strategy, or a typical user of the Internet or typical application for the Internet. There also was no such thing as an advanced plan for the Internet, and no single organization orchestrated the design, building, and operation of the Internet. The relevant experiences span multiple generations of participants from a varied set of backgrounds—for example, government laboratory managers, university computer science graduate students, Internet service providers and their commercial cousins in bulletin board firms, start-up veterans and founders, and platform software makers, among many other participants.

That requires a book that mixes stories, economic insight, and general lessons. Accordingly, this book employs a framework for each chapter that generates this mix. Each chapter will begin with one story. Each story motivates a broader examination of a specific question or set of questions about commercialization, which the chapter pursues. In the end, each chapter provides a few general economic insights and lessons. The conclusion reviews those insights and shows how the lessons fit together under one framework.

What role do the stories play? This is easier to illustrate than to explain in general terms. Here are three examples of such stories:

- Chapter 2 begins with a story describing the experience of assistant attorney general William F. Baxter. He visited the White House just prior to the divestiture of AT&T. The White House did not intervene in the divestiture, and that nonevent is the first of many to motivate inquiries about planning the Internet. Did any single decision maker or executive orchestrate the Internet in a top-down fashion? Generally no, and, as later chapters show, despite some bumps in the road, it turned out well for society.

- Chapter 6 begins with a historical story, the beginning of the California gold rush in 1848. This story motivates analysis of the conditions that produced the temporal concentration of economic activity, which common language labels as a "rush." Understanding the detail of the story begins the broad inquiry into whether events in 1995 actually resembled a gold rush. It did, but not for too long, and, as later chapters explain, something other than a gold rush explains why the boom sustained itself and eventually crashed.

- Chapter 13 starts with a discussion about the policies that governed National Science Foundation (NSF) funding of research. It shows how the NSF's flexible policies helped two Stanford professors, Hector Garcia-Molina and Terry Winograd, and their students, among them Larry Page and Sergey Brin. The latter two founded Google with a project that started in their professor's labs. This story begins a larger narrative about how markets renew themselves with new ideas that run contrary to assumed wisdom. Did the NSF intend to renew the market? No, that was not the direct intent of its funding. However, the flexibility of their funding process helped indirectly, because it raised the chances that the research would be relevant. In the end, society benefited from that flexibility.

These are just three examples among many, and they illustrate the general challenge in a book with these goals. Commercialization of any major technology, including the Internet, does not involve one individual in one location in one time period. Each participant's story draws on details that reside in different organizations and distinct time periods. Each story illuminates distinct economic forces, decisions, and policies. In each case the story drives toward understanding the sound economic reasoning illustrated by events. The larger narrative is comprised of many of these stories and insights because no single insight or story could or should address the key questions motivating the book. This topic requires an economic narrative with wide scope that integrates many insights.

Innovation from the Edges

This book is more than stories; it describes general economic principles and analyzes connections between cause and effect using economic analysis. It shows how different factors worked in the same direction or against one another to produce the observed outcome. The book distinguishes among three categories of causes—economic archetypes, government policies, and influential institutions:

- *Economic archetypes* are patterns of economic behavior that reflect economic forces and principles that manifest repeatedly in different episodes. Economic archetypes are not unique to the Internet and have appeared in other markets or time periods.
- *Government policies* shape behavior and outcomes with the force of law or regulatory authority. These policies are either inherited, reflecting the legacy of prior legal or regulatory decisions, or they are chosen for anticipated impact, reflecting the preferences, wisdom, and foolishness of those with legal or regulatory authority.
- *Influential institutions* describe business practices and social norms that shape actions, though not necessarily with economic motive as the primary driver. These norms often exist for sensible reasons, and sometimes they exist for independent reasons that are unconnected to their economic impact.

What is one goal of the book's analysis? Said succinctly, this book identifies the economic archetypes, government policies, and influential institutions that shaped the growth and evolution of the commercial Internet. More specifically, the book asks whether specific economic archetypes, government policy, and influential institutions encouraged or discouraged innovation from the edges. It also analyzes which economic archetypes, government policies, and influential institutions played an essential role in generating a large economic impact from innovation from the edges.

Longtime aficionados of communications policy may recognize the phrase, "innovation from the edges." In its original use it typically describes experiments in communications markets, often using new wireless technologies outside of major urban markets, where the impact is (typically) small but the discretion to experiment is large. This book appropriates the phrase and employs a more expansive meaning. For the purposes of this book, *innovation from the edges* describes innovation being commercialized by suppliers who lacked power in the old market structure, who the central firms regarded as peripheral participants in the supply of services, and who perceived economic opportunities outside of the prevailing view. This definition embeds three related interpretations—stressing place, power, or perceptions.

Consider the interpretation around "place." An *edge* can refer to a distant *place*, an area far from a central location, such as the edge of town. *Innovation from the edges* refers to innovations coming from a dispersed set of places, and each place is located away from a central location. In that sense *innovation from the edges* refers to a pervasive feature of the Internet historical experience: many key innovations for the Internet came from contributors in a widely dispersed set of places. Those innovations were added to, or competed against, the contributions that came from the central locations. The book asks: How and why did some innovations come from places outside the center, and why was that largely a positive experience?

There is another way to interpret *innovation from the edges*. It brings to mind "power" structures in markets. For example, in many markets a large powerful firm inhabits the leadership position, while many less powerful firms live in its shadow in the periphery. In this sense *edge* refers to less-powerful peripheral supplier and their customers, and accordingly, *innovation from the edges* describes innovation arising from firms and users that leading firms perceived to be on the periphery. That sense also fits a pervasive feature of the historical experience for the Internet: many of the key innovations came from the seemingly less powerful and more peripheral participants—research laboratories, bulletin board firms, start-ups of all stripes, consultancies, and iconoclasts working with distinct outlooks. The book asks: How and why did so many seemingly powerless players have such a large influence on so many commercial episodes, and why did that have such a positive influence on outcomes?

A third interpretation of *innovation from the edges* refers to "perceptions." The sources of information reflect the edges of perception at the leading firms. In this sense, the edge refers to a place beyond the horizon of a vision, a perception that fell outside of known forecasts or prevailing points of view. That captures one other pervasive feature of the historical experience: many of the key innovations fell outside known forecasts and predictions and were unanticipated by established firms in computing and communications. The book asks: How and why did the Internet's deployment lead many firms to reconsider their perceptions about how the Internet could contribute to the generation of market value, and how did changing perceptions shape outcomes?

Why did innovation from the edges play such a large role? Many chapters will stress the importance of uncertainty over the level of value the Internet could create, and how it could be created. To say it concisely, there often was genuine disagreement among experts about the sources of value in Internet markets. The situation supported different opinions about the strategic actions for firms to take. Not every participant perceived the value of the opportunities, or possessed the same assets for taking advantage of the opportunities. Decentralized decision was far better at enabling exploratory actions than a central decision-making process, often because it enabled actions by entrepreneurial actors with distinct points of view.

As it turned out in the United States in this time, innovation from the edges also played a large role because policy allowed it to. Many innovative participants who came from the edges were unrestrained by barriers or frictions, and policy played a role in fostering the low barriers and frictions (in a sense explained in the book). These aspects of the situation are complex or involve obscure detail, so they are often underappreciated. Accordingly, the book spends some extra effort providing details about policy and explaining their pertinence to economic behavior and outcomes.

Schumpeter would have forecast the narrative arc of this book: mainstream firms who had traditionally assumed leadership roles were threatened by innovation from others, and they reacted by innovating. The book also argues that much of this innovation would not have occurred in the absence of innovation from the edges. By fostering creative destruction, innovation from the edges created value much faster and with greater success than any single organization ever could have.

The Layout of the Narrative

The book makes one additional important compromise: it starts its narrative in the late 1980s when the Internet began to "privatize." Privatization involved the change in the ownership status of public assets associated with operating the Internet, changing them into private assets. Privatization involved a complex process, withdrawing the government from ownership and management of the Internet backbone, and substituting private or collective not-for-profit organizations in every instance. The earliest two chapters describe this process.

There is a reason to start then, and it goes to the core of this book's novelty. First, while it is always possible to go further back in time, for this book's purposes most of the important commercial events take place after privatization, primarily in the 1990s. Second, the book focuses on something only peripherally explored by others—namely, the links between innovation, privatization, and the birth of the commercial Internet. Again, the key events for that purpose occur after privatization. Said another way, this book has little new insight to offer about events in the 1970s and 1980s, prior to privatization. Many scholars and commentators have covered these events, as the footnotes and references will document. The book develops plenty of novel insight about later events, and that is where the book focuses its attention.

That does not mean the book can ignore events prior to privatization. Privatization occurs after the Internet already has incubated under government stewardship for a considerable time in the 1970s and 1980s. At first a military research organization had sole responsibility for managing the precursors to the Internet. A new era began in 1985, when the National Science Foundation accepted responsibility for managing the aspect of the Internet that supported research throughout universities. Privatization began during this second era, around 1989, and eventually brought about the end of government stewardship.

For readers not steeped in the history of the Internet, it will be challenging to appreciate the narrative without understanding a few events prior to privatization. Chapter 2 must recall some of these events. In addition, the end of this introduction presents a brief explanation of events prior to privatization—just enough to meet the needs of a novice to this topic. (A reader who knows the history of the Internet's invention can skip this section and go to chapter 2.)

The logic about where to start the book also determines where to end it—namely, around 2003. The book focuses on a number of events shaped directly or indirectly by privatization. That encompasses many of the events affiliated with the economic boom of the late 1990s. It does not include many events after the dot-com bust, but it does include some important events whose origins can be traced indirectly to privatization, such as, the birth of wireless Internet access, commonly called Wi-Fi, which has deep roots dating to policy decisions in the 1980s. It also covers the rise of search supported by advertising, as founded by Google, which also traces its origins to research conducting just as privatization got underway.

Now I will describe the organization of the book. The book collects its chapters into three distinct sections that cover partially overlapping sequences of related events. The first section contains four chapters. It focuses on understanding how privatization occurred and why it had such a large impact on commercial markets. The second section contains five chapters. It focuses on understanding why so many disparate participants seem to act in concert after privatization, all investing at the same time, fostering a boom in economic activity. The third section contains four chapters. These chapters highlight how and why many participants in the economy did or did not undertake "exploratory" actions, creating and developing new commercial services embedding Internet technology.

Begin with the first group of chapters. Seen from the perspective of participants in 1989, the Internet had accumulated many of the pieces of the modern Internet. For example, the infrastructure had been successfully engineered to support a packet switching network, and it daily handled a large volume of electronic mail and file transfers, and demand appeared poised to continue to grow. The most vexing issues about privatization were not technical, but institutional, legal, and commercial in nature. The first group of chapters is called "The Transition," and it is comprised of chapters 2 through 5. These chapters identify factors in privatization that created innovation from the edges. Table 1.1 presents a chronology of the notable events touched on by this group of chapters.

As chapter 2 describes, the Internet should not be understood solely as a network technology. Even prior to privatization, groups met regularly to facilitate the Internet's growth and development. While no single administrator controlled or planned the Internet, the outlines for what became the Internet's "governance" already existed in this era. That insight helps understand what had to change to accommodate privatization, which is the topic of the next chapter.

Chapter 3 focuses on the privatization process itself and highlights several key policy decisions that shaped the evolution of the Internet. It highlights the decisions that turned out to be crucial for later commercial experience, such as NSF's decision to set up the commercial Internet as a competitive market and not a monopoly. Although that might seem like an obvious policy

TABLE 1.1. Chronology: The Transition
Selected notable events from chapters 2, 3, 4, and 5

Year	Chapter	Notable Event
1990	2, 3	NSF conducts conversations about privatization
	3	PSINet and UUNET begin first full year as private firms
1991	3	High Performance Computing Act of 1991 passed
	4	Tim Berners-Lee downloads code for web to shareware sites
	3	Commercial Internet eXchange (CIX) founded
1992	3	Network Solutions takes control of domain name system
	3	Rick Boucher sponsors a bill to amend NSF charter
	3	Internet Society founded and IETF becomes part of it
1993	3	Final NSF plan for privatization emerges, and NSF solicits bids
	4	Mosaic browser made for Unix and Windows OS
	5	Earliest ads for ISPs appear in *Boardwatch Magazine*
1994	4	Founding of the World Wide Web Consortium
	4	Mosaic Communications Company (MCC) founded
	4	MCC changes name to Netscape, and releases a beta browser
1995	4	Apache formed from different versions of NCSA HTTPd server
	3	NSFNET shutdown, and Internet backbone privatized
	5	Netscape IPO and Windows 95 launched in same month
1996	5	Congress passes the 1996 Telecommunications Act
	5	More than 2,000 ISPs advertise in *Boardwatch Magazine*

choice in retrospect, the NSF did not reach it by a straight path. The chapter explains how that happened, and begins to explain why the consequences from privatization turned out to be so difficult for contemporaries to forecast.

After commercialization of the Internet many participants online tended to treat the Internet and the web as synonymous, even though their blending obscures the origins and economic functions of the network and the software layered on top of it. The Internet refers to the vast networking infrastructure that connects computers, while the World Wide Web became a layer of software that enables browser-based applications over the Internet. Chapter 4 considers how a number of policies shaped the transfer of the web's technology out of universities and into commercial markets. Once again, these events were crucial for later commercial outcomes and are often unappreciated.

The Internet did not grow in an isolated research lab, and it did not privatize in a commercial setting that started from scratch. Chapter 5 puts the spotlight on the eclectic and entrepreneurial communities outside of the government who would play a crucial role in building commercial Internet service providers, or ISPs. ISPs provided access to the Internet to homes and businesses in exchange for a fee. The ISP market was not particularly large until after privatization, and this chapter helps understand where many of the entrepreneurs came from. Many came from the bulletin-board industry. This chapter also focuses on understanding why—a short time after privatization—their presence fostered innovation from the edges.

The book then turns to explaining how the Internet "gold rush" emerged—when investment, adoption, and new formation of firms all grew at the same time. It concludes by showing that the metaphor of the "gold rush" both informs and misleads. The metaphor describes only an early part of the experience, while later chapters show that other metaphors provide a more satisfying economic explanation for why growth persisted. A deeper explanation analyzes the new commercial value chain for services related to the commercial Internet. A value chain is a set of interrelated activities that together produce a final product of value greater than the incremental value of each part. All mature industries have a value chain. The next section, chapters 6 through 10, examines events in the middle of the 1990s, when this value chain grew. These chapters compose the section "The Blossoming." Table 1.2 provides a chronology of notable events from this group of chapters.

The first chapter in this group grapples with the economics of a gold rush. Chapter 6 explains the relationships among privatization, the creation of the web, and the timing and bunching of investment at one time. The creation of the first commercial browser, in particular, resulted in a catalyst for action by many private actors. Why? It was a catalyst, because it was a working prototype of a commercial product that showed how to deliver valuable functionality to users. While plenty of technical histories

TABLE 1.2. Chronology: The Blossoming
Selected notable events from chapters 6, 7, 8, 9, 10

Year	Chapter	Notable Event
1992	7	David Clark speaks of "Rough Consensus and Running Code"
	7	Internet Society founded and IETF becomes part of it
	7	Tim Berners-Lee first visits the IETF to standardize the web
1993	8	Louis Gerstner hired as CEO at IBM
	7	CERN renounces ownership rights to World Wide Web code
	8	Earliest ads for ISPs appear in *Boardwatch Magazine*
1994	6	Vermeer founded, begins work on web-authoring tools
	7	Tim Berners-Lee founds the World Wide Web Consortium
	6	Brad Silverberg organizes team at Microsoft to examine web
1995	6	Gates circulates the memo, "The Internet Tidal Wave"
	6, 7	Netscape IPO and the launch of Windows 95
	9	HoTMaiL founded, and "viral marketing" is invented
1996	8	Microsoft offers Internet Explorer at a price of zero
	8	AT&T WorldNet sold at $19.95 for unlimited service
	8	AOL implements all-you-can-eat pricing
1997	8	56K modems first introduced
	10	Tiered structure emerges among Internet data carriers
	9	Netscape and Microsoft reach parity in browser features
1998	10	WorldCom merges with MCI, spins off backbone assets
	8	Over 65,000 phone numbers available for dial-up ISPs
1999	9	Dot-com boom reaches greatest height
	10	WorldCom proposed merger with Sprint is called off
2000	8	*Boardwatch Magazine* records over 7,000 ISPs
	9	Internet adoption nears saturation at medium/large businesses

have made such an observation, this chapter places an emphasis on the underappreciated role of commercial markets. It stresses what firms could have done had they known how to deliver value. How did value get delivered to users? Technology alone could not do it. Firms also had to observe a working prototype of a functioning and viable business.

Chapter 7 contrasts the commercial operations of the Internet with the commercial operation of the personal computer market. In 1995, the value chain for the commercial Internet was quite young and still undergoing dramatic change, while the PC market was almost two decades old and dominated by Microsoft and Intel. Despite overlapping in some respects, the two value chains differed in many subtle ways, and those differences will help explain how and why the process of creative destruction took root.

Even after a new value chain comes into existence, its existence alone does not explain why it delivers value. Chapters 8, 9, and 10 explain the economic growth affiliated with building the commercial Internet and web. These chapters analyze how value was created in different sectors—Internet service providers, households, business users, consultants, and other suppliers in established and entrepreneurial firms. These three chapters provide many illustrations of private actors adapting the Internet to their needs in specific market and organizational circumstances, arguing that such adaptation was crucial for economic growth.

These chapters stress how investment in one sector complemented the other. That illustrates an important observation about economic growth in this period: the creation of value in one sector reinforced its creation in another, raising incentives to invest in the Internet. In this instance, such reinforcement generated a "network effect," in which one decision maker's participation in the Internet economy raised the value to another's participation, and it operated at an economy-wide level. It also played out over time as "a virtuous cycle," in which investment by one actor encouraged investment by another at a later time, and on and on in a chain across multiple sectors. That pattern also provided strong incentives for impatient investment behavior. That is an important economic explanation for why firms continued to invest at the same time in the late 1990s, and it is distinct from the factors that catalyzed investment in the middle of the 1990s.

These chapters explain why the Internet boom may have started as a gold rush, and how it was sustained by a virtuous cycle. That explanation also will play a role in the dot-com bust, when the virtuous cycle came to a halt.

Exploratory behavior arises in all the chapters that compose the last section, titled "Exploration and Renewal." Chapters 11 through 14 largely cover events in the late 1990s and the beginning of the new millennium, until the dot-com bust led to a decline in investment and entrepreneurial activity. In other words, these four chapters stress several different exploratory episodes unleashed by innovation from the edges during the first wave of investment. Table 1.3 provides a chronology of this group of chapters.

Chapter 11 focuses on how Microsoft reacted to the new prevailing view about the prospects for the Internet. It perceived a commercial threat and acted to redirect behavior unleashed by innovation from the edges. This event became popularly known as the "browser wars," and it shaped the commercial Internet for many years. The chapter focuses on understanding the strategic behavior of Bill Gates, and why he sought to discourage Netscape and its business partners. The analysis leads to several insights about how and why leading firms do and do not have incentives to encourage innovation from the edges.

Internet exceptionalism comes in for scrutiny in chapter 12. This chapter analyzes how this ideology shaped behavior of many participants within financial markets and distorted the growth of electronic commerce. Said simply, this chapter identifies many of the factors that distorted the economics of what was popularly called the dot-com boom and bust. The chapter places particular emphasis on impatient exploratory investment, and how financial markets encouraged those distortions. The chapter also explains why these distortions came to an end. Some of the end was inevitable—a by-product of overshooting in the virtuous cycle. Some of it resulted from a distortion, a product of an Internet exceptionalism allowed to run rampant.

Chapter 13 describes one mechanism for renewal of growth after the dot-com bust. It examines the creation of Google, which arose from innovative software created in a university with funding from the NSF. It is not widely appreciated that these innovations originated from government-funded research, so the chapter begins by focusing on the policies for transferring the results into private markets. The chapter then examines how Google continued to explore new features in a commercial setting,

TABLE 1.3. Chronology: Exploration and Renewal
Selected notable events from chapters 11, 12, 13, 14

Year	Chapters	Notable Events
1994	13	Lou Montulli invents the cookie at Netscape
	13	Sergey Brin begins his graduate studies
1995	11	Bill Gates writes "Internet Tidal Wave"
	11	Netscape IPO and Windows 95 launched in same month
	13	Larry Page begins his graduate studies
1996	11	Microsoft begins pressuring partners not to support Netscape
	12	Greenspan makes speech about "Irrational Exuberance"
	12	Wave of new entrants marks start of dot-com boom
1997	14	FCC issues final draft of Part-15 rules for spectrum
	11	Jobs makes deal so IE becomes default browser for Apple
	11	Netscape and Microsoft reach near parity in browser features
1998	11	Senate hearings about Microsoft
	13	Google founded by Larry Page and Sergey Brin
	11	Netscape coalition collapses, AOL eventually buys Netscape
1999	12	Dot-com boom reaches greatest height
	12	Telecom meltdown begins after rule change for CLECs
	14	IEEE committee 802.11 issues design a & b, labeled "Wi-Fi"
2000	11	Judge Jackson issues judgment that finds against Microsoft
	12	NASDAQ reaches its peak in stock valuations of dot-coms
2001	14	Wi-Fi becomes available on Windows-based systems
	12	PSINet declares bankruptcy
	12	9/11 terrorist attacks on World Trade Center
	11	DOJ settles with Microsoft
2002	12	Internal accountant discovered fraud at WorldCom
	13	Google scales quality-weighted second price auction
	12	Economic decline reaches its nadir
2003	13	Google launches AdSense
	14	Intel launches Centrino

developing both new technologies and new business processes, using automated auctions to sell advertising. It developed a novel approach for keyword search auctions that supported advertising focused on the needs of users.

The final chapter of the narrative, chapter 14, examines the creation of the market for wireless Internet access, which added an important functional capability to the Internet. This innovation was more difficult to create than commonly appreciated, in part because the rules for spectrum use emerged out of a long and complicated policy debate. Like prior chapters, the analysis focuses on the mix of technology and commercial incentives that led firms to explore developing new technical features and new business processes. In this instance, Wi-Fi emerged from a mix of collective private action from a standards committee and entrepreneurial action from several different firms. The chapter ends with general lessons about how firms explored innovative activities in commercial markets, and why some market settings encouraged or discouraged such innovative exploration.

Such an extensive narrative needs a summary and a synthesis of the main lessons. Chapter 15 provides these, and it is called "Enabling Innovation from the Edges." First it provides a synthetic summary of the book's story for how and why the commercial Internet grew and evolved. It next provides the summary to the set of questions that motivate the book: What economic archetypes, government policies, and influential institutions encouraged or discouraged innovation from the edges, and why? After reviewing the list of influential factors, the conclusion highlights why innovation from the edges emerged. It also summarizes why rapid market-based learning played a big role in magnifying the impact of innovation from the edges.

The last chapter also offers a surprising set of conclusions. The list of important causes is long and varied. It is not surprising that no single economic archetype or policy alone accounts for such a broad array of events, but this raises a curious observation. Despite the absence of any large coordinating government planner, many independent factors tilted in the same direction, reinforcing one another at a market-wide level. How could that have happened? It was as if innovation from the edges arose from either a vast web of coordinated action or an impressive conspiracy of propitious accidents, and neither is plausible. The book ends with a set of observations about how institutions tended to push different events toward similar policies and, hence, toward the operation of economic archetypes that generated similar types of outcomes. This helps explain why events appeared to be coordinated, even when most were not.

The book also offers lessons for how society can try to rely on systematic policies—and more than mere luck—to produce similar results in the future. It suggests how policy could be tailored to shape events in the future. Most readers already can anticipate the big theme that runs throughout this part of the conclusion. Government policy can fruitfully address many crucial open issues about a firm's action or a government's policies by organizing the inquiry around a broad question: does an action encourage or discourage innovation from the edges? Addressing that key question provides the crucial insight for understanding why outcomes acquired their specific economic characteristics and contours.

How It All Started

Many key inventions for the Internet began with military funding. Yet the military's sponsorship is easy to misunderstand. It may be tempting to compare the Internet to historically archetypical big invention sponsored by hierarchical government organizations, such as the Manhattan and the Apollo projects. These archetypes for developing technical breakthroughs are not good models for understanding what happened during the military's sponsorship. The Internet was not a single urgent project in a single lab devoted to engineering a single object.

This early history is not widely appreciated. That is the point of this section—to introduce a novice reader to a few known and crucial details about the origins of the Internet.

Another popular myth about the Internet's military origins also interferes with understanding its invention. According to this popular myth, the government developed the Internet in order to survive nuclear war. There is a grain of truth to this myth because Paul Baran's theoretical work at Rand was motivated by a research quest, to design networks that remained robust to damage from war.[2] Frontier computing also had played an important role in military applications, and this was widely under-

---

[2]Although his insights were widely unappreciated at the time, Baran later became well known for this early vision. For more in-depth analyses of Baran's contribution, see, e.g., Abbate (1999), Waldrop (2001), or Norberg, O'Neill, and Freedman (1996).

stood inside the military.[3] However, this myth points in misleading directions. Surviving nuclear war was, at most, one of many motivations for the funding for the invention of what became the Internet. More concretely, it had little influence on the actual inventive activity of the researchers who did the inventing.[4]

What should replace the popular myths?[5] The military did not take action in an isolated research laboratory. Rather, the military funded several inventions, and so did other parts of the government, and so did private industry. Sometimes these inventions complemented one another, and occasionally they substituted for one another. There were (occasionally) porous boundaries between the communities who invented for the military and for private industry, so lessons learned in one domain (eventually) spilled into another. There also were multiple efforts outside the United States, most prominent among them was OSI, which later chapters will discuss, and the efforts competed with one another, and imitated one another.[6]

The Internet's early development, largely but not wholly located in the United States, fit into an economic archetype often called "collective invention." Collective invention "is a process in which improvements or experimental findings about a production process or tool are regularly shared."[7] What we today call the Internet began as a series of loosely connected engineering projects, with military funding supporting some of those projects. Those projects eventually involved a vastly dispersed set of technically adept participants with a shared interest in the project, but otherwise heterogeneous needs and outlooks. The Internet developed slowly throughout the 1970s and 1980s and accumulated capabilities over time from an enormous number of contributors. Researchers with government sponsorship contributed some of the primary innovation, while plenty were borrowed from the active private sector.[8]

Five partially overlapping groups had major roles in shaping the attributes of the Internet that commercialized in the 1990s. Each group valued

---

[3]See, e.g., Flamm (1988), or Edwards (1997).
[4]Again, see e.g., Abbate (1999), Waldrop (2001), or Norberg, O'Neill, and Freedman (1996).
[5]For an extensive development of this view, see Greenstein (2010b).
[6]See Russell (2014).
[7]See, e.g., Allen (1983), Meyer (2003).
[8]For an extensive development of this view, see, e.g., Campbell-Kelly and Garcia-Swartz (2013).

distinct dimensions of functionality, and each altered the accumulation of innovative features over time.

The first two communities were the primary decision makers at funding agencies—the Department of Defense (DOD) and the National Science Foundation. The remaining three, no less important, were programmers/developers/inventors, administrators, and application users. Many were funded by the government agencies and given considerable discretion. Others became participants over time and added their own contributions within their own budgetary limitations. An extensive group of inventors also remained active outside of government circles, and, as this book will discuss in several chapters, had a large influence on how the Internet commercialized after privatization.

The earliest funding for the Internet took a form unlike a traditional military procurement project. The Defense Department organized the project in a subagency called DARPA (Department of Advanced Research Projects Agency), which focused on fostering pathbreaking invention.[9] What became the Internet was but one of many projects on the frontiers of computer science funded by a special office within DARPA.[10] The project, building of prototypes for a packet switching data-communications network of networks, pushed the boundaries of network computing at the time.

A packet switching network sends messages between computers. It translates the zeros and ones from one computer into many discrete "packets" of data, each of a fixed size. Large packets are divided into many smaller packets, and those packets are then sent between the computers. The computers sending and receiving the packet use the same processes, or "protocols," for creating and assembling packets. Each packet reserves room at the beginning for identifiers and other code, put there by the computer sending the message. The computer receiving the packet can use the identifiers and code to reassemble those packets, and put them back together in the right order.

DARPA's program officers understood from the outset that research in packet switching would represent a technical break with prior precedents. Chapter 2 will go into greater detail about how the operations for this

---

[9] This organization was originally founded as the Advanced Research Projects Agency, or ARPA, and for the sake of simplicity I will use only one name throughout, DARPA.

[10] See Aspray and Williams (1994), Norberg, O'Neill, and Freedman (1996), Edwards (1997), Roland and Shiman (2002), or Russell (2014).

technology required more than merely a few inventions. It is sufficient for this backstory to understand that initially packet switching was a budding theoretic concept for how a network should operate. It had not been implemented in the 1960s and could have been implemented in a variety of ways in the 1970s. DARPA's administrators wanted innovations in the form of ideas, new designs, and new software. The inventive goals were large and ambitious, as well as open ended, and that meant the opportunity could not be addressed by a single organization, or by the insight of one lone genius. The inventors and DARPA administrators also understood the goals broadly and did not presume to know what specific designs and applications would suit their needs.[11] They broadly funded pie-in-sky research as well as inventions addressing pragmatic problems with anticipated military applications.

As it turned out, the project accumulated capabilities and became very useful for quite a few purposes, such as transferring files, electronic mail, and other forms of communications. Gradually new purposes were invented for the network, and functionality grew and accumulated. Different audiences perceived that open-ended opportunity in different ways and added distinct inventions to the existing packet switching network.

Military needs also overlapped with civilian needs, and that facilitated moving this technology out of the military in the middle of the 1980s. Why? In part, this was an explicit goal. Administrators at DARPA desired that all of these innovations be portable to military operations in the long run. Such an outlook was required under a statute called the Mansfield Amendment (stipulating that Department of Defense funding be relevant to military's mission).[12] Many of the computers used in the military came from civilian suppliers, so such a pragmatic goal inevitably oriented the project toward the similar problems computer users outside the military experienced.

---

[11] David Clark, private communications, September 2008.

[12] Norberg, O'Neill, and Freedman (1996) stress that DARPA's funding of packet switching research in the 1960s and 1970s met concerns about whether the funding was relevant to a military mission, as required by the Mansfield Amendment, which was proposed several times, and eventually passed in 1973. The research anticipated enhancing the "command and control" capabilities of commanders increasingly reliant on their computing resources. Flamm (1988) also stresses the overlap in government procurement requirements for computing and civilian needs. For a large class of activities, making progress on a military problem overlapped with progress on a similar or related civilian problem.

What issues did the US military face with its own computing facilities and operations?[13] For one, as hinted by the earlier references to nuclear war, the military sought a robust design for a communications network, and the potential value of robustness was self-evident. Keeping communications functioning in spite of a blown or cut line has military value in hostile battlefield conditions. In theory, an inexpensive packet switching network could do this because the path taken by the packets did not matter, and, in principle, could follow many different routes. Thus if one route was damaged and another remained open, then the messages could continue to go through.

An additional technical and pragmatic aspiration also motivated funding. An ideal network could facilitate the movement of data between distant computer systems, and with as little human intervention as possible in the intermediary points of the network. A packet switching network could cover vast geographic distances, which could support the sharing of expensive computing resources between faraway places, and without the use of operators at switches. That too had self-evident military value, as it would for any large computer user. Coordinating the exchange, combination, and filtering of data between computer systems in different locations generated numerous potential gains for operations.

Several prototypes for this packet switching network were engineered with DARPA's funding. With additional funding, these innovative designs turned into a prototype of an operating network, operated by managers from Bolt, Beranek and Newman (BBN), a research contractor subcontracting through DARPA. A number of researchers and their students became familiar with its principles. The network grew from this unusual origin, covering more locations and more research laboratories. Eventually the system became reliable and could exchange data between computing systems without frequent human intervention. Once again, such automation had value inside the military as well as outside of it.

By the early 1980s the network had value to a community of researchers with few connections to the military research projects, and with even fewer to military operations. A considerable community of hobbyists and

---

[13] There has been considerable writing on this question, and this summary skims the surface. See, e.g., Abbate (1999), Aspray and Williams (1994), Norberg, O'Neill, and Freedman (1996), Edwards (1997), and Roland and Shiman (2002).

commercial firms with interests in frontier information technology also existed outside of the military circles. Yet access to the military network required military backing. The military grew tired of the inconveniences of managing participation among researchers with sporadic military funding, and, for this and other reasons, spun off a part of the network to researchers.

The NSF Era

The second era started when the National Science Foundation (NSF) began managing a network for the benefit of the research community in the United States. It was more than a simple change in management, but it would have taken uncommon prescience to understand how crucial it would be for fostering innovation from the edges at a later date. The consequences are easier to see in retrospect.

The NSF invested in the Internet with several motives, principally among them to stretch the Internet's capabilities as an input into research and higher education. That motivation built on a long history of supporting computer science inside universities.[14] In this case, the NSF sought to use the network for more than just computer scientists, and sought to invest in turning the Internet into a large-scale network for researchers, professors, or students coming from a variety of disciplinary backgrounds. Much investment was aimed at aiding basic tasks, such as sending electronic mail.[15] The NSF also aimed to use the Internet to facilitate connecting with supercomputers, making use of the capacity. Supercomputers were expensive fixed investments with no geographic mobility. Some of the core development, especially for software to make the network operate, continued to be managed by the NSF and by the military.

The NSF's investments began to focus on scaling the network as traffic grew, and early into its stewardship it standardized the protocols in its network. It chose a protocol that the military network also had adopted several years earlier, called TCP/IP, which stood for transmission-control protocol and Internet protocol. TCP defined the protocols for sending and receiving packets. IP defined the design of packets and the information

---

[14]See, e.g., Aspray and Williams (1994).
[15]See Abbate (1999). Other factors also shaped investments, as discussed below.

contained in each packet. TCP/IP had been defined many years earlier with DARPA funding, and the military also used it.[16] This was a crucial choice, as the commercial Internet still runs on TCP/IP to this day.

The NSF aimed to build a routine and reliable network infrastructure, making it easy to adapt and spread to every university, community college, and research institute.[17] By 1989 the NSF had rationalized the processes and infrastructure underneath the Internet. That investment gave a wide range of participants—students, faculty, and administrators—a taste for what the TCP/IP packet switching network could do to help them in their work—namely, transmit e-mail, send and receive electronic files, and do both reliably over long distances. By this point virtually all users had begun to shorten "inter-network" to "Internet," which was a more convenient label.

After a few years under the NSF's stewardship, the Internet had a different look and feel than it had had in the earlier military era. All participants in the earlier era experimented and explored the frontiers of networking, inventing new capabilities for the nascent network. Some continued to do that in the second era, but many of the new users had no intention of inventing anything, and most had no idea how the entire system operated, nor did they want to know. The Internet was merely something they used in their research and work.

Scale brought with it a new set of managerial questions: could private firms perform the same activity as efficiently, or more cheaply? If they could, how should they be organized? These questions would not—could not—be definitively addressed by the NSF. Several later chapters will explain how these questions were addressed, and why the answer coincided with the emergence of innovation from the edges.

A related pragmatic aspiration—cost reduction—came along with the concern about reliability at large scale. That emerged as a central concern

---

[16] Russell (2014) stresses that DARPA supported scientific inquiry with a robust and questioning conversation, but its sponsor also modulated many forms of dissent and discretion. The US military had a lot of leverage because it could withhold funding, and such coercive tactics proved rather effective in getting TCP/IP adopted. Russell also mentions government representatives could compel TCP/IP compatibility through procurement, as they eventually did by requiring TCP/IP in all forms of Unix sold to the military. Russell stresses that these instruments worked because TCP/IP was not an empty promise. The protocol had been effectively deployed and reflected a clear conception of how it should operate.

[17] See, e.g., Frazer (1995), Leiner et al. (2003).

at the end of the 1980s because, in part, the NSF did not have a large or reliable budget for operating the Internet or upgrading it. Every large investment required a large appropriation, and that required congressional approval. Congress was not known for writing blank checks to the NSF.

When he took the job of managing the Internet for the NSF in 1986, Stephen Wolff believed the Internet would be useful for a wide set of potential users in all research communities. An engineer by training, Wolff enjoyed working with the network in his position at a government laboratory, the army's research network at Aberdeen, which had a connection to the network sponsored by DARPA.[18] Wolff's attitude, common to the earlier generation of Internet pioneers, combined idealism—belief that the deployment of the Internet could be transformative—with an engineer's pragmatism. Looking back on his experience, with characteristic laconic description, Wolff thought the NSFNET "looked like a good project with good values."[19]

Stephen Wolff did not take the job of managing the Internet at NSF in order to privatize the network. Rather, that proposal emerged from daily experience with the reliable network, and from confronting the budgetary realities of operating the network at NSF. He eventually concluded that private firms probably could handle all the relevant tasks. Wolff made an educated guess that the costs for universities and researchers could be lower if private providers supplied services to both his constituents and private users. The budgets for many networks also could improve if there were multiple source of revenue.[20]

The proposal for privatization did not emerge overnight. Cautiously at first, Wolff widened the conversation, seeking to figure out how universities could share the infrastructure with private users. In 1989 Wolff began meeting with other stakeholders in the academic Internet and so began a series of conversations about introducing private enterprise into the Internet's operations. Many of these conversations took place at the Harvard

---

[18] That also was near the University of Delaware, the research home to David Farber, one of the key participants in building the network at that time.

[19] Stephen Wolff, private communications, July 2008.

[20] Stephen Wolff, private communications, July 2008.

Kennedy School of Government, organized by Brian Kahin, director of the Harvard Information Infrastructure Project.[21]

The participants left copious records of their perceptions at the time. They generally acknowledged that the research-oriented Internet had matured, moving beyond its "nuts and bolts" stage of development.[22] While no serious networking engineer thought the Internet's technical capabilities had stopped evolving, by this point the Internet had acquired many appealing attributes. It was a large-scale and reliable data communications network with a documented code base upon which many participants could build additional layers of applications. Most of the participants worried about losing those accomplishments if the privatization became neglectful of key aspects of the operations. Most of them did not give any thought to fostering anything related to innovation from the edges.

---

[21] These meetings are documented in Kahin (1992), which provides a marvelous record of the diversity of thinking at the time. See also November 1990, Request for Comment 1192, titled "Commercialization of the Internet Summary Report," which provides the initial report of the meeting, accessible at http://www.rfc-editor.org/rfc/rfc1192.txt, accessed July 2009.

[22] This is the phrase used by Mandelbaum and Manderbaum (1992). They meant that the Internet had moved beyond the stage where just installing it and getting it to work was the primary objective of many IT managers. See also the description of the transition to the T-1 backbone in Frazer (1995), pp. 24–26. Participants faced numerous initial complex technical issues, but overcame them, resulting in a widely recognized technical achievement.

THE TRANSITION

Chapters 2, 3, 4 and 5 cover the transition from a government-sponsored and research-oriented Internet to a privately owned and operated network. This transition did not go smoothly and required government managers to rethink their strategies for achieving policy goals. The experience changed key features of the commercial network, irreversibly, and in ways that encouraged innovation from the edges.

TABLE 2.1. Selected notable events from Chapters 2, 3, 4, and 5

Year	Chapter	Notable Event
1990	2, 3	NSF conducts conversations about privatization
	3	PSINet and UUNET begin first full year as private firms
1991	3	High Performance Computing Act of 1991 passed
	4	Tim Berners-Lee downloads code for web to shareware sites
	3	Commercial Internet eXchange (CIX) founded
1992	3	Network Solutions takes control of domain name system
	3	Rick Boucher sponsors a bill to amend NSF Charter
	3	Internet Society founded and IETF becomes part of it
1993	3	Final NSF plan for privatization emerges, and NSF solicits bids
	4	Mosaic browser made for Unix and Windows OS
	5	Earliest ads for ISPs appear in *Boardwatch Magazine*
1994	4	Founding of the World Wide Web Consortium
	4	Mosaic Communications Company (MCC) founded
	4	MCC changes name to Netscape and releases a beta browser
1995	4	Apache formed from different versions of NCSA HTTPd server
	3	NSFNET shutdown and Internet backbone privatized
	5	Netscape IPO and Windows 95 launched in same month
1996	5	Congress passes the 1996 Telecommunications Act
	5	More than 2,000 ISPs advertise in *Boardwatch Magazine*

2

The White House Did Not Call

Q: How many Bell Labs vice presidents does it take to change a light bulb?

A: That's proprietary information. Answer available from AT&T on payment of license fee.

In 1981 William F. Baxter Jr. became assistant attorney general for anti-trust in the US Department of Justice (DOJ). Due to recusals, Baxter had an unusual degree of authority. He became manager of two of the largest, longest-running cases in US antitrust history. The first case against IBM had been filed in 1969 and accused IBM of subverting the competitive process in a variety of settings. It had continued seemingly without end, accumulating over sixty million pages of documents. The second involved a case against American Telephone and Telegraph, or AT&T. This company descended from the firm founded by Alexander Graham Bell and was known as Ma Bell for short. The largest telephone company in the world had been a source of concern in government circles for decades. This antitrust case had been filed in 1974, and was one of the three rings in a political circus fixated on AT&T's future—the others were at the Federal Communications Commission and Congress. All had been trying to re-shape the company and the US telephone system.[1]

The DOJ had come to a decision: it planned to announce settlements to both cases on the same day in January 1982. The IBM case would be closed,

---

[1] Two histories of this period are Temin and Galambos (1987) and Coll (1986).

FigURE 2.1 Vint Cerf, Robert E. Kahn, creators of TCP/IP and President George Bush (White House photo by Paul Morse, November 9, 2005)

FigURE 2.2 Stephen Wolff, division director for Networking and Communications Research and Infrastructure, National Science Foundation, 1986–94 (Photo by Marshall Clarke; photo from June 1, 2011)

"dismissed without merit." The case against AT&T would have a different experience. The prosecution had just presented its case in a major antitrust trial, and the judge indicated that AT&T would face a high hurdle if it tried to make a plausible defense. Rather than finish the trial, AT&T decided to come to a negotiated settlement.[2] The settlement would break up the company and become known as the AT&T divestiture.

The AT&T divestiture contained a formidable amount of detail. Even the outline was daunting. The old firm would break itself up into eight organizations, comprised of seven regional local telephone carriers, dubbed Baby Bells, and one long distance carrier, which retained the name of AT&T. Western Electric, the telephone equipment producing arm of the old AT&T, became affiliated with the long distance firm.[3] Consent decrees barred the local telephone companies from offering products and services in competitive markets, such as computing and other information services. Once AT&T no longer managed any local telephone services, Western Electric would become free to compete with any other firm, including IBM, in any other competitive market, including computing markets. Eventually the presiding judge, Harold Greene, would supervise the Modification of Final Judgment, which would take effect on January 1, 1984.

Baxter drew a formidable assignment. He had to travel to the White House to present the DOJ's decisions and the negotiated settlement to President Ronald Reagan and his staff.[4] The attorney general normally would have handled this activity, but he was recused from the AT&T case. Baxter had to single-handedly manage the interface with the White House.

As Baxter prepared to do this, he was acutely aware of the delicate nature of the relationship between executive authority, political considerations, and major antitrust actions. The daily tug of politics at the White House normally did not affect antitrust matters inside the Department of Justice. However, there were exceptions for cases like AT&T and IBM. The

[2] The judge, Harold Greene, had inherited the case on his first day on the bench in 1978. After the prosecution rested their case, midway through the trial, he issued a ruling framing several key questions, signaling to AT&T the burden it had to meet.

[3] In addition, the settlement split Bell Laboratories between AT&T and a consortium of the Baby Bells. The settlement also passed control over cellular networks to the local telephone companies.

[4] Later, after he retired, Baxter was fond of telling his students about the moments just prior to these historic announcements. I was privileged to have heard it, as were many others. I would like to thank Greg Rosston and Eric Talley for confirming these memories of Baxter's story, and adding details to my imperfect remembrance.

announcement would receive considerable publicity. The settlement with AT&T would restructure the firm and an important US industry—the executives at both firms were well known, and the companies employed many people. The country's prosperity depended on the telephone system. At a minimum, the White House would have to be informed in advance. This situation was worse than typical, because they were being informed at the end of a long series of events. Both cases had long histories behind them and had been managed by several prior administrations. Baxter worried that President Reagan and his advisors might raise objections—for whatever reasons, political, or philosophical—and it might lead them to request or demand changes in the negotiated settlement. Baxter did not know what to expect.

Baxter would later admit to being nervous and caught up in the moment as he made his presentation. He finished and paused, waiting for any reaction. After a moment of silence President Reagan spoke. He asked if the telephones would still continue to work after the breakup. Baxter replied that the phones would continue to work as they always had. Reagan asked nothing else. There was another pause, and nobody asked any questions. The pause signaled that the meeting should come to an end. Baxter left the room.

On his way back to the DOJ Baxter replayed the meeting in his head. It then dawned on him that he had made a mistake. At the conclusion of the meeting nobody had said, "Go ahead" or "Stop." Only Reagan had voiced concern, and some might have interpreted that as caution. Baxter had not pushed the point to resolution and had not received either a definitive yes or no. What an omission! He was about to authorize the DOJ to undertake one of the largest restructuring efforts in the history of US antitrust and he was doing that without an unambiguous endorsement from the White House.

Baxter pondered the situation. He weighed the options and considered one question in particular. If the White House did not say "no," did that give him permission to use his discretion? Baxter recognized that constitutional lawyers could debate such a question for days. Baxter did not have time for such a long debate. A news conference had been scheduled. He considered it and eventually he persuaded himself that, indeed, the lack of a definite command to stop did give him permission to act.

As it would turn out, the White House never called. Baxter went ahead and later made the announcement.[5]

The announcement made headlines, its significance widely recognized. It also set off a great deal of speculation. Freed from its previous constraints, analysts anticipated that AT&T would invite a great confrontation with IBM, since computer and telephone equipment used many of the same electronic components. Western Electric possessed the manufacturing capacity and distribution network to reach scales only a few other firms (other than IBM) could hope to achieve. The lifting of the case against IBM, in turn, freed management from the large distraction it had faced for many years. IBM seemed poised to compete vigorously as well.

Speculation is one thing, competitive action another, and, as it turned out, actual customer purchases are another thing altogether. Baxter's first forecast did come true. The phones continued to work as they always had, though with one intended change: users got their telephone service from more firms and smaller organizations. In addition, AT&T took numerous steps to enter various aspects of the computing market, while IBM tried to develop various services in networking. But IBM was unable to dominate the competitive supply of personal computers or networking in the late 1980s and 1990s, and neither was AT&T. Competitive events in computing and communications took a number of unanticipated turns, as this and later chapters will describe.

All the contingencies and unanticipated outcomes beg the question: had antitrust been a waste of time and effort? As it would turn out, antitrust would be crucial to future outcomes, and for reasons consistent with the spirit of the antitrust actions. However, that was easy to miss. The biggest impact arose in an unexpected arena.

Although not anticipated, the Internet's commercial future became linked to both AT&T's divestiture and IBM's inability to dominate any markets other than its traditional market, large-scale computing. Both AT&T and IBM would enter the personal computer market, but only IBM experienced initial commercial success before losing its leadership position

---

[5] The Reagan White House tended not to make confrontational decisions on the spot. If, after Baxter left the room, Reagan and his advisors decided to put a stop to something, they almost certainly would have sent word or phoned directly. Thanks to Bill Draper for this insight about the workings of the Reagan administration.

in the late 1980s.[6] Lack of a dominant firm in computing or communications would be crucial for the Internet's growth. Not only did it eliminate the possibility that decisions in a single boardroom could act as a bottleneck in any specific decision, but also the divestiture of AT&T created multiple decision makers in many technical and commercial arenas relevant to communications. It accelerated steps toward a new era marked by decentralized decision making, where multiple organizations had discretion to act. Indeed, they would act in distinct ways. The theme arises in many places; decentralization was crucial for the Internet's growth.

Less appreciated at the time was the second consequence. As this chapter explains, not only had AT&T confronted challenges in legal court, but all the publicity and public discussion placed the firm in a poor light among the community of computer scientists building the Internet. Most computer scientists had faced AT&T's infamously bureaucratic billing and marketing practices, or had encountered its stubbornly selfish and legalistic actions in regulatory hearings, or had confronted engineering plans that presumed only one official design for a service and locked out others. While most participants in the Internet could not articulate precisely how the Internet would be governed, most had an almost visceral dislike for the centralization at Ma Bell. Most desired anything other than a single decision maker or a single executive at the heart of the Internet.

Only a few years later, the preferences of the computer science community would matter a great deal. While the Internet started within DARPA, a single hierarchical organization, this chapter discusses how the Internet's transfer to the National Science Foundation (NSF) would lead to more dispersion of leadership. That left NSF in charge of a crucial component—the Internet's backbone. In 1989 the director of the Internet for the NSF, Stephen Wolff, would pose a seemingly narrow question about how to privatize the Internet backbone. That narrow question eventually would lead NSF to a much broader set of questions about how to structure the supply of services supporting the Internet.

While many questions were unanswered in 1989, the participants knew one thing for certain: they did not want the next communications network to resemble Ma Bell or to be dominated by IBM. The purpose of this chap-

---

[6] As it happened, IBM also had successful entries into minicomputers, though it did not dominate this market as it did large-scale systems. Its position in the networking market will be discussed in later chapters.

ter is to recognize the symptoms of those preferences, identify their main features, and explain their origins. Those observations will become relevant to many later events in the commercial Internet, when the preferences and habits of the computer science community will play an unexpectedly large role in fostering innovation from the edges. What were those preferences and habits? This chapter focuses on understanding those that had a large impact in later events.

Architecture

To any denizen of the commercial computing or telecommunications world, the Internet of the early 1990s would have seemed shockingly naive for its trust in decentralization of authority and lack of hierarchy. What prevented myriad endless disagreements and a collapse of the whole enterprise underneath the weight of uncoordinated quarrelsomeness? The answer could not be found at any single location, person, or design. Rather, it would be seen in the origins of the Internet in the 1980s and interplay of several different informal practices, principles, and norms, which are seen within a few related organizations.

To begin with the architecture, the Internet's designers thought of it as a "platform."[7] Later chapters will discuss platforms in greater detail, so this chapter begins with a broad outline of how a platform works. A computing platform is a standard bundle of components. The components are used together in a system that regularly delivers valuable services to users. Platforms in computing typically embedded modular architectural designs and aimed for a balanced use of resources. The modularity emerged from the standards. Each component employed standardized interfaces compatible with the other components within the platform. Modular designs allowed for changes in one component of hardware and software without changing another. In most platforms someone or some organization has designed those interfaces, standardized them, and managed how the components worked together.

---

[7]Much of this discussion about platforms can be found in accounts about the Internet's invention. See, e.g., Hafner and Lyon (1998), Abbate (1999), Waldrop (2001), Norberg, O'Neill, and Freedman (1996), or Ceruzzi ([2006] 2008). It is also a well-known concept in computing. See Aspray and Campbell-Kelly (2004).

Computing platforms perform two distinct functions that complement each other. First, a platform reduces technical variety by embodying specific choices for standards that all applications use. Most platforms do that in the service of reducing design costs for widely used technologies, as well as a second goal, to foster expansion in the functionality of the platform through growth of a variety of applications. A well-designed and sagaciously governed platform succeeds in attracting useful applications. Additional applications do not have to replicate the shared aspects of the platform, which makes their development less expensive. That helps the platform scale to more users, which helps the platform thrive over time. A functional platform with inexpensive applications attracts users, and a growing number of users entice the design of more applications. In the ideal case, a virtuous cycle emerges.

By 1989 such a virtuous cycle had arisen in the NSF's Internet. The design and governance both were responsible. The Internet's core design embedded one particular design for packet switching, TCP/IP. It had demonstrated that it was modular and possessed many functional merits, and many administrators, programmers, and users were satisfied with its design and could envision a path toward improving it with additional functionality.

What about governance? In 1989, the governance of the Internet did not resemble any organization any telephone engineer had ever seen. The Internet operations involved a set of collective decision-making bodies that users and administrators had built for the benefit of the US scientific and research community. It was suited to the wide dispersion of technical skills and administrative discretion among its participants.

One principle, "end-to-end," played a central role as both a design principle and a governance norm.[8] End-to-end networks placed the "smart" computing for applications at the devices and clients, such as the PCs, not in the middle of the network, the servers. The switches for the network, the routers, would retain general functionality, but remain "dumb." They only moved data between computers and did not perform any processing on the contents.

---

[8] The paper that first defined this phrase is Saltzer, Reed, and Clark (1981), commonly cited as Saltzer, Reed, and Clark (1984).

There was direct pragmatic benefit to this design, and each network administrator knew it. Administrators in different locations had one less issue to worry about. Said simply, the applications in one location might work in another because nothing in the middle of the network altered the data as it traveled between the ends. If something went wrong, then administrators did not have to consider problems with the transmission of data from point to point; rather, they could focus on an issue at the application or at the installation. This property was well known to engineers in the phrase "The intelligence resided at the edges of the network." That is, nothing in an application depended on any functionality within the routing of the data.

As Blumenthal and Clark (2001) stated in a retrospective look:

> When a general-purpose system (for example, a network or an operating system) is built and specific applications are then built using this system (for example, email or the World Wide Web over the Internet), there is a question of how these specific applications and their required supporting services should be designed. The end-to-end arguments suggest that specific application-level functions usually cannot and preferably should not, be built into the lower levels of the system—the core of the network.

When first proposed in the early 1980s, end-to-end was a radical engineering concept, and its merits were debated frequently. It differed from the principles governing the telephone network, where the switching equipment performed the primary and essential processing activities, and where the telephone handset contained little functionality.[9]

End-to-end was more than merely an abstract engineering design principle by the late 1980s. It was also a governing principle, one founded on a nuanced understanding of how administrators used their discretion. End-to-end increased the chances that administrators at the edge could add a new application. Deploying applications did not require coordinating with the carriers of the data—usually a telephone company—each time there was a transaction or an addition of a new application.

---

[9]End-to-end also differed with most large computing systems at the time, such as mainframes, which put the essential operations in the central processing unit in the center of the system. There was little for the terminals to do except display results and take input, so they became known as *dumb* terminals.

End-to-end also fit the organizational realities of the network at the time. It was well suited for organizing a network not operated by a single supplier. It suited a network with diverse and dispersed investment and management, and with shared goals among a wide range of participant— found throughout universities and research laboratories in many locations. It was meant to guide investment decisions made by hundreds of network administrators in scores of locations who also wanted their applications to work with each other.

How did consensus hold? In part this was a legacy of DARPA's management of the development of TCP/IP, which managed the network to prevent a plethora of varieties from emerging. The same protocols were widely adopted among early adopters, and later developments built upon that unified core. In part it emerged by gentleman's agreement among the NSF's managers. To be successfully deployed, new functionality also had to involve the complicity of many administrators. It also held due to the virtuous cycle between the growing number of users and the growing functionality of the network. While the growing size of the Internet made it more difficult to monitor the behavior of any individual administrator, conversely, it generated increasing incentives for any individual to follow everyone else in order to remain compatible with others.

End-to-end played an enabling role in fostering innovation from the edges because it gave discretion to others. How did participants use that discretion? Several norms and institutions shaped behavior during the era of NSF governance.

Inventive Specialization

Inventive specialization thrived in the Internet of the 1980s. Distinct subcommunities became organized around operating and improving different parts of the whole system. Inventive specialization was crucial because it facilitated the growth of distinct bodies of knowledge devoted to improving distinct functions on the platform.

Why did inventive specialization arise? It was not due to the death of renaissance men. It was not impossible for any potential inventor to be a generalist, that is, to have familiarity with enough technology to make suggestions for all parts of the network. In the 1970s and early 1980s a first-rate programmer could read the source code for any application, often in less than a week, as long as they could get access to the Unix applications.[10] However, knowing anything in principle was not the same as knowing enough in practice to usefully invent new improvements. It was possible, but ultimately infeasible, to know everything simultaneously. An inventor typically chose to make improvements to one piece of the whole.

Improvements became embedded in a working prototype, which is a new design whose purpose it is to show that an invention will do what it proposes. Done well, the act of building a prototype can also expose the designer to unanticipated technical issues. A prototype must work well enough to demonstrate "proof of concept," which was another widely accepted norm. A working prototype did not need to be perfect or even reliable enough for a mainstream user. It just needed to allow any competent observer to understand the new functionality, and potentially imagine improvements beyond it in a broader or more limited range of circumstances. Others might make suggestions to the inventor, who would improve the working prototype. In the best case, the invention would be refined and become something others could use.

Inventive experience within the community of e-mail inventors can illustrate the point. Even the most specialized of subfields divided problems into distinct domains. For example, from the outset electronic mail had been conceived as a series of layered abstractions. Moving from one body of knowledge to another took time and effort.

Ray Tomlinson placed the "@" at a crucial dividing point between (a) the message itself, and (b) transportation to an address.[11] After the invention and diffusion of the "@" in e-mail addresses, every insider began to talk about this divide. To say it in a stylized way, some inventors focused on the "left side" of the @—how users interact with e-mail, as determined by the design of the user mailbox. Other inventors focused on the "right side" of the @—how a message was routed, as well as how it was hosted on a user's machine. Each body of knowledge accumulated incremental

---

[10]Craig Partridge, private communication, July 2008.

[11]Tomlinson explains why he chose that symbol: "I am frequently asked why I chose the at sign, but the at sign just makes sense. The purpose of the at sign (in English) was to indicate a unit price (for example, 10 items @ 1.95). I used the at sign to indicate the user 'at' some other host rather than being local." Tomlinson discusses his experiences in http://openmap .bbn.com/~tomlinso/ray/firstemailframe.html, accessed February 2014.

suggestions from distinct groups with only a little overlap of personnel.[12] Groups of inventors specialized in one or the other.

Inventive specialization in the Internet also was nurtured by the repeated success in accumulating working prototypes from a geographically dispersed set of contributors. One inventor's improvement led to well-documented applications and experiences that inspired others to suggest new ideas for improvement. Each working prototype built on the other, even though inventors came from different organizations in different places.

The accumulation of improvements from inventive specialists did not happen by magical technical glue. Stepping back from daily events, it was possible to see a set of norms—largely borrowed from the governance of science and research communities—governing many decisions over time and in many locations. The community largely operated under the norms of a technical meritocracy—a social norm, whereby individuals advance in standing through commonly recognized technical achievements. Importantly, the technical meritocracy for the Internet survived in an informal consensus process in the 1970s and much of the 1980s. Eventually it would be formalized in processes discussed at length in this chapter and the next.

Where did this norm come from? It was founded on a shared model among engineers and computer scientists about what constituted a sound technical solution. In any given area, the group of researchers and administrators tended to be small enough that a technical consensus could emerge comparatively quickly after a proposal was introduced and demonstrated. Those norms reflected a convention—an accepted way of doing things— quite common among technically oriented engineering communities in which everyone participated in the peer-review system both as reviewer and author. The community assigned hierarchical status for the quality of the technical contribution.[13]

---

[12]The observations about how distinct bodies of knowledge accumulated within different communities of inventors who built upon one another come from David Crocker, private communication, August 2008. For a general theory for how such processes led the Internet to become a "generative" technology, one that spawns many new insights, see Zittrain (2009).

[13]Turner (2006), 135, attributes this norm to the "hacker ethic." This ethic and identity began to gel in the early to middle 1980s among early pioneers in information technology, and they expressed a norm that, says Turner: "work should be organized in a decentralized manner and individual ability, rather than credentials obtained from an institutions, should determine the nature of one's work and one's authority." He places particular importance on a 1984 conference organized by Stewart Brand of the Whole Earth Catalog, which identified hackers and their individualism as a positive norm.

The model played itself out in numerous settings. For example, Craig Partridge was a recent Harvard graduate in the early 1980s, employed at BBN, one of the central contractors doing work for the Department of Defense. While many years later Partridge's contributions to the Internet would be widely recognized, at this point he was rather green—articulate and bright, to be sure, but a few years out of school, and many years away from completing his PhD in computer science.

Partridge had been part of a small team assigned to a problem that interested Vint Cerf, one of the coauthors of TCP/IP. Cerf first called the research vice president at BBN one morning to learn about progress and consider solutions. Cerf had not found a satisfactory answer from the vice president, so Cerf next did something considered quite normal at the time: he directly called the researcher assigned to the problem. In this case, the researcher was Craig Partridge. Partridge was in his office and knew nothing about the prior phone call or, for that matter, Cerf's status. Nonetheless, he quickly discerned that Cerf knew his subject. They had a conversation, coming to a resolution that satisfied both of them.

Having been unexpectedly interrupted, Partridge went back to work on what he had been doing and did not find the time to report the conversation to his supervisor before the vice president suddenly called an unplanned meeting. When all the researchers gathered, the vice president announced that the group needed to discuss the strategy for answering Cerf's concerns. At that point Partridge blithely reported on his early phone conversation with Cerf, and its satisfactory resolution, to the surprise and pleasure of all.

In a setting that operated under command and control, such as the military, Partridge would have been reprimanded for having a conversation without authorization. In BBN, however, Partridge was not reprimanded because the computer scientists were organized around an informal technical meritocracy. Partridge resolving the technical issue with Cerf, thus, was celebrated. Indeed, as a result of this incident, Partridge found that from then on out he was always included in key technical conversation at his department within BBN.[14] That was but one example, but it reflected a wider social norm that celebrated technical achievement.

[14] There is an oral history within the Internet community of similar experiences. Reportedly, Phil Karn had a similar experience at BellCore after his algorithm appeared in print. Jeff Case, an assistant professor at the University of Kentucky, and among the most junior colleagues

Acknowledging technical achievement, and making use of its fruits, also aligned with another convention, a willingness to allow technically flawed ideas to fail, so all could move on. That held regardless of the identity of the author or other facets of the origins of the idea. Consider the following illustration of a failed protocol proposal, described by David Crocker:

> Eventually, the specification stabilized and we published it. A few people decided to implement but it soon died away, in spite of his publishing a revision a bit later. . . . Almost no one knows of this protocol today, but I consider it a superb example of the real "decision" process of the Internet community. Someone suggested an idea. Some others fleshed it out. Still more people tested it. No one complained about authority or scope of responsibility, or following a particular process. No one worried about egos or power. The focus was on the problem and its possible solution. The problem was serious enough and the idea appealing enough to get some people interested in exploring it. The idea failed, but it failed on its merits.[15]

These developments became self-reinforcing. Inventors could specialize in one part of the system, each participant having reasonable faith their efforts would not be wasted, expecting others would do complementary efforts in other parts of the system. In the same way, useful working prototypes would integrate back into the whole.

Consider the results produced by the technical meritocracy over many years. The group of inventors for e-mail involved many exceptionally talented inventors, later receiving multiple awards for their contributions.[16] Most of the significant inventions that composed e-mail networks in the 1970s and '80s came from a community that exceeded four-dozen individuals. The suggestions came from all types of participants with a wide va-

---

within his department, suddenly became known around the world for his work on simple network management protocol (SNMP). Partridge, private communications, July 2008.

[15]See http://bbiw.net/amj/AMJ-20-ChangingTheWorld.html.

[16]Partridge (2008), 23, notes that many contributors to e-mail's development are Institute of Electrical and Electronics Engineers (IEEE) and Association for Computing Machinery (ACM) fellows. He also singles out IEEE award winners, David Crocker, Steve Crocker, Paul Mockapetris, and Ray Tomlinson, the IEEE Kobayashi award winners, Vint Cerf and Van Jacobson, and ACM Sigcomm Award winners, Vint Cerf, Van Jacobson, Paul Mockapetris, Jon Postel, and Larry Roberts.

riety of backgrounds. Several of these inventors were responsible for more than one significant invention while many inventors made only one.[17]

What happened in e-mail occurred more widely across the Internet community. The community of e-mail developers was but one of scores of subcommunities that contributed to building the Internet.[18]

The combination of inventive specialization with the informal technical meritocracy also fostered competition among designs. Distinct designs generated distinct experiences in terms of functionality and costs. Administrators recorded these outcomes and, in time, supporters of distinct approaches would compare and contrast their assumptions and results. Administrators would listen, debate among themselves, and vote with their own decisions, adopting the choices that best suited their own experience.

Competition allowed some installations to experiment with new deployments of frontier equipment while bringing economic considerations into the debate, such as the cost of installation and operation. In this way, the administrators for Internet applications began to taste the improvements in electronics occurring in mainstream markets for personal computers, workstations, local area networks, printers, external storage, displays, and a wide range of equipment.

Competition among designs introduced tension into the early Internet that would later create headaches for the privatization of the Internet. Up to a point, disagreements could survive without splitting up the entire system.[19] TCP/IP's definition of technical standards for different technical layers quarantined most fights to one area at a time, leaving other layers to progress at their own pace. Up to a point, each layer progressed according to the localized logic of competition among component providers.[20]

[17] This observation has been noted by both Partridge (2008) and Crocker (2008).

[18] This is one of the key themes in Abbate's (1999) account of the wider community.

[19] For example, the commercial networking industry of the 1980s was undergoing a technical and commercial debate about the most efficient design for local area networking. IBM had put forward a proprietary architecture known as "token ring," while many other firms put forward proprietary solutions based on Ethernet design principles. A young start-up, 3Com, founded by Robert Metcalfe, one of Ethernet's technical pioneers, put forward another design, one that was not proprietary. Initially endorsed by Intel and Digital Equipment Corporation, it was gathering some adherents too. All three designs had received endorsements from the IEEE standards committee for data transfer in local area networks. Most academics preferred Metcalfe's design, but as a small buyer their influence was trivial on market success. For an analysis of the evolution, see Burg (2001).

[20] These layers were: application, transport, network, datalink, and physical layers. A layer is a collection of related functions that provides services to the layer above it and receives

This feature underwent reconsideration whenever a major dispute emerged. One of the earliest principles arose from the success of Ethernet. Many researchers favored making the Internet optimized to local area networks using Robert Metcalfe's designs for Ethernet, while others favored retaining a structure for TCP/IP that could accommodate more local area networking designs. Eventually, the latter path was chosen in deference to the principles of preserving technical simplicity and choice, even in the face of more potential simplicity.[21]

The center did not hold after every fight, however. Since cooperation was voluntary, there was always risk for breakaway subcommunities of inventors. In fact, the US community did experience several breaks away from unity in the early 1980s. It had its own fractious communities, each organized around different preferences for the operation of a national packet switching network.[22] E-mail systems in North America became embedded in four national networks with distinct technical features. Those networks were called CSNET, Bitnet, UUCP, and the TCP/IP Internet. In each case, e-mail was implemented in slightly different ways to accommodate differences in the administrative and technical preferences of each community of a network's administrators, and separate bodies of knowledge accumulated for each community.

Eventually this fractiousness would generate a significant operational cost, as it interfered with establishing a unified communications network throughout the country.[23] As described in the next chapter, these communities were brought together in 1987 by a combination of a clever technical invention and governance mechanism, which was part of the domain name system. While unification was an important step, it did not come for free. It required intelligent management of the domain name system. Privatizing the domain name system eventually would cause many issues.

---

service from the layer below it. The boundaries between the functions in each layer are defined so that functions in one layer can be altered but still interact with other layers without disabling the entire system.

[21] David Crocker, private communication, August 2008.

[22] The origins of these differences have been described in detail in Abbate (1999), among others. For its effects on e-mail development see Partridge (2008).

[23] To achieve unification, some clever inventors would have to learn to make e-mail move seamlessly between distinct networks. This accomplishment also came with its own set of costs. It is discussed in subsequent chapters.

The combination of inventive specialization and technical meritocracy played a crucial role in helping the Internet improve under government stewardship. That experience raised questions about whether it would continue after the privatization of the Internet. As later chapters show, it did continue to play an important role because its technical and institutional determinants stayed in place.

Governance at the Edges

DARPA had ceded to NSF a set of modular architectural principles for internetworking, and NSF had to implement these within the university system of the United States. DARPA had always permitted some degree of discretion to accommodate the geographic dispersion of its community, and the NSF scaled that discretion to many decisions. The NSF dispersed discretion over investment to many participants, reserving very few investment decisions for the center. This governance structure would have profound unforeseen consequences. Once the Internet backbone privatized, it would be easy to give discretion to private firms to invest. They inherited a structure that presumed widely dispersed and unrestricted initiatives in an end-to-end network.

How was discretion over investment given to many distinct participants prior to privatization? Several organizations nurtured the network's daily operations behind the scenes, while others administered operations within universities. All of these organizations were nonprofit entities with a variety of noncommercial goals, and each would adjust to the commercialization of the Internet in different ways.

Although key personnel were widely dispersed, there were four primary groups for managing and governing the NSF's Internet. Several of these were formal organizations.

1. The NSF: A US government agency providing most of the funding for some of the other organizations that also had other key managerial roles.
2. Mid-Level Networks: This heterogeneous group was comprised largely of nonprofit organizations that built and operated networks in distinct regions of the United States—for example, they provided connections between labs.

3. The Internet Activities Board (IAB): An organization comprised of key engineers and computer scientists who had designed the Internet in the earlier era, as well as many more who volunteered their time and managed changes to the design of TCP/IP compliant software and hardware.

4. Network administrators: Dispersed among scores of universities and research locations, this heterogeneous group oversaw investment at locations that affected user experience. This group pursued their own interests while also adhering to the previously discussed principle end-to-end.

All but the first organization, the NSF, would survive in an evolved form after privatization and take on new functions to suit the new era. To contemporary observers in the late 1980s it went without saying that this four-pronged governance structure did not look like the management for other communications networks. It certainly did not look like AT&T. Looking back on events, the director of the Harvard Information Infrastructure Project, Brian Kahin, observed,[24]

> The Internet began as an internetwork of special-purpose networks for an academic elite and evolved into a general-purpose internetwork open to commercial interconnection and uses. The public internet benefited from private campus-area and corporates internets needed to make disparate LANs work together.

This governance structure had emerged gradually in response to the pushes and pulls of inventive computer science emanating from researchers directly funded by the Defense Department and then the NSF. It did not have a hierarchical logic; no order came from a central chief executive officer or a chief technology officer. Instead, it emerged from a give and take between those in positions to make investments and invent new functionality. These institutions and processes were untested in commercial markets but contained a feature that made them resilient: they had accommodated the wide dispersion of technical skills and administrative discretion among participants in the research-oriented Internet.

Also, the NSF did not dictate to private participants, which would be important for later events. Private firms had always played a role in the NSF-

---

[24]Brian Kahin, private communication, October 4, 2013.

NET, but neither the sales volumes nor the prices were high for the equipment. The TCP/IP-based Internet by itself was not a big market, so NSF did not have much negotiating leverage. The local area network market was big, but largely unrelated. DEC, IBM, and others perceived nothing wrong with selling networking equipment that only worked with their own proprietary designs. Other firms in the data-communications business also provided related equipment, such as 3Com and Ungermann-Bass, again using their own proprietary designs. A few companies were in the business of making routers and related equipment. This was not a lonely business, but it was not a priority investment for most of the commercial participants except, perhaps, the start-ups. For example, during the 1980s Cisco was a small router company, a spin-off started by a few administrators from Stanford, and its business entirely depended on growth in data networking.[25]

Importantly, business was involved in managing the NSF backbone. Although the operation has many positive aspects, as the next chapter describes, unwinding the existing system also would cause many problems for privatization.

The arrangement started innocently enough. In 1985, after gaining stewardship of the Internet from the military, the NSF sought some form of private/public partnership to bring about upgrades (to a speed of 56K). The NSF had to follow standard government procedures, however. It received a budget from Congress for the project and solicited bids to build the network to increase its speed.[26] In 1986, the NSF received several bids for five-year contracts, set to run from 1987 to 1992. It selected a joint bid from MCI and IBM with MERIT (Michigan Education Research Information Triad) acting as the managing contractor.

---

[25] A division at IBM was another such supplier, though it had less strategic importance than the division that sold Token Ring, a proprietary IBM design. Wellfleet, a small mid-1980s start-up from the Boston area, Protean, another small start-up, and BBN, a contractor for DARPA, also made routers. For more on this industry in the 1980s, see Burg (2004).

[26] The initial investments sought to raise the speeds of data transfer between five supercomputer centers and researchers at other universities. In a few years the goal expanded to include connecting the entire university system and many research laboratories, not just a few elite research institutes and some big computer machines. The upgrade to the NSFNET from 56K/sec to 1.5M/sec with the installation of a T-1 line came about due to the call for such an upgrade from a report issued by the Office of Science and Technology Policy. The report, *A Research and Development Strategy for High Performance Computing*, was written after Senator Al Gore introduced a law in 1986 requiring the agency write it. That law passed.

These organizations had a range of assets and experience. MCI was a telephone company that provided the long-distance lines to carry the data from point to point. IBM provided the computer equipment, principally the routers, staff, and software to make the network work. The staff at MERIT had experience with operating a network for the research and educational community in the state of Michigan, which has some similarities, albeit at a smaller scale, to operating one for the entire country. Ultimately, this bid won as it significantly underbid other proposals. The low bid resulted from the actions of the state of Michigan, IBM, and MCI, who each contributed some of their own funds into the proposal.[27]

It is not clear why IBM and MCI's managements took this bidding strategy, and whether long-term monetary gain, the prospects for technical learning, or just plain public-spiritedness motivated the underbid. Because a mix of motives was not unusual for a private/public partnership involving major corporations, it is most likely that a combination was at the root. In addition, building the backbone for the NSFNET was technically challenging for the time and involved addressing a vast array of engineering experiments.[28] Many ambitious employees and managers were eager to work on these problems. The project also had a high profile and projected good images for the firms, but ultimately only involved small, specific divisions of each company.

As might arise from this mix of motives, over the next several years on some occasions the managers of the firms would act as if nonimmediate, nonmonetary motives were paramount, such as the pursuit of scientific knowledge. At other times, the monetary issues were at the forefront of

[27]Later the actual contribution of IBM and MCI to the building of the NSFNET became a point of contention. See the summary of these issues in Cook (1992–94), which is quite skeptical, and also Kesan and Shah (2001), which provides statistics about IBM and MCI's original bids.

[28]Looking back many years later for a retrospective look by NSF, Stephen Wolff said,

> There was an extraordinary commitment from MCI, from IBM, from MERIT and also from the state of Michigan—who put money into this partnership as well. It was clear from the outset that IBM thought it was learning something new about networking that it didn't know. It was also clear that MCI was learning about data networking, which it had zero experience in at this point. So both the major providers were learning something from this experience, but above and beyond that, they seemed dedicated to make it work.

See http://www.nsf.gov/news/special_reports/nsf-net/textonly/80s.jsp, accessed December 2014.

their actions. Such seeming ambivalence about motives was not particularly noteworthy until the movement toward privatization gained momentum, when the profit-making and non-profit-making goals came into conflict.

NSF used a standard agreement with MCI, IBM, and MERIT. This was less expensive than a cost-plus contract (where the price was not fixed by the bid) and less rigid than a fixed-price contract (where changing anything was difficult). It seemed to suit the project well at first, as it allowed Stephen Wolff to discuss developments with MCI, IBM, and MERIT as issues arose.

By 1988, NSF's management began to look ahead and anticipated finding itself in an unfamiliar position. Users had started to employ the backbone so intensively that it would require an upgrade soon. The contract with MCI, IBM, and MERIT was due to expire in 1992. It was easy to forecast that the network could exceed its capacity before this date. Either the NSF would have to consider rebids for the backbone or develop some other structure comparatively quickly.

Conversations about upgrading the backbone began quite early, around the same time as the conversations about privatization. Upgrading and privatization required planning in advance of 1992. Conflating the two topics was inevitable, and, as the next two chapters describe, led to controversy as the Internet privatized.

No Network Is an Island: The Mid-Level Networks

The NSFNET differed from the phone network in another respect. There was no dominant decision maker in the Internet. In part this was because the NSFNET did not live in isolation. Rather, it lived in a sea of other networks, and it connected to all of them. Coordinating with all of them produced many managerial challenges. Connecting all these "networks" with the NSFNET backbone made the Internet a "network of networks." The NSFNET had to become quite flexible and adaptable. Once again, this flexibility was adopted for parochial reasons, not with foresight about its positive consequences for the growth of the Internet after privatization.

The organizational structure for the NSFNET and its arrangement with other networks had arisen over time. The NSFNET connected with multiple regional networks around the country, generally known as *mid-level networks*. No single experience characterized all these relationships, nor could it. Virtually all of these mid-level networks were bottom-up efforts, organized to help regional participants, each structured in its own way. Many of the regional networks were not managed by established corporations with histories, like MCI and IBM. Rather, they were not-for-profit organizations that either provided networking services in regional areas or were quasi-public organizations with limited mandates to provide networking services for several universities.

These mid-level networks differed in size, experience, and managerial sophistication. Some involved small regional areas, such as BARRNET for the San Francisco Bay Area. Others involved multistate areas, such as SURANET, which focused on a large number of universities in the southeast.[29] Some had considerable experience with frontier networking issues. Many of them had come into existence to support supercomputer research communities or extend the NSFNET to some specific community.[30]

The mid-level networks gave the Internet wide geographic reach. Through the judicious use of subsidies, the NSF had shaped the coverage of the research Internet, and many of these mid-level networks also lived off funding from the regional universities they supported.[31] This geographic reach would be crucial after privatization, as others could build incrementally off what was already there. With only incremental investment the Internet could (and would) become available almost everywhere.

Figure 2.3 shows a picture of the fastest parts of the NSFNET backbone in 1991, just prior to its privatization. The backbone connected all the supercomputer centers and had two key features. One key feature was its bandwidth. It had replaced lines from a much slower national network, one that could not support remote access to supercomputers. Second,

[29]Specifically, LSU, Florida State, University of Alabama, Georgia Tech, Clemson, University of Tennessee, North Carolina's research triangle, University of Kentucky, Virginia Tech, University of Maryland, University of West Virginia, University of Delaware, and JVNC (at Princeton, NJ). See the description in Mandelbaum and Mandelbaum (1992), 63.

[30]The complete list of mid-level networks (and headquarters) in 1988, listed in Frazer (1995), pp. 25, were BARRnet (Palo Alto, CA), JVNCnet (Princeton, NJ), MERIT (Ann Arbor, MI), Midnet (Lincoln, NE), NCAR/USAN (Boulder, CO), NCSA (Champaign, IL), NorthWestNet (Seattle, WA), NYSERNet (Ithaca, NY), Pittsburgh Super Computing Center, San Diego Super Computer Center, SEQUINET (Houston, TX), SURANet (College Park, MD), WestNet (Salt Lake City, UT).

[31]Frazer (1995), for example, describes the process of moving mid-level networks to the high speed NSFNET in increments, as one successful demonstration motivated more networks to connect, and so on, resulting in over 170 networks being connected by July of 1988.

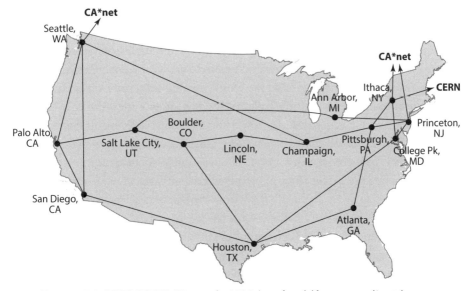

FIGURE 2.3. NSFNET T1 Network, 1991 (see ftp://ftp.uu.net/inet/maps /nsfnet/, accessed March 2004)

hundreds of universities and laboratories hooked into the NSF backbone. Many of those universities received their connections from regional networks, which connected into the NSFNET. That gave the network nearly national geographic coverage. Many participants anticipated a faster network with a greater number of users after the prior upgrade provided much evidence of the benefits of higher bandwidth.[32]

There were various ways to measure the growing size of the subnetworks that composed the Internet in the United States. In addition to the mid-level networks in the United States, there were many other networks throughout the globe. Most of them were not compatible with TCP/IP during the 1980s, but some began to be so at the end of the decade.

Symptoms of growth partly showed up in problems managing and documenting progress. For example, Ed Krol's 1987 *Hitchhikers' Guide to the Internet* mentions that three hundred networks attached to the Internet. Krol remarks that this size of a network presented considerable issues.[33]

---

[32]It also added connections to the increase in bandwidth for national data traffic. It was a T-3 bandwidth, i.e., 3X larger than T-1.

[33]For a copy of the original August 1987, draft, see http://www.gutenberg.org/dirs/etext 92/hhgi10.txt.

In 1990, the global networks that would become the Internet still remained just small enough for one extraordinary individual to document
them all in one book. John Quarterman published his 719-page reference
manual of every network on the globe, titled *The Matrix: Computer Networks
and Conferencing Systems Worldwide*, which became required reading for any
networking engineer and manager at the time. It provided the core reference material for every network and how to contact it. In just a few years,
however, after thousands of networks joined the Internet, such a book
would be impossible for any individual to produce. Instead, administrators
and users began to refer to an interconnected "network of networks."

Process as Governance

If central hierarchy existed anywhere in the Internet, it would have existed
at the Internet Architecture Board (IAB). It served as the formal organization in which groups of Internet specialists considered, debated, and ratified new design modifications for TCP/IP.[34] Yet, once again, as elsewhere
in the Internet, this organization adopted a range of institutional processes
that made it very unlike AT&T.

The IAB in the late 1980s had grown out of earlier institutions developed under the Department of Defense. The prior arrangement involved
a small group of designers who had been with the Internet almost from its
inception. It had been an invitation-only discussion between researchers
and the earliest government sponsors for the Internet. The invitations
went to researchers with long and trusted histories, such as David Clark,
Vint Cerf, David Farber, and Bob Kahn.

In the late 1980s, participants in the Internet sometimes quipped—sometimes sarcastically—that IAB was a council of elderly wise men.[35] The
quip embedded both respect for those involved and resentment over its
closed structure, which did not reflect the egalitarianism and hierarchical
fluidity affiliated with intellectual and engineering accomplishment, found
virtually everywhere else in the Internet community. Within a few years

---

[34] It began under DARPA's sponsorship under a different name and was renamed the Internet Advisory Board in 1984, then the Internet Activities Board in 1986, and in 1992 the Internet Architecture Board, the name it retains today. See Abbate (1999) and Russell (2014).

[35] Russell (2014) provides a summary of the evolution of governance and places it in
broader context.

that resentment would boil over and force a change, but in the late 1980s those events were still on the horizon.

The transition to wider participation came gradually. As the Internet transferred to the NSF, the participants in the IAB sought to develop an institutional structure that broadened participation and included more voices. This aspiration led to the establishment of the Internet Engineering Task Force, or IETF, as the organization in which to conduct most discussions for redesigns of Internet standards. The IETF initially began in 1986 to bring together all US-funded researchers with an interest in engineering standards for the Internet, but it quickly expanded to include vendors and many subgroups. In the late 1980s, the IAB selected the chair of the IETF, who then established chairs for subgroups to consider specific topics.

From the outset the IETF adopted principles for widening participation. Anybody was allowed to attend meetings for these subgroups. These were not conversations among invitation-only participants.[36]

That did not mean these groups lost their elite origins overnight. The general mission for this group, while not a secret, was inaccessible to anyone without appropriate technical training and experience. The group approved design modifications arranged by and for a consensus of technical experts. The norms were also well known, reflecting only slight modification of the norms that governed the technical meritocracy (with which most engineers were familiar). No expert had singular formal authority. Rather, one expert asked other experts for their opinions before deciding anything, and if one design were superior, then most experts would come to the same conclusion or consensus. After decisions were made, the recommendations were endorsed. That still left a great deal of open-ended procedural choices.

The IAB and IETF revolved around an item called a Request for Comment (RFC). These were technical and operational proposals, circulated primarily among the cognoscenti, but any interested party could find

---

[36] The formation of the IETF has been discussed by various authors, e.g., Abbate (1999), Leiner et al. (2003), or Simcoe (2006). Russell interprets its founding as a deliberate attempt by the Internet's earliest designers to widen participation in the discussion about the direction of design change—outside of the small invited club of insiders. Russell argues that the IETF was a way to do this without the insiders completely giving up control over its direction.

them.[37] There were informational RFCs, proposed RFCs, and even final RFCs. The former progressed to the latter, and, crucially, in the latter the writing and ideas had been vetted. Prior to the emergence of formal procedures, RFCs circulated among a small set of concerned administrators and designers, none of whom would unilaterally act without requesting and receiving feedback and comments from others in positions like their own.

The seemingly polite label, "Request for Comment," was inherited from its informal origins, though it belied its actual purpose in later years. An RFC could bring about real changes in procedures for many participants in the Internet. The topics could engender serious and passionate debates.

The role of the IAB and IETF in the late 1980s was most notable at the time for what it was *not*: beholden to the managerial auspices of a major corporation, such as AT&T or IBM. For that matter, these committees also did not simply ratify the design decisions of Intel or Microsoft or DEC, who were leading firms in personal computers and minicomputers. Although those firms, in principle, could send representatives to have a voice in shaping outcomes, at this point most did not. The Internet was not large enough to get much attention from the large firms, and they invested little in the standardization efforts, treating it like any other niche technology.

The operations of the IAB and IETF also were not anything like the operations of the Federal Communication Commission (FCC), the federal agency that regulated voice communications and broadcasting networks in the United States. The FCC had the force of law behind its rulings, and any given ruling faced court review about whether its rulings stayed within or strayed from statute. In contrast, the US government did not put the force of law behind many of the IAB or IETF standards except in one key area—in the supply of computing for defense. For example, the Department of Defense required all Unix-based systems to be compatible

[37]Their informality is noted in a description of the process before the IETF. Krol (1987) says,

> The internal workings of the Internet are defined by a set of documents called RFCs (Request for Comments). The general process for creating an RFC is for someone wanting something formalized to write a document describing the issue and mailing it to Jon Postel (postel@isi.edu). He acts as a referee for the proposal. It is then commented upon by all those wishing to take part in the discussion (electronically of course). It may go through multiple revisions. Should it be generally accepted as a good idea, it will be assigned a number and filed with the RFCs.

with TCP/IP.[38] That procurement requirement de facto led to standardization of TCP/IP across a wide range of systems.

The majority of RFCs *mandated* nothing, requesting only voluntary compliance. For most administrators compliance with a few key standards was voluntary in name, but mandatory if they wanted a functional Internet that remained compatible with TCP/IP.[39] Why did anybody comply with new proposals? Compliance occurred because the engineering meritocracy within the community of Internet inventors often did its job well. The new proposals often were better than what came before.[40] Administrators would adopt as part of deliberate upgrades of facilities or as a by-product of purchasing new Unix servers.

Rivalry also informed this arrangement. Many members of the IAB proudly contrasted their processes with those of the ITU, the International Telecommunications Union. The ITU is a quasi-international agency operated under the auspices of the United Nations. By the late 1980s the ITU had become involved in another effort to tame networking around the world. This effort was known as the open systems interconnection (OSI) model, and the model had become the principal rival to the US-led Internet effort.[41]

OSI began in the late 1970s, and the initial intent of OSI appeared rather laudable. The effort sought to develop a framework that anticipated incompatibilities between widely used communications and computing technology, and sought to ease their interoperability. It sought to ease the entry of competitive new products and data services by fostering their integration with existing services, speeding their deployment into widespread use. For some developers this effort aimed to break the hold of some major markets by established firms, such as IBM or AT&T.

For a time the movement also made progress—for example, developing and publishing a reference model that became widely quoted in textbooks

---

[38] Bill Joy was told to write and insert TCP/IP code into Berkeley Unix. Also see Abbate's (1999) account.

[39] See the discussion in, e.g., the Internet protocol, RFC-791.

[40] Occasional disagreement permitted multiple implementations (e.g., in how e-mail services operated), but as long as these stayed consistent with relevant RFCs, then different networks worked with one another.

[41] There have been many accounts of the ITU process, both complimentary and derisive. For more on this debate, see, e.g., Drake (1993) or Russell (2014).

and contemporary presentations.[42] That progress came early, and it became a mixed blessing. It made OSI a magnet for additional attention. In practice, the OSI involved efforts from many established companies, especially telephone companies in Europe and Asia. The attention brought extra personnel from many companies, and the extra resources helped in some of the efforts affiliated with OSI. Not all of the attention helped the movement succeed at its goals, however. Established industry players would send representatives to meetings and sometimes find ways to delay outcomes they did not support.[43] Many subgroups at OSI also became known for conducting thorough discussions of every suggestion from original thinkers with one more idea to consider. Among its critics in the United States, OSI developed a reputation for holding discussions that could bog down.

More to the point, the OSI effort led to several engineering designs that ostensibly performed many of the same functions as those performed by the TCP/IP-based Internet in the United States. For a time, especially in the 1980s, OSI had an air of slow inevitability about it, and its early progress also meant its detractors took it very seriously. That gave a sense of competitive urgency to the group growing around TCP/IP.

Strains of nationalisms also became mixed into the rivalry between OSI and TCP/IP communities. TCP/IP was funded by the US military and was identified with the US military until the transfer of the governance of research-oriented activity to the NSF. OSI was a multinational multilateral effort, and for some participants, was aimed at reducing the control of US firms, such as IBM and AT&T.

Many participants in both efforts tried to rise above the rivalry, but no amount of diplomacy could ever wipe away the undercurrent of the technical meritocracy. Despite equal accomplishments in some areas, some gaps between the accomplishments of the two efforts began to become apparent in the late 1980s. When OSI's plodding pace lay behind its unrealized aspirations, a group of TCP/IP's supporters began taking overt pride in their seemingly scrappier and more grounded effort, and the way

---

[42] The OSI model had seven layers: Application, Presentation, Session, Transport, Network, Data Link, and Physical Layers.

[43] Russell (2014) singles out IBM—which tried to extend its dominance in mainframes and PCs to networking—for such behavior.

it produced protocols that worked in practice immediately.[44] The rivalry would eventually come to a head, and on the eve of privatization.

Governance at the Core

By 1989, just prior to privatization of the Internet, the IAB and IETF were evolving toward many of the features of a mature standard-setting organization. While a set of informal norms governed activities, one unresolved tension lay at the core of the organization. At the cost of getting ahead of the events, it is useful to articulate this tension, as it reflected the strengths and weaknesses of a nonhierarchical research organization.

While the core of the design was inherited from a military research effort, the community growing around it preferred administrative processes that reflected the norms they all shared. While the technical meritocracy of those norms respected the conceptual and vocal clarity that emerged from the hierarchical process, it also desired a process open to a wide participation and considerate of a variety of opinions. It also favored giving large discretion to users to implement designs, and it desired pragmatism—namely, solutions that worked today.

At a practical level it meant the IAB and IETF were forums where those who cared about the operations of the Internet could meet, compare notes, make suggestions, and, if necessary, put forward technical fixes to common problems. More broadly, it also meant the decisions involved a combination of theory and implementation, frontier scientific debate, and pragmatic compromise. Unlike the military era, participation was not restricted.

A shared sense of commitment to the success of the technology united the participants even when they disagreed on the details of how to achieve it. Hence, many participated in good faith. There was little presumption that others deliberately obstructed progress for private gains. Not that private opinion and disputes were absent. Rather, as in any organization involving so many technical experts, specialists began to stake out expertise on specific issues.[45]

---

[44] Russell (2014) provides extensive analysis about this point.

[45] The line between scientific judgment and prejudice is a fine one, and would play a large role in later events. For example, the working group for hypertext would greet Tim Berners-Lee's suggestions for the World Wide Web with considerable skepticism. He encountered opposition even though he had a proposal that already worked and was widely adopted. It was inconsistent with the views of many of the participants, however. See chapter 7.

Not all specialists came to agreement, and those disagreements eventually had to be settled with intervention from the center. While potential disputes were channeled through a process that most participants regarded as fair and open to argument, there was some latent tension between the bottom-up nature of the IETF's subgroups, and lack of democratic processes for appointing the leadership of the IAB.[46] The IETF's committees adopted the principles of dispute resolution by peer review from academic computing science—any proposal with a reasonable articulation received a hearing, but no proposal was accepted without peer review. All relevant parties had a right to comment on proposals and argue about their merit, but any disagreements were settled through analytic argument, empirical demonstration, and scientific judgment. Yet final authority rested with senior leadership of the IAB, which had not changed in years, and was comparatively closed to new invitations.

This arrangement had its defenders and its critics. To defenders this arrangement mixed an academic debate society with urgent needs of a network operated in the present moment, where many of the suggestions came from its operators and users. All participants shared respect for the importance of a working prototype. As noted earlier, a working technical prototype is a new design whose purpose it is to show that an idea will do what it proposes. Yet respect for the working prototype could go only so far in limiting the ad hoc and arbitrary decision making that was typically produced by dominant personalities and prejudice. While it is too simple to say that prototypes trumped theory, participants would support a prototype that worked *today* instead of a proposal that might work perfectly sometime in the future. The emphasis on working prototypes also reduced delays and moved matters forward.

To detractors this arrangement did not generate principles for resolving disputes between competing prototypes. At some point the leadership and the participants had to have distinct perspectives, and were bound to disagree. Any disagreement would require the center to assert its authority. Yet the center did not derive its authority from the participants through any formal process.

The impending privatization highlighted this tension. Privatization was about to introduce a new constituency of users, entrepreneurial firms,

---

[46] See Russell (2014).

and designers, who had little patience for hierarchical practices that did not reflect market realities. In other words, there was going to be strong pressure to get rid of the "council of elders" at the IETF and replace it with a process supportive of the users of the privatized Internet. What shape would it take? This was an open question in 1989. As chapter 7 describes, the council of elders would bow out just prior to privatization and adopt a new structure of leadership.

The Economic Consequences of Governance

By the time the community began discussing the privatization of the Internet in 1989, it possessed many of its recognizable features. First, end-to-end became a design principle for achieving functionality in spite of heterogeneous capital at local settings. Despite such differences, all installations could communicate with one another.

Accommodating heterogeneous deployment overlapped with the economic benefit; while administrators deployed some capital specifically for the Internet, the network repurposed existing capital. Repurposing of existing capital had a pragmatic economic advantage. It reduced costs for administrators with limited budgets.

A related economic pattern had begun to emerge. The entire system did not come crashing down simply because there was a technical and commercial disagreement over the next direction of improvement to embed in a working prototype. For example, one user could choose to physically implement his or her local layer in one way, while another person could choose a different method.

Isolating disputes and accommodating heterogeneous installations supported another—and, in the long run, especially important—economic feature of TCP/IP: It permitted users with distinct *economic* conditions to *participate* on the same communications network and use its applications; for example, exchange e-mail.[47] In many research environments with limited funds, such technical and operational flexibility had a strong appeal. In the commercial market after privatization this feature would be crucial for fostering greater participation from households.

---

[47] In the research environment of the 1980s this was not a trivial benefit. It gave TCP/IP a chance to spread out from the pioneering universities, Stanford, MIT, UCLA, to other elite universities, Illinois, Michigan, Georgia Tech, and far beyond, to those who normally could not afford to participate in a frontier technology.

Finally, as it had deployed, the Internet possessed technical features and governance processes well suited for sustaining a virtuous cycle. Increasing participation brought with it a larger community of networks. More users further led to a larger array of suggestions in the IAB, on shareware sites, and in discussion groups for improving the technology. These improvements would accrue as new designs, new applications, and a well-functioning network. Eventually that led to more participation. Participation on the TCP/IP-supported Internet handed back something valuable in exchange—a group of other participants in other locations. That is not circular logic, but a statement about coordinating around a shared platform.

How would this arrangement support the growth of innovation from the edges in commercial markets? Several features of the Internet at this point would become essential for outcomes in later events. To summarize, among them, the Internet accommodated considerable heterogeneity across network installations that remained TCP/IP compatible. It aided the repurposing of capital from other parts of computing—that is, the use of a piece of existing equipment for a purpose other than the one originally motivating its purchase, as long as it remained TCP/IP compatible. It also insulated developments on one component of the Internet, such as the transport layer, from a technical disagreement in another, such as the application layer. Finally, it permitted users from distinct economic conditions to participate as long as they remained TCP/IP compatible. That is a formidable list of positive attributes for encouraging adoption and widespread use.

3

Honest Policy Wonks

Well, I will be offering—I'll be offering my vision when my campaign begins. And it will be comprehensive and sweeping. And I hope that it will be compelling enough to draw people toward it. I feel that it will be. But it will emerge from my dialogue with the American people. I've traveled to every part of this country during the last six years. During my service in the United States Congress, I took the initiative in creating the Internet. I took the initiative in moving forward a whole range of initiatives that have proven to be important to our country's economic growth and environmental protection, improvements in our educational system. During a quarter century of public service, including most of it long before I came into my current job, I have worked to try to improve the quality of life in our country and in our world. And what I've seen during that experience is an emerging future that's very exciting, about which I'm very optimistic, and toward which I want to lead.

—*Al Gore, March 9, 1999*[1]

What did Al Gore invent and when did he invent it? The topic became a guaranteed laugh line during the presidential campaign of 2000. The joke was so well known that even the candidate could poke fun at

---

[1] The quote came in response to a question from Wolf Blitzer on CNN's Late Edition. He asked: "I want to get to some of the substance of domestic and international issues in a minute, but let's just wrap up a little bit of the politics right now. Why should Democrats, looking at the Democratic nomination process, support you instead of Bill Bradley, a friend of yours, a former colleague in the Senate? What do you have to bring to this that he doesn't necessarily bring to this process?" See Wiggins (2000), McCullagh (2000), and Agre (2000).

FIGURE 3.1 Al Gore, US senator and vice president
(photo from January 1, 1994)

FIGURE 3.2 Rick Boucher, representative from Virginia's 9th District,
1983–2011 (photo from official 109th Congress
Photo, photo taken July 28, 2007)

himself and expect a response. On September 26, 2000, with the election less than six weeks away, Gore participated in a town hall meeting as part of MTV's *Choose or Lose* series. Students attended at the Media Union at the University of Michigan. Gore quipped, "I invented the environment." The friendly audience erupted in laughter.[2]

How did a senator's involvement in Internet policy in the 1980s evolve into a joke? What distance lay between joke and fact, and what did that distance say about the development of the Internet under government sponsorship?

One element of this situation appears in the quote at the start of this chapter. The interview occurred in March 1999, well before the presidential race heated up. Out of all the muddled sentences, one would eventually garner the most attention: *I took the initiative in creating the Internet*.

Initially the interview received little public attention, but one reporter made a story of it, and political insiders used it as fodder for a few jokes.[3] Senate majority leader Trent Lott, no political ally of Gore's, issued a press release ridiculing the interview. Lott sarcastically claimed to invent the paper clip, adding cheekily that "paper clips binded the nation together." Vice president Dan Quayle, poking fun at his own less-than-stellar orthographical reputation, said, "If Gore invented the Internet, then I invented Spell-Check."[4]

Professional advisors to politicians stress the importance of controlling the message. In this instance, Gore gradually lost control. He fought back with quips[5] and self-deprecating humor,[6] but neither slowed the onslaught of mockery. Other public figures picked up the meme about invention, and gradually it gained traction as a source of humor. With frequent retelling, Gore's awkward phrase about creation morphed into a ripe and exaggerated claim about invention. For example, late night television entertainers Jay Leno and David Letterman worked humor into their monologues

---

[2] Recounted in Wiggins (2000).

[3] McCullagh (2000) and Agre (2000).

[4] Wiggins (2000).

[5] The quip by Trent Lott about paper clips was returned with the volley, "It's no surprise that Senator Lott and his fellow Republicans are taking credit for an invention that was created a long time ago. After all, they're the party whose ideas will take us back to the Dark Ages."

[6] "I was pretty tired when I made that comment because I had been up very late the night before inventing the camcorder," Gore told the Democratic National Committee on Saturday, March 20, 1999.

about other things Gore invented. In Letterman's case, his writers also created a "Top Ten List" of things invented by Gore. Journalists eventually began to quote the exaggerated claim as if it was fact, and George Bush campaign television commercials used it as well.[7] By the end of his presidential campaign most audiences assumed Gore had not merely fumbled over his words in a television interview, but had *actually* claimed to be the inventor of the Internet.

What does the evolution of this joke illustrate? For reasons explained in later chapters, by the time Gore ran for president, the origins of the Internet had become buried in all the flotsam and jetsam the blossoming of the commercial Internet generated. While it was not readily apparent to the man on the street who had invented what and when, it also was obvious that no single individual could take credit for inventing the Internet. Such a claim came across as absurdly funny, and from a politician it came across as an egotistical fantasy, the delusions of someone who overestimates their own power and significance. More to the point, it was a powerful slogan, and persuasive to the uninformed.

Perhaps more remarkable, except to a cynic about public discourse, once the joke about Al Gore's exaggerated claims gained credence, the actual words of the interview and the actual facts of the Internet's invention did not play a role in popular conversation. That observation begs the deeper question: If the actual facts had been widely known, would they have helped or hurt Gore? The answer is not so clear. Looking closely, more accuracy might have suggested Gore had had good intentions, but it also might have suggested an ambiguous interpretation of Gore's actions. That ambiguity also touches on a theme in this chapter, so it merits understanding.

Gore did have a record to stand on, and that seemed to work in his favor. Although congressional records are typically pockmarked by many more symbolic initiatives than actual accomplishments, Gore's interest in the Internet was not in dispute, and neither were his legislative accomplishments. As early as 1986, for example, then-Senator Gore made speeches on

---

[7]In a January 2000 written column, Steven Roberts and Cokie Roberts reported on a series of person-in-the-street exchanges. They started with: "When Gore does try to assert himself, it often backfires—witness his claim that he helped invent the Internet." The announcer on a Bush commercial states, "If Al Gore invented the Internet, then I invented the remote control." Recounted in Wiggins (2000).

the Senate floor supporting basic research in computer networking. He compared it with public support for highways. He referred to the information superhighway, a metaphor Gore would use frequently over the next few years. For example, inserted into the congressional record is the following from 1986 (excerpted):

> In order to cope with the explosion of computer use in the country, we must look to new ways to advance the state-of-the-art in telecommunications—new ways to increase the speed and quality of the data transmission. Without these improvements, the telecommunications networks face data bottlenecks like those we face every day in our crowded highways.
>
> The private sector is already aware of the need to evaluate and adopt new technologies. One promising technology is the development of fiber optic systems for voice and data transmission. Eventually we will see a system of fiber optic systems being installed nationwide.
>
> America's highways transport people and materials across the country. Federal freeways connect with state highways which connect in turn with county roads and city streets. To transport data and ideas, we will need telecommunications highway connecting users coast to coast, state to state, city to city.[8]

Gore eventually would become chairman of the Senate Subcommittee on Science, Technology, and Space. He would conduct hearings in 1989 about upgrading the Internet backbone. Those hearings, in turn, would lead Gore to sponsor a piece of legislation in November of 1991: The High-Performance Computing Act of 1991, passed by both houses and signed by President Bush.[9] The act provided a framework for funding the National Science Foundation's efforts to upgrade the Internet backbone and support use of supercomputers in universities. These efforts directly produced a key component of the Internet, its first long distance high-speed lines. It also indirectly funded other inventions discussed in the next chapter, the NCSA (National Center for Super Computing Applications) Mosaic

---

[8] Wiggins (2000).

[9] That does not complete the privatization of the Internet, however. The next fall Gore ran as the vice presidential running mate to presidential candidate Bill Clinton, and could not take steps in Congress. This chapter describes the last steps, sponsored by representative Rick Boucher.

browser and the inventions that would become the most popular web server. As several later chapters describe, these inventions became essential for catalyzing growth of electronic commerce.

Gore's record also was not in dispute a decade later. Not many other contemporary national politicians in the 1980s had shared Gore's interest in large-scale networking. It gave Gore a distinctive legacy.[10]

Why all the fuss over such a legacy? Political opponents sought to undermine any gains Gore might accrue from having such distinctive tastes. Of course, part of the motivation arose from naked political desires to have George Bush Jr. elected president. In addition, the debate about Gore's record also served as a proxy war for a big and long-standing ideological fight about the role of the government in subsidizing invention and technical advance, particularly when many aspects of that advance, such as its market value, could not be predicted or anticipated with certainty. The computer industry offered one of the best cases for such government involvement in an industry that faced unpredictability about its value. Hence, undermining the view that government played a salutary role in this specific industry also undermined the broader assertions about government's positive role.

Long before the actions of the NSFNET grabbed the attention of the US electorate, the US computer industry and federal government coexisted in a mutually beneficial relationship. The US computer industry employed many inventors, as did many US research laboratories and universities. The US computer industry commercialized those inventions, and the federal government bought frontier computers and applications at uncommonly high prices. NASA, the Department of Defense, the US Census, the Federal Aviation Administration, and the National Security Administration all had served as the lead buyers for frontier computing of the 1950s, 1960s, and 1970s. Both sides could see plenty of benefit from the relationship. Through its procurement of frontier computing, the US government indirectly subsidized a part of the innovation in the US computing indus-

---

[10]Several participants in the government-sponsored Internet, especially those involved in building and governing the network, remembered Gore's interest, and during his presidential run would affirm that Gore made significant contributions, highlighting the 1991 legislation. This included quotes from Vint Cerf in *Time Magazine,* June 14, 2000, and a widely quoted Internet mailing from Bob Kahn and Vint Cerf on September 28, 2000. See additional observations about attempts to set the facts straight in public discourse in Agre (2000).

try. US agencies gained advantages in new capabilities, new military strategies, and new types of information.[11]

US firms gained from the government's demand for frontier computing. This demand also gave them a leg up in learning how to meet the private demand that arose not long after government demand. The learning could have great strategic importance, because private demand tended to grow exponentially, eventually overwhelming any government demand. The pattern had played itself out in numerous technologies: time-sharing, client/server computing, graphics, LANs, workstations, graphical user interfaces, VLSI design, RISC processors, relational databases, parallel databases, data mining, parallel computing, RAID/disk servers, portable communications, speech recognition, and broadband.[12]

By the time Gore ran for president, the Internet appeared to be yet another example in a long string of examples where government subsidies played a role in fostering frontier developments—except that this one differed in an important respect. In a short time—by 1999—it was obvious that nobody a decade earlier, not even the most optimistic visionary, could have forecasted the direction the Internet took in commercial markets. After privatization, too many contingencies and surprises shaped outcomes, making the ultimate economic outcome fundamentally unknowable in advance. It strained credibility to believe one politician or one government policy had had much foresight about the specific consequences that would result from subsidizing invention of the Internet. Any statement suggesting such foresight invited ridicule.

This chapter begins to set the record straight. What actions had government managers taken, and when had they taken them? Privatization involved more than just privatizing the Internet backbone, as this chapter describes. The actual record contains complications and requires a nuanced understanding. Broadening use of the Internet occurred with the

---

[11]See, e.g., the comprehensive accounting of these relationships in Flamm (1988), and a summary of some of the transfers of inventions from universities to industry in National Research Council of the National Academies (2003).

[12]See, e.g., the page 6 and 7 of National Research Council of the National Academies (2003). It covers a range of computing technologies, including those mentioned above and the Internet and World Wide Web. In some cases industry laboratories precedes university work, but in most cases university work precedes work in industry laboratories, and spills into it.

blessing of government managers, and certainly not with complete foresight about the consequences of their policies.

The Symbiosis between Government and Industry

The happiness with the symbiotic experience in computing contrasted with the results from many other federal programs to subsidize large-scale innovative activities. The list of unsatisfying experiences with federal subsidy of technology was long. The supersonic transport, the communication satellite, the space shuttle, the Breeder reactor, the synthetic fuels program, and the photovoltaics commercialization program, to name a few, had been funded with high hopes and big promises.[13] While large-scale innovative activities funded at the federal level might yield big scientific demonstrations, the projects yielded mixed results for commercial success.

The details differed, but the general character of the problem did not; something disorderly always emerged. Once the industry became dependent on funding from the federal government, it became difficult to untie the relationship, and attempts to do so came after enormous political efforts. Sometimes simply managing the relationship placed unusually large strains on all parties. The profits and stockholder value of commercial firms became tied to the nuances of policy decisions in direct ways. The employment of workers in politicians' districts depended on whether technological projects reached intermediate bureaucratic benchmarks. That induced wrangling and negotiating over the use of public dollars and assets, not to mention self-dealing in the setting and design of benchmarks for policy decisions, which could not be divorced from the self-interested actions of firms and employees. Scandals and the hint of corruption made headlines, often overshadowing good intentions and technical accomplishments.

Those unsatisfying experiences framed many questions prior to the privatization of the Internet. Would privatization of the National Science Foundation's (NSF's) backbone resemble most of the experiences in computing, helping the industry generally, or would it lead to a disorderly process, as occurred in other large-scale technologies when government handed assets to private firms? As it would turn out, events would con-

---

[13] For analysis of many experiences in the 1960s and 1970s, see Cohen and Noll (1991).

tain a bit of everything. Privatization initially involved disorderliness and eventually gave industry a tremendous boost.

Disorderliness during the privatization of the NSFNET did not arise from lack of planning or poor engineering. There was no disorderliness with many aspects of the planning. Starting with the meetings in 1989, the National Science Foundation conducted robust conversations with a wide variety of stakeholders, such as the IETF and regional network operators.[14] There was no disorderliness with the engineering. Throughout the first half of the 1990s, every day users woke up, logged on, sent electronic mail, and the Internet continued to work well.

To the extent that it arose, disarray and confusion arose from a combination of political, administrative, and economic issues. As this chapter explains, extracting the NSF from the Internet involved greater complications than any of the management at the NSF had anticipated. By mid-1992 it was clear that Wolff could not merely turn off the NSFNET or just hand it over to IBM, MCI, or any other organization operating the Internet backbone. Several other firms also had staked out commercial positions, and they did not want the transition to provide IBM or any other insider with a competitive advantage in the soon-to-arrive competitive world where the NSF no longer played a role.

As it turned out, the resolution of these issues changed the plans for privatization. Those changes left irreversible marks on the structure of the commercial industry, and generally for the better. The chapter provides the long explanation for how that happened, but a short summary will give a sense of where the detail leads. Stated succinctly, after taking some questionable actions that received considerable scrutiny, Wolff listened to the advice of many honest policy wonks and put their advice into practice.

What was an honest policy wonk? Describing an honest policy wonk is a bit like describing an elephant for someone who has never seen one. A description in words will sound odd. An honest policy wonk was someone who worked in government and sincerely aspired to make policy decisions as part of serving a reasoned conception of the public interest. It was easier to say what an honest policy wonk was not: it could not be bribed; did not suppress information, even to save someone in a powerful

---

[14]See Brian Kahin, Request for Comment 1192, Commercialization of the Internet, Internet Engineering Task Force, http://tools.ietf.org/html/rfc1192, accessed February 2014.

position from embarrassment; did not decide new rules behind closed doors after consulting with a few executives; did not tow a demagogic line merely because the party in power desires it; did not abandon ideals or dreams for mere material reward or short-term payoff.

Most honest policy wonks arose in less-than-glamorous places within government service: at the FCC, at the NSF, at DARPA, and elsewhere within the broader technology policy community in Washington, DC. The Internet inspired honest policy wonks. It appealed to the utopian ideals of the global communication network. Many could speak of a vision, working for a better day, vaguely in the future, when networks could connect the world and permit participants from far reaches of the earth to communicate with one another.[15]

Getting a Kick out of Acceptable Use

The NSF operated under a charter—granted by the US Congress several decades earlier—that most of its employees found inspiring. The charter gave the NSF a grand purpose: to stretch the frontier of science and aid the institutions of discovery. Most employees believed in the power of science to make the world a better place. Notwithstanding the higher ideals, some words in the NSF charter put limits on the scope of the NSF's mission, and did not inspire such love. While the NSF's mission allowed the NSF to directly help research in the United States, it did not give the NSF permission to start an industry that could compete with others already in existence.[16]

The charter embodied a convenient fiction. The NSF occasionally subsidized industry without admitting to it directly. If scientists conducted science as an end in itself, then the NSF's mission remained safely distant from the interests of commercial firms. Scientists would make discoveries with the aid of public moneys and firms would use what they considered valuable. However, the separation of science from industry was a fiction in areas where scientific discovery could have immediate pragmatic applications, as in some parts of frontier computing. In these cases, the NSF would pay for discovery that firms could put to use. Often at the same time the NSF would subsidize training of computer scientists that indus-

---

[15]A great deal has been written about the ideal visions that propelled the networking community. See, e.g., Edwards (1997), Hafner and Lyon (1998), Oxman (1999), Castells (2001), Markoff (2005), and Turner (2006).

[16]This is described in Abbate (1999) and Kesan and Shah (2001).

try could put to work on the same technologies. In a few well-known cases, the NSF had funded research that had led to inventions that made venture capitalists rich.

The growth of the Internet under the NSF management put strain on that fiction and exposed its weakness. More to the point, the charter did not give the NSF permission to build the Internet with taxpayer money so firms could conduct commerce over that network. The precedent had been set some time ago: if the NSF ever stepped over those bounds they could expect a congressional hearing to bring the agency back in line. But there was little precedence for the situation the NSF faced: what if the technology could do two types of activities—help scientists conduct scientific research *and* help private users conduct commercial transactions?

The acceptable use policy, or AUP for short, was the policy for addressing this type of question. The policy issue did not present itself in a clean way in practice. A common situation from the late 1980s illustrates one aspect of the issue: could students at a university hold a flea market online, one selling, say, tickets for a college football game to another? If it was done informally over electronic mail, there was not much anybody could do about that transaction. However, if the owner of the tickets advertised their existence on a university owned and operated server, then it potentially violated the AUP, as the advertisement used university resources to support commerce. University administrators might take the post down and advise the student to post outside the Internet, in a privately operated bulletin board network. The student might complain, and with some merit, that most of the potential buyers—other students—were not using the privately operated bulletin board network. Requiring all transactions to move off the Internet was not in the interests of either buyer or seller.

Carriers faced a more complex set of questions, and these arose from the same origins. If a network carried traffic from the NSF-sponsored Internet, was it acceptable to carry traffic from anyone else over the same lines? At first the answer was *absolutely not*. If the US government paid to set up the infrastructure, as it did with the NSFNET, carrying commercial traffic could be interpreted as a violation of the NSF's charter.

Most engineers despised this policy for no reason other than its pointless rigidity. Engineers saw quite clearly that economies of scale would be easier to achieve by putting as much traffic as possible over the backbone lines. Anything else—such as separating lines into NSF traffic and non-NSF traffic would be inefficient, a ridiculous limitation on achieving an optimal use of expensive resources.

All could see that once the government no longer owned and governed the NSFNET, questions about the AUP did not have to stand in the way of sharing traffic. That was partly what motivated the plan to privatize in the first place. However, it also introduced a hitch. What policies would apply during the transition, the time between the announcement that the NSF would privatize the Internet and the moment that it actually happened?

This was not a trivial question. Discussion about privatization began quietly in 1989 but had become public by 1990. In the meantime, the NSF-NET had to operate, make upgrades to accommodate growing traffic, and provide service for academic users. Foresighted entrepreneurial firms had to keep earning revenue and covering as much of their operating costs as possible. Yet the NSF did not—could not—act quickly. As delays began to creep into the schedule for privatization, firms looked after their own interests. Disorderliness lay around the corner.

Entrepreneurs Taking Action

In 1989 three entrepreneurs saw an opportunity and acted: PSINet and UUNET started their businesses. PSINet (PSI = Performance Systems International) had been founded by William Schrader and Martin Schoffstall in late 1989 by privatizing the lines that supported the NYSERNET, the regional network that Schrader had managed until that point. UUNET was founded at roughly the same time by Rick Adams.

As participants in operating parts of the network, Schrader, Schoffstall, and Adams were familiar with the plans to privatize the NSFNET and thought about commercial issues the same way. They went into the business of carrying TCP/IP-based traffic in advance of the growth of the market, and viewed themselves as foresighted entrepreneurs. They anticipated a big growing market in the near term. They also could see that many Internet insiders did not care to start businesses, nor did many established firms, such as telephone companies. Unlike these established players, these entrepreneurs forecast that the new market would be a good future for an entrepreneurial firm.[17] They located their firms near each

---

[17] Bill Schrader, private conversation, July 2008.

other in northern Virginia, a stone's throw from Washington, DC, which they regarded as necessary to deliver lobbying that might protect their young firms.

How did they each start their firms? Rick Adams merely changed the status of his organization. He turned the nonprofit organization by the same name—a hosting site that facilitated Usenet, e-mail, and text exchanges between bulletin boards—into a profit-oriented firm that provided backbone services independent of government backbone assets. Schrader and Schoffstall cut a sweetheart deal. They bought assets from the state of New York and NYSERNET, turned around and rented services back to the very same customers. The university users liked the deal because they began getting services from a large, growing private firm that realized greater efficiencies and passed some of the savings to the users. The state government of New York liked it because it could claim that its public expenditure had spawned private enterprise. For PSINet the situation was as close to ideal as any entrepreneurial company could desire. They gained working assets on day one, as well as a set of paying customers.[18]

The founding of two entrepreneurial firms changed the chess game for IBM. IBM no longer could anticipate being the sole beneficiary of privatization. IBM would face competition from these upstarts, and potentially others that followed their example, adding to what IBM anticipated from others (such as Sprint). The entrepreneurs also would add their voices to the policy discussion, pushing for policies IBM did not favor.

As delays mounted in the privatization plan, IBM devised a strategy for the time period before privatization completed.[19] It established Advanced Network Services (ANS) as its commercial division for the private Internet. IBM's managers sensed that it could gain an advantage for ANS's services by interpreting the AUP in a self-serving and narrow way, one that yielded strategic gains during the transition. As figure 3.3 illustrates, the NSFNET provided national coverage. De facto, so too would ANS. IBM's management believed that ANS's geographic scope would provide it with advantages when bidding for new business. It believed it could keep the advantage to itself if it did not allow any interconnection with a competitor.

---

[18] Bill Schrader, private conversation, July 2008.
[19] Cook (1992–94) provides a detailed account of these steps.

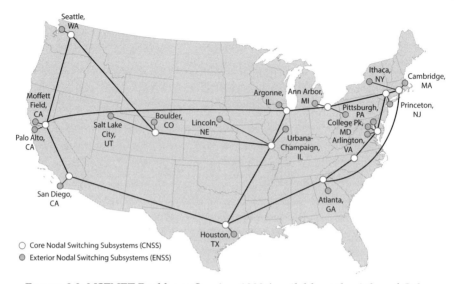

FIGURE 3.3. NSFNET Backbone Service, 1993 (available at the Atlas of Cyber Spaces, maintained by Martin Dodge, http://personalpages.manchester .ac.uk/staff/m.dodge/cybergeography//atlas/geographic.html, accessed March 2004)

IBM's lawyers wrote a self-serving legal opinion. The opinion stated, in effect, that IBM and its newly established division, ANS, could not inter-connect with others because it would lead to mixing of traffic from research-oriented and non-research-oriented sources, violating their lawyer's inter-pretation of the AUP's application to the NSFNET. Since they did not want to violate the law, the opinion said, IBM's managers had no choice but to refuse interconnection to the NSFNET to any other firm carrying traffic from sources other than the research community. That meant practically everybody would be denied interconnection, especially PSINet and UUNET, since much of their new growth was coming from outside the research community.

Through additional maneuvers IBM tried to tip the scales in its own favor. Its lawyers split ANS into two firms, one for profit and the other not for profit. When ANS managed to carry commercial traffic it involved the for-profit company. When it carried NSF traffic it involved the not-for-profit organization. Of course, in either case, the traffic traveled over the very lines that ANS refused to connect with others carrying commercial traffic. However, through this legal technicality, the traffic was not mixed.

There was one more aspect, and it infuriated observers who cared about Internet policy.[20] IBM's split gave it a way to interconnect with other regional networks already in the NSF network. When this was announced, it was quite controversial, especially because the NSF seemed to initially accept the proposal. ANS's managers put forward a settlement plan for interconnection with the for-profit part of ANS. In this plan, other firms paid ANS an interconnection fee for the volume of traffic another network put on ANS's lines. These actions were designed to leave ANS as the biggest operator of the national backbone, with no close rival, and in a position to collect money from others.

Outraged observers cried foul.[21] Bill Schrader gained attention by accusing ANS of gaining a competitive advantage against PSINet with the help of the NSF, violating the NSF's charter. It eventually would lead to an investigation from the Office of the Inspector General and a congressional hearing.

With the benefit of hindsight it is possible to see why ANS's proposals and behavior generated outrage. First, it raised issues about the different conduct appropriate for assets when they are both public and private. In the eyes of many participants of the research-oriented Internet, IBM's assets were supposed to be operated in the public interest until the NSF was privatized, not prior to it. A second issue arose over the unilateral and nontransparent way in which IBM received these decisions. ANS's actions were not conducted in broad daylight. The Internet community was accustomed to participatory decision making for changes in the use of public assets. Instead, these actions were taken without consulting the broader Internet community, and with only consulting Stephen Wolff. Wolff had been involved because the cooperative agreement between IBM and the NSF had to be modified.[22]

As it turned out, one congressman was paying attention and decided to take action. Rick Boucher of Virginia chaired the subcommittee that oversaw NSF's activities. His subcommittee eventually would conduct hearings

---

[20] This is described in detail in Cook (1992–94) and Kesan and Shah (2001).

[21] The nontransparency for the legal maneuvering magnified the outrage. Stephen Wolff was notified, though no others knew about the actions. See Cook (1992–94) for a summary.

[22] The outrage shows up in the accounts of Cook (1992–94) and Kesan and Shah (2001).

in March 1992. A number of people testified, including Schrader, Wolff, and others. These hearings highlighted the confrontation and would change the shape of the commercial Internet, leaving an indelible mark.

Organizing against IBM

Before Boucher held his hearing, one other significant event had profound long-term consequences for the Internet. PSINet and UUNET took action designed to bypass ANS's maneuvers, and, in doing so, PSINet and UUNET created their own interconnection policy. Starting from conversations in late 1990,[23] and involving Susan Estrada, who operated CERFNET (California Education and Research Foundation), based in San Diego, this team established the Commercial Internet eXchange, or CIX for short.[24] The conversations came to fruition in the summer of 1991. CIX solved the interconnection problem all three of them faced.

The engineering behind CIX was straightforward. CIX placed a router and a series of interconnecting lines from the three providers in Washington, DC. Users of one firm's network could send direct messages to users of another firm's network. CIX resolved interconnection issues with an innovative contracting solution. All firms who joined the CIX brought their traffic to the router at the center of the exchange and agreed to take traffic from every other firm who deposited traffic at the same location. Each member of CIX paid a flat fee to support the cost of the equipment and maintenance, and each agreed *not* to charge each other on the basis of the volume of traffic they delivered.

Soon thereafter CIX opened another router in Santa Clara (eventually moving it next door to Palo Alto), and another in Chicago a year later. CIX quickly covered the needs of the burgeoning private industry in the entire country. CIX's actions offered a solution to support interconnection between networks. CIX's solution put all the costs in fixed fees and left none of it to volume pricing. It contrasted with ANS's model, which charged in proportion to volume of traffic.

---

[23]See Hussain (2003a, b, c), and, in particular, see the CIX Router Timeline (2003a).

[24]Hussain (2003a), footnote 1 for the CIX Router Timeline, makes an interesting point about CERFNET, which, like many of the other regional networks, helped to connect the San Diego supercomputer. It was a for-profit organization, and as one, it had more natural alignment of interests with PSINet and UUNET. Also see the discussion in Oxman (1999).

As it would turn out, the CIX model became the predominant model for interconnection for the next five years. Very quickly other commercial providers of services, notably Sprint, signed up. From there, the momentum kept building, with agreements with small Internet service providers as well as some of the regional networks. Just a little less than a year later, CIX essentially had everyone except ANS.

By the time Boucher held his hearing, ANS had become isolated, substantially eroding their negotiating leverage with others. By June 1992 ANS's settlement proposals no longer appeared viable. In a very public surrender of its strategy, it agreed to interconnect with the CIX on a seemingly short-term basis and retained the right to leave on a moment's notice. In fact, it never rescinded the decision.[25] From then on every provider "peered" with every other in CIX at no cost.

This confrontation was more than a mere hiccup on the path to privatization. Out of the confrontation with ANS were born the institutions that defined the relationship between the multiple providers of data services in the US national network. Once it was formed, CIX held together for several years. No firm had an economic incentive to depart from this solution, as no carrier was large enough to go its own way without cooperation from others. Peering in this way would continue to be practiced until the NSF put forward a plan that imitated CIX's ideas and rendered CIX's contribution less essential.

Why was this arrangement so crucial? It held together long enough to get the industry off to a competitive start, not close to a monopoly in its backbone. As it would turn out, this feature did not change. The backbone market remained competitive for most of the 1990s. Indeed, nothing would threaten to change that until the largest backbone providers of Internet services, MCI and WorldCom, proposed to merge, generating a government-mandated divestiture as a condition to achieve the merger. Similar issues arose, once again, when MCI/WorldCom tried to merge with Sprint near the end of the decade. That proposal would collapse over antitrust issues.

Did this disorderly crisis with ANS result in a healthy, privately operated commercial Internet? In the long run it did. With a touch of irony and

---

[25]The agreement was forged by Mitch Kapor, who became chairman of the CIX after Marty Schoffstall stepped down. The rivalry between PSINet and ANS made it difficult for Schoffstall to act both as CIX chair and as PSINet executive, while forging a compromise with ANS.

the sense of relief that comes with retrospective hindsight, it is possible to say, "Thank goodness for IBM's self-serving behavior!" Without it, perhaps no firm would have been motivated to explore solutions to the hard questions about how firms would interconnect. And without it, perhaps NSF would not have taken a new approach to peering.

The Setting, Planning, and Anticipation

The episode with ANS and CIX had an irreversible effect on the privatization of the NSFNET. Wolff found himself facing more scrutiny than any government administrator would prefer. The NSF needed to reassess, figure out what was possible, and revise its plan. Pragmatically speaking, how does a government agency respect such processes and still transfer the backbone to private parties? To make a long story short, the NSF, with Wolff as the leader on these initiatives, held meetings and hearings, adopted a plan, obtained comments, and revised the plan while simultaneously responding to commentary from Internet administrators and policy wonks all over the country, who—to say it charitably—willingly provided advice, kibitzing every step of the way.[26] All the honest policy wonks—and more!—had their say.

The final plan emerged in May 1993.[27] It had two broad goals: First, it proposed a timetable for turning off the NSFNET, effectively transferring the assets to IBM and MCI. Second, it established institutions, modeled after CIX and described below, that helped the commercial Internet operate as a competitive market after the NSFNET shut down. The second goal supported competitive interconnection in the newly privatized Internet and provided a significant lasting legacy from the privatization of the NSF-NET. Much of this became implemented more than a year later, when firms were selected to implement various elements of the plan.

[26]This included an audit from the Office of the Inspector General, principally looking at whether changes in the contracting arrangement between the NSF and MERIT had violated federal law. For a summary, see the Cook Report (1992–94).

[27]That simplifies a long planning process that stretched over many years. The basic elements of the redesign were first proposed by the NSF in late 1991, reacting to proposals by others. In June 1992 the NSF released draft solicitation for public comment, receiving a wide array of comments. The final draft—what was called the "revised solicitation"—was released May 6, 1993. The bid winners and final look of the plan were released in September 1994. A detailed summary of these steps is provided in Kesan and Shah (2001).

The shutdown date for the NSFNET finally was set for the spring of 1995. The process behind the shutdown was genuinely complex. That made it hard for anyone outside of the most experienced Internet insiders to understand the consequences of what the NSF had proposed.

Stepping back from details of events and seen in retrospect, NSF's actions raise a puzzle. The United States was the first country to privatize a carrier industry for data using TCP/IP protocols, so the NSF had no precedent to follow. Every action and policy had to be invented from scratch, without any clear consensus on how to proceed. Despite being the forerunner in developing a commercial Internet, the US experience did not set a precedent for other countries. In contrast to the United States' competitive data carrier business, in many countries foreign carrier services were handed over to each country's telephone company, resulting in monopoly provision. Why did the United States take such a unique path?

As chapter 2 implied, the answer has much to do with timing. Had commercialization in the United States occurred in a setting resembling the market structure several decades earlier, the new communications technology would have been handed to the largest communications company in the country, AT&T. It would have been an exclusive franchise (if AT&T's management had cared to commercialize it, which they may not have). Instead, the United States got a competitive data carrier business because it was possible to take advantage of the recently created competitive telephone industry. Credit for that should go to the United States' unique set of antitrust laws, which had broken up AT&T.

Divestiture created a market structure where a dozen different firms possessed the ability to perform commercial data carrier services. More specifically, in late 1992 there were seven regional Bell operating companies,[28] three major long-distance services plus many small firms,[29] a large geographically dispersed local telephone company,[30] many local telephone

---

[28] Bell Atlantic in New England, NYNEX in New York and environs, Bell South in the Southeast, Southern Bell Company in the mid-south region, Ameritech in the Midwest, US West in the Rocky Mountain states and environs, and Pacific Bell in the far west regions. However, due to ongoing debate about the permissible line of businesses for local telephone firms within Judge Harold Greene's court, it was unclear how many different business lines each local telephone firm could enter.

[29] The major long-distance companies for home and business long distance included AT&T, MCI, and Sprint.

[30] General Telephone and Electric (GTE) owned and operated a large number of geographically dispersed franchises all over the United States.

firms in several medium-sized cites,[31] and a small but growing cellular telephone market.[32] In addition, at least two entrepreneurial entrants, UUNET and PSINet, had made their presence known. Finally, IBM and its division, ANS, stood poised to offer service. Soon there would be others who would try. In short, many firms possessed the necessary technical and commercial assets to reach the technological frontier and offer a viable service. If they did not possess such assets, it was possible to quickly assemble them by combining existing assets with those they purchased from markets.

Other high-tech markets such as the computing and telecom equipment markets had a similar feature. The ability of multiple actors to take action on the technical frontier was sometimes called *divided technical leadership*. Although familiar to computing, it was a structural feature novel to the communications carrier sector—and one the trustbusters had artificially nurtured. Industries with divided technical leadership innovate more quickly than monopolies. Monopolies typically prefer a quieter life of controlled experimentation to one of unrestrained experimentation in the service of competitive goals. With divided technical leadership, in contrast, no single firm controlled the direction of technical change, nor could any single firm block a new initiative. NSF operated in the midst of completely new territory, fostering private initiatives.

What to Do with Divided Technical Leadership?

In June 1992, Boucher introduced a small amendment to an existing bill. It was a deft legal solution. It changed the charter of the NSF, altering the legal definition of NSF's mission just enough to permit the NSFNET to alter the AUP. That change in the AUP permitted others to share traffic. The key change was seemingly small. It read:

> Section 3 of the National Science Foundation Act of 1950 (42 U.S.C. 1862) is amended by adding at the end the following new subsection: (g) In carrying out subsection (a)(4), the Foundation is authorized to foster and support the development and use of computer

---

[31] This list including local franchises, such as Rochester Telephone, Southern New England Telephone, Cincinnati Bell, and many rural co-ops.

[32] At this point, every major city in the United States had cellular services provided by a duopoly, where one provider was the local telephone monopoly and the other was another firm.

networks which may be used substantially for purposes in addition to research and education in the sciences and engineering, if the additional uses will tend to increase the overall capabilities of the networks to support such research and education activities.

That slight change in words made all the difference. It meant that the NSF did not violate its charter when it shared lines with private users because sharing those lines lowered the costs to researchers in the sciences and engineering fields.[33] Additional uses actually did increase the overall capabilities of the networks, as the statute said.

The amendment passed in October. Once it passed, IBM's lawyers could not plausibly offer a narrow interpretation of the AUP as an excuse for not interconnecting. It also meant that other firms could bypass ANS altogether, using the CIX method to interchange traffic. That did not enable the Internet to grow right away—it would take time for private firms to appreciate what they could do with the Internet—but it was a crucial step.

Introducing competition had one drawback. It added a high degree of unpredictability to the privatization efforts. Even knowledgeable observers of communications markets were not quite sure what features the final industry structure would have and how it would operate. While there was some experience with competitive telephony and some of the digital technologies that supported it, there simply was not much experience with the competitive supply of data carrier services organized around a packet switching technology, such as one where all computers used a TCP/IP network. Only a few companies had ever offered similar services, and it had been at a smaller scale. The NSF's plan ultimately used the division of

---

[33] The hearings took place in the House Science, Space, and Technology Committee's science subcommittee, chaired by representative Rick Boucher (D-VA), which has jurisdiction over the NSF policy. Boucher held hearings on March 12, 1992, after reporter Brock Meeks published several articles about procedural irregularities in *Communications Daily* (on February 4, 1992; February 6, 1992; and February 21, 1992), according to Hauben and Hauben (1997), chapter 12. This was introduced in the 102nd Congress as the modification to the NSF's charter in 1992 and Amendment to the National Science Foundation (NSF) Act of 1950, H.R 5344, which was introduced June 9, 1992, "to authorize the National Science Foundation to foster and support the development and use of certain computer networks." See http://www.lib.ncsu.edu/congbibs/house/102hdgst2.html, accessed July 2009. It was passed by the House on June 29 and was signed into law October 23.

technical leadership to nurture a market structure that began to head in a direction that most observers of communications markets had never before seen.

The consequences of the NSF plan were hard to understand for another reason: there were many compromises embedded in the details. It was not an ideal plan in many respects. Rather, it was tailored to the NSF's strengths and weaknesses in the role of sponsoring federal agency.

The NSF normally subsidized research at US universities. From time to time, NSF funded research that directly and quickly led to new products, or saved costs in production of existing products. Most of these gains to private industry happened in a piecemeal fashion, and out of NSF's control. NSF was not normally in the business of launching new industries or regulating ongoing industries. It did not possess the best set of tools for the task. It also did not possess the legal authority to regulate economic activity other than the conduct of research. In this case, it lacked authority to regulate the commercial Internet once it grew out of its research orientation.

Regulatory agencies, such as the FCC, have two broad tools, which might be simplified as either carrots or sticks. Carrots come in many forms, and the NSF did have several carrots when it used its budget judiciously. For example, NSF's managers knew how to use solicitation of bids, and through solicitation the NSF could subsidize the establishment of an activity that might not otherwise have occurred. Sticks also come in many forms—but they usually involve a lawsuit to make someone cease and desist from performing an activity. The NSF, however, had few sticks and few staff with relevant experience. In short, the NSF plan relied on carrots because those were the tools it possessed.

At a broad level, the launch of the private and commercial Internet involved four related actions. First, technical planning for the Internet had to move out of government hands. This was substantially accomplished by removing sponsorship of the IAB, which acted as the organizational home for standard-setting activity at the IETF. It moved the groups to private not-for-profit sponsorship, and called the new organization The Internet Society. It evolved on a track independent of other actions, but like the others, it was essentially a government gift.

Second, the NSFNET had to cease to operate, and the retirement date for the NSFNET was announced as April 1995. This date brought up an additional distraction and controversy because it extended IBM and MCI's contract a second time beyond the original granting date.[34] These concerns partly reflected a lack of experience with the recent change in the Acceptable Use Policy. As it turned out, this extension was less controversial. While it mildly benefited ANS directly, as long as all networks interconnected, this extension did not hurt the other commercial networks. The announcement of the date also anticipated that private firms would step in to provide service after that time.

Third and fourth, there needed to be additional access points for interchanging data, and privatization of domain name systems had to occur. These parts of the plan had very distinct experiences. The former encouraged the development of competitive markets, while the latter resulted in monopoly. After the fact, the former received few complaints, while the latter became the focus of enormous amounts of attention.

The Plan for Network Interconnection

The NSF's plan altered the structure of data exchange among backbone firms. This was the most technically challenging piece of the plan, and, in comparison to the casual discussions prior to 1991, also the aspect that underwent the largest change. It was also the most unpredictable piece. There was no precedent for operating a commercial carrier service on a national scale with many data-exchange points. It had not been technically feasible for most of the 1980s due to the routing protocols in use, which assumed a single backbone. The stage was set after moving to a new protocol, known as "best-effort routing,"[35] which allowed for multiple backbone providers.

While no serious observer was 100 percent certain how well the NSF's plan would work in practice, the uncertainty should not be exaggerated. The federally sponsored network had several data-exchange points. While the NSF was planning the shutdown, the CIX was already operating its precedent-setting servers. Most of the uncertainty concerned economic conduct: how would firms behave?

---

[34] The original contract had been set to expire in 1992. It was extended twice before the NSFNET was retired in 1995. See Kesan and Shah (2001) for a timeline.

[35] In part this was due to the work on the border gateway protocol (BGP), which accommodated multiple backbone providers. The first RFC for BGP was published in June 1989 (RFC 1105), replaced a year later by RFC 1163 and 1164. It continued to evolve over the next few years.

The plan for network interconnection underwent a noticeable revision because of the controversy over ANS and the AUP. Chided by the negative attention, the NSF attempted to be more transparent and put out its plan for comment from many of the Internet's participants. It received suggestions to support multiple data-exchange points in multiple locations, as well as encouragement to support a competitive market. The attention bore fruit; rather than anticipating one commercial backbone, the NSF's 1993 plan anticipated and accommodated multiple backbone providers.[36]

The plan relied on two stylized versions of textbook economics and one leap of faith in competitive incentives. The subsidization of the establishment of several network access points, or NAPs, was the first strategy that relied on a version of textbook economics—it aspired to avoid bottlenecks. If there had been only one place for backbones to interconnect, then it would have been easier for a single entity to erect a bottleneck to new entrants and thereby control a monopoly. Instead, there were multiple points of interconnection, so such bottlenecks could not arise.

For the second version of textbook economics, the NSF's plan set the rights to operate a NAP out for bids in an auction. In theory the highest bid would come from the potential owner who foresaw the lowest costs. While each NAP operated on its own and with a distinct owner, the NSF anticipated a grander geographic logic to this structure. Every NAP stood at the center of a regional collection of backbones and networks operated by many other firms, and served as a single place to collect and exchange traffic. The geographic structure of the Internet backbone and regional networks determined the geographic shape of the network. It followed the limits and pathways determined by the geographic dispersion of the US university system. These aggregated into regional alliances to support

---

[36]This also was anticipated in Aiken, Braun, and Ford (1992), "NSF Implementation Plan for Interim NREN." Insiders appreciated that the technical experience with exchanging data in the last few years had helped spur new thinking about how to design more efficient points for exchanging data. Already there were plans for what would become a Metropolitan Access Exchange, or MAE. These plans called for a MAE East and MAE West. The number of network access points (NAPs) did not remain fixed at two. Eventually, the NSF increased the number.

sending traffic between campuses, and those alliances followed rather natural geographic groups.[37]

The leap of faith relied on the owner of a NAP to do everything necessary to keep a NAP operational after it was established, such as manage it, collect revenue to cover costs, respond to unanticipated crises, and so on. Thus in one of its more questionable choices, the NSF did not place any additional restriction on the operations of NAPs. Bidders were not required to operate with rules similar to CIX. While it would have been reasonable to assume the NAPs would operate in a manner similar to CIX in 1992, that presumption was not made explicit.

The plan relied on competitive discipline to keep quality at an acceptable minimum. The reasoning went as follows: If multiple backbone providers had choices among multiple NAPs, then it put pressure on NAP owners. NAP owners would have incentive to make sure users of the NAP did not move their data elsewhere. In brief, each NAP competed with the other for the fees provided by interconnecting carriers. That generated incentives for each of them to lower cost and raise quality.

Consider the inherent effectiveness of such discipline. This could be most effective when all carriers participated in NAPs, since then every NAP would be competing for the connection fees of every other carrier. That also implies the opposite: This discipline could be less effective if some carriers found reasons to bypass the NAPs altogether. Indeed, if backbone carriers abandoned NAPs, exchanging their traffic elsewhere, it was clear what would happen to NAPs—they would wither.

The NAPs were put out to bid and awarded in 1994. The NSF held several different auctions for the right to be the NAP provider in different designated locations as potential data-exchange points. Three were called Metropolitan Area Exchanges, and the acronym was pronounced as MAE, as in Mae West, the actress. In total four NAPs arose in four locations: San Francisco (called MAE West, operated by Pacific Bell), Washington, DC

---

[37] In an intriguing footnote, Abbate (1999, p. 239), states that this structure was probably inspired by the structure of the telephone industry at the time, which had a mix of regional networks and national interconnection. It is unclear how much of this inspiration was loosely "conceptual." In fact, the resemblance was coincidental, not causal. The data networks followed their own regional logic, based on the alliances formed in the mid-level networks and geographic constraints. Stephen Wolff, private conversation, September 2008.

(called MAE East, operated by Metropolitan Fiber Systems), Chicago (called MAE Central, operated by Ameritech), and just outside New York (operated by Sprint).

Even though the financial support for NAPs would not be strong, the backbone market was born as a competitive market, and that competitiveness would persist long after birth, even after NAPs diminished in importance. Later events would show the wisdom of starting the industry off with a structure that fostered multiple access firms and competitive supply. That wisdom would become apparent even though NAPs would not retain a central place in the long term.

The Soap Opera over Domain Names

Almost from the outset a conflict emerged around the privatization of the domain name system, or DNS for short. The foregoing provides a brief overview of why the privatization of the DNS began to interfere with the privatization of the Internet.[38]

For all intent and purposes, the large-scale domain name system came into existence in 1987. To make a long story short, a small team of researchers—with the help of DARPA funding and directives—invented the domain name system in order to address the incompatibilities across distinct networks in the United States (whose origins were discussed in chapter 2). The incompatibilities shaped almost every action, even the simplest, such as sending e-mail. It was possible to send e-mail between the Internet and the other networks in the country—Bitnet, UUCP, or CSNET—but it required the sender to specify the path for the data to take. It took so much technical knowledge that only the most technically skilled sender could do it.[39]

Networks had "gateways," protocols that allow messages to pass between mail servers at individual locations and one of the networks. The domain name system was part of a solution to allow individual sites to move from CSNET/BITNET/UUCP to the Internet by reconfiguring only the mail server to deliver mail via TCP/IP on the Internet.

---

[38] These events have received extensive treatment elsewhere. See, e.g., Mueller (2004), or Kesan and Shah (2001), and Goldsmith and Wu (2006) for a full description.

[39] See Partridge (2008). Some of this text also comes from Partridge, private communication, 2008.

The new design was modular, allowing for different ways for data to move in and out of a gateway. That unified all e-mail from different networks. It also enabled new building blocks to be added. In the short run it accomplished its primary goal of unifying all communication. In the long run it would have profound consequences. After privatization, this design would enable a multiplicity of e-mail programs to thrive at households and business establishments.

The unification had an asymmetric effect on the four different networks it brought together. It allowed all to survive, and each network could grow at whatever pace its users preferred. As the largest and most widely supported network among them, it would favor further growth in the TCP/IP network. In turn, the growing user base encouraged further improvements, which further encouraged more users.

The privatization of the domain name system occurred in a two-step process. First, in 1991, the US government reasserted its authority over the domain name system, taking control of part of it from Jon Postel, a well-known Internet pioneer, who had been among those who helped to invent the DNS. After its inception he had almost single-handedly managed and operated the system.[40] On one level removing Postel from operations was straightforward: he worked under a contract from DARPA to manage the domain name system, and when the old contract expired, the Defense Department sent it out for new bids. Second, and relatedly, a private firm won the right to manage domain name services. The text related to the root server was transferred to a company called Network Solutions, which was based in Virginia, just outside of Washington, DC.

Neither step was particularly well received by the Internet community at large. Every experienced administrator knew Postel, and many insiders had known him for more than a decade or two. Known for his extraordinary intelligence, lack of self-serving behavior, and hardheaded yet gentle persistence and stubbornness, Postel's conduct was trusted by virtually every longtime participant. In contrast, the managers at Network Solutions, as well as their motives, were unknown. Trust would have to be earned. No amount of prospective efficiency gains from privatization would wipe away the suspicion inherent in this transition. No abstract argument about the need to routinize and scale the domain name system

---

[40]See Mueller (2004), and Goldsmith and Wu (2006) for a full description.

for prospective growth of the Internet could eliminate Jon Postel's personal authority, or reduce the sense that something was being taken away from a mainstay of the old guard.

The transition was jarring for another reason. The domain name system was an essential function for operating the Internet, and it had operated with a mixture of formal and informal principles. This transition began steps toward the elimination of that informal element and replaced it with a process managed at a firm. For example, prior to this change an Internet administrator could simply send an e-mail to Postel or buttonhole him at a conference and casually raise issues. It also potentially altered the habits of every Internet administrator and designer connected to Postel—every major contributor to the Internet up until that point.

Privatizing the domain name system underscored an unsettled question among many Internet participants—namely, once a government or private firm operates the domain name system, what policies should govern an operation that many others depend on? Should it depend on Jon Postel's judgment, or should it depend on institutional rules founded in government decisions? No law had compelled any participant in the Internet to cooperate with Postel, and everyone did so voluntarily. Why should everyone remain so cooperative in a formal system? No satisfying answer to this question was found over the next decade. Indeed, there could not possibly be one, since many inconsistent opinions existed and any action necessarily left many insiders unhappy with the outcome.

The transfer of authority over the root server to Network Solutions set the terms for this debate and drove the transition forward by rolling two functions into one. The first function was the management of a database that associated domain names underneath *com, edu, net, gov,* and *org* with appropriate IP addresses. The second function involved notifying other participants on the Internet about new names and the IP address associated with it.[41] The latter also enabled the transfer of existing names and eventually would set the bounds for operating a secondary market in domain names.

The computer science behind this registry was straightforward. This involved maintaining the registry, updating it, and providing this information to others. However, as the Internet grew these processes became

---

[41] Mueller (2004) provides a comprehensive history of this function.

much more involved than anticipated, because the central registry also had to delete old registered names from those who no long wanted to keep a name or (later, after their establishment) failed to pay their fees. Network Solutions needed to make available those names to others, as well as make it feasible for new applicants to apply for new names. From the outset there were clearly many open questions concerning the registry's pricing for services, its processes, and its involvement in the secondary markets. Critics began to worry that Network Solutions could (and would) employ its controlling position to gain self-serving ends in other operations within the Internet.[42]

In retrospect many aspects of that choice are easy to question.[43] For example, why was the contract for five years and not shorter? Why grant a sole provider but not embed the contract with an assumption about regular review? Why did the contract not include any specification about the minimal quality of services offered?[44] Why was *com* not given to one firm, *edu* to another, *net* to another, and so on, so some form of competition between these names could exist from the outset?

The contract also was incomplete in some essential business matters, such as the pricing of domain names. Perhaps that made sense in 1992, since there had been no charge for registering names in the informally operated research-oriented Internet. In 1995, however, this policy was changed at the request of the owner—a decision that was quite unpopular with the existing Internet community.[45] Once again, such an action touched on core policy philosophies surrounding an essential asset. Should a firm be allowed to charge revenue for this action and profit from it? If so, should their actions be held in check by any regulatory mechanism? What form should that mechanism take?

By the standard norms of network economics, the governance of domain names lacked solid foundations. The manager of the top-level domain names occupied a monopoly position and an essential function inside the network's operations. That combination required some sort of regular oversight to prevent self-dealing by Network Solutions, and from

[42] See Mueller (2004).

[43] Indeed, many observers have done so. See, e.g., Mueller (2004) or Kesan and Shah (2001).

[44] For a discussion, see Mueller (2004).

[45] This occurred after Network Solutions Incorporated was purchased by Science Applications International Corporation.

using the monopoly position to subvert the competitive process in other areas related to domain names. Oversight would have placed limitations on the firm that performed the function. It might have limited its pricing or its ability to achieve other self-serving goals. However, the NSF did not put in place any oversight on the private firm. Later observers became outraged at the lack of oversight.[46]

The reason behind the absence of oversight goes back to carrots and sticks. How was NSF supposed to do that using carrots? It is normally the purview of the US Congress to design regulatory institutions. If the US Congress wanted to regulate the DNS system, it could have done so at any time. It just did not.

Stepping back from the soap opera's details, perhaps Congress did not act because there was not a sufficient crisis. The most important economic goal for the transition was avoiding disaster, and that was achieved. The transition to a privately managed domain name system did not cripple the commercial Internet, nor particularly handicap its global operations. Long after the privatization, prices stayed low. The cup was partially empty as well. The domain name system was not a blindingly efficient system in 1995. Recycling retired names involved a particularly cumbersome process, for example, and trademark holders did not have an easy way to address complaints of infringement.[47]

In short, there were no major delays or costs preventing other parts of the Internet from growing. CNN found a way to own CNN.com and IBM found a way to own IBM.com. Even Encyclopedia Britannica owned both encyclopediabritannica.com and eb.com and began experimenting with them. An active secondary market for domain names also began to emerge, some of which became quite valuable as the potential for the Internet became more apparent.

In many respects the initial actions in the early 1990s kicked the policy issues down the road and turned any little event into an engaging sideshow for insiders. After privatization Postel still existed and continued to tinker with improvements to the Internet. Network Solutions still operated under contract. Not surprisingly, therefore, tension did not diminish after privatization and received considerable attention in Internet forums

---

[46] Kesan and Shah (2001) summarize these positions.
[47] For a discussion, see Mueller (2004).

and conferences. The Internet community sensed the gap in governance and made attempts to assert its independence from government control. Perhaps egged on by his friends, or frustrated by their lack of progress, Postel eventually made one last attempt to reassert his control, but that failed.[48] In the greater scheme of things, none of these events fundamentally changed the commercial domain name system, which continued to operate under the contracts it had.

In 1997 and 1998, in response to the perceived need, the Clinton administration set up ICANN (Internet Corporation for Assigned Names and Numbers) under the domain of the Department of Commerce, with an understanding about moving the agency out of US government control sometime in the next decade. This creation was contentious, and those difficulties made for salacious stories among Internet insiders and compelled many observers to wonder why nothing had been done sooner.[49]

For all intent and purposes, the establishment of ICANN sealed the issues within the boundaries of one institution. While many squabbled over the behavior of ICANN and its core principles, the Internet continued to function as it always had.

A New Industry Structure

Years later, after the commercial Internet grew to a gargantuan size, a myth arose that the policies behind the privatization of the Internet succeeded because the stakes were too low to attract attention. That myth is misleading. The privatization cannot be characterized as a quiet walk in the park. The stakes were high enough to attract action from many concerned firms, inventors, and entrepreneurs. The countervailing stakes of different parties attracted the attention of congressional representatives on oversight committees, and eventually attention from the investigative arm of the US government.

There is also a myth, popular among cynics, that all regulatory decisions eventually become "captured" by private interests with high economic stakes in swaying decisions in their favor. Again, this view is misleading. The privatization of the Internet involved complex decisions in which a

---

[48] This is a well-known story, and is recounted in both Mueller (2004) and Goldsmith and Wu (2006).

[49] This is a longer story. See also the accounts in Ceruzzi ([2006] 2008); Aspray (2004), chapter 3; and Mueller (2004).

few very large firms had very high stakes in the outcome. According to the standard theory, the situation was ripe for capture, and, indeed, IBM tried. Yet that does not characterize events accurately either. Although the process was disorderly and messy, the outcome *was not* captured by a single firm.

Appeals to higher ideals motivated actions and had an enormous influence over decisions. The ideals of many honest policy wonks came to the center of the conversations about the policies for privatizing the Internet. They generated a reaction at the NSF, and their actions could not be characterized as convenient or the path of least resistance. The NSF's managers took very costly and inconvenient actions to meet the ideals of many honest policy wonks. By the time the 1993 plan was developed, it no longer focused on only cost savings from privatization. It also aspired to nurture conditions that would allow the commercial Internet to flourish—such as supporting multiple backbone firms and developing interconnection policies to enable multiple firms to thrive.

Wisdom did not prevail in every policy action affiliated with privatizing the Internet, and it would be saying too much to claim that government policy makers always got it right. DARPA and the NSF privatized the domain name system without fully addressing long-term governance issues. While this part of privatization achieved minimal functional goals, the initial clumsiness generated complaints and resentment, and the issues continued to fester for many years thereafter.

More to the point, though honest policy wonks had their day, there was no consensus forecast among them, and the participants only knew one thing for certain: after privatization every firm would have a fighting chance to compete. Nobody had ever seen a market structure like the one the NSF proposed, and the lack of experience stood in the way of making any grounded forecast about the features competition would display. It also interfered with forecasting the scale of adoption, and the best strategic actions for capturing value as a large-scale commercial service. As later chapters will explain, largely unforeseen at the time, that also set the stage for the emergence of innovation from the edges.

4

A Taste of Champaign

DAVE: Open the pod bay doors, HAL.
HAL: I'm sorry, Dave. I'm afraid I can't do that.

In 1968, Arthur C. Clarke published *2001: A Space Odyssey*. Thanks to Stanley Kubrick's movie, the oddly wired and soft-spoken computer HAL became a classic canonical cinematic figure. In the book, Clarke imagined a world in which HAL would be a midwesterner at birth, becoming operational at the HAL plant at the University of Illinois at Urbana-Champaign on January 12, 1997. In the movie, HAL was five years older, born in 1992.[1]

While enough time has passed to see that no computer resembling HAL has been created in either Urbana or Champaign, or in 1992, Clarke should not be regarded as a technological Nostradamus who missed the target. Clarke's writings were somewhat prescient. He picked the right location and almost the right year for the emergence of a revolutionary invention in computing. Around 1992 the campus gave birth to an important prototype software application for the Internet called *Mosaic*. It was a browser.

---

[1] As Dave disconnects HAL, HAL resorts to his most basic programming. He states: "Good afternoon, gentlemen. I am a HAL 9000 computer. I became operational at the H.A.L. plant in Urbana, Illinois on the 12th of January 1992. My instructor was Mr. Langley, and he taught me to sing a song. If you'd like to hear it, I can sing it for you." Dave states that he wants to hear the song. As HAL is being disconnected, HAL sings the song "Daisy Bell," which is called "Daisy" in the movie. Arthur C. Clarke inserted that song as homage to a synthesized version he heard at a technical demonstration at Bell Labs in 1962. It used an IBM 704.

FIGURE 4.1 Tim Berners-Lee, creator of the World Wide Web, and founder
World Wide Web Consortium (photo by Paul Clarke, 2014)

Mosaic was nothing like HAL, and neither was the birth of the browser, and the differences would shape how the browser commercialized. Clarke had presumed premeditated development of a large computer system by a single, hierarchical, and deliberate organization. In other words, HAL could have been developed by the IBM of the 1960s, the most familiar archetype for a successful computer company. Hal was conceived as an instrument for a closed world, a spaceship. The central drama of *2001* revolves around Hal's interactions with the crew within that closed space.[2]

Mosaic, in contrast, was a child of the Internet's decentralized, cumulative, and unpredictable development. It emerged from a small project inside of a research institute funded by the National Science Foundation, which, ironically, operated a big box computer pushing the frontier called a supercomputer. Mosaic built on top of, and openly imitated, many working prototypes created elsewhere by others. The project had goals that loosely connected to the primary purpose of the organization. Deliberate and hierarchical did not describe the manner of Mosaic's invention. Nor was it an instrument for a closed world, unless the expanding, unpredictable, and fast-growing Internet were considered closed.

[2]See, e.g., Edwards (1997), 307–8, and 322–24.

FIGURE 4.2 Robert Cailliau, helped Tim Berners-Lee create the World Wide Web (photo by en: CERN, 2005)

FIGURE 4.3 Marc Andreessen, co-creator of Mosaic, and cofounder of Netscape (photo by Elisabeth Fall, September 24, 2013)

As one piece in a much bigger system, Mosaic was yet another software contribution from one set of developers adding to the end-to-end Internet. Mosaic was a piece of code for PCs and worked with other layers of the World Wide Web—namely, HTML (hypertext markup language), the hypertext transfer protocol (HTTP), and URLs (uniform resource locators). The web had been designed by Tim Berners-Lee to work with the domain name system that had become a standard piece of Internet infrastructure, all of it broadly based on TCP/IP.

Mosaic's birth led to the birth of another piece of software, the Netscape browser, and many later chapters will discuss how Netscape catalyzed commercial events. The Mosaic browser was not the first browser; rather, it was the first one whose use exceeded more than a million users. Mosaic was a catalytic commercial prototype for the entire Internet because it led to the founding of Netscape. Netscape's browser was catalytic for commercial markets because it eventually caused virtually every participant in the commercial computing and communications market to alter their investment plans and strategic priorities.

How did Mosaic initially cross the boundary from research tool to commercial software? Some of the key decisions did take place in seemingly unlikely places. One was Champaign, Illinois, and though it was the fictional home to HAL, it was a likely source for invention. It had a long and proud history as one of several leading academic centers of research in computer science in the United States. The second was a bit more unlikely, at a lab in Switzerland called CERN, which is home to the largest collection of high-energy physicists in the world.[3] Only the third could have been predicted with near certainty: many other key decisions occurred in Silicon Valley, where venture-funded firms predominated.

How did a European physics lab and a public university in the Midwest enable prototype software to transition from the research-oriented Internet to the commercial Internet? Even an inventive writer of science fiction such as Arthur C. Clarke could not have imagined the unlikely consequences of the combination of parochial events.

Looking more deeply, it was not just the coincident discoveries of a few blind squirrels finding their nuts. There was an underlying economic ar-

---

[3]CERN is located just outside Geneva. It is a French acronym for Organisation européenne pour la recherche nucléaire (originally Conseil européen pour la recherche nucléaire).

chetype at work, and one familiar to the Internet—namely, inventive specialization. The Internet of the early 1990s was reliable enough, dispersed enough, and modular enough that the network could support a range of new applications invented by specialists. Several different foresighted inventors considered different ways to take advantage of the potential and aspired to realize their visions, and, collectively, altered the value users gained from the Internet. Just as had occurred in the past, in the 1990s the Internet's architecture could nurture decentralized invention and independent application development.

What was new? There was one key difference with the era in which NSF governed the Internet: privatization allowed inventions to move rapidly into private use and into commercial sale. More to the point, because the difference between the research-oriented network and the private Internet were small, an innovation like the browser—one seemingly from the edges of the network—could become available to commercial users and quickly become adopted. In this case, private firms had incentives to get it adopted, and that helped it move quickly into widespread use and catalyzed a set of actions that transformed the world.

Connecting Continents

Prior to 1989, the physics research community in Europe expressed impatience with its inability to electronically communicate with its North American colleagues, who had been using the research-oriented Internet for some time. In 1989 Europe contained very few users of the TCP/IP-based Internet. In that year a group of researchers successfully ignored all the cross-continental rivalry in the Internet/ISO debate and negotiated to establish RIPE, a European-wide network of connections to the Internet in North America.[4]

That connection alone did meet some of the needs of researchers, since it made sending electronic mail and transfer files possible. Yet researchers wanted more. The Internet in North America had evolved into a complex, interconnected set of computing facilities from a heterogeneous set of universities, research laboratories, and academic departments. That size and

---

[4]While not the first TCP/IP connection in Europe, RIPE was significant for bringing institutional cooperation to the spread of the Internet. RIPE had to overcome the national rivalry that had European and US researchers pursuing incompatible networking protocols.

complexity highlighted an overwhelming problem for both newcomers and longtime users: how could one navigate the myriad sites all over the Internet?

Some software tools helped in searching on the Internet,[5] but there was a long conversation among computer scientists about numerous ways to improve upon these tools. The bigger challenge was designing something that others on the research-oriented Internet would use. It had to be functional, intuitive to the user, easy to explain, and not too expensive for administrators to install.

Robert Cailliau and Tim Berners-Lee were colleagues at CERN, which had TCP/IP connectivity. Both had an interest in developing tools to aid physicists in the sharing of information. Both independently pursued their interests. Both were focused on improving the search and sharing tools for their constituent community, researchers who came up against these constraints regularly in their scientific pursuits.

But in 1989, Cailliau eventually abandoned his own efforts, combining them with those of Berners-Lee's, who was building key parts of what would become the World Wide Web. In addition, Berners-Lee later organized the pieces of code by establishing the World Wide Web Consortium (W3C), which standardized many protocols, with Cailliau helping to organize the W3C at its first conferences.

Berners-Lee was far from the first programmer to try to devise a hypertext system, and he was aware of prior efforts. At the outset, Berners-Lee's goals were modest and were heavily informed by both the prior experience of his own previous efforts and others. Berners-Lee had experimented with making computing tools for physicists in the past, and despite his best efforts had seen prior innovations go unused. That experience taught him the importance of compromising technical ambition in order to foster adoption: users adopted software when it was easier to use and its functionality was readily apparent. He also continually faced questions from his management about how his inventions would aid the physics research community.[6] That kept his attention focused on meeting pragmatic goals, inventing software his user community would find valuable. While the

---

[5] For example, Gopher and WAIS were two such tools for indexing users and topics in a network. See Frana (2004).

[6] This is described in somewhat different language and at some length in both Berners-Lee and Fischetti (1999), and Gillies and Cailliau (2000).

project was not starved for resources, the setting also forced a certain efficiency and resourcefulness on the design and the process for building it.

Although there had been years of discussion within computer science about how to design such a system, one of Berners-Lee's core insights was *not* to design a perfect system. Rather, he designed one that improved performance for his community, making them better off than they were, motivating them to try the software and use it regularly. Berners-Lee deliberately kept the complexity low in spite of his ambitions. In a conscious attempt to make his invention easy to install and use, he reduced the scope of functions his software could perform. He also made it *backward compatible* with some other tools in widespread use—other tools worked within the system designed by Berners-Lee. Backward compatibility was a concession to the habits of his constituency—once again, something he did for the sake of promoting adoption by offering a migration path from old processes to new that involved few frictions.[7]

The community at CERN turned out to have propitious attributes as lead users. They were technically oriented but were not computer gurus—that is, they were physicists who needed to send files easily to one another and make them available for downloading. Although they did not know all the ins and outs of each computer system, these users did not require the type of easy-to-use designs and instructions that computing needed to appeal to the mass market. The lead users at CERN did not fear technical difficulties, they could learn new procedures, and they would follow directions to achieve desired ends. They also tended to work in environments with technically skilled systems administrators, who could take care of a few installation difficulties.

In addition, this community was already accustomed to the idea of electronic communication, if not the actual process. Berners-Lee faced no difficulties explaining his goals to this user community. Instead of spending time on demonstrating the software, he just had to get something that

---

[7]Backward compatible designs give users of the prior program a migration path to the new. For example, on his FAQ page for the World Wide Web, Berners-Lee goes to some lengths to show potential users that his creation would work with the most common tools in use, WAIS and Gopher. See the discussion in Frana (2004). Also see the historical documents, housed at http://www.w3.org/History/19921103-hypertext/hypertext/WWW/FAQ/WAIS andGopher.html, accessed June 2008.

worked for them. If he could get some to adopt an invention and see its value, those first users would motivate others to adopt as well.

Berners-Lee came up with a comparatively simple model for hypertext computing where all information, whether text or graphic, was presented to the user in one format. Navigation was accomplished via links between files, where the user could either follow a link or make a query in search of a page where lists of documents existed. The code aimed to do a lot with as few steps as possible.[8] In summary, Berners-Lee's narrow search for a new invention yielded a rather simple but elegant result, and one with unexpected and wide breadth.

Adoption was always a priority, and that led Berners-Lee to develop working prototypes for his own lab and others. For example, during the period of experimentation at CERN, one of Berners-Lee's first illustrations was administrative, not scientific. He used his invention to make available the document known as the telephone directory for CERN. His administrators could see the value of that.[9]

After numerous trials at CERN, in 1991, Berners-Lee decided to make the key inventions, HTML, HTTP, and the URL, available for others on shareware sites.[10] Together these formed a hypertext language and location labeling system that made it possible to transfer textual and nontextual files. Once installed in a host computer these were well suited to Berners-Lee's constituency in two specific senses: (1) They helped users organize transfers of previously known files, and (2) they helped make files available to others without a tremendous amount of searching prior to transferring.

The URL and HTML system was not the only application on TCP/IP for organizing many firms. It diffused quickly for several reasons: It appealed to system administrators who perceived its value for a problem many of them had in common, such as making large directories widely accessible on a local area network; the spread of the Internet itself also contributed to the ease many users had contacting the sites where this shareware resided; compatibility with preexisting search tools, such as WAIS (wide area information servers) and Gopher appealed to many users, who could either continue to use as always, or in conjunction with

---

[8]See, e.g., Berners-Lee and Fischetti (1999) and Gillies and Cailliau (2000).

[9]See, e.g., Berners-Lee and Fischetti (1999).

[10]In 1993 CERN agreed to make the code available as open source code.

Berners-Lee's invention; in February 1993, the University of Minnesota, the home of the inventors for Gopher, announced the intention to charge a licensing fee for its use, and that raised a concern among many insiders that the university intended to charge for all extensions as well, which motivated many administrators to abandon investing in Gopher and make use of HTML and the URL.[11] Berners-Lee and Cailliau put considerable effort into publicizing their invention and making it known, investing more energy in marketing and distribution than typically found among computer programmers in the academic world. Perhaps most importantly, the software enabled users to do something demonstrably useful right away—namely, it brought text to life, allowing users to add color, graphics, and sound. Because its value was easy to illustrate, leading users became advocates for its diffusion.

In due time the new would replace all others, and it is easy to have a retrospective bias. The diffusion of the web did not seem inevitable at the outset. With additional functionality the web and its hypertext would attract more users, and the entire system would become self-reinforcing. After privatization of the Internet, many commercial applications would be built with the tools of the web, and that would lead the other tools to fade into obscurity.[12] None of the early users saw that coming, however. At the outset users spread the web by word of mouth.

Word of mouth worked like this: One pair of researchers at distinct installations would use HTML and URL, like it, and then ask other administrators at other installations to get involved. They would, and then one of them would tell another friend, who would tell another, and so on. In brief, successful use motivated an exponential increase in adoption and use, and it operated both across departments within a single location and between institutions across locations. Such "word-of-mouth" marketing brought about a seeming explosion of use over the next several months. The technical community liked Berners-Lee's invention and began installing it to use within research-oriented computing.

The invention of the popular browser Mosaic helped spread HTML and URL even further throughout universities, a topic discussed at length later

[11] Many fans of Gopher would blame the University of Minnesota for implementing a clumsy licensing program, which discouraged use of Gopher and interrupted momentum behind its diffusion. See Frana (2004).

[12] See Frana (2004).

in this chapter. As they spread, Berners-Lee forecast the need for an organization to assemble and standardize pieces of codes into a broad system of norms for operating in the hypertext world. He founded the World Wide Web Consortium (or W3C) in 1994 for this purpose.

While seeking to found the W3C, Berners-Lee gradually concluded that CERN would not be the most hospitable home. In part this simply reflected what CERN's administrators told him: it was a physics laboratory and not a natural home for an organization to support worldwide use of software. In large part, this conclusion reflected Berners-Lee's considerable experience with the global computer science community and his impression about how well different locations served as hospitable homes for development.[13]

Berners-Lee established the offices for the W3C in Cambridge, Massachusetts, at the Massachusetts Institute of Technology. This was a key event, which will receive more attention in a later chapter. The organization ultimately helped diffuse many of the software standards and tools that became important for operating on the commercial web, fostering growth around nonproprietary protocols endorsed by the consortium. The timing was propitious as well. This software—the URL, HTML, and HTTP—was established and institutionalized just as the privatization of the Internet was nearly completed. It was ripe for commercialization, as well as ripe to support the development of other new commercial applications.

Standing on the Shoulders of Giants

As with other inventions for the Internet, the technical path for the browser involved several researchers building on each other, using the institutions of shared science common to the research-oriented Internet. Specifically, several researchers had used the World Wide Web, devised improved versions of rudimentary browsers Berners-Lee had experimented with, and made them work on Unix operating systems. Many technically skilled Internet users understood Unix, so developing for these systems was the

---

[13] This decision is described in detail in Berners-Lee and Fischetti (1999), and Gillies and Cailliau (2000). CERN did not want to offer support, but MIT was willing to do so. CERN's managers did not view providing institutional support for the W3C as within its domain, whereas the experience with supporting the consortium at MIT gave Berners-Lee a model for how to proceed.

obvious first step to take. Throughout 1992, several browsers were in use among technically skilled programmers in the research community.[14]

The improvements accumulated on top of each other and set the stage for a pivotal development, the creation of Mosaic by a team at the University of Illinois. This team was situated at the National Center for Super Computing Applications (NCSA), an NSF-funded research center that supported and housed supercomputers. Its founding in 1985 was one of the direct results of the initiatives to gain congressional support for the NSFNET. NCSA received national funding from general NSF research support for computing, as well as the recently passed High Performance Computing and Communications Act of 1991, which Al Gore had sponsored. The NCSA housed supercomputers, to be sure, but it also housed many of the support facilities for using the Internet to access the supercomputers, which was a function that many other researchers used.

Larry Smarr, the enterprising director at NCSA, was a physicist by training but had not set up the NCSA solely for physics. Rather, the NCSA supported a large range of projects, principally involving a network of researchers who did a variety of frontier science in computing and networking. The center regularly built shareware software, used it, and made it available to others. It also employed many graduate students and undergraduates from top-ranked hard sciences departments, as well as many of the social sciences, where mathematics and networking played a role. The undergraduates were predominantly midwesterners attending the Illinois flagship university.

The activity at the NCSA can be viewed in both a positive and negative light. On the one hand, it could be seen as part of a broad mandate to experiment, invent new software for the Internet and supercomputers, as well as make it available for others. On the other hand, Smarr's pervasive push of technology at the center could be seen more cynically, as an attempt to invent uses for the overly abundant computing capacity and justify the existence of the NCSA in time for the next application for more funding. Entrepreneurial presentations by Smarr around campus aimed to recruit faculty for the center, and fueled both views.

A more measured assessment emanates from a different premise—it recognizes the value of sponsoring a portfolio of research activities in the

[14]See Gillies and Cailliau (2000).

presence of a range of risks over the payoff of any specific project. While many, or perhaps even a majority, of projects at the NCSA were not expected to yield high returns, a few with very high returns justified the expense on the whole portfolio. Indeed, as it turned out, one project by itself, Mosaic, resulted in gains to society that paid back the expenses at that center many times over.

Mosaic initially appeared to be a routine project making mundane and incremental progress, seeking to design an easy-to-use browser for nonresearchers. That is, it was an attempt to improve on one aspect of the shareware Berners-Lee had made available less than a year earlier and to which others had added improvements. The project gradually became anything but routine. Mosaic's team of programmers included an undergraduate, Marc Andreessen, and a graduated master's student, Eric Bina, who had joined the NCSA as a full-time employee in 1991. Andreessen and Bina had a talent for programming and design. The browser was called Mosaic to reflect the team's aspiration that the browser would open up a world of different pictures to student users.

Building on the inventions of others was not unusual in the technically oriented Internet, which operated under the norms of academic computer science. As long as credit was given to earlier inventors, standing on their shoulders was acceptable. With a seemingly cavalier attitude, Mosaic's earliest prototypes liberally borrowed from prior designs for browsers. Andreessen and Bina made no secret that they were borrowing, and, following norms for open science, communicated with many of those prior designers, who expressed no interest in further developing their version of their own software.[15] That was the best of all possible worlds for

---

[15]See the account in Kesan and Shah (2004). A lengthy list of browser prototypes influenced Mosaic. Consider this brief account by Berners-Lee (quoted from Robert X. Cringely, 1998b):

> I wrote the first GUI browser, and called it "World Wide Web" for NeXT-Step. (I much later renamed the application Nexus to avoid confusion between the first client and the abstract space itself.) Pei Wei, a student at Stanford, wrote "ViolaWWW" for UNIX; some students at Helsinki University of Technology wrote "Erwise" for UNIX; and Tony Johnson of SLAC wrote "Midas" for UNIX. All these happened before Marc (Andreessen) had heard of the Web. Marc was shown ViolaWWW by a colleague (David Thompson?) at NCSA, Marc downloaded Midas and tried it out. He and Eric Bina then wrote their own browser from scratch. As they did, Tom Bruce was writing "Cello" for the PC which came out neck-and-neck with Mosaic on the PC.

Andreessen and Bina, since it meant there was little rivalry, no frictions to slow them down, and they possessed discretion to do as they pleased.

Aside from refining and improving the software there were a couple of aspects that distinguished Mosaic from other NCSA projects. First, it was not a project pursued by just a single researcher. The NCSA's institutional support helped the team design the software, and diffuse it, as well as help fund improvements to it over time. The institution paid for equipment and other support, and its endorsement also helped give Mosaic credibility with university administrators, which fostered adoption. Over time, the NCSA browser eventually was built for several operating systems. Crucially, that would include a Windows-based system from Microsoft, at that time the most widely used operating system worldwide for PCs.[16]

While releasing a version for Windows might seem like an obvious thing to do in retrospect, until then it had not occurred to any designer in the technically adept community of Internet programmers to write a browser for a nontechnical user, save one. They had taken care of their own parochial needs first, for which Unix-based browsers were sufficient. More than invention also played a role, as Berners-Lee later recalled:[17]

> Marc and Eric did a number of very important things. They made a browser that was easy to install and use. They were the first one to get inline images working—to that point browsers had had varieties of fonts and colors, but pictures were displayed in separate windows. Most importantly, he followed up his and Eric's coding with very fast 24 hour customer support, really addressing what it took to make the app easy and natural to use and trivial to install. Other apps had other things going for them. Viola, for example, was more advanced in many ways, with downloaded applets and animations way back then—very like HotJava.
>
> Marc marketed Mosaic hard on the net, and NCSA hard elsewhere, trying to brand the WWW and "Mosaic": "I saw it on Mosaic" etc. When Netscape started they of course capitalized on Mosaic as you know— and the myth that Mosaic was the first GUI browser was convenient.

---

[16]This version was released many months after Mosaic had spread to Unix-based systems, so its release received little attention in the technical community. In fact, the browser was built for several different operating systems, such as Unix, Mac, and Windows.

[17]Cringely (1998b).

The release of the Mosaic browser for Unix-based systems began in the spring of 1993, and it immediately began to receive attention and adoption. It was followed by the release for the Windows system in late fall of 1993. It too became available on shareware sites aimed at making software available to other university users. NSF's accounts about the browser say,[18] "In less than eighteen months after its introduction [Mosaic] became the Internet 'browser of choice' for over a million users."

Andreessen increasingly spent all his free time on the browser. Initially, he had helped program it, but increasingly he was helping debug it and responding to requests and suggestions from users.[19] Throughout the academic year of 1993, he continued in this role with others at NCSA, performing what a software firm might call "support," and "feature upgrades," improving the browser's design.

Two intricately related events next shaped the direction of Mosaic. First, Marc Andreessen graduated in December 1993, leaving the Midwest for a software-programming job in California. Second, the browser became available for ISPs in a variety of commercial formats. These two events were linked, as NSCA was on its way to licensing the software. The latter did not sit well with the programmers. Charles Ferguson, an entrepreneur aspiring to make tools for browsers, recounts what was widely believed at the time:

> Smarr and his managerial team had moved to assert control over Mosaic. The development team got thousands of emails a day with fixes, complaints, and questions, which placed them at the very center of the ferment. Smarr decided to route the email to a generic response desk and then told the developers that they could not even see it, because it interfered with their work. When Andreessen graduated in December, he was offered a $50,000 salary to stay at NCSA—high by university standards—but Smarr would not let him manage Mosaic development. Andreessen quit and headed for California, where he got a job at EIT (Enterprise Integration Technologies), which was, however ineffectually, exploring commercial opportunities on the Internet.[20]

[18] See http://www.nsf.gov/about/history/nsf0050/internet/mosaic.htm, accessed September 2012.

[19] Kesan and Shah (2004).

[20] Ferguson (1999), 52.

That account accords with the version of events Netscape later told about itself. It is, however, perhaps a bit unfair to the university and to Smarr in particular. In December of 1993 Andreessen was young, footloose, ambitious, and, by all accounts, headstrong. It is not obvious that any offer from the university would have kept this young talented programmer in Champaign, or for that matter, the state of Illinois.

Growing a Business

As Mosaic grew in popularity (measured by downloads), the managers at the NCSA realized this invention had commercial potential. While they anticipated that the browser would diffuse into popular use through shareware, which was free, they did not view that as sufficient to support a sustainable software business over time. The university administrators arranged for commercial licensing of the browser.

There were numerous justifications for initiating a licensing program. Any popular piece of software requires extensive support. One way to do that involves seeding a firm to perform that support. Commercial licensing of the software was a viable way to seed such a firm.

The University of Illinois initially tried to license the software itself and then decided to work through a known channel, an existing software firm, which was given a master license. It was managed by a third party, a company known as Spyglass, who had helped commercialize other inventions out of the NCSA in the prior years, and though none of them were as large as the browser, the company had worked appropriately in the past.

This effort began with good intentions. Universities with rich technical histories, such as the University of Illinois, are frequently pressured by state oversight committees to find ways to translate their faculty's inventiveness into innovations that help society at large (and their state in particular). Other universities, such as MIT, had seemingly shown the way. Their licensing offices turned patents for faculty inventions into lucrative licensing deals. The arrangement with Spyglass appeared to be an answer to such a request: It was actively speeding the commercialization of software invented at the NSCA, and benefiting an Illinois-based firm as well.

One path was chosen and another was not. An active licensing program precludes an alternative—namely, leaving things to chance and shareware. Once the university puts the underlying software on shareware sites, it must passively wait for an enterprising software firm to imitate pieces of it and put it to use in commercial applications.

A licensing program also precludes another alternative, releasing the underlying software code, which would make it difficult to establish unique ownership over a piece of software. Accordingly, though the university had released earlier versions of Mosaic's code for all to see, they did not do so on the last version.

The university administrators started the licensing program without anticipating what actually happened: the programmers left the state altogether, an action that did not benefit the state at all. As noted, first Andreessen left for California. A few months later, so would Bina and many others, as part of an effort to start a new firm.

Worse yet for the university, that same team built software that eventually competed with the university's licensing program. Specifically, the newly graduated Marc Andreessen, who had moved to the area between San Francisco and San Jose popularly known as Silicon Valley, had previously struck up an e-mail conversation with Jim Clark. Clark had used Mosaic and was curious about it. As it happened, Clark had founded Silicon Graphics many years earlier and was well known in the industry. Clark and Andreessen hashed through a variety of predictions for the future of browsers, starting with interactive TV.[21]

Clark was tiring of his role at Silicon Graphics and its strategic fights and decided to step down as chairman of the board in February 1994. After that point he wanted to start another company. Not long thereafter, Clark and Andreessen's relationship coalesced into a business plan in April 1994. After considering Internet television as a business application for browsers, they eventually settled on selling the browser alone, enabling surfing on the web. They called themselves the Mosaic Communications Company and sketched a plan to make money selling a browser and the servers to go with it.

Clark openly admitted that the business plan was sketchy, but viewed it as a by-product of the enormous opportunity in front of Mosaic Communications Company. Approximately two million copies of Mosaic had been downloaded in the spring of 1994, and millions of more Internet users had never tried it. He reasoned that they could displace Mosaic with

[21] Cusumano and Yoffie (1998), 20.

a new and better browser and generate millions of new users. Although he initially did not have a plan for generating revenue, ever known for his understatement, Clark was sanguine. As he said later, he saw twenty-five million users on the Internet in April 1994, and he expected that to double by the time the company shipped a product. He expected the product to appeal to all of them, and, thus, a rather simple business plan was born:

> You've got to be able to make money with fifty million users using your product.[22]

Eventually Clark and Andreessen's company gave away their browser for free to households, but charged businesses for licenses and support. The free downloading was necessary to compete with Mosaic, which, as an academic program, also was free to students and households. Many enterprise customers were willing to pay the fees, however, as they began to build applications around browsing. Eventually this plan would expand far beyond the browser. It blossomed into an extensive business plan to support a range of complementary activities around their own browser, server tools, and range of services.

One of the notable features of this business plan was the absence of concerns about the underlying substrates of the Internet, such as the presence of the backbone, ISPs, and routers. Andreessen knew that structure well from his days in Champaign, and so did many of the other employees he and Clark would soon hire. They had confidence that their browser would work on a privatized Internet and commercial adaptation to the World Wide Web. They only had to build the browser, not any of the other pieces.

At the outset the newly formed team moved quickly. In part, as with any entrepreneurial firm, their urgency arose from the desire to get their product to market fast. Urgency also arose because this team was concerned about competing with others seeded by Spyglass's licensing program, which held the University of Illinois's master license.

Clark helped the business in a variety of ways. First, he put in as much as $4 million of his own money to finance the start-up, and had connections for collecting more. The team applied for and received venture funding from the same venture capitalists that had backed Clark's earlier

[22] Interview in Cringely (1998a).

efforts—Kleiner, Perkins, Caufield, and Byers, one of the premier venture capitalists on the West Coast. Founded in 1972, this firm was well known for its investments in information technology over many years, including firms such as Compaq, SUN Microsystems, and the predecessors to AOL.

While the financial backing was helpful, the endorsement and connections from L. John Doerr would be especially useful, particularly for recruiting new executive talent.[23] Doerr was already well known, having funded a string of other start-ups, including Compaq, Intuit, and Clark's prior firm, Silicon Graphics. In addition, Clark's connections with the West Coast computing community and his stellar reputation also helped recruiting.

Throughout the spring of 1994, Clark, Andreessen, and Doerr started recruiting employees. Their first action was telling. Immediately after getting the funding in May 1994, they hired many of the same programmers who had worked at the NCSA in Champaign.[24] With that one blow, they cornered most of the market for insider knowledge about the browser (outside of Spyglass's programmers). Whether it actually mattered or not is an unanswerable question, but the appearances did make an impression. It looked like a very astute business move.

After that, the young company went on a crash course to become a large organization supporting worldwide use of their browser. Clark's and Doerr's energy and ability to interest world-class executive talent with experience made for eye-popping headlines among the executive insiders of Silicon Valley during the spring and summer of 1994. For example, they hired as chief operating officer Jim Barksdale, CEO from AT&T wireless (and, before that, at McCaw Cellular Communications, which AT&T bought out).[25]

Even before the young company shipped a product, others specializing in start-up markets began to take notice. This commercial start-up had financial backing from strong venture financing. Moreover, the enterprise had a famous founder, and he and his backers were actively recruiting world-class executive talent in addition to the programming talent.

---

[23]Cusumano and Yoffie (1998) stress this point.

[24]As Sink (2007) recounts, Champaign's computer science community was small enough that it became known immediately who were asked to join and who were not, setting off jealously, envy, and admiration.

[25]See the account in Cusumano and Yoffie (1998), especially page 42.

An Early Confrontation

Back in Champaign, the movements of the university's former students could not help but raise eyebrows. On the one hand, the university had arranged for diffusion, support, and further development of its inventions through two channels, shareware and licensing. These students had introduced a third and unexpected channel: an enterprise based on the West Coast, founded on the knowledge of several programmers' deep familiarity with the inner workings of Mosaic.

Spyglass's managers concluded (correctly) that the new venture aimed to make Spyglass's actions less valuable and potentially obsolete in the marketplace. They responded as any manager in their shoes would have: since Spyglass had been given the right to license the trademarked name *Mosaic*, Spyglass's management decided to defend its intellectual property. It had its lawyers contact Mosaic Communications Company with the intent of getting them to stop using the name *Mosaic*.

The lawyers' actions had two effects. Firstly, in November, Clark and Andreessen chose to end the problems by finding a new name for their firm, renaming it Netscape. Secondly, they did some additional programming, making certain their software did not overlap with the intellectual property owned by the university, eliminating any risk of such claims.[26]

A tussle over a name, by itself, would not be sufficient to deter any new enterprise, and it did not in this case. However, unsurprisingly, Netscape employees resented the actions—especially those who had recently graduated from the university. They did not blame Spyglass as much as they blamed their alma mater for licensing the software in the first place, rather than making it available as shareware, which was the normal practice. They viewed these actions as a clumsy nuisance, arriving at a moment when their time was precious and their commercial needs urgent.

It is not a foregone conclusion that every start-up will succeed, even those with such a strong set of advantages at a young age. Personalities can clash in unexpected ways under the stress of entrepreneurial life, for

---

[26] Netscape's management later claimed it would have reprogrammed the browser from the ground up in any event because they were developing software to support their long-run goals, which required starting from scratch. However, the concerns about intellectual property made that goal a necessity rather than a luxury.

example, or technical issues can emerge that nobody foresaw. If this had been a weak start-up, perhaps this little tussle over a name would have mattered. As it turned out, it was a minor blip.

One early test of a start-up's management is whether it can ship its first product on or close to its self-assigned shipping date. Netscape's management gave itself a four-month timeline for shipping a beta browser. They came close to making that goal. The beta browser was released in November 1994, with its final release in December. Commercial versions were available by February 1995. In other words, the newly founded firm released its first beta just six months after founding, and its first product in less than a year.

This speed got the firm attention because it was fast by the norms of Silicon Valley start-ups. Looking behind the curtain, such speed was not magical. The firm succeeded in being so fast not only because it had a good programming team, but also because it had things few start-ups ever have: it was *not* creating a design from scratch, but rather was starting from a working prototype, and it employed the original designers of that prototype, who were given the opportunity to do a makeover (albeit under a deadline). Moreover, they did this with deep familiarity and near certainty about what features users wanted.

Although Andreessen and Clark already knew from experience that there would be a market for something similar to Mosaic's product, there was considerable uncertainty about how large that market would be, and what form competition would take. In this setting, Netscape had one strategic advantage. Their biggest risk was Spyglass, but because Netscape's staff members were the original designers of Mosaic, they could improve upon anything Spyglass did without any learning-curve lag time. This provided the firm with a competitive advantage in a race with Spyglass.

As it turned out, demand for Netscape's product grew in spectacular fashion through the early winter of 1995, much of it coming from displacing the Mosaic browser, as Clark had forecast. Netscape gained market share and publicity throughout the winter. Andreessen's and Clarke's initial strategy had been correct, and with every successful day the company embarked on an even more ambitious plan for growth.

A Host of Ironies

It is worthwhile to pause and observe several ironies in this brief tussle over a name. The form for diffusing innovations out of the nonprofit sector into commercial use has consequences for how much of society benefits, how quickly, and which firms reap the most benefits. These events illustrate that no licensing program is totally neutral in its consequences.

Most research-oriented universities make it a primary goal to invent new knowledge and diffuse it into widespread societal use. That is as true of the University of Illinois as it is of Stanford University and the University of California at Berkeley, the two large research universities located near the Silicon Valley. Many universities also pursue these goals with a parochial regional focus, if at all possible. This was also true of the three universities just mentioned.

The West Coast universities, however, had lived physically next door to a thriving industry for decades and evolved a set of norms that differed significantly from norms found at most other universities. Both Stanford and Berkeley had licensing programs, but they used comparatively light touches for enforcing them outside of the biological sciences. At both universities it had become quite common for former employees and graduate students to walk out with knowledge of innovations made on campus. The students could start new firms or contribute to the efforts of existing firms, sometimes without any university license at all. Often, however, these firms were within a short drive of campus, and the university retained a relationship with the former students in a variety of ways—through graduate advisors, other friends who remained on campus, and connections to other alumni.

As a former professor from Stanford, Clark was familiar with that norm, and he had taken advantage of it in his prior firm. He was also far from alone. For example, SUN Microsystems involved the teaming of Andy Bechtolsheim, a PhD student at Stanford, and Bill Joy, a programmer at Berkeley. Although SUN directly built their firm using inventions made in the university, neither Bechtolsheim nor Joy ever formally paid the university for its part.

Did the universities eventually get paid? Yes, the money came back to Stanford and Berkeley through later donations and through supporting a local industry that hired its graduates.

Clark and Andreessen established their firm using the norms with which Clark was familiar. They never had any intention of directly paying the University of Illinois for anything invented while Andreessen had been at the NSCA, but something would come back to the university eventually.

The University of Illinois had taken a different path. Although it had taken a light touch in the past, by the early 1990s it was using a heavier hand by initiating a licensing program. That program, in turn, led the university to de facto use a commercial channel for diffusing the invention, for which it needed to establish clear property rights over the work done by its employees and students.[27] In many respects this was an appropriate strategy because the primary user of the technology was not expected to be geographically near. The local economy could be helped through commercialization of technology, and raising revenue became the dominant priority.

The law of unintended consequences rebounded on the university. The university was explicitly encouraging a commercial channel in the hope it would further speed diffusion. Yet in order to do that properly, the university had to establish clear property rights—a step that angered Andreessen and his friends, who reputedly became irate that the university was not assigning credit to the programmers. To make matters worse, the university handed the property rights over to Spyglass, which had to take actions that actively discouraged another competitor, while it licensed Mosaic widely. In other words, Spyglass's fight over the name of the Mosaic Communications Company represented a by-product of the fight between the norms of the light touch and the heavy hand of active promotion. The university's attempt to speed adoption, therefore, partly helped, but also eventually backfired, in achieving its primary goal.

A further irony only became apparent over time. Ultimately, Netscape became fabulously successful for a few years, making several alumni of the University of Illinois quite wealthy. Yet many of the university's former students resented their experience tussling with the university over ownership of the browser. None of them made major donations back to the university.

One might conclude that society was fortunate that the dispute between the University of Illinois and Mosaic Communications Company only involved a naming right and not an issue that might have deterred or slowed Netscape further. Netscape's actions would go on to become catalytic for Silicon Valley and other incumbent firms in commercial computing. That is, virtually every computing and communications company in the United States altered its investment and strategic plans as a conse-

---

[27] This explanation gets more emphasis in the account of Kesan and Shah (2004).

quence of actions Netscape took. Spyglass's actions also did compara-tively well, generating interest among many firms, but it simply did not have as catalytic an impact as Netscape's throughout 1995 and later.[28]

What a set of ironies! The university's administrators discouraged the very channel that eventually succeeded in having the most impact. The uni-versity's failure ultimately ended up having positive results, as the failure of Spyglass eventually helped the university achieve its broader aims—namely, diffusing the browser into wide use.

Champaign's Second Gift

While the events at Netscape garnered much attention, Netscape was not the only software descendant from the NCSA at the University of Illinois. In fact, the NCSA gave society one other invention, a set of standards and protocols for the web server software that worked with the browser—the NCSA HTTPd server. This was the most widely used HTTP server soft-ware in the research-oriented Internet.

The server software was the yin to the browser's yang. The latter would not have been catalytic without the former. The browser was useless with-out the server to support it. The team at Champaign had sensibly under-taken a project to design server software to work with their browser.

While it is not surprising that NCSA had some server software, that fact alone does not explain why this specific software, NCSA HTTPd, became the seed for the most widely used server software. There would be other server software, but no other server software would become as popular as the descendants of the version written at NCSA.[29] Moreover, in strong contrast to the browser this invention leaked to society without much ex-plicit push from the university. It developed along a path quite unlike that of the commercial browser, eventually becoming an open source project. How did that happen?

The server was a collection of technologies that supported browsing and use of web technologies. Along with that came a key invention, pro-tocols for supporting CGI script, which moved data from browsers to

---

[28]Spyglass sold a total of 108 licenses. See Cusumano and Yoffie (1998), Kesan and Shah (2004).

[29]Spyglass also released a server program in 1995 and had some commercial success, for example, selling licenses to Oracle for the product, which resold it under its own brand.

servers and back again.[30] As it would turn out, that tool would become an essential building block for electronic commerce.

From the outset the server software had been available for use as shareware, with the underlying code available to all. Many webmasters took advantage of it by adding improvements as needed or communicating with the lead programmer, Robert McCool. McCool, however, left the university along with all the others to work at Netscape in the middle of 1994. Throughout the fall of 1994 and the first quarter of 1995, therefore, there was minimal maintenance of the software at the university. Webmasters and web participants became frustrated with the lack of response to identified new bugs, or suggestions for improvement in the design.

Netscape had just released its commercial browser, but had not yet built server technologies. It aspired to do so, and would eventually try, but the young company's first product had stretched itself as far as it could go. (At this point, Microsoft did not even have plans to build any server programs for the Internet, a set of priorities that would change shortly.) Frustrated developers and impatient webmasters had nothing else to use except the descendant of the NSCA HTTPd.

The code was available on shareware sites, and many teams had improved it. At the time, there were eight distinct versions of the server in use, each with some improvements that the others did not include. These eight teams sought to coordinate further improvements to the software descended from the NCSA server. They combined their efforts, making it easier to share resources, share improvements, and build further improvements on top of the software.

The eight versions were combined and called Apache. The name *Apache* was a play on words: the first February 1995 effort involved bringing together a piece of software that involved many software "patches," a colloquialism for additional code to repair problems. That led insiders to refer to their own project as "a patchy" piece of software. In a later interview Brian Behlendorf, one of the founders of Apache, acknowledges the pun, but claims it did not motivate his initial thoughts about naming the project Apache. He also referred to the Native American tribe, stating "It just sort of connoted: 'Take no prisoners. Be kind of aggressive and kick some ass.'"[31]

---

[30]CGI stands for Common Gateway Interface. It was first introduced in December 1993 (see RFC 3875) and became a common element in implementing dynamic web pages.

[31]McMillan (2000).

In April 1995, NCSA administrators tried to revive their support for server software by hiring new employees. Upon learning about the Apache effort, however, administrators quickly changed plans and cooperated with the team behind Apache.[32]

Apache worked well with browsers, and many webmasters adopted it, sending suggestions and improvements back to the Apache team. It became the most widely used server on the commercial Internet, eventually competing with, and besting, Netscape and Microsoft's versions of similar software. Spyglass also had a version, which did not diffuse widely. It did, however, become pieces of other software, most notably as server products from Oracle.

Apache played another role. Throughout the 1990s Apache became one of the most widely adopted open source projects, and became widely known as the first case of large-scale open source software that was not descended from Unix, as Linux was, the most widely used open source software at the time. Apache became known as one the "killer apps" for Unix, that is, an application on top of Unix whose value alone merited supporting the operating system.

With such widespread use, Apache's organizers were able to influence others. As such, they became leading defenders of many nonproprietary protocols and standards for the commercial web. For example, CGI script became a widely used nonproprietary standard, and Apache insisted it stay that way.[33]

Becoming a champion of nonproprietary shareware, Apache led many other firms in the commercial computing industry to alter their strategies and investment priorities. It achieved such change because throughout 1995 and beyond, Apache's and Mosaic's users illustrated a working prototype for this novel approach to the organization of commercial computing.

Why did contemporaries consider the pair of server and application software novel? First, until then, personal computing was dominated by an interface known by the acronym WIMP, which stood for the predominant features of a personal computer, Windows, Icon, Menu, and Pointer. These all had proprietary code supporting them. Computing built around browsing appeared to differ significantly. It allowed users to open a window

---

[32]See Mockus, Fielding, and Herbsleb (2005).
[33]See, e.g., Behlendorf (1999), Mockus, Fielding, and Herbsleb (2005).

to other information, but potentially without the operating system, Windows, and with a new set of distinct icons and menus.

Second, the client-server interactions built between any browser and an Apache server did not involve proprietary code. They had the potential to allow users not to use proprietary software in their client-server applications. To many industry participants, that opened the potential for an enormous number of possible futures. For example, it implied that users would not necessarily have to buy everything from IBM or Microsoft to ensure it worked together, but instead could purchase server software from one firm and applications for browsers from another, just so long as both worked with the nonproprietary standards and protocols in wide use. This potential grabbed the attention of many, including Bill Gates. As discussed in later chapters, he reversed his previous position about staying out of the browser business, writing a memo in May 1995 about the change in direction for Microsoft. It was called the "Internet Tidal Wave."[34]

The lack of prices became essential to the operation and success of the project.[35] The absence of pecuniary transactions first arose at the beginning of Apache's existence, when the University of Illinois collected no licensing fees for its use as shareware. It continued as Apache relied upon donations and a community of users who provided new features for free. Apache eschewed standard marketing/sales activities, instead relying on word-of-mouth and other nonpriced communication online. Apache also did not develop large support and maintenance arms for their software, although users did eventually find ways to offer free assistance to each other via mailing lists and discussion boards. Eventually, a foundation was established to support Apache and to provide some of these functions.

Altogether, this added up to yet another irony. The university's neglect of the server software at a crucial moment led to the development of multiple improvements, independently made by others. That later led to an effort to unify the software, which became named Apache. That fostered the retention of nonproprietary software as a crucial component of the commercial Internet. That example, in turn, contributed to an enormous

---

[34] See Gates (1995).

[35] The Apache Software Foundation argues that the lack of price encourages the commitment of the community, and this community would likely fall apart if its products were not free. "Why Apache Software Is Free," http://httpd.apache.org/ABOUT_APACHE.html, accessed July 11, 2011.

institutional shift in the practices that supported the commercial web. Hence, it is not much of an exaggeration to say that one university's neglectful behavior led to an institutional novelty for supporting widely used software in commercial markets.

Microsoft's Action after Licensing

There was a further irony from the University of Illinois's licensing program and that arose from competitive events between Netscape and Microsoft, which later chapters will discuss in much more detail. To appreciate it requires a few more details about the University of Illinois's role in Gates's actions after May 1995. A fast-forward on future events will show the full picture.

Specifically, after Microsoft set on a course to offer a browser, its executives had to determine how to build one quickly. The fastest way to enter the browser business was through remodeling the browser Spyglass offered. Due to Gates's late decisions about browsers, however, Microsoft's entry into the browser business actually occurred in a somewhat roundabout way.

As part of an internal debate about the Internet, several Microsoft executives had arranged to license the browser from Spyglass in January 1995. They gained rights to fully access the code and modify it under their own brand. After May, as Gates authorized the change in direction, Microsoft added a few features, rebranded the browser, and unveiled what they called Internet Explorer 1.0 (IE 1.0) in August 1995 along with the release of Windows 95.

Spyglass's licensed browser hastened the entry of Microsoft into the browser market, saving the Redmond-based company at least several months of development time by providing it with a working version of the software whose code it could examine and from which it could build. The value of that lead time was not apparent to others in January 1995, though it was to the team at Microsoft.[36] It would be more apparent later, as Microsoft competed with Netscape from the position of an underdog. The Spyglass license was extraordinarily valuable to the Microsoft programming team in the second half of 1995. It gave them a working prototype

---

[36]Private communication, Ben Slivka, October 2008. Slivka headed the programming team for Internet Explorer 1.0, 2.0, and 3.0.

as a starting point, just as Andreessen and Clark had had a working prototype in Mosaic.

IE 1.0 was not much more than what Microsoft had licensed from Spyglass, with many of the same features Spyglass had programmed into the browser, including some of the same bugs.[37] Microsoft included it in a separate "plus-pack" that accompanied Windows 95. They did not make it central to the marketing surrounding the unveiling. In August 1995, IE 1.0 received little notice and made little market impact.

By the end of 1995, however, Microsoft began to devote enormous resources to improving the browser and supporting it.[38] Eventually a thousand programmers would multiply to four times that in the entire Internet Products and Tools Division.[39] Within two years, that investment would motivate all other licensees of the Spyglass browser to move their activities to Microsoft's, effectively ending Spyglass's ambition as the primary supporter for this software category.

Seen in retrospect, it was as if events were fueled by a propensity for unexpected consequences. First, Netscape had not put Spyglass out of the browser business. Spyglass's last licensee did. Second, the University of Illinois sought to speed the diffusion of the innovation into widespread use. It succeeded in doing so by licensing their invention to the world's largest software company. As a by-product of doing so, the university unwittingly took sides in a brewing competitive fight, helping the very firm that would compete with Netscape, which was founded by the university's own graduates.

Was the licensing deal a good deal or a poor one? The deal in January 1995 between Spyglass and Microsoft initially was for $2 million. It also paid Spyglass a minimal quarterly fee for the Mosaic license. In a notable departure from Microsoft's usual practices, the company agreed to pay a royalty from Microsoft's Internet Explorer revenue. As it turned out, however, this royalty did not matter in practice, as IE 1.0 did not sell very well. Microsoft altered its strategy in December 1995, bundling IE 2.0 and later

[37] See Sink (2007).

[38] See Sink (2007). He argues that Spyglass's management was quite elated to get Microsoft as a licensee, which implied the management did not forecast this possibility. After they licensed the browser, Microsoft increasingly positioned itself as the primary firm to support other application development. All the other licensees eventually chose to either get support from Microsoft or Netscape; none continued with Spyglass.

[39] Bresnahan, Greenstein, and Henderson (2012).

versions with the operating system, pricing the browser at zero. Hence, Microsoft only paid Spyglass the minimal quarterly fee after December 1995. After Spyglass threatened an auditing dispute in 1997, the companies settled for an additional $8 million.

Ten million dollars looked like a good deal in some respects. If the alternative were shareware and open access to code, which yielded the university fame but no fortune, then some money would have been better than none. In that sense it was a good financial deal. Moreover, at that time, it was one of the most lucrative deals ever for any invention out of the University of Illinois.

By the norms of Microsoft, in contrast, the amount of money was trivial, and the deal was a steal. The licensing deal helped its strategic interests in Windows, a business worth billions. It also accelerated the development of a project in a technology in which the firm had invested minimal resources, software that became a strategic priority to which the company would soon devote several thousand programmers. For a pittance, Microsoft bought the right to climb high and stand on the shoulders of others.

Does Public Funding Pay Off?

Even the best operated government funding of R&D is, by definition, difficult to assess, because of two criteria common to subsidies for R&D: specifically, that the activity funded yields large benefits, and secondly, that these activities should be actions not otherwise undertaken by the private sector. The first action leads government funders to avoid funding research projects with low rates of return. This sounds good because it avoids wasting money. However, combining it with the second criterion has some nonobvious consequences. Private firms fund scientific R&D where the rate of return can be measured precisely—where they can *observe* the return. What is left for government to fund? Governments fund activities where returns are imprecisely measured. In other words, governments tend to fund scientific research in precisely the areas where the returns are believed to be high, but where there is little measurable data to confirm or refute the belief.

The NSF accomplished a great deal of impressive science. In 1989, after only a short period, the transfer of the Internet to private ownership was on the near horizon. More to the point, the technology and the operations had approached the level of maturity required for commercial markets. The Internet had acquired most of the attributes that eventually would lead to the transformation of every part of information and communications markets around the world—except one attribute, software that compelled widespread use for any function other than electronic mail. In 1989 the software to support the web was not built. Needless to say, all the web pages later built by hundreds of thousands of webmasters with Berners-Lee's software were even more unimaginable.

Table 4.1 provides a sense of what had been accomplished before privatization, as well as what was about to occur after privatization, due to the growth of the web. The table provides a summary of the growth of the Internet in terms of its "host" computers on the Internet. A host is a physical node in the network and has an IP address assigned to it, and it provides information to others on the network.[40] This is one standardized way to measure growth over both the precommercial and postprivatization Internet. The table shows enormous growth rates, with the size of networks doubling one year to the next.

Table 4.1 frames Stephen Crocker's well-known comment in his August 1987 RFC. In his retrospective about the Internet's growth he wrote: "Where will it end? The network has exceeded all estimates of its growth. It has been transformed, extended, cloned, renamed and reimplemented. I doubt if there is a single computer still on the network that was on it in 1971."[41]

Crocker turned out to be right. The prior growth was remarkable, and it would not end.

This growth was accomplished at a remarkably small cost. The total cost to the government of creating the Internet is difficult to ascertain, but its ballpark estimate cost is well known. It is known that during NSF's management (approximately 1985–95) the agency invested $200 million in building and managing the Internet.[42] Since the Internet would grow into

---

[40] Although printers and other devices may have IP addresses assigned to them, they tend not to have IP hosts in this sense. In addition, many hubs and switches may not be designated as nodes in the network, and thus will not serve as hosts.

[41] Request for Comment 1000, http://www.faqs.org/rfcs/rfc1000.html, accessed August 2010.

[42] See Leiner et al. (2003), and the longer explanation in Greenstein and Nagel (2014).

TABLE 4.1. Number of hosts on the Internet, 1981–98

Date	Hosts
August 1981	213
May 1982	235
August 1983	562
October 1984	1,024
October 1985	1,961
November 1986	5,089
December 1987	28,174
October 1988	56,000
October 1989	159,000
October 1990	313,000
October 1991	617,000
October 1992	1,136,000
October 1993	2,056,000
October 1994	3,864,000
January 1996	9,472,000
January 1997	16,146,000
January 1998	29,670,000

Source: Coffmann and Odlyzko (1998).

a multi-billion-dollar worldwide industry only a few years later, it is tempting to compare the result against that $200 million figure and assert that the US government got an enormous rate of return for its investment.

Such a conclusion fosters the myth that governments can financially support new technological development for cheap. This conclusion is not correct. It is conceptually inaccurate, most of all. Such a conclusion presumes the funding for basic research about the Internet arose out of cost and benefit calculation designed to accelerate the arrival of economic gains. This grafts a viewpoint on the participants that simply did not motivate events. The cost of the Internet or its future economic benefits did not shape the aspirations of the government.[43] The NSF invested in developing Internet technologies to meet its agency mission, not with the intent of producing large economic gains.

In terms of accounting, the $200 million figure is also too small. It does not include the funding that paid for most of the early invention in the 1970s and early 1980s. While the financial commitment to what became the Internet was undoubtedly considerable, no historian of these events has made a precise estimate of its size. The entire expenditure for the Information Processing Techniques Office (IPTO), the agency within the Department of Defense that funded most of the Internet, did not exceed approximately $500 million over its entire existence (1963–86), and the funding for what became the Internet was but one of many IPTO projects.[44]

In addition, the cost tally of the Internet is further complicated by the distributed investments by others. The NSF paid for investments in backbone facilities and facilities for data exchange but offered only minimal support for investing in installations at universities. Most universities invested heavily in their own computing facilities, paid for by university funds.

There is a deeper observation lurking behind this point. The Internet is more than merely one particular implementation of packet switching at any point in time. Much additional invention had to occur after 1973, and also after 1989. The NSF invested in improving the backbone and supporting high-volume exchange of data, and that led a set of administrators and researchers to invent ways to make the Internet easier to use. In 1993 one research organization contained a small team who designed some software applications on top of Tim Berners-Lee's inventions, and thus were born the browser and web server.

The US economy got innovation from the edges without the NSF fully intending that specific software as an outcome of its investment. Browsing

[43] This is especially so for the period prior to NSF's stewardship. DARPA quite explicitly did not use economic rationales to fund projects. DARPA funded high risk projects that "dealt with the development of fundamental or enabling technologies with which to reach newly defined DOD objectives. . . . When DARPA judged success, it applied technical rather economic measurement standards." Norberg, O'Neill, and Freedman (1996).

[44] The cost of the Internet would also include the substantial number of failures that were part of a broad portfolio of investments in computing science more generally. For example, it would include funding for a range of computer science efforts that did not work out as well as planned, such as in artificial intelligence. It also does not include a range of other experiments in computer science that NSF paid for and from which the general community of researchers learned. Norberg, O'Neill, and Freedman (1996).

made it possible to commercialize services founded on the World Wide Web, thereby increasing the value of the Internet infrastructure, which the NSF had helped to develop. That began at the same time the NSF privatized the backbone, which gave commercial firms permission to build an entirely new commercial use for the Internet. Later events did not merely provide a payoff from one investment in invention. Instead, society got a return on an innovation that enabled a large range of additional innovations across the economy.

5

Unleashing Commercial Iconoclasts

In IBM we frequently refer to our need for "wild ducks." The moral is drawn from a story by the Danish philosopher Søren Kierkegaard, who told of a man who fed the wild ducks flying south in great flocks each fall. After a while some of the ducks no longer bothered to fly south; they wintered in Denmark on what he fed them. In time they flew less and less. After three or four years they grew so lazy and fat that they found difficulty in flying at all. Kierkegaard drew his point: you can make wild ducks tame, but you can never make tame ducks wild again. One might also add that the duck who is tamed will never go anywhere any more. We are convinced that any business needs its wild ducks. And in IBM we try not to tame them.
—*Thomas J. Watson Jr.*[1]

Wild ducks has been a colloquial term in computing for decades. By the early 1990s few remembered that it originated with Thomas Watson Jr., the charismatic chief executive officer (CEO) who inherited IBM from his father, and who built IBM into a computing powerhouse in the 1960s.

Watson Sr. encouraged social conformity in his firm because he believed it made his sales force more effective. Salesmen had to wear blue suits, for example. Watson Jr. continued with that practice, but also came

---

[1] Watson (1963).

to a different understanding with his technical talent, which he labeled *wild ducks*. Watson's wild ducks had permission to be diverse—that is, they did not wear blue suits—so long as they invented.

Wild ducks are a particular group of technically adept innovators, often considered social outsiders by those controlling funding. In this sense "outsiders" is a relative term, defined against another norm for routine behavior. Outsiders could exhibit a range of behaviors and social differences, which are regarded as potentially disruptive and costly to the regular operations of an organization. The reverse also often holds—that is, wild ducks regard the practice of those involved in regular operations as interfering with their inventive activity.

In Watson's world wild ducks also were avant-garde thinkers, often chasing visions they saw as aesthetic, potentially running contrary to received wisdom. Yet they were essential for keeping an organization vital.[2] The value of their ideas could defy evaluation ex ante, and in many technical cases it was hard to evaluate even after a prototype was developed. In addition, wild ducks in a laboratory setting could be willing to take a distinct labor contract from others, such as those in sales. A wild duck might take a cut in pay in exchange for (what was regarded as) a more favorable working environment, such as one permitting lab workers to have more research freedom.[3]

Watson Jr. reiterated these points publicly with a purpose. Wild ducks could serve a useful purpose, but only if an organization made explicit policies to accommodate them. While IBM had made an arrangement to

---

[2]Thomas Watson Jr. reiterated the point in multiple occasions. Consider the following:

> I talk a lot around here about wild ducks, and people kid me a good deal about my wild ducks. But it takes a few wild ducks to make any business go, because if you don't have the fellows with the new ideas willing to buck the managerial trends and shock them into doing something new and better, if you don't have those kind of people, the business pretty well slows down. So I would tell a 21-year-old I.B.M.'er what I've told a lot of 21-year-old college people . . . that is, that the priceless ingredient that a youngster has when he starts in business is that sense of not compromising beyond a certain point.

Quoted in http://www.nytimes.com/1989/05/07/business/l-wild-ducks-048289.html, accessed May 2010.

[3]This theme extends into other industries as well. For broad views on this topic, see Christensen (1997), Stern (2004), Rich and Janos (1994), and for its application to the early Internet, see Greenstein (2010a).

accommodate its wild ducks, their behavior raises a broader question: what arrangement had society made? As this chapter describes, to the extent that the United States had a policy for its wild ducks in computing, the absence of policy was its most salient feature. On first glance, the absence of policy arose as part of a long-standing social compact to live and let live, and not interfere with freedom of expression.

The symptoms were readily apparent in public conversation. A large and vociferous debate preceded and accompanied the NSF's privatization of the Internet. In contrast, no loud national policy debate informed or shaped the emergence of the commercial Internet access market built around a browser. Why the difference? The short explanation is straightforward: the wild ducks of private industry had lived without public scrutiny for years and wanted it to stay that way.

But that misses something deeper that is not widely appreciated. At the time, activities in the commercial industry seemed unworthy of debate or notice to many managers in leading firms. That is more than just a statement about the fickleness of managerial attention. Rather, the different participants in the nascent Internet access market—many of them wild ducks—took actions that they viewed as both technically incremental and straightforward business decisions, but not as big news. The *New York Times*, *Wall Street Journal*, and *Washington Post* might have written about the Internet when NSF managed it from Washington, DC, but these leading news outlets did not write about the emerging situation in markets, nor was this an obviously wrong decision by editors. For years computer systems had evolved and broadened the scope of their activities into reservations, banking, logistics, and other network services, but rarely did the launching of a new service deserve headline in national news organizations. It merely reflected the normal parochialism of a longtime participant in high technology communications markets.

The full and longer explanation might start on the western side of the Great Plains, in Colorado, in a suburb just outside of Denver. That was the unassuming home for *Boardwatch Magazine*, the primary trade magazine for firms that offered bulletin board services (BBS). Each BBS existed merely to supply its customers with services for which they were willing to pay. No government agency directly subsidized the BBS industry in anticipation of its crucial role in the commercial Internet, nor did its suppliers get into the business with that eventual goal in mind. Many in the mainstream treated them as merely another breed of wild duck, eccentric marginal actors who satisfied a few fanatics with their services. At best, BBSs were viewed as harbingers of a far-off electronic future.

The most common BBS was a comparatively simple technology by the norms of frontier Internet computing, it was the result of years of exploration in online information services, and it was largely invented and used by a community loosely connected with those involved in the TCP/IP-based Internet. Despite differences in background, the BBS community shared a passion with the community that had grown up around TCP/IP—namely, a defining interest in networking technology and in its uses.[4]

The name, *bulletin board system*, suggests a metaphor for what a bulletin board did. It was the electronic equivalent of the corkboards of classrooms, where various articles were tacked to the wall, ready for others to examine; it was essentially an electronic message center that catered to people with a specific hobby or interests. The messages accumulated and generated a conversation. Sometimes this conversation took the form of a "chat," where multiple users typed in their text, responding to one another. It also offered additional services, such as forums for news groups, shareware sites for articles, and electronic mail among members. Many BBSs also had a large menu of online games. Some even attempted to set up marketplaces where users could shop.[5] For many participants it became an addictive habit and the means through which they expressed their social existence.[6]

With a BBS, a set of users would phone a particular telephone number, usually a local one, and plug their computer into the call. Using (typically) a PC, or (among the technically adept) a workstation, the users would then establish a connection with a server at that phone number. The server contained files for downloading. Seen from the perspective of the Internet, these BBSs would give users information from only a local server and contain no connection to the Internet.

In more advanced configurations, one BBS could call another in serial, sending messages in an architecture called "store and forward," reminiscent

---

[4]For a history of the earlier generation of experiments, see, e.g., Hauben and Hauben (1997), Banks (2008), Turner (2006), or Campbell-Kelly and Garcia-Swartz (2013).

[5]These shopping sites largely did not succeed prior to the rise of the commercial web. See Banks (2008), or Campbell-Kelly and Garcia-Swartz (2013).

[6]See especially Hauben and Hauben (1997) and Banks (2008).

of classic telegraph systems. These were BBSs, however, which made them more effective than any telegraph ever was. One received the message, automatically sent the message to another, who received it and spread it along. Through such architectures every system could get the same message, and rather quickly. While admired by the wild ducks when they first came out, seen from the perspective of later developments, this was a clunky and cumbersome method for connecting many servers.

In other words, in the early 1990s BBSs occupied a position quite distinct from the Internet. Although the personal computer, modem, and related electronic software played essential roles in both the Internet and the BBS, for many Internet users, the BBS was an afterthought, an alternative they occasionally used, but not the center of their activity. For many outside the research communities with access to the Internet, in contrast, BBSs offered the primary channel for receiving frontier commercial services, such as community discussions, schedules and lists, and a variety of electronic documents. As this chapter explains, the blurring of those lines in the early 1990s had enormous consequences for the emergence of innovation from the edges.

The Internet and BBSs shared one similarity: how they took advantage of local telephone calling rules and regulations. Users typically paid for the service, but not the telephone call, because state regulators in virtually every state compelled local telephone companies to provide unmeasured pricing for local calls over short distances (with some exceptions in some areas in which the local caller incurred small per minute charges). In urban areas these distances ranged from a ten- to fifteen-mile radius, but were larger for rural areas. Local calls involved extremely low costs per minute, if any, except to those who called from outside the local area. While the specific features of these policies differed from one state to another, their general features were similar everywhere. States required low prices for local calls as part of a broad program to encourage universal service in telephone use.

The BBS operators were operating under the existing regulatory setting, made by distant regulators. Like the citizen-band radio community and the early PC market, the community of bulletin board providers drew from a wide swath of eclectic wild ducks that could be found all over the country. Some BBSs had purely commercial motives and others were hobbyists. Some operated their bulletin boards as part of a technical obsession or hobby, others as part of their upstanding commercial business where they took professional pride in the delivery of their services. Still others—indeed, a substantial number—operated the BBS as part of the pornography business and preferred to remain out of the center of the public eye in communities that regarded such activity as salacious and unsavory.

When the Internet became available, there were thousands of BBSs throughout the United States, and there was no national policy debate about what they should do when the NSFNET privatized. Many did not even participate much in the Internet at that point, and those that did, such as those who cooperated with UUNET's nonprofit activities, were not central to the debate about the NSFNET's privatization. Yet virtually all of them eventually became active in the commercial Internet by the mid-1990s. Its services were ideal for hosting content and providing other services related to Internet-supported browsers.

With nonchalance at first, beginning in the early 1990s, and becoming visible around 1993, many BBSs decided to become torchbearers for the accelerated arrival of the commercial browser-using Internet. These participants in the BBS industry became familiar with HTML, URLs, and the technical methods for making PCs accept TCP/IP software. This chapter explains how, in a short time, they joined the commercial-oriented Internet. As far as most of those in the BBS industry were concerned, it was not a big deal. They were wild ducks, they were used to being ignored by the mainstream, and they were accustomed to sharing their passions among themselves. They did not see any point in trying to bring more attention to their actions than necessary to generate advertising that attracted customers. They would propel the commercial Internet forward quickly, and, importantly, they did so almost everywhere in the United States.

The Last Mile

The facts on the ground provided no reason for optimism about the Internet's prospects in the early 1990s. All prior attempts to develop electronic mass markets had crashed on the shores of what was perceived to be "the last mile problem." The *last mile* concerned the supply of infrastructure services for delivering data between the national/global data grid and end users.

In the early 1990s, US national regulatory policy focused on growing infrastructure—namely, it focused on a solution employing telephone companies.

These companies would deploy technologies that allowed for higher data-transfer rates over telephone lines, such as ISDN (Integrated Services Digital Networks), which supported bandwidth speeds of 128K. Regulators debated how changes to access and interconnection policies altered investment incentives for incumbent local exchange providers. Considerable momentum built up inside telephone company bureaucracies to support the deployment.

By 1994 it was clear that ISDN had a problem, and it was simple to describe: There was not much demand for it. It was too expensive on a monthly basis for most households and too cumbersome to install. Few households or businesses wanted the service. Inside the industry a joke had emerged about ISDN, that it stood for "I Still Don't Need it."

Odd as it may seem in retrospect, many contemporary managers within telephone companies did not recognize that there was no need to upgrade the speed of data transfer with an expensive technological solution. The existing telephone service was more than adequate for most TCP/IP-based applications, such as electronic mail and simple browsing. The last mile issues did not need new infrastructure or new technology at this time. Rather, the situation needed new business processes and a viable commercial plan for raising revenue to meet the operational costs of offering e-mail and a browser and supporting those applications.

A commercial service over regular dial-up telephone services based on a resource-sharing protocol, TCP/IP, had not been on this list of solutions to last mile problems until the NSF finished its privatization. With the newly privatized industry demonstrating its feasibility every day, the advantages to the Internet were becoming obvious to those who understood how it worked. TCP/IP worked with minimal installation at a home. Due to long experience with NSF and the military, long-distance data carriers used compatible digital processes; so too did data-exchange carriers, and equipment providers of routers, such as Cisco. Units from MCI, Sprint, BBN, and IBM, as well as entrepreneurial spinoffs such as UUNET and PSINet had operations and provided Internet service.[7] Every regional carrier knew how to operate the underlying protocols as well, since it merely involved moving digitized data.

---

[7]For an examination of the technical and business issues of developing services, see, e.g., Marcus (1999).

In addition, the Internet provided some (but limited) international communications abilities. While many other developed countries had their own networking technologies (for example, France, Germany), and some countries had oriented themselves to international efforts (such as those at OSI), there were operating TCP/IP networks in many parts of Europe. The working prototypes of the TCP/IP Internet worked robustly now and allowed for vendor and user participation.

It just needed one thing: commercially viable Internet service providers in most locations. That explains why there were many potential disadvantages to the commercial Internet, especially in 1994. Norms for providing Internet service to the business enterprise market were not settled. The servers were usually Unix based, and these offered the most technically straightforward route to TCP/IP compatibility. Using them, however, also required hiring technically oriented staff, which only the largest installations tended to do.

The software issues were complex. Because local area network (LAN) equipment had to be made more usable, some standard retrofits had emerged, but better software upgrades were anticipated. Novell's Netware, the most commonly employed network and server software, did not blend with TCP/IP-based networking very easily.[8] In addition, Microsoft's server software, Windows NT, was slated to have TCP/IP compatibility, but that product's release date was slipping, not due until the middle of 1995.

The workstation was the most common client for accessing the Internet, but that was not a general solution. Internet connection software was not easy enough to figure out for a novice user. As with the servers, TCP/IP-based traffic and web-based traffic worked easily on Unix-based computers in a client role, but that appealed only to technically adept users. Many participants awaited the arrival of Windows 95 for the PC, which promised better compatibility with the core plumbing of TCP/IP.[9]

Nor did the Internet's proponents have a sexy value proposition to support its widespread use. In early 1994, before Clark and Andreessen formed their company, there was no palpable buzz in Silicon Valley about Mosaic.

---

[8] Forman (2005) describes these issues and offers statistical evidence about their consequences for how fast enterprises adopted the Internet.

[9] Numerous retrofits and add-ons had enabled users of Windows and DOS-based machines to get functional service over dial-up networks and local area networks, but these technical solutions were ad hoc.

It had diffused throughout the research and university user community. That working prototype had not yet turned into a recognizable commercial industry of web services. Aside from an abundance of web pages from researchers and university users, there were no start-ups or provocative initiatives. The biggest news in early 1994 came from the venerable *Encyclopædia Britannica*, which had released a web-compatible version of its text in January. That was interpreted as a notable technical accomplishment, and potentially a competitive response to Encarta, a CD-ROM encyclopedia from Microsoft, but not a motivation for starting any entrepreneurial Internet businesses.[10]

Household service for novice users also was a big question mark. Some of the existing national bulletin board firms, such as Genie, Prodigy, CompuServe, and AOL, had adopted Internet e-mail by 1994, and retrofit it into their services with varying degrees of success.[11] Some firms, such as MCI, had tried offering proprietary electronic mail services but had not enjoyed much commercial demand and had made efforts to offer TCP/IP-based e-mail. No norm had emerged for how services for households should operate in a bulletin board that also provided access to the Internet. For example, there were open questions about whether to charge per time period, per traffic flow in bits, or simply for the connection. There were also unanswered questions about how to charge a premium for increasing the quality of services. Nobody was quite sure what novice consumers would want and what they would do in the face of different prices.

How would the commercial Internet get out of this position? A most unlikely coalition of iconoclasts and visionaries took the first step, and many came from the BBS industry.

From BBS to ISP

Even prior to the privatization of the NSFNET some BBSs began developing a commercial Internet service. A few of those tried commercializing a browser. They all acquired the new label, Internet service provider, or ISP.

Operating an ISP was similar to operating a BBS. It involved much of the same equipment to handle phone calls, as well as the same software to handle password authentication and monitoring. In addition, the modem

---

[10]See Greenstein and Devereux (2009).
[11]See the extensive discussion in Banks (2008).

TABLE 5.1. ISPs listed in Boardwatch Magazine, 1993–99

Dates	11/93	1/95	5/96	8/96	3/97	1/98	1/99
Directory Firms	24	35	2050	2934	3535	4167	4511

bank and the arrangement with the telephone company remained the same. With an ISP, however, there were the added features of software that enabled a caller to use the Internet and a connection to the Internet that allowed the ISP to carry the traffic. For most BBS operators, additional features to enable Internet traffic were not technically out of their reach, though not technically simple. That also had an implication for the ISP business. Billing the customer could remain the same, or the ISP could reconsider whether to bill for time or not. Most of the additional investment would go into software development and customer support.

Watching the changes at *Boardwatch Magazine* were a good barometer for noting what happened to the commercial Internet access market. The earliest advertisements for ISPs in *Boardwatch Magazine* appeared in late 1993, and the magazine's staff thought a few of these developments were worthy of news stories. As it turned out, advertisements grew slowly until mid-1995, at which point the operation became so large that *Boardwatch Magazine* began to organize the presentation, showing many pages of tables in the format of a directory.

Table 5.1 presents the number of ISPs listed in *Boardwatch* for several different years. The data gives a good sense of the timing behind the growth of dial-up ISPs. In November 1993, only twenty-four advertised; in January 1995, there were thirty-five. By May 1996, however, those numbers had exploded to over two thousand. It would become over 4,500 by January 1999.

The advertisements in *Boardwatch* were not the idiosyncratic result of something only the magazine experienced. They accurately reflected the trends seen in other publications.[12] By 1996, however, the situation had changed in books, just as it was changing for *Boardwatch Magazine*.[13] In

---

[12] In one of the earliest Internet "handbooks," Krol (1992) lists forty-five North American providers (eight have national presence). In the second edition of the same book, Krol (1994) lists eighty-six North American providers (ten have national presence). Marine and colleagues (1993) lists twenty-eight North American ISPs and six foreign ISPs.

[13] For example, Schneider (1996) lists 882 US ISPs and 149 foreign ISPs.

other words, the industry began to explode with an entirely new wave of participants.

An Unlikely Partnership

The BBSs operated as part of an unlikely, uneasy, and asymmetric partnership with the telephone companies. The partnership shaped innovative behavior in both good and distortional ways, yet it was not a voluntary relationship, but rather one born from necessity and from reasons idiosyncratic to the United States, founded on years of lawsuits between AT&T and regulators. Local telephone firms and bulletin board operators' relationships were defined by years of lawsuits, regulatory disputes, and distinct differences in the attitudes of managers and employees about how to employ technology and operate a firm. Such a legally enforced partnership contained multiple recriminations and tedious disagreements over lines of law, and it was a relationship marked by frequent suits, countersuits, and new suits.

Partnership itself was not a barrier to innovation. Partnerships were not unusual in technology markets. The history of commercial innovation contains many famous teams in which tension between the members fostered creativity and rivalry, fueling outcomes that neither individual would have achieved on his or her own. Such teams inside one firm were a staple of high technology lore: Wozniak and Jobs at Apple, Gates and Ballmer at Microsoft, or Bechtolsheim and Joy at SUN.

Fruitful partnerships among firms were also not unusual in spite of the complexity of managing a (possibly) contentious relationship across firm boundaries. For example, Microsoft and Intel had a partnership that dominated the PC industry in the 1990s. Bill Gates at Microsoft and Andy Grove at Intel each had distinct upbringings, ages, ethnic backgrounds, and managerial philosophies about what was best for their firms. In spite of those differences, though, they found common ground to make the situation work profitably for both.

To be precise, however, in all of high-tech lore, there was no precedent for an innovative *involuntary* partnership among firms resulting in much of anything. In such a partnership, loud bickering and lawsuits would have been expected to lead to little or no innovative performance. In the case of the telephone companies and the BBS industry, that would have been reasonable to expect as well.

First, consider the telephone company. Telephone companies in the United States performed an enormous and essential economic activity.[14] These firms primarily had one responsibility: to operate and maintain the world's largest and most sophisticated landline telephone system. Regulators had long ago found numerous ways to place demanding performance requirements on telephone companies, requiring build-outs into expensive low-density areas so the entire population could receive service. Regulators had also demanded capacity decisions that supported completing calls at all times under all settings, even in the face of extraordinary demand, while also requiring low expenses for the service.

Over the years, the largest telephone companies had evolved to accommodate these stipulations. They were accustomed to routine market demands, predictable investment trajectories, and long regulatory review prior to any change. They had evolved into stable utilities and had grown bureaucratic organizations suited to stable investment under regulated conditions, with little competitive threat.

Telephone companies and BBSs could not be more different in their organizational structure or market orientation. There was no such thing as a typical BBS, but three types of bulletin board operators were predominant in the 1980s and early 1990s: national online service providers, specialized online service providers, and operators who supported online pornography. Each had a distinctly different type of relationship with telephone companies and regulators.

The national online service providers (for example, AOL, Prodigy, Genie, CompuServe) had entrepreneurial roots, but, unlike the other two groups, had experience in state and national regulatory arenas. They viewed the phone companies as cooperative partners in some respects. In part this was due to their size. They regularly negotiated contractual agreements with high-level executives from many firms, and, at least in principle, had their concerns addressed directly. Moreover, as national firms they would not hesitate to hire lawyers to lobby the federal regulatory apparatus to settle disputes.

These firms also had been in business for years. Some, like CompuServe and Prodigy, had corporate parents with ambitious aims and long-term

---

[14] In 1992 the telephone industry generated 171 billion dollars of revenue, with the three largest components going to local service ($43B), long distance ($69B), and network access ($31B). *Annual Survey of Communications Services*, US Census. http://www.census.gov/services/sas/historic_data.html, accessed July 2009.

visions for their services. All offered service using extensive proprietary content, as well as proprietary features underlying the standards and protocols. Some also managed to resell proprietary content from other online services, such as LexisNexis. Others sold access to news and other features, such as airline flight schedules.

In 1992, these BBS providers and their standards and protocols were very different from the Internet. Their managers experienced a balkanized world of electronic commerce, one in which users signed up for proprietary services. Communicating between different firms would require bilateral arrangements between firms, and those did not exist as often as they did exist. The national providers encountered difficulties getting their e-mail clients to work with each other, and users could only get content for which their sponsoring firm had arranged in advance.

Prior to the mid-1990s, this group of BBSs had difficulty widening their appeal beyond technically sophisticated home PC users. Their services were cumbersome to set up and operate, and only a technical sophisticated user was willing to learn the precise steps and diagnose the issues. Yet due to their corporate sponsorship, these BBSs tended to have the largest customer bases and the most experience with large-scale marketing and operations. Most important, because their outlooks tended to differ from those found in academic computing and networking, they viewed commercial opportunities in a more competitive light.

For some time, mainstream computing had treated the online providers as prototypes for a distant revolution. For example, when Microsoft sought to establish its own online service (launched in 1994 and named MSN for Microsoft Network), Microsoft's management thought the revolution was far off in the future. It first approached AOL to buy a piece of it, then after being rebuked, it explicitly modeled its service after AOL, believing it had plenty of time to catch up.[15] Because Microsoft also saw the online services as prototypes for futuristic online services, its management concluded that

---

[15] Ferguson (1999), 53, reports a story that commonly circulated at the time. He says Gates approached Case, CEO of AOL, on the recommendation of Russ Siegelman, the head of the Microsoft Network, MSN. He then reports,

> With his characteristic delicacy, Gates said to Steve Case, "I can buy twenty percent of you, or I can buy all of you, or I can go into this business and bury you." Displaying considerable courage, Case replied that AOL was not for sale, so Gates decided to bury him. That same day, Gates authorized Siegelman to proceed with development of the Microsoft Network."

the biggest growth for MSN was many years into the future, most likely coincident with the diffusion of high speed services to homes, delivered by fixed wireline broadband more advanced than ISDN and much cheaper. The expected time of arrival was sometime in the next millennium.[16]

Few forecast that the demand for, and ultimate arrival of, the browser-based commercial Internet access market would come so much sooner. Nevertheless, just a few years later as Internet demand boomed, the national BBSs attempted to become national ISPs. As early as 1995, several of these providers had well-functioning connections to the Internet for most of their user base. By this point, AOL had gotten into its "carpet-bombing" campaign, blanketing households with free start-up disks. It was the brainchild of Jan Brandt, AOL's marketing director, and Steve Case, its CEO.[17] It simplified installation and gave free demonstrations before it began billing, and user response was positive.

AOL's method for developing an installed base came in for considerable attention, and ridicule in technical circles. Part of its approach addressed an actual problem—lack of user experience with online services made many potential users reluctant to adopt—by giving them a free look, and, charged them only if they stayed with the service. Some of the ridicule reflected one generation feeling superior to another, with the earlier adopters pointing at their own sophistication. It also reflected something else. Part of its approach involved hustling and garish marketing, distributing the disks by a variety of means—direct mail, newspaper insert, and any other manner that put the disks in the hands of potential users. This type of activity focused on commercial goals, flaunted its unconcealed marketing aims, and appealed to nontechnical users. Such activity had not been part of the NSF-sponsored Internet, and to many longtime participants in the Internet it looked novel, and foreign. To longtime participants in bulletin boards, however, it looked like a further extension

---

[16] For a longer explanation, see Greenstein (2008a), Haigh (2008), or Bresnahan, Greenstein, and Henderson (2012).

[17] Banks (2008), 135, reports that the first experiment with carpet bombing began as a direct mail campaign to households, in which Brandt included free time with the disks. Steve Case expressed skepticism, but authorized a small experiment with 200,000 people at a cost of $250,000. After an astounding 10 percent response rate, AOL began expanding the approach with more direct mailings and other approaches. AOL's campaign was so large that in some weeks of 1998 it bought the world supply of disks. Stated Brandt, "At one point 50% of the CD's produced worldwide had an AOL logo on it." See Siegler (2010).

of years of the commercial hustling, long found among the spreaders of online services.

The second set of BBSs resembled the first group in technical operation, but tended to be much smaller, focusing on one or a small number of locations. These were specialized organizations that attempted to accomplish a specific function, such as product support or sales (for example, information sales or product manuals), club support (for example, airplane hobbyists), or games (for example, groups devoted to Dungeons and Dragons). Some provided limited user-group functions, such as daily updates of news, organized Usenet group postings, or periodic e-mail. Many of these smaller organizations operated BBSs as a side business, or, perhaps, as one of many activities related to a hobby, a community, or as a service to the local friends.

Some of these, such as the WELL, acquired a loyal following of users who regularly phoned in to take part in long discussions, a precursor to the emergence of electronic communities.[18] The WELL achieved a cult-like status among its users, as well as considerable coverage from general media.[19] Indeed, many of the online service providers took notice of WELL's success and began to imitate its practices, viewing community building as a source of loyalty for their national services.[20]

Most important, the participants from this second group had perspectives that differed from the NSF descendants. They might not have cared as much about stretching frontier computing for its own sake, or about high-minded public debates about the use of public assets. Instead they focused more on making their systems easy for a nontechnical user. Many of them also focused on a local area, providing service to a niche set of customers or community.

Their leaders also differed from many mainstream executives in computing, taking on the role of both a user and supplier of services. They also tried different pricing scenarios. For example, when a small BBS supported another activity, such as local PC repair service, the operator might

[18]In 1985 Stewart Brand and Larry Brilliant founded the Whole Earth 'Lectronic Link (WELL, for short), starting a virtual conversation between the writers and readers of the *Whole Earth Review*.

[19]See, e.g., Markoff (2005), or Turner (2006).

[20]See, e.g., Swisher (1998).

only have cared about covering their costs, not necessarily about finding ways to maximize revenue.

Because they were present in many cities nationwide, the entrepreneurs among them offered views that differed from technology business leaders in places like Silicon Valley, New York, and Boston. For example, many were often content to supply service to a small town that would appear unprofitable to a major corporation. Many would focus on providing local news or specialized information that national outfits would otherwise ignore.

Some of these smaller bulletin board operators did later become ISPs.[21] As was previously mentioned, supporting such groups led to the founding of some commercial ISPs, such as UUNET. However, the vast majority became smaller ISPs, often with a geographically local focus, just as they had done with their BBS.

The third type of BBS, and arguably the most numerous and geographically dispersed, was the operator who supported pornography. Although any individual firm tended to be small, these operators were present in every city in the United States. *Boardwatch Magazine* listed thousands of them among their BBSs in the United States.

It is an open secret of US communications policy that pornography proliferated on the frontiers of information technology. Suppliers of pornographic material had a history of crashing through convention in order to exploit a new technical opportunity, and they had a history of experimenting with a variety of pricing and marketing models on the frontiers. Moreover, their experiments provided a forecast. Not infrequently, commercial mainstream suppliers would come along a little later with less salacious applications of the same technical and business elements a pornographer had successfully pioneered.

Many of these operators were comfortable with commercial practices the NSFNET descendants and national firms did not employ. They also had two key differences. The pornographers were social pariahs in many cities, protected under the First Amendment, and defended by such groups as the ACLU (American Civil Liberties Union) in light of the perceived larger principles. Yet, mainstream computing firms, as well as many other BBSs, shunned open associations with them. Suppliers monitored the

---

[21] This transition is very apparent in the directories of the 1997 and 1998 editions of *Boardwatch Magazine*.

experiments of the pornographers and learned from them, and typically did so without giving credit to them as a group or attributing the lessons to any specific firm.

In addition, many pornographers operated profitable businesses outside of the spotlight. Profitability was important for these prospective ISPs. They found it easy to get the cash from their own operations to become ISPs. That gave them the freedom to invest according to their entrepreneurial instincts, without interacting with banks or other formal financial institutions whose oversight might have altered their investments. In some cases, that led them to develop other functions in the commercial Internet, such as becoming content providers and hosting sites. Unsurprisingly, as the Internet commercialized some of them moved into the lucrative online pornography business.

Like most service industries, the BBS support staff was local, with employees who lived nearby. The infrastructure for supporting the market already existed in the early 1990s due to the spread of the PC. Surveys showed that more than half the US adult population used a computer regularly by 1995, with the percentage among college-educated young men approaching more than three-quarters, albeit, the number with a PC at home was considerably smaller.[22] Nonetheless, that was sufficiently large to support repair services for PCs in most cities of any significant size. And there were always retail outlets for peripherals, such as modems, printers, and software. National mail order catalogs also supported specialty purchases.

That BBSs supporting pornography could be found everywhere in the United States is a literal statement about simple supply and demand. The supply of technically skilled entrepreneurs throughout the United States who could operate a BBS for pornography responded to a demand for the service virtually everywhere, and the business made enough revenue to cover the costs, even in a small isolated town. As a result, any location that contained sufficient density of human settlement to justify a hair salon, a grocery store, and a street light at a busy corner also had at least one BBS providing pornography, and usually more.[23] Said another way, because of

---

[22] Table 1138, Adult Computer and Adult Internet Users by Selected Characteristics: 1995 to 2005, *Statistical Abstract of the United States. 2007. The National Data Book.*

[23] See the discussions in Aspray (2004), chapter 2, and Cronin (2006). As further evidence, the 1996 edition of *Boardwatch Magazine*'s directory makes it apparent (from examination of

the pervasiveness of pornography BBSs, every small town had at least one potential BBS that could convert to supply ISP service.

In contrast, geographic pervasiveness was not a goal of the national firms. They did not find it profitable to establish local telephone service in geographically isolated small cities, because in small cities the subscription levels just did not generate sufficient revenue to cover operating costs. For the same reasons, the hobbyists and national providers also focused on serving most medium-sized and large cities.

Many of the local BBSs brought with them a hacker ethic, and in one area it contrasted with the commercial online services. Many hackers believed information should be free, and they eschewed the institution of copyright licensing.[24] They did not hesitate to download software for sharing. On their bulletin board systems they made available news items for sharing. Their attitude toward paying for content was almost cavalier, if it was present at all. Even if they did not hold this attitude for ideological reasons, many small BBSs turned a blind eye to this behavior among their users because it helped business. They had no incentive to police it.

The hacker ethic had existed prior to privatization, but the NSF had held it in check with the rules for acceptable use. Just as with enforcing restrictions on commerce, some universities had turned a blind eye to violations of copyright by its students, while other universities had policed such activity, preventing it from blossoming. The NSF would be gone after 1995. Without oversight, where would these attitudes take sharing of information and copying of copyrighted material? This was an open question as the BBS providers became ISPs, melding their actions with the newly privatized Internet.

In summary, as the NSF privatized the Internet in 1994, the BBS industry had outlooks that differed from telephone companies. There was no single typical response from these firms. They had widely different backgrounds. They did not speak with a single voice on any of the key questions regarding forecasting, strategy, or public policy, which is what made the innovations that evolved from their unlikely partnership with the telephone companies so unpredictable at the time, and incredible and surprising in retrospect.

---

the names of many of these BBSs) that BBSs that specialized in pornography were geographically dispersed across the country.

[24] For longer discussions, see, e.g., Markoff (2005), or Turner (2006).

Rules, Regulations, and Restrictions

The partnership between BBSs and telephone companies got much of its animus from prior disputes over regulatory rules. Many local telephone companies tolerated the BBSs because they had to, not necessarily because they wanted to. Many BBSs did not trust the telephone companies and remained wary of any action they viewed as a betrayal of precedent.

The FCC compelled local telephone companies not to "discriminate" against BBSs, or any others that were classified as "enhanced service providers." These complex regulations grew out of years of antitrust and regulatory lawsuits and inquiries at the FCC, focused on preventing AT&T from blocking development of new services complementary to the telephone system. They governed the designs for communications equipment firms and the operations of information service firms, where competitive supply conditions prevailed. They also governed how both types of firms interacted with monopoly telephone companies and aimed to prevent the monopoly from shaping competitive conditions in distortionary ways.

The set of regulations changed over time, and became known as Computers I, II, and III. By 1993 and later, only Computers II and III were in effect.[25] Computer II would play a profound role during the commercialization of the Internet. Yet Computer II's adoption and design arose from many motivations, and some of those were only loosely connected to the Internet. This is worthwhile to understand in detail, except that the legal nuances would put to sleep all but a couple dozen wonkish addicts of telephone regulation. What follows is a compromise between a brief synopsis and a full explanation.

Computer I began in 1966, resulting in an order in 1971. The issues motivating Computer I predated the design of TCP/IP and concerned issues more fundamental to the regulation of telephone systems. It began to put in place rules for mediating the relationship between the telephone company (who had rights because it "owned" its equipment), and others with computing equipment (who had to have legal "permission" to attach to the network).

---

[25]There is a very long history behind these events, and this chapter reviews only a part. See, e.g., Noll and Owen (1989), Werbach (1997), Oxman (1999), Cannon (2001), Owen (2002), Hogendorn (2005), and Nuechterlein and Weiser (2005).

Computer I would accommodate computer modems and did not anticipate what those modems would be used for. That would prove awkward for the FCC in the 1970s, especially as the earliest experiments in commercial packet networking became available for private users. Computer II, issued in 1980, was designed to resolve these tensions and was viewed as an improvement to Computer I. Should the telephone companies have monopoly rights to these packet network services? (No). If multiple firms provide such services, then should they be regulated like monopoly local telephone service? (No). If these are not regulated as monopolies, then should there be a bright regulatory line between them and the telephone? (Yes). What are they to be called to distinguish them from telephone service? ("Enhanced Services"). Can an enhanced service get access to a business line from the telephone company, then resell access to it as a BBS? (Yes). Once again, notice the timing: Computer II was put into practice long before DARPA transferred stewardship over part of the TCP/IP network to NSF. Its motivation is connected to the rise of packet networking and services using digitized data over telephone lines, which loosely connects it to the rise of the same technical factors that yielded the Internet.[26]

Computer II had a seemingly straightforward purpose: to preserve and nurture competitive markets in services and products that worked with the telephone system. It did so by tightly describing the obligations of telephone providers and circumscribing their ability to escape these obligations. Computer II achieved this objective with two interrelated requirements.[27] First, it permitted telephone firms to enter these same markets only if the telephone firm contained a structurally separate division offering services that competed with new entrants. Second, Computer II designed the form of the protection in a way that made it easy to monitor. Telephone firms were compelled to offer a competitor what it would offer to its own division.[28] The first provision permitted phone companies to

[26] This should be read as a statement about the origins and adoption of these rules. Their merits were revisited periodically, as circumstances and the ideology of policy changed. In particular, these rules were revisited just as the commercial Internet was developing, and retained. The rule about reselling business lines was key to developing a competitive dial-up ISP industry. See Oxman (1999).

[27] This is a necessary oversimplification. Cannon (2001) provides a history of these rules and how they changed over time.

[28] Under Computer III, a telephone company could have an integrated division as long as it also had a very detailed and approved plan for supplying interconnection to other providers. The first Computer III order was issued in 1986 and underwent subsequent revision and

use their expertise in new markets, while the second provision limited the ability of the phone company to put a potential rival at a disadvantage.

Most relevant to what follows in later chapters, by the early 1990s, every manager at a local telephone company had lived with these rules and knew them well. They required the telephone firms to treat a competitor the same as its own division, and they applied to BBS operators, just as they applied to any other electronic service, such as ISP lines to university networks. More to the point, the FCC would face questions around the time of privatization about whether to revisit these policies as BBS operators considered carrying Internet traffic, and the FCC would largely choose to leave the policies unchanged. That left all potential parties in a familiar regulatory environment with known regulatory obligations.[29]

These rules were incredibly important to BBS operators. The long fights to develop the rules left an uncomfortable legacy with many BBSs. Many believed they could not order lines from telephone companies and resolve technical issues to make their modem banks operate efficiently without the routine cooperation of the local telephone firm. Many managers also believed those local telephone firms would not be cooperative without being compelled to do so.

If the Internet did not originally motivate the design of these rules, what motivated them in the first place? It is easy to conceive of them as a by-product of specific legal cases, though that is too narrow. Seen in a broader light, however, they can be interpreted as reflections of two long-standing tendencies in US antitrust law and regulation. For one, US antitrust law enforcement agencies have a long history of attempting to prevent a dominant incumbent telephone company from using its dominance in one market (for example, local telephone service) for commercial gain in another where competitive entry and innovative activity might emerge (for example, selling data or selling services that use digitized data). Another distinct motivation arose out of common carrier regulation, which had been applied to telephone companies for many decades. It required monopoly utility carriers to refrain from using their monopoly to benefit one business partner at the expense of another market supplier, that is, not

---

court challenges. At the dawn of the commercial Internet Computer III was still undergoing change.

[29] This is a necessary oversimplification. See Cannon (2001) and Oxman (1999).

to discriminate against any potential business partner.[30] The phrase "common carrier" embodies the principle: carriage has to be provided as a common good, available to all on the same terms.

Summarizing, the broad principles of antitrust law and common carrier regulation were widely appreciated, and the details of each underwent frequent reapplication to suit new circumstances and technologies. These rules were regarded as a nuisance for local telephone firm operations in the details, but, as a technical and operational matter, they were also a fact of life in the business. Any such engineering details had long ago been worked out, and new services in the later part of the 1980s and early 1990s tended to raise incremental issues, at most.[31] The daily issues behind compliance were routine. Because the bulletin board volumes were comparatively small in relation to voice telephony, most local telephone firms and local regulators thought the burdens were a manageable nuisance. The timing and features of calls to bulletin boards looked distinct from voice calls, placing peculiar demands on capacity during peak load times, but most often at nonpeak times, after business hours. They were also a small source of revenue, since they led users to demand second lines.

A slight fast-forward can also illustrate a related point. The first major restructuring of US communications law since 1934 took place during the writing of the 1996 Telecommunications Act. The act borrowed much of its wording for the sections regarding enhanced information services from Computer II and embedded it in the legislation's language. The act retained the architectural logic of the regulations—its seemingly bright line between the monopoly provision of local telephone access and competitive provision of enhanced services.

Additional evidence of its acceptance can be found in the priorities of the White House after commercialization. A memo from Ira Magaziner became well known, as it argued that many aspects of the network's commercial evolution was too complex and contained too many unknowns, and did not lend itself to government intervention.[32] Despite that stance,

---

[30] In addition, Judge Green administered the modified final judgment of the divestiture of AT&T with bright lines regulating local telephone firm involvement in enhanced service markets. See Noll and Owen (1989) or Nuechterlein and Weiser (2005).

[31] This is a simplification for the sake of brevity. Vendors did learn what was possible, but the engineering challenges turned out to be manageable. See Werbach (1997), Oxman (1999), or Nuechterlein and Weiser (2005).

[32] Brian Kahin, private communication, September 27, 2013.

the Clinton administration was busy negotiating with Congress on many legislative fronts related to the Internet and would choose to focus its attention on issues such as provisions for the Communications Decency Act, the Digital Millennium Copyright Act, and the establishment of ICANN. It did not return to the regulation of ISPs until the Internet Tax Freedom Act, passed in October 1998, which placed a federal moratorium on taxing the provision of Internet access.[33]

Summarizing, the commercial market for dial-up Internet access emerged at a time with comparatively favorable regulatory environment for ISPs, due to Computer II. The presence of a monopoly provision of local telephone access did not delay the rollout at most ISPs, nor did the need to adjudicate and tailor a new set of regulatory rules put new frictions in front of an entrepreneur selling ISP service. Entrepreneurs everywhere focused, instead, on something other than the debates inside Washington, DC; they focused on developing their Internet service.

An Implicit Policy

In the research-oriented Internet, users employed dial-up services operated by their universities. In 1994 the open question was whether a similar service would arise for commercial users of the newly privatized Internet. Initially, a few commercial ISPs forged ahead, presuming that they would absorb the regulatory norms from the BBS industry. At first, telephone companies did not deter them. Those that tried did not succeed in suppressing all the experimentation. That lack of opposition did not change for most telephone companies until the mid- to late 1990s, when the ISP business started to become large. In other words, neither US telephone company executives nor regulators initially assumed that the telephone companies should be the only providers of Internet service.

Was that policy the outcome of a great, deliberate procedure? No. It was a policy based on historical inertia over a set of regulatory rules adopted in an earlier era for a related but distinct set of market circumstances. Why did that policy matter? Later events in other countries would illustrate

---

[33]The market's young status justified the law, according to supporters, who worried that excessive local taxation could deter growth for the new nationwide commercial applications of electronic commerce.

why. Regulators in many other countries did not inherit any tradition of separation between carriers (telephone companies) and content providers (BBSs/ISPs). As the Internet commercialized in their countries, they just handed Internet service to their telephone companies without debate. Pricing and service norms evolved in the context of the distribution of service from that monopoly provider.

Not so in the United States. In principle, BBSs were not precluded from turning themselves into ISPs and trying to offer Internet service if they so wanted. This leeway gave US ISPs the opportunity to act and, crucially, it gave them some discretion with which to act without interference from their business partners, the telephone companies. That is, ISP managers perceived that they could explore commercial possibilities without telephone companies constraining their actions—a situation that was protected by the ample precedents embodied in Computer II.

As the commercial Internet began to develop, some BBSs began experimenting with offering service, a few as early as 1993 according to the ads in *Boardwatch*. By 1994 all the national BBSs were experimenting with some form of Internet access, albeit, often it was limited in its capabilities. Clearly, however, retail services had started sooner than that for some customers, especially in business. For example, PSINet and UUNET sold service as early as 1990 and offered backbone services to others comparatively early as well.[34]

The date of the first BBS turning into an ISP is less relevant than the fact of its transformation as a precedent. Even in 1994, few ISPs existed, and their total national revenue amounted to little. Prototypes do not have to be large, nonetheless, to demonstrate the viability of their commercial service.

Events in 1994 helped crystallize the viability of the BBS as an ISP. A BBS needed to add two things to become an ISP, and neither was out of its technical reach. First, a BBS had to arrange to make a connection to the Internet. That would involve establishing contractual relationships with another firm to carry data, and it usually involved setting up an additional server to handle the management of data traffic between the Internet and

---

[34]It became something of a point of pride to claim to be the first provider in a local area. From quick examination of the *Boardwatch* advertisements, the earliest entrants tended to be in major urban areas, such as Chicago, Boston, New York, San Francisco, and so on. Of the national online service companies Banks (2008), 165, reports that Delphi first found a way to get TCP/IP e-mail in 1992.

the user.[35] That was feasible to do in most major cities in the United States, because by 1994 the NSFNET was in the midst of privatizing the Internet in many locations around the country, and its plans had fostered a competitive supply of backbone providers. Sprint, AT&T, PSINet, and others offered backbone interconnections to any ISP, and a market for interconnection between ISP and backbone had begun to spring up in virtually every major city.[36]

Second, a BBS/ISP had to add software to enable the browser to work. That was not trivial because the conception of the business changed. Previously, the bulletin board provided all the information in proprietary services. A browser transformed the BBS into an ISP with extraordinary capabilities. An ISP gave its users a window on visual information provided by sites all over the Internet.

In 1994, at a time before many web pages existed, the change in business begged questions about where content would come from. While universities' websites tended to be the primary providers, e-mail was another common early use. The questions soon ended as new providers of content flooded in from a variety of sources. As it turned out, Tim Berners-Lee's software was easy to use, and self-publishing web pages became one catalyst for growth of the web.

It also was possible to simply be an ISP without any content. For example, like many ISPs offering retail access accounts, Netcom began business well before Internet privatization was finished. Established in San Jose, California, by Bob Reiger, an information systems engineer at Lockheed, Netcom grew into a provider of Internet access to students off campus. Reiger never had a business as a BBS and never felt he had to. Instead, he always focused on improving the quality of the ISP service. He became particularly well known for making tools so the service worked well with Windows 3.1. Furthermore, Netcom's business grew with the web. By the

---

[35] The protocols for doing so improved over this time. ISPs first employed SLIP, or serial line Internet protocol, which was written by Rick Adams, founder of UUNET. See, e.g., RFC 1055. This was later replaced by PPP, or point-to-point protocol. The latter was first proposed in the IETF in 1989, and improved over the early to mid-1990s. See, e.g., RFC 1661, from July 1994.

[36] Seen through the historical lens of frequent interconnection disputes in telephony, the presence of multiple backbone firms left no backbone firm in a position to be a monopoly provider, except in low density areas, where it was possible to charge high rates for access to lines. Said succinctly, lack of monopoly in urban areas eliminated the viability of using interconnection as a strategic tool to advance business aims in retail markets in urban areas.

mid-1990s, Netcom became one of the leading providers of Internet access, at its peak in early 1996 claiming close to half a million worldwide users.[37]

Overall, in 1994, the browser was an incremental change to a BBS already offering Internet service. That is a key observation and worthwhile to highlight: the browser depended on a set of standards, the World Wide Web, which was a layer of software on top of the TCP/IP stack. An ISP enabled this to work if it downloaded the appropriate shareware software and sent one piece to its user.

Any BBS could easily learn the additional steps necessary to make it work with the World Wide Web. Many technically adept engineers with experience with PCs already knew the basics and could open an ISP from scratch, once again, tweaking it to work with the World Wide Web.

As ISPs began to grow in number and size, an additional requirement became more salient: the need for more telephone lines. When BBSs were small, this had not been an issue, but the growth of ISPs soon generated a need for many phone lines. Most ISPs could not arrange for that capacity from their phone companies overnight. Soon, getting these lines would become a contentious issue in many areas.

An identity began to coalesce at about the same time. Some self-aware ISPs characterized their place as outsiders, as rebels within a bottom-up movement. Their labels said it all. They began to cast themselves as "Net-heads," in contrast to the "Bell-heads" who did not perceive the Internet on the same terms.[38]

Enabling Vital Visionaries

The first entrepreneurial ventures in Internet access were largely undertaken by commercial iconoclasts. These entrepreneurs occasionally rejected conventional wisdom, maintaining a view about the future that differed from the majority. Often, as in this case, the majority treated these visionaries as eccentrics to be ignored, or, perhaps, lone wolves that are allowed to howl at the moon as long as nobody else loses money on behalf of their idiosyncratic views. Mainstream industry considered the iconoclasts to be peripheral participants, living on the edges.

[37] This included customers all across the United States, as well as in Canada and the United Kingdom.
[38] See, e.g., Friedan (2002) for further discussion.

The academic community was one source of potential iconoclasts for the commercial Internet, but it did not become a major source. Although that community had developed many prototypes, it did not seed many firms. Only a trickle of firms showed up with this background, such as PSINet, UUNET and Netcom. Had that been the only source of entrepreneurs for the commercial Internet access business in the United States then the access market probably would have grown, but not as fast as it did, and not in so many places.

The BBS industry provided another source of potential entrants, and, as later events would show, an abundant one. Many were far more optimistic about the business prospects than many administrators with academic experience.

The commercial Internet gave commercial iconoclasts the discretion to act in the Internet access market. That occurred for numerous reasons: The NSF backbone connected them all at low cost; the presence of multiple backbone providers largely supported multiple points of interconnection in major urban areas; the end-to-end architecture of the Internet gave potential ISPs discretion; US regulatory rules reduced the frictions of setting up modem banks; the shareware norms of academic computing gave Apache to everyone; and many BBSs decided to act, and act in ways they perceived to be incremental.

For a time these iconoclasts did something they perceived to be so incremental that at first these actions hardly received notice from those to whom it would later appear to be radical. Only as it started to gain scale in the market—by signing up customers all across the country—did other participants in the Internet realize that these innovators had come from the edges, and had operationalized all the elements of a new and potentially mainstream business.

THE BLOSSOMING

Chapters 6, 7, 8, 9, and 10 analyze the blossoming of the national dial-up network. The market had the air of an impatient gold rush. These chapters show how innovation from the edges shaped the timing of investment and actions. Investment by one type of participant increased the value of action by another, accumulating in a virtuous cycle of value creation.

TABLE 6.1. Selected notable events from chapters 6, 7, 8, 9, 10

Year	Chapter	Notable Event
1992	7	David Clark delivers "Rough Consensus and Running Code"
	7	Internet Society founded and IETF becomes part of it
	7	Tim Berners-Lee first visits the IETF to standardize the web
1993	8	Louis Gerstner hired as CEO at IBM
	7	CERN renounces ownership rights to World Wide Web code
	8	Earliest ads for ISPs appear in *Boardwatch Magazine*
1994	6	Vermeer founded, begins work on web-authoring tools
	7	Tim Berners-Lee founds the World Wide Web Consortium
	6	Brad Silverberg organizes team at Microsoft to examine web
1995	6	Gates circulates the memo, "The Internet Tidal Wave"
	6, 7	Netscape IPO and the launch of Windows 95
	9	HoTMaiL founded and "viral marketing" is invented.
1996	8	Microsoft offers Internet Explorer at a price of zero
	8	AT&T WorldNet sold at $19.95 for unlimited service
	8	AOL implements all-you-can-eat pricing
1997	8	56K modems first introduced
	10	Tiered structure emerges among Internet data carriers
	9	Netscape and Microsoft reach parity in browser features
1998	10	WorldCom merges with MCI, spins off backbone assets
	8	Over 65,000 phone numbers available for dial-up ISPs
1999	9	Dot-com boom reaches greatest height
	10	WorldCom proposed merger with Sprint is called off
2000	8	*Boardwatch Magazine* records over 7,000 ISPs
	9	Internet adoption nears saturation at medium/large businesses

6

How Not to Start a Gold Rush

I'd say there was a fair amount of skepticism at the time about whether the Internet held any promise. And of course I felt that it did.

—*Jim Clark*[1]

Just as the California gold rush of 1849 involved rigorous and concerted exploration of natural resources for commercial gain, a gold rush in a technology market can be an intensive exploration of a specific product's commercial value. In mid-1995, especially after Netscape's first browser and Netscape's initial public offering (IPO), the commercial Internet turned into something akin to a gold rush, experiencing intense exploration by a large number and wide range of firms. Many established firms altered their investment plans to take advantage of the new business opportunities the commercial Internet offered. Many newly founded start-ups, attempting either to displace incumbent firms or establish service in areas incumbents had not addressed, also tried to take advantage of these opportunities by becoming dominant in specific activities.

Examining these events leads to two economic questions regarding the ways that firms invested their resources in the commercial Internet: Why did they explore and invest simultaneously? Why did the Internet gold rush not occur sooner?

[1] BrainyQuote.com. August 4, 2010. http://www.brainyquote.com/quotes/quotes/j/jim clark406158.html. Accessed September 2013.

FIGURE 6.1 James H. Clark, cofounder of Netscape
(photo by Knnkanda, July 14, 2013)

FIGURE 6.2 Bill Gates, cofounder of Microsoft
(photo by Simon Davis/DFID, July 2014)

The beginning of the explanation lies in Coloma, California, and in lessons learned from the history of the California gold rush. Coloma gets its name from a Native American word for beautiful. It deserves the label. Located on the southern fork of the American River, just over fifty miles east of Sacramento, it retains an abundance of oak trees and other flora. These dot the rolling foothills, which lie at the base of the Sierra Nevada mountain range. It is not an easily accessible place today and can be reached only by way of hilly roads off major highways. It was regarded as an even more remote location when it first gained notoriety, as the location for the discovery of gold in California in 1848.[2]

Contrary to popular romantic conceptions, *gradual* exploration is the norm for metal mining, and that is how most of gold in the Sierras eventually was mined. It is *not* what happened in Coloma. There are several seams of gold in the Sierra Nevada, put there hundreds of millions of years ago by natural forces. Millions of years ago plate tectonics formed the mountains and pushed several of the seams close to the surface. Miners eventually explored many of those seams using underground tunnels.[3] However, glacial erosion did much work to expose one of those seams, combined with wind and rain. The southern fork of the American River happens to travel over one exposed seam, taking flakes from the rock, depositing it a little downriver.

Spanish settlers had been in California for more than seven decades. Evidence of gold occasionally surfaced in rock in the Central Valley—over hundreds of thousands of years rock easily could have moved down the hills in cataclysmic landslides and landed in the valley, far down from its sources in the Sierras. Yet the Spanish had never identified the origins in the mountains, many miles east and much higher up in elevation. Nobody had traveled to the exact place in the mountains because it was remote from the Spanish settlements in California, and it was not easy to find. The weight of gold also helped keep it hidden. The American River joins the Sacramento River upstream, but far downstream from the exposed gold seam over which the American River traverses. Gold flakes are too heavy to travel far in water, even in a fast-running river like the South Fork of the American during a snowmelt in spring.

An enterprising American commercial iconoclast and entrepreneur, John Sutter, decided to be the first person to go high up on the South Fork of the American River. He was seeking fresh timber, not gold. He established his mill in Coloma in an attempt to get timber nobody else had harvested. In 1848, in the midst of building that enterprise, one of his

---

[2]Coloma today supports a well-functioning, if somewhat sleepy, national park. The area also supports an active white-water rafting industry.

[3]After being discovered in the mid-nineteenth century, it took decades to recover the precious metal thousands of feet below the surface. Only a few of those mines operate today.

employees, John Marshall, discovered gold flakes in the water tracings of the mill, which had turned over sediment around the river. Weeks after Marshall's discovery the word was out. The mill site was soon overrun with prospectors. The following year the hills contained as many prospectors as oak trees, the "49ers" of the California gold rush who panned for gold.

What are the lessons from this story for the Internet gold rush? Stated broadly, gold rushes possess four features:

1. The value remains unknown for some time and is discovered to the surprise of the discoverer and all others.
2. Once the value becomes known, knowledge about it spreads rapidly.
3. Many prospectors explore and invest in the hope to gain later.
4. Every prospector takes action quickly, believing that only the earliest movers will reap part of the newly discovered value.

There is another lesson embedded in this story, which later chapters will return to: a few of the earliest pioneers profit in the long run, but only a few. That last lesson, however, requires several steps to illustrate, and the first of which is explaining the rush. This chapter discusses the first step, why circumstances led to the Internet gold rush—namely, the simultaneous exploration of value by many market participants. That is also equivalent to asking why everyone waited until a specific moment in time, so an oversimplified statement can summarize the puzzle one must explain: if a gold rush begins when a great deal of activity follows a quiet moment, what triggers the change? To understand the timing of a rush it is necessary to explain what circumstances prevented the Internet rush from happening earlier. As the above story suggests, typically some new information acts as a catalyst, and the crucial question becomes a query about what action led to new information, and whose knowledge changed and why.

Looking at it from this angle, the puzzle requires stretching the metaphor about the gold rush to make it fit events in the Internet. There were, in fact, two overlapping periods of exploration. The first period involved many prospectors looking for Internet gold, but nobody shouting, "Eureka, I found it!" Stephen Wolff's discussions to privatize the Internet started this period of exploration. It led to the founding of the for-profit data carriers PSINet and UUNET in late 1989 by William Schrader and

Martin Schoffstall, and Rick Adams, respectively. It also led to a slow trickle of entry by commercial ISPs into the US market for such services, by firms such as Netcom. It also led a few intrepid BBSs to add an Internet service. It also led CompuServe, a very large information service using BBS technology, to offer Internet service. As earlier chapters discussed, these were interesting events among the cognoscenti of the Internet. To the core of the communications and computer industry, however, a new valuable market had not been found.

The introduction of Netscape's first commercial browser eventually started the second and much noisier rush. By the end of 1994, *many* commercial computing and communications firms had seen a beta version of Netscape's product, and *many* were on the way to altering their plans. By the end of the summer of 1995, after Netscape's IPO, *every* market participant was evaluating the value chain for the commercial Internet and web. Many venture capitalists were beginning to assess the prospects for newly founded firms in a variety of applications. A few of the early pioneers also began to reap large rewards about this time. Like a gold rush, new information about the source of value triggered these actions.

To summarize, by the end of the summer of 1995 events were set in motion that would last for a considerable length of time, events that contemporaries would label as a boom in investment. Netscape's IPO is, therefore, probably the best symbolic event for marking the birth date of the commercial web, and, accordingly, the beginning of events that resembled an Internet gold rush.

The above also suggests why the metaphor about the gold rush fails eventually. While the Netscape IPO did generate a short and intense period of prospecting by entrepreneurs, the boom was sustained by more than just the immediate and one-time reaction to new information. Different factors explain why the boom sustained itself long after the initial rush of 1995 and 1996.

This chapter, in contrast, focuses on understanding the sense in which the metaphor about a gold rush actually explains events. It focuses on commercial markets before the Internet rush, say, in early 1994, before participants were informed about the value of the Internet. Why had only a few major commercial firms prospected for value in the commercial Internet up until that point? This chapter explains why circumstances left many potential participants in doubt, and that illuminates why those who came from the edges would have such a large impact on catalyzing commercial markets.

The Collective Shrug of '94

Looking back at the commercial computing market in 1994 requires a big change in perspective for an observer from the future. While years later it would be obvious that the privatization of the Internet resulted in an extraordinarily valuable gift to the US economy, most contemporaries in 1994 did not appreciate the value of that gift at the time it was given. Most contemporaries did not appreciate the NSF's plan to privatize the Internet. Most of them just shrugged.

The marketplace primarily attracted prospectors from the edges. By early 1994 the catalytic pieces were all in place for motivating investment to meet the anticipated demand. The plans for privatization of the Internet were almost complete and the web was beginning to diffuse, available as shareware for anybody to use and assess. Several commercial iconoclasts had made investments in carrier markets and access markets, demonstrating the viability of providing commercial services.

The actions of those early pioneers did not generate a reaction. No prominent business magazine in early 1994 hailed PSINet or UUNET as leaders of an Internet revolution. No Wall Street analyst changed his or her recommendations in early 1994 from sell to buy for the stock of prospecting firms who had a great deal to gain from privatization. No venture capitalist made an explicit effort to round up the leading talented Internet entrepreneurs in early 1994 and fund a portfolio of the most sensible plans for new Internet services, even though later events illustrated beyond any doubt that it would have been extremely profitable to do so.

No three established firms could better illustrate the causes of the shrug than the three firms best positioned to take advantage of the commercial Internet. IBM, MCI, and Cisco each held a unique position. Each firm had experience serving the need of users in the research-oriented Internet. If anybody would invest heavily in anticipation of the coming Internet gold rush it would be these three firms.

Both IBM and Cisco focused a substantial fraction of their business on enterprise computing, and there was a straightforward explanation in 1994 for the lack of investment in Internet products and services. Most customers did not ask for it in 1994. Most customers were in the midst of converting large-scale computing to client-server architecture or any other form of local networking. Client-server computing was the *revolution-du-jour* among IT consultants and others in the enterprise computing market. It typically had a workstation act as *server* of data, while personal computers on a local area network acted as *clients*, or receivers of data. According to the standard mantra, the Internet contributed to client-server networks in some useful ways, since exchanging data between computing systems on different local area networks could be cumbersome in other formats.[4] Some consultants were disdainful, however, and recommended that secure electronic commerce use another approach, something called electronic data interchange (EDI), not the protocols of the Internet.

Forward-looking management should have been able to see beyond short-term demand, nonetheless. The short-term focus of customers on client-server should not have deterred investments by forward-looking managers into TCP/IP services, which were about to grow in demand.

IBM would have had the best position if it had only acted on it. IBM had a unique position within the NSFNET backbone. IBM also had strategic advantages in enterprise equipment markets. Its involvement with the NSFNET gave its employees in the research division early insights into how to make TCP/IP-based equipment, especially routers. There was one obvious hitch. IBM's research division handled the activity, and that needed to be translated into viable businesses in other divisions within IBM. Even though the wild ducks had a good idea this time around, their initial experience inside IBM would be mixed.

As it turned out, by 1994 most of the attempts to translate the research division's insights into products did not pan out. One of these initiatives was touched on in prior chapters. For example, it had become rather clear by 1994 that IBM's data carrier, ANS, did not and would not be able to assume a dominant position during the transition to privatization.

That was not the end of the commercial opportunities, however. ANS did not dominate the backbone, but IBM did operate one of the largest worldwide ISPs for its clients for the next few years. While ANS eventually was sold to AOL to enhance its consumer business, IBM's access business for commercial clients did thrive for a few years, being regarded

---

[4] For a study of the challenges from that conversion, see Bresnahan and Greenstein (1997).

as one of the largest and most reliable access businesses for large business users.

The commercial experience with the equipment business has its roots elsewhere inside IBM. In the early 1990s, IBM's enterprise division refused to be involved with any equipment using Internet protocol. Its division favored selling proprietary equipment, such as Token Ring and OS/2, which yielded higher margins for its sales force. Symptoms of the broad commercial problems affiliated with this practice were already apparent by 1994. While a few loyal buyers continued to use only IBM equipment, by the early 1990s many enterprises had made a deliberate choice not to, investing in much less expensive nonproprietary configurations of client-server networks. These consisted of Ethernet-based local area networks, Microsoft operating systems in clone PCs, as well as servers coming from many firms, such as SUN Microsystems. By the early 1990s others firms—such as Cisco, 3Com, SUN, Compaq, and Novell—had taken advantage of the situation and established strong commercial positions.

Louis Gerstner was hired from outside as CEO in April 1993 with a mandate to change the financial situation in the organization. He was brought in because the company was in the midst of a financial crisis, ostensibly caused by declining demand for its mainframes (being replaced by client-server architectures), a crisis exacerbated by an almost willful lack of planning by Gerstner's predecessors for the structural changes wrought by client-server architectures. As an outsider and former consultant for many of IBM's clients, Gerstner perceived the crisis in broad terms, and also blamed the crisis on policies that placed too much emphasis on selling proprietary equipment instead of listening to customer preferences.[5]

Gerstner met with tremendous internal resistance trying to move the firm to support non-IBM technologies, such as Unix and Microsoft-client software. In that light it is hard to know just how much of IBM's subsequent failures were collateral damage from the reorganization and how much were a by-product of prior myopia. In any event, IBM never became a strong router and switch supplier for enterprises.[6]

---

[5]See, e.g., Gerstner's (2002) account, which argued that, in retrospect, these changes were among those that were most beneficial for the long-term health of IBM.

[6]Perhaps just as interesting, IBM's close rival, Digital Equipment Corporation, faced a similar problem. Its own internal division committed to a proprietary local area network technology for enterprises, called DECNet, and put up considerable resistance to moving the

The silver lining of Gerstner's strategy became more apparent after the Internet gold rush began. It positioned IBM for what turned out to be an enormous market opportunity. As IBM's employees became more vendor neutral in their advice, their consulting business for enterprises would thrive. Later chapters will describe how this vendor-neutral approach became the foundation for the financial rejuvenation of IBM.

Cisco's actions illustrate what commercial opportunity IBM lost in equipment markets. Cisco began as a supplier of routers and hubs for academic ISPs and operations. The company had specialized in the routers and hubs that stood between different computing systems, reading addresses on data packets and redirecting the packets from one computer to another. As late as 1993, it was justifiably obscure in comparison to the leading computing equipment firms in the world.

By 1994 Cisco's management had adopted a strategy to expand far beyond just hubs and routers, positioning Cisco as the leading Internet equipment supplier for enterprises. Cisco's strategy would have been a good idea whether or not the commercial Internet grew at a fast or slow rate, but it looked like a spectacular idea when the gold rush arrived. Cisco's organizational change positioned the company for dramatic growth in response to increases in demand for its products. It also put Cisco in a good position to supply products it had not anticipated with appropriate research and development; Cisco planned to buy a leading product through acquisition of start-ups. Indeed, many years later it would be apparent that (perhaps) nobody profited more from the commercialization of the Internet than Cisco's stockholders.

The most radical feature of this new strategy was its stated reliance on acquisitions, which left much of the risk for technical inventions to others and deferred the growth of Cisco's product line until the company's management needed it. The firm declared that acquisitions would become a deliberate piece of its strategy to grow, making this one of the firm's core tenets. Normally a firm that acquires others faces risks related to overpaying, not getting sufficient value from the acquisition for their money. In addition to that risk, there were two primary strategic risks in Cisco's declaration, and these would have sunk most firms: Cisco's management had

---

firm to support other technologies. DEC's equipment division for enterprises was, therefore, poorly positioned for the Internet gold rush.

to absorb new acquisitions fast enough; firms had to supply acquisition targets fast enough. If Cisco failed at the former, it would drive up the internal cost within Cisco's organization. If the latter did not occur, it would drive up the external price to Cisco's stockholders, which would reduce the potential gains.

Realizing the ambition set Cisco on a path that no firm had ever pursued at such a large scale. Cisco would invest in lowering the transaction costs and frictions normally affiliated with so many acquisitions. It routinized processes for acquisitions and began educating others about its aspiration. Altogether Cisco made seventy-two acquisitions between July 1994 and December 2000, with sixty-five of them after January 1996, and twenty-three in the year 2000. During the Internet boom its market capitalization was valued at over $500 billion (in 1999), making it the most valuable company in the world for a short time. As later chapters will discuss, the stock market eventually came back down to earth, but for most of the late 1990s it valued Cisco highly, which helped it make stock-only deals for acquisitions, further lowering the price of an acquisition.

Cisco's early repositioning contrasts with its other competitors in 1994. Most equipment firms took partial steps toward strong positions in markets related to the Internet, such as enterprise servers. This included companies like Nortel, Novell, Alcatel, and 3Com. None of them made such overt changes in strategy as early as Cisco. The equipment division of AT&T, which became Lucent in a few years, also did not take action to anticipate the Internet. In general, these firms did not consider changing their strategic direction until the winter of 1995, when such changes become part of conventional wisdom for everyone who had observed the functionality of Netscape's first commercial browser. In that sense, Cisco was a rare early prospector.

MCI's experience after the NSFNET also contrasts with IBM's. First, MCI had developed skills and assets it could translate into a business for national data transport over its own fiber network; later acquisitions further enhanced that capability. Second, MCI could offer ISP service for both homes and businesses in the coming commercial data market. This business was further enhanced by MCI-mail, an Internet-compatible service. After the Internet gold rush arrived MCI gained a large amount of business, especially for service to homes.

MCI's actions resembled that of two other early movers and incumbents, Sprint and BBNNET. Each had significant experience carrying international data traffic for the NSF. Each also managed to adjust to privatization, at least at first, positioning for further business.[7]

MCI, Sprint, and BBNNET can also be understood in contrast. They were the exceptions that identified the rule. There was no better illustration of their uniqueness than to contrast them with AT&T, the telephone company headquartered in New Jersey. Divestiture had spun the local telephone companies off as separate firms, leaving AT&T as a long-distance company, competitor to MCI and Sprint, as well as an equipment supplier, which would eventually be spun off as Lucent. AT&T did not move as aggressively into Internet services. It was only when the Internet began to enter widespread discussion in 1995 that AT&T moved into providing backbone and access services, both to businesses and to homes. In brief, AT&T was later than its most direct rivals, MCI and Sprint.

AT&T's managers were not alone in their hesitance. Their closest cousins, the seven other local telephone companies created by divestiture, also did not invest in Internet service. Most had no immediate plans to provide Internet service in 1994. Instead, they spun their wheels on many projects that did not pan out.[8]

Why did so many firms such as IBM and AT&T ignore investing heavily in the Internet just prior to the boom? Overall their lack of action can be interpreted in three (overlapping) ways:

- a situation in which the Internet lacked internal "champions," perhaps because of the expectation that Internet services would cannibalize too many revenue streams at existing business;
- a misunderstanding of the potential for the Internet, perhaps due to a commitment to an alternative technological vision or forecast;
- a situation in which the Internet benefited many users at once, perhaps because no single firm had incentive to nurture adoption that seemingly did not directly contribute to their own bottom line.

[7] For more on Sprint's commercial actions, see the account in Hussain (2003c), or Meeker and DePuy (1996). The chief architect for BBNNET wrote about his lessons from that experience in Marcus (1999).

[8] Ferguson (1999), pages 54–55, provides a sarcastic and caustic recounting of many of these business adventures, including deals with Ziff-Davis, 3DO, General Magic, and Lotus.

In practice these three motives yielded similar outcomes, no investments in Internet technologies. It left market opportunity available to firms, such as Cisco and MCI, who had short-term market reasons to act, as they met immediate market demand.

Errors in the Consensus

In early 1994 Microsoft was one of the largest software companies in the world, and, by many accounts, possibly the best managed. By the early 1990s Microsoft had a track record of successfully forecasting the commercial value affiliated with new technical opportunities in personal computing. Management in Redmond believed its success partly arose from its systematic studying of the actions of many other firms before settling on strategic plans.

Due to this systematic approach, Microsoft's actions reflected a critical analysis of the consensus of views elsewhere in the industry. Microsoft's mistakes can illustrate the types of forecasting errors made elsewhere at the same time.

Microsoft's decisions occurred within the context of several complex events. In early 1994 Microsoft was in the midst of developing a product that later would be called Windows 95. Since 1992, long and elaborate planning had gone into its design. This product was supposed to replace DOS (disk operating system) as the standard OS (operating system) in PCs. Windows had been an application built on top of DOS, and Windows 3.0 and then 3.1 were the versions of Windows most widely in use in 1994. Microsoft sought to make a better version of Windows the next widely used operating system in PCs, and, at the same time, cement itself as the central coordinator of application software development for the PC. By 1994, the company was late in executing these ambitious plans, but no viable competitive alternative had arisen, so it appeared it would succeed, nonetheless.[9]

At around the same time, management began making plans for and subsequently investing in MSN, a proprietary network that would have content for home users. The management in Redmond made plans that called for a gradual development cycle over many years, anticipating that the mass-market opportunity for MSN would emerge slowly, giving the

---

[9]See Cusumano and Selby (1995) for extensive discussion.

company enough time to learn from its experience offering a proprietary dial-up service.[10] In short, in early 1994 the architects of Windows 95 and MSN were confident that the main competitive issues affiliated with the Internet *had* been addressed, and the biggest concerns were far into the future.

Microsoft's plans for servers reflected the same outlook. Reading TCP/ IP compatible files had been a standard feature of Unix systems for some time, as it was an outgrowth of the military's procurement requirement— all Unix systems had to be TCP/IP compatible. Unix was commonly used in enterprises as a server in a client-server architecture. To compete with Unix-based servers, Microsoft made Windows 95 and its server compatible with TCP/IP,[11] anticipating that others might build Internet applications on top of the OS. In these plans Microsoft accepted the conventional wisdom that the Internet would become one of several pieces of plumbing for servers, but largely reside in the background. Placing TCP/IP in its servers illustrates one additional aspect: the standard assessment relegated the Internet to status as internal plumbing for an IT system, not as a customer-facing aspect of software.

One of Microsoft's most successful enterprise applications in the 1990s, e-mail for business enterprises, ended up benefiting from the Internet, but even this experience shows the way in which Microsoft misperceived the future. In the early 1990s Microsoft's strategists (correctly) anticipated demand for business-oriented e-mail, and they had begun designing an application, later known as Exchange. Like many of Microsoft's other products in the early 1990s, Exchange was not conceived as a part of a broad Internet strategy. Instead, Microsoft sought to develop applications for enterprise users of Windows NT and its other server software employed in mainstream client-server architectures. This software would reside on local area networks (LANs) inside enterprises.

Exchange's design process followed the textbook for an exemplary product development. Not long after taking responsibility, Todd Warren,

---

[10]See, e.g., Swisher (1998) for an accessible comparison of the AOL/MSN differences and similarities—especially their market positions and strategic approaches during the mid-1990s.

[11]Under the original design plans for Windows, there were two target markets, one aimed at PC clients and one at servers. TCP/IP compatibility had value for server software as a direct competitor to Unix systems. It also had value because it eased data exchange between server and client.

the group product manager for mail products from 1990 to 1993, led his team on an analysis of the strengths and weaknesses of all competitive LAN-based electronic mail products. In Warren's words,

> Exchange was an amalgam of all features of competitive products at the time, prioritized by customer wants and needs.[12]

What was the best design for electronic mail for business in the early 1990s? Microsoft's team concluded that Lotus Notes, designed by Ray Ozzie and his colleagues at Lotus, offered an attractive model for users, and it embedded a vision of the future that Microsoft would have to match in functionality. From former IBM employees who had moved to Microsoft, the Microsoft design team also learned greatly, embedding Exchange with multiple features needed at enterprises, such as calendar systems, designed specifically to meet the needs of a senior executive. On Bill Gates's insistence, Microsoft designed its standard implementations to work best with the SQL server and Microsoft's other LAN products.

Lotus contained one crucial design feature, its reliance on a proprietary solution for internetworking. Lotus Notes had a tight and elegant integration, which worked optimally within one corporate network under one manager's control, and Notes addressed internetworking issues with the same elegant solution. That solution came at a drawback: it could not integrate easily with other types of systems, and especially not with systems owned by others in different locations. It was potentially not a drawback; it was the largest enterprise e-mail system in use at the time, and as long as it retained its status as the largest, most systems would conform to it.

Microsoft's designers anticipated the spread of some general standards for internetworking, such as those coming from OSI. They expected generic standards for internetworking would eventually play to Microsoft's competitive advantage because it played to Lotus's competitive disadvantage. They anticipated "loose coupling of networks," giving Exchange a technically viable path for linking up geographically dispersed e-mail servers and clients provided by multiple firms. In other words, with a viable internetworking solution from a third party, Microsoft could be a late entrant into this market and viably compete. It did not have to engineer solutions to internetworking issues and could take for granted that estab-

---

[12] Todd Warren, private conversation, May 29, 2009.

lishments would be able to manage the internetworking functions without Microsoft's help.

Consistent with this forecast, Microsoft designed Exchange with flexibility at the enterprise gateway. At this point they made their fateful—though, as it turned out, not fatal—choice and embedded the erroneous forecast in their design. Their analysis did not conclude that SMTP, the standard mailbox for Internet e-mail, would be as competitively important. Rather, they concluded the OSI had a strong likelihood of being widely adopted, and its electronic mail design, known as X-400, offered a useful roadmap for desirable features. Microsoft followed this road map, using the Internet gateways to hand off electronic mail flowing outside a corporate enterprise.

As earlier chapters have already hinted and the next few chapters will discuss, OSI did not become widely adopted in the 1990s. Like others who believed this consensus forecast, Microsoft's forecast turned out to be wrong. However, sometimes it is better to be lucky than right, and, as it turned out, X-400 was sufficiently flexible to serve Microsoft's strategic aims. Exchange could be tailored to fit TCP/IP traffic. In other words, in spite of the forecasting error, Microsoft's system handed off traffic at the gateway, and the firm got the competitive advantage it sought, just not by the path it anticipated.[13]

What lesson does this illustrate? Like the prior examples, the consensus view about e-mail turned out to be mistaken, because it did not anticipate a central role for the Internet in the design of enterprise electronic mail. Even at one of the best-managed firms at the time, the newly designed electronic mail product reflected this small role for the Internet based on TCP/IP.

Heeding Cassandra's Warning[14]

Microsoft's approach to the Internet came straight from Gates's assessment of the conventional wisdom, and after he did his homework. When

---

[13] Todd Warren, private conversation, June 5, 2009.

[14] In classic Greek mythology Cassandra can foresee the future but her prophecies are never believed, and her warnings never hinder her friends and family from taking tragic action.

Microsoft made an error it illustrated something unique about Bill Gates and something general about the prevailing view.

The unique part of Microsoft was Bill Gates's managerial style. Bill Gates constantly sought to educate himself and use his learning in every aspect of decision making. He was technically skilled enough and energetic enough to debate virtually any employee about the strategic merits of a decision. He also had an extraordinary amount of personal authority, so his judgment carried the day during disputes.[15] In short, employees and other executives took it for granted that little got done without Gates's understanding and approval.

Gates's reasoning about TCP/IP and the web arose from the consensus in commercial computing. In the spring of 1994 Microsoft had held a major strategic meeting to discuss the Internet, as part of potential design changes for what would become Windows 95. After long discussion Gates concluded—like much of the rest of the software industry at the time—that browsers could not be a profitable stand-alone business and, therefore, would not make much money in commercial markets. It was not difficult to understand the origins of this point of view. Mosaic had built functionality on nonproprietary protocols and standards, which rendered them vulnerable to imitation, widespread entry, and intense competitive rivalry, which inevitably would reduce the software's price. So went this view, anything built on top of such common elements would become—in the lingo of the time—a "commodity," and any such application could not and would not generate much revenue for long.

Most important, Gates made a decision that showed how certain he was that the consensus had it right. He did not concede to the Internet enthusiasts that there might be some set of market circumstances that could conspire to produce a profitable Internet service or application worthy of Microsoft's attention. Rather, Gates concluded that no investment in Internet applications on the desktop had any potential payoff, not for Microsoft, nor for much of anyone else.[16] Hence, he chose not to invest in *any*

---

[15] This partially arose out of Gates's driving personality and his smarts. It also arose from experience, as the leader of Microsoft when it displaced IBM as leader of the PC industry. See the discussion in Cusumano and Selby (1995), or Bresnahan, Greenstein, and Henderson (2012).

[16] In this view, electronic mail would make its revenue through licensing the Exchange server, which supported Outlook on the client.

application development, not even development of working prototypes of web-based applications.

The forecasting and strategic flaw became apparent later, but not at the time. Had Gates had even a modicum of doubt, it would have been strategically sensible to authorize a few exploratory projects in April 1994. These would have involved a few employees, and would not cost much money. With the benefit of hindsight Gates certainty appears, at best, to be penny wise and pound foolish. A less flattering characterization would say he was—take your pick, as none of these are a compliment—rather unimaginative, too distracted to be thorough, overconfident in his judgment, or merely arrogant.

Microsoft employed a number of wild ducks who disagreed with Gates, however, and, to the eventual benefit of the firm, they had the courage of their convictions. In the summer and autumn of 1994, a small group inside Microsoft undertook a review of trends; Brad Silverberg, a comparatively senior manager who reported to members of the strategy team, organized this group.[17] These employees ostensibly did something that was not unusual at Microsoft, thinking about new initiatives. What they actually did, however, was start an unauthorized skunk works devoted to examining the commercial potential of the Internet and web, and in depth.

A skunk works could be an organizational home for wild ducks, seemingly mixing metaphors from the animal kingdom.[18] It is housed away from the main operations of an organization, sometimes in secret or with organizational barriers, and often with top management support for these barriers.[19] Typically the development projects involve something of value to the future of the organization but are not directly connected to its

---

[17] Ben Slivka, private communication, October 2008.

[18] The phrase, skunk works, originated from the aeronautics industry. A project for the air force at a division of Lockheed in Burbank, California, had called itself the "Skonk Works" in a bit of salty humor about its own secrecy. The phrase came from Al Capp's *Lil' Abner* cartoon—the skonk works was a "secret laboratory" that operated a backwoods still. The label became well known throughout the industry, in part because it was considered humorous and saucy. *Lil' Abner*'s publisher eventually asked Lockheed to change it, and "skunk works" emerged from there because the Lockheed facility was next to another plant that emitted fumes (Rich and Janos 1994).

[19] The legendary leader of the skunk works at Lockheed was Clarence "Kelly" Johnson. He also helped establish these precedents. He was known as a technical leader who kept outside meddling and paperwork to a minimum, albeit, he would not be characterized as a wild duck.

present operational or service missions. Sometimes a skunk works has the approval of senior management, and sometimes, as in this case, it does not.

No one paid much attention to the team studying the Internet, and, by the same token, they received few resources. As events began to unfold in the fall of 1994, however, this team decided to come out of hiding and conduct many wide-ranging conversations with existing stakeholders inside Microsoft. They eventually received permission to license Mosaic, finishing negotiations in January 1995. They refined their vision about the future and Microsoft's potential strategy for addressing it, and they internally publicized their views and efforts. A member of this team, Ben Slivka, articulated the vision in a widely circulated memo titled "The Web Is the Next Platform."[20] Eventually this memo would go through redrafts, finishing on version 4.0, and would provide the beginnings of a framework for Microsoft's Internet strategy. Slivka would later be rewarded for his efforts with an extraordinary responsibility, as lead programmer for Internet Explorer, and he stayed there through versions 1.0, 2.0, and 3.0.

The group eventually did change Gates's mind, but much later than the change in the consensus. As later events would illustrate, this turned out to be early enough to allow Microsoft to participate in the Internet gold rush, though that was far from assured when Gates first announced the change in direction. The key event happened in April 1995, and it illustrates Bill Gates's stubbornness and the opposite, his willingness to change his mind in the face of contrary evidence. It also illustrates where the common consensus went wrong.

The team organized an evening of surfing for Bill Gates, with instructions about where to go and what to look for. Gates had not tested the web extensively with Mosaic, and he had not gone back to the web after the explosion of the entry of Netscape's browser in February/March 1995. He was unfamiliar with the range of capabilities the browser could perform by this point. Gates spent the better part of the night surfing, and it changed his view about the commercial potential of the software. A month later he issued a memo titled "The Internet Tidal Wave,"[21] which other

---

[20] See Slivka (1995) for the fourth and final draft of this vision statement. A publicly available copy is at http://www.usdoj.gov/atr/cases/ms_exhibits.htm, exhibit 21.

[21] A publicly available copy of Gates (1995) is at http://www.usdoj.gov/atr/cases/ms_exhibits.htm, government exhibit 20.

prior chapters have mentioned, and later chapters will return to. It was especially significant, because it announced the realignment of priorities for strategy inside Microsoft.

Having won the argument in principle, at the same time Slivka issued the fourth and final version of his memo. Slivka's memo goes to sixteen single-spaced pages while Gates's goes on for nine, so Slivka's provided more detail about both the opportunities and potential competitive issues. Nonetheless, Gates was CEO, so his memo had authority as official policy. After May 1995, many executives inside Microsoft debated how to address "The Internet Tidal Wave," as the memo took on canonical status inside the firm.

Referring to Netscape in his memo, Gates states, "A competitor was born on the Internet,"[22] that is, a competitor to Microsoft. He goes on to outline why he interprets a browser company as a threat. It was not the company, per se, that posed any threat to Microsoft's interest, but the potential for its product to support an entire ecosystem of applications. Its standards were becoming pervasive on virtually every PC, which other applications would use.[23] Gates worried about two scenarios in which Microsoft's operating system could become "commoditized." One scenario involves Netscape directly, where Gates asserts:

> They are pursuing a multi-platform strategy where they move the key API[24] into the client to commoditize the underlying operating system.

Translation: Netscape helped to coordinate developers whom Microsoft would have been coordinating, and if those developers provided functionality equivalent to PC software, Netscape's browser substituted for Microsoft's operating system as the point of access for those applications, which reduced the value of Microsoft's operating system.

The other scenario is less specific about who will take the action. It involves the combination of several component firms developing a new device. In this vein he says:

---

[22]Gates (1995), 4.
[23]See Bresnahan (2003).
[24]An API is the application programming interface, that is, the frame seen by programmers when interacting with the program.

One scary possibility being discussed by Internet fans is whether they should get together and create something far less expensive than a PC which is powerful enough for Web browsing.[25]

While the memo also remains rather unspecific about the timing for this particular forecast, the fear and paranoia comes through. Events could generate an outcome that threatened a very profitable business at Microsoft.

Gates makes it clear that the browser was the most urgent concern. Browser technology held the potential to radically change the way a mass market of users employed the PC, possibly leaving Microsoft outside its central standard-setting position, or leaving Microsoft in the central position of a less valuable PC.

Immediate events appeared consistent with the paranoia. Netscape had begun to make money from sales to businesses and employed a unique distribution mode involving "free" downloads by households and students, anticipating revenue from business licensees.[26] Importantly, Netscape had begun a program to invite third-party vendors to make applications compatible with the Netscape browser, practices aimed at influencing the rate and direction of innovation. Netscape had also begun to expand its product line into complements to browsers, such as products for servers and areas of related networking.[27] This market-development activity would bring the browser and the Internet into play as an effective way to achieve mass-market e-commerce and content. Responding to it all would eventually become a matter of competitive urgency at Microsoft.

What do these later actions say about Microsoft's earlier errors? There was never any *technical* error at Microsoft. Both Microsoft's strategy and conventional wisdom were based on up-to-date technical information that someone with sufficient technical skill could understand. Rather, Gates misinterpreted the value of the Internet's commercial prospects. This error would take three interrelated forms in its conventional assessment:

[25]Page 4 of Gates (1995). Attempts to realize this forecast were tried shortly after Gates predicted it, though the attempts largely failed in the marketplace. See Bresnahan (1999). They came to be realized much later, in the form of smart phones and tablets.

[26]As discussed in chapter 4, the browser was free, only for evaluation and educational purposes. They attempted to establish usage share through households by making it free, while collecting significant revenue from business licenses.

[27]Cusumano and Yoffie (1998) have an extensive description of how Netscape explored the commercial potential of many complementary service markets through site visitation of lead users and interaction with many user and vendor experiments.

1. Underestimating the Internet's value to users;
2. Underestimating the myriad and clever ways entrepreneurs and established firms would employ Internet and web technologies to provide that value for users;
3. Underestimating the ability of Internet firms to support applications that substituted for Microsoft's in the marketplace.

These three errors were common at other firms in the spring and fall of 1994. Only two additional errors were unique to Microsoft. First, Bill Gates recognized months later than did most computing industry participants that the first three errors had occurred. In addition, Gates had not authorized any investments in the event that the conventional assessment was in error, so by the spring of 1995 Microsoft had limited short-term ability to follow through on the anticipated growth in demand for Internet services. In particular, the first browsers in Windows 95 were not designed to support HTML, so, as a result, software application firms got their tools and solutions in 1995 and 1996 from shareware and other firms, such as Netscape.[28]

Microsoft's unique problems would have consequences for others, however. If applications could come to users without using Microsoft's OS then such applications held the potential to reduce the prices Microsoft could charge for its OS in the near-distant future. That made the Internet a threat to Microsoft's interest in its biggest market. This was not an outcome Bill Gates would accept passively. He would resist it, let others know about his resistance, and try to realign the actions of other market participants. Later chapters will describe these actions in detail.

In contrast, in 1995 virtually every participant in commercial computing looked at prototypes for the commercial browser in a more positive light than Gates. Many participants in computing and communications first experienced the Mosaic browser or the Netscape browser with a sense of joy at the technical and commercial possibilities. The browser illustrated the potential to help create value that had not been as apparent to observers only a short time earlier.

For many of these observers, the Netscape IPO confirmed the unique status of Netscape's browser. The IPO followed an atypical script.

---

[28] This is a necessary summary of a long set of complex events. See, e.g., Haigh (2008), Bresnahan and Yin (2007), and Bresnahan, Greenstein, and Henderson (2012).

At a typical initial public offering, or IPO, a young firm receives money from investors in exchange for shares of common stock. (Before the IPO, the shares are privately held by founders and venture capitalists. After the IPO, the shares can be traded on a stock exchange, such as the New York Stock Exchange or NASDAQ.) Typically, the number of shares to be issued and the price are decided by the company's investment bankers (also known as underwriters) in consultation with management. The underwriters have two objectives that run in opposing directions. First, as agents of the company, they want to raise as much money as possible for a given number of shares. Second, to protect their own firm from loss and to maintain their reputation in the marketplace, the underwriters want to be sure that all the shares on offer are sold in a short amount of time (a few minutes after the offer "goes live").

The bankers' success in balancing these two objectives can be gauged by looking at the performance of the stock in the days and weeks after the issue date. On the one hand, if the stock price goes down significantly on the first day of trading (or after a short time, say, a couple weeks), then initial buyers will be faced with a loss; as a result, they may felt cheated and lose faith in the underwriter who sold them the stock. On the other hand, if the price increases significantly on the first day (or after a short time, say, a couple weeks), then the young firm's management may feel cheated. They could have sold the same number of shares at a higher price or sold more shares at the same price. Either way, if the price rises, post IPO, the company has left money on the table. (Academic research indicates that the deck is stacked somewhat in favor of investors and against the companies. IPO stock prices typically rise on the first day of trading and stay at the higher level thereafter. Gains are typically on the order of 16 percent.[29])

Netscape's IPO departed from the standard script, and it was never settled whether the departure was accident or deliberate. In the first day of public trading, the stock started around $28 a share and then shot up to over $75.[30] After the fact, nobody would admit publicly to a mistake. While the run-up conferred instant paper wealth to the founders and key management, the gain came at a seeming cost to the young organization.

---

[29]See Beaty and Ritter (1986), and Ritter (1991).
[30]See Cusumano and Yoffie (1998) for a fuller account.

By setting a higher initial price, Netscape could have raised several hundred million dollars more than they did, while issuing the same number of shares (thus suffering no more dilution).

It gave the impression that Netscape was so confident it could cavalierly throw away wealth. Garnering attention from many corners, Netscape's IPO became one of the most successful publicity stunts a young firm could have done.

This event had one other consequence, entirely unforeseen at the time. Later on, as more Internet and web businesses engineered their IPOs, many founders wanted to imitate Netscape's pattern—namely, generate large run-ups in the stock price on the first day of trading. Such run-ups were viewed as a sign of success. Cooler heads could not prevail against the request in many later cases. Hence, many of the IPOs in what became known as "the dot-com boom" became lucrative for those who got access to new stock, who often profited merely by acquiring it at the IPO price, and holding it for a short period of time before selling.

The Cost of Oversight to Investors

The shrug of '94 was costly for investors, because indifference led many investors *not* to invest in ways that would have been extraordinarily profitable. For example, foresighted investors who made propitious investments in 1993 and sold the shares between 1997 and 1999, or even 2003, would have made significant financial gains. Said another way, in retrospect two comparatively rare types of investors principally gained: those who invested in the equity of the right established firms, and those who invested in the right start-ups.

Specifically, investments in established companies that later directly benefited from the growth in the Internet—such as IBM, MCI, PSINet, UUNET, Cisco, and Intel—would have yielded huge returns on the dollar. To be sure, such investors would have needed considerable courage to follow their convictions. None of these firms, with the possible exception of Intel, were considered to have large growth potential in early 1993.

Table 6.1 gives a flavor for how large the gains could have been. Specifically, it answers the question: if an investor put $100 into company x on June 30, 1993, how much money would that investor get back on June 30 in 1994? What about the year after that? And so on. This is a standard financial exercise. The table calculates the date at which the maximum return would have been realized, and it shows these returns over a ten-year horizon, providing a flavor for both the up and down.

Table 6.2 shows that valuation of most of these companies between 1993 and 1994 did not change dramatically, reflecting the grip conventional wisdom had on investor assessment of these firms' prospects. No major change in mainstream investing priorities occurred until 1995—and even then, the revaluations did not begin to accrue until a few months prior to (and then especially after) the Netscape IPO in August 1995.[31] The first high-profile analysis of the Internet access market on Wall Street did not arrive until Mary Meeker's at Morgan Stanley, which then resulted in a publication for general audiences in 1996, after her team had done related work for clients.[32] By June 1996 the news had caused a change in views. Any general investor in the sector from June 1993 would have done rather well. That continued to hold through June 1997, '98, '99, and early 2000, and even later for some companies, such as IBM and Cisco.

A similar insight holds for venture capitalists. There was no noticeable change in the rate of first-stage investing by venture capitalists in computer and communications equipment companies in 1993 or 1994, nor in PC or networking software firms. Similarly, there was no significant change in the number or rate of initial public offerings by related firms. Later chapters will say more about this nonevent.

One example can illustrate how the consensus of conventional wisdom held back new entry. Indeed, this example illustrates the exception company that ran against the herd, and profited from it. In 1994, a few intrepid visionaries started Vermeer, a company seeking to develop server software tools and related Internet applications to take advantage of the newly developing World Wide Web. They later developed a software-authoring tool that ultimately became a Microsoft product called Frontpage.

This tale is well known because, several years after he sold out his shares, one of the company's founders, Charles Ferguson, published an articulate memoir about his perspective on his start-up's experience.[33] As

---

[31] Krol (1994) gives a good sense of movement prior to 1995. For a description of the type of resistance foresighted entrepreneurs encountered during this time, see, e.g., Ferguson (1999).

[32] See, e.g., Meeker and DePuy (1996). This team of analysts was not the first one to organize a systematic analysis of the vendors in the market. The first-stage venture capital firms certainly were earlier. A few of these stories are described in later chapters.

[33] See Ferguson (1999).

TABLE 6.2. Returns from investing $100 on June 30, 1993 (June 30, 1993 = 100)

Company[1]	Date of max value	94	95	96	97	98	99	00	01	02	03	04
IBM	7/13/1999	121	201	215	386	495	1120	954	989	595	732	787
MCI	6/21/1999	77	77	88	134	204	375	300	97	n.a.	n.a.	n.a.
PSINet	3/8/2000	n.a.	100	76	49	85	287	330	2	n.a.	n.a.	n.a.
UUNET	6/21/1999	100	106	254	459	696	1236	988	318	1	5	n.a.
WorldCom[2]	6/21/1999	96	148	302	351	531	944	755	243	1	4	n.a.
Cisco	3/27/2000	85	185	426	490	1,009	2,119	4,179	1,197	861	1,104	1,558
Lucent	12/20/1999	n.a.	100	124	237	549	891	784	87	28	33	64
JDS	3/6/2000	97	259	894	1,412	3,044	8,049	46,497	4,848	993	1,356	1,470
Corning	9/1/2000	100	103	125	217	138	283	1,097	205	42	91	160
Intel	8/31/2000	107	232	276	521	546	878	1,975	866	521	621	827
AMD	6/21/2000	104	151	58	149	71	75	320	240	76	53	132
DEC	1/26/1999	47	98	110	85	137	114	124	75	47	68	68
SUN	9/1/2000	70	164	409	503	586	1,860	4,911	1,698	510	502	468
Oracle	9/1/2000	152	235	357	460	337	763	3,456	1,562	740	988	981
Novell	2/17/2000	64	77	53	27	49	102	36	22	11	12	32
Dell	3/22/2000	141	321	548	2,505	7,920	12,629	16,832	8,926	8,588	10,868	12,227
Compaq	3/22/2000	198	277	306	609	870	728	789	475	300	431	433
Microsoft	12/27/1999	100	117	205	278	574	985	1,640	1,455	1,327	957	935

Note: n.a. means "not available." This arises in the table when a stock has ceased to publicly trade or reaches a low number, becoming virtually worthless.

[1] This accounts for the value of subsequent acquisitions.

[2] WorldCom tracks LDDS.

Ferguson's account makes abundantly clear, the commercial vision of his firm for the World Wide Web was not largely shared by others in the summer of 1994. He had a difficult time convincing anyone that a market need existed or that a firm started by outsiders had commercial potential, and he was met with considerable skepticism about the prospects for his firm.

> We were dangerously ahead of the Internet curve; nobody knew what the hell the Internet was, and the Internet industry didn't exist. And finally, we had a truly original product that didn't fit into neat, established categories, so VCs perceived us as risky—particularly because a lot of them didn't understand anything we said.[34]

Being so unusual initially made it difficult for Ferguson and his business partners to raise money for Vermeer, but later that same uniqueness conferred enormous competitive advantages. It allowed Vermeer to position its product where few others could create equivalent value. It released its authoring tool in beta format in September 1995, not long after Netscape's IPO.[35] Only a few months after its product release, Vermeer auctioned itself off in a bidding war between Netscape and Microsoft, making all the founders and investors quite wealthy.

Did that make Vermeer the canonical gold rush pioneer that made out well? This example illustrates another misleading aspect of the gold rush metaphor. In a gold rush the pioneers find the largest chunks of gold by virtue of being early. Vermeer is similar in that respect, in that they had the right idea in advance of the Internet rush. Yet, notice the key differences too: pioneers in a gold rush get their payoff comparatively quickly, if they get one at all. In contrast, Vermeer had little value at first, and really had no prospects to cash out early. Vermeer did not realize the gains from that idea until several years after the entrepreneurs hatched the idea. While comparatively quick, the risks also were enormous. A VC had to finance their firm in the interim, and share the risk with them over whether there would be a payout at all. In short, Vermeer did not arrive quickly and pan for gold in the hopes of a quick payout; it had pursued a unique path prior to the rush, built an enormous apparatus, and once the other gold diggers arrived, it sold its position.

---

[34] Ferguson (1999), 71.
[35] http://www.seoconsultants.com/frontpage/history/, accessed July 2009.

Working Prototypes and the Consensus

Why did the near future remain elusive? The complexity of privatization made it difficult for any observers—both those close to it and those distant from events—to grasp the consequences of the NSF privatization. Even if Stephen Wolff had taken out a full-page ad in every major daily newspaper in the summer of 1994 and explained the NSF privatization in great detail, few participants in the computing or communications industry would have grasped the implications.

It was not impossible for an imaginative technologist to foresee much of what commercial markets might be able to do, and that yielded a few entrepreneurial prospectors. Management at PSINet, UUNET, MCI, Sprint, and Cisco invested in anticipation of the commercial Internet, and, to their credit, before the summer of 1994. Ben Slivka at Microsoft foresaw what was coming, and in detail, and in the fall of 1994. Jim Clark and Marc Andreessen and Charles Ferguson also saw opportunities and acted on their visions. There were a few others, and those few did not work in influential positions in private firms.

Everyone else in commercial markets was hesitant, even though later events would make it abundantly clear that early actions would have yielded enormous payoffs. What were they waiting for? A compelling working prototype from a commercial firm had to be sufficiently advanced in its operations to sway more than a visionary technologist. It had to be compelling enough to sway entrepreneurs and VCs who would invest time and money in new ventures. It had to be good enough to convince CEOs at established firms to gain board approval to commit to major investment projects. These people needed to observe an entire system operate with all its layers working together, delivering service to users, under reliable contracts, supported by established firms. In short, it had to demonstrate how the technology could generate revenues from applications.

The NSF-sponsored Internet produced plenty of the working prototypes, but not those needed to overcome the hesitance found within commercial markets. A commercially viable working prototype could not exist until the NSF finished announcing its privatization plan, as it had in the fall of 1994. That made the Internet ready for a catalytic working prototype, one that would generate a killer application in the market. Netscape walked into that situation, and its browser dazzled.

The same prototype was shown to just about everyone only a few months apart, so perceptions about the commercial opportunities changed nearly everywhere, and did so at just about the same time. Very quickly the consensus changed, and the shrug of '94 disappeared. Many established firms recognized that they had to respond, and quickly. This realization initially would generate activity, and resemble an Internet gold rush. It would begin with a decided tilt toward entrepreneurial activity and innovation from firms who had previously been on the edges.

7

Platforms at the Core and Periphery

The remarkable social impact and economic success of the Internet is in many ways directly attributable to the architectural characteristics that were part of its design. The Internet was designed with no gatekeepers over new content or services.

—Vinton Cerf, codesigner of TCP/IP[1]

In 1994 a company called Spry Technologies Inc. developed an endearing little product called "Internet-in-a-box." Quaint by modern standards, it appeared to be a CD for downloading a program to generate an Internet connection to a dial-up ISP, including a licensed version of Mosaic. In fact, it was a clever attempt to create and package everything a user needed to get on the web. It turned a complex process into something simpler. It filled in the technical pieces a user needed to have access to the web. The box was designed to appear familiar, which was thought to be reassuring to the mass-market user. It appeared to be packaged software, just like every other application software for personal computers, and it was sold on the same shelves in retail outlets.

The product generated $40 million in revenue its first year, which was enough to suggest Spry was on to something. That early success in the

---

[1] Vint Cerf and Robert Kahn are co-creators of TCP/IP. At the time of this quote Cerf held the title of chief Internet evangelist for Google. The quote comes from a letter to the US House of Representatives, Committee on Energy and Commerce, Subcommittee on Communications and Technology, November 9, 2005. See Cerf (2005).

FIGURE 7.1 David D. Clark, chief protocol architect, Internet Architecture
Board, 1981–89 (photo by Garrett A Wollmann, March 19, 2009)

market attracted the attention of CompuServe, who bought the firm in the
middle of 1995. It used Spry's assets to develop its Internet strategy.[2]

Those events illustrate a phenomenon that would repeat itself in many
forms in the commercial Internet. As many chapters will discuss, the commercial form of the Internet and web permitted many small-scale businesses
to enter and generate revenue in excess of their costs. Many of them aimed
to simplify the Internet for users, making it more useful. Just as the modular
organization of the Internet in the academic setting had enabled specialization in invention, its commercial arrangement permitted a few (and eventually a flood of) specialists, but in this case, they came in commercial form.
These specialists primarily worried about their business application and
could take for granted the workings of the remainder of the system.

Stepping back from this specific example, another observation leads to
a deeper lesson. Spry sold the Internet to users in a format that referenced
familiar features of the commercial PC software industry, even though the
Internet was nothing like it. The Internet was not a corporal good. The
Internet could not be touched, unpacked, or shipped in a turnkey form.
This rendered the business proposition for the Internet rather inchoate in
comparison to the PC, even though users wanted it to be easy to use, like

[2] Wilder (1995).

the PC. Users needed the technology to work easily. Users needed a low price in a standardized format. Just like the packaged software business, many users wanted firms to offer products, promise to provide service for them if they did not work, and back up those promises.

The value chain for the Internet differed in a marked way from the value chain for the personal computer. A value chain is a set of interrelated activities that together produce a final product of value greater than the incremental value of each part. All mature industries have a value chain. In 1995, the value chain for the commercial Internet was quite young and still evolving, while the PC market was almost two decades old and largely settled.

The value chain for the PC involved a wide set of firms. The typical PC used a microprocessor (usually from Intel or AMD), a motherboard design that descended from IBM's 1981 design. It contained several standard upgrades to the memory (from one of many firms) and an input/output bus (redesigned by Intel), an operating system (typically from Microsoft), and an internal memory device (from one of several hard-drive firms), as well as many other parts. These were assembled together by one of several firms (Compaq, Dell, Gateway, IBM, and so on) and distributed to users along with other compatible peripheral components, such as printers (most often from Hewlett-Packard, but also from many other companies). Users acquired the products either directly from the assembler (Dell, Gateway) or from a third-party retailer (BestBuy, Circuit City). Standard software applications included office-oriented applications (from Microsoft, Intuit), games (from a variety of firms), and several utilities (Norton, McAfee). Any PC also could accommodate thousands of niche applications.

In comparison, by early 1995, the commercial Internet's value chain had resolved some open questions, and a few remained. The best-laid plans at NSF had come to fruition. Not only had the commercial Internet survived its transition from public funding to privatization, but a regular routine for exchanging data and settling accounts between private parties had also continued and made a transition into a marketplace. With the release of the web, the prospects for growth looked promising. The market prospects for Internet services were improving, and awareness was growing outside of the cognoscenti into a mass market.

The two markets did have many economic similarities. Both the Internet and the PC had platforms at their core—namely, a standard bundle of components that users employed together as a system to regularly deliver services. In North America, the Internet and the PC also both drew on a similar knowledge base and similar pools of programming talent who shared lessons with one another, sometimes reluctantly. The most talented developers and programmers moved between multiple platforms, whether it was a Unix-oriented network software or C++ for a PC.[3]

The PC and Internet also shared another feature, discretion to make modifications after purchase. The IBM PC (and its descendants) had allowed for user modification ever since its introduction, through user additions of electronic cards, peripherals, or software applications. The Internet also gave considerable discretion to users. If any administrators or users found existing code unsatisfactory, they were at liberty to propose a new addition or retrofit another.

One key difference struck all observers. Unlike the PC market, there was no profit-oriented organization providing platform leadership for the commercial Internet in mid-1995. That difference received considerable attention from contemporaries. The PC bundle was developed and sold in a proprietary environment, while developers called the Internet more open. There was only one problem with that label. *Open* was inherently vague. To a contemporary, it elicited about as many definitions as an Inuit had for snow.[4]

Looking behind the scenes more deeply, there were meaningful differences in the processes for decision making. Two commercial firms in the PC market, Microsoft and Intel, retained and guarded their right to make unilateral decisions about the pervasive standards embedded within the most common configuration of the PC platform. Microsoft's processes were proprietary, resulting in limited rights for other market participants. Only the platform leaders had unrestricted access to information. The Internet, in contrast, employed a consensus process for determining the design of pervasive standards and protocols. The processes employed documented standards and did not restrict access to these documents or their use by any participant in the Internet.

If pressed, many inside the Internet argued that proprietary platform

[3]For more on moving between the Unix and Windows programming environment, see, e.g., DiBona, Danese, and Stone (2006).

[4]For an analysis of the wide range of meanings, see, e.g., West (2007).

leadership represented the antithesis of what they aspired to achieve. Yet on the surface it was unclear why Microsoft inspired so much opprobrium. Many of Microsoft's practices were not appreciably different from those found at other well-known and successful software firms, such as Oracle, Apple, SAP, or IBM. Moreover, Microsoft was astonishingly efficient at supporting a wide and diverse group of application developers. Its managers knew how to reach the organizational frontier for production of large-scale mass-market software in ways few others did.[5] Shouldn't that have inspired either reluctant or approving admiration?

As the Internet began to commercialize in 1995, this topic often generated more heat than light and obscured the plain economics. Both processes had strengths, and both platforms could support innovative outcomes, often with only minor differences in performance. However, proprietary platforms possessed a major strength that open-source software lacked: their ability to execute on a "big deliberate push" toward a new frontier, especially if it were coordinated inside of a well-managed firm. Open platforms, in contrast, had an extraordinary strength that proprietary platforms lacked. Openness nurtured radical exploration around unanticipated and underanticipated value, and that could lead to growth around a platform at a rapid pace. That was especially so if existing firms had been reluctant to pursue the unanticipated value, and many entrepreneurs perceived the opportunity.

Both strengths shaped outcomes in the commercial Internet at a watershed moment in 1995. Microsoft was in the midst of demonstrating the principal strength of proprietary software development during its rollout of Windows 95. At about the same time, the birth of the commercial web would demonstrate the principal strengths of open governance, and its ability to enable radical transformation. Markets rarely allow for such direct comparisons of the relative strengths of starkly alternative organizational forms at the same time, but in this case events conspired to sharpen that comparison. Those similarities and differences are worth exploring, and that is the purpose of this chapter. It will frame topics found in many later chapters, such as why the Internet diffused so quickly, and why this contrast lay at the heart of the largest market conflicts of this era.

[5]See, e.g., Cusumano and Selby (1995).

Computing Platforms and the Internet

To disentangle the consequences of the economic differences between proprietary and open platforms, it is essential to view the functions of platform leadership broadly. According to Bresnahan and Greenstein (1997),

> A computing platform is a reconfigurable base of compatible components on which users build applications. Platforms are most readily identified with their technical standards, i.e., engineering specifications for compatible hardware and software.

The failure or reduction in performance of any of the essential activities can lead to inferior outcomes. Well-designed platforms encourage successful innovation from multiple parties in settings where no single firm can easily develop and provide a majority of the applications. All platforms—whether open or proprietary—share four functions, and all the leaders of platforms aspire to provide these functions:

- Designing a standard bundle of technical implementations that others use in their applications;
- Operating processes to alter those standards and inform others about the alteration;
- Establishing targets and roadmaps to coordinate complementary developer and user investment;
- Providing tools and alternative forms of assistance to others who wanted to build applications using their technical standards.

Unilateral and consensus processes perform these functions in very different ways. In addition, proprietary and open processes employ distinct policies for releasing information.

The Proprietary Side: Windows 95

In early 1995, the PC platform was in the midst of an upgrade to Windows 95, which was due in the summer of that year. The upgrade was a culmination of a major transition away from DOS as the predominant compatible system for IBM PCs. As a text-based operating system, DOS, along with several upgrades, had been the operating system since 1981.

Yet getting from blackboard conceptions into mass-market products had vexed many firms. By early 1995 it was apparent that Microsoft had found a way to make that transition for users of descendants of the IBM PC, and simultaneously keep the Redmond-based firm at the center of the industry.[6]

What had Microsoft done? In short, Windows 3.0 had been an addition, residing on top of DOS, and later improved in Windows 3.1. Microsoft also had lined up every major application firm around a new development, later to be named Windows 95. The new operating system would resemble a more polished version of Windows 3.1 in its user interface but would include many improvements. In addition, Windows 95 would reside at the core of the operating system, which would yield numerous technical benefits and functional improvements.[7]

The project imposed a set of rules and policies on application developers. Microsoft defined a technical layer, invented on one side of it, and then enabled peripheral developments at the other side of the layer. It was a base for developers to build upon. These boundaries between the layers were called APIs (application programming interfaces). The use of APIs was typical for a proprietary platform. Other proprietary software firms (for example, Apple, Oracle, and SAP) used similar practices to organize a community of others. If anything was novel, it was the scale of the community involved in Windows 95, extending to tens of thousands of firms, many of whom were very small. The number of participants in the PC community in the mid-1990s exceeded anything ever organized by Apple, IBM, or SUN, for example, or by Microsoft, for that matter.

This strategy produced many challenges in execution. Microsoft's employees worked hard to provide inviting pervasive standards on which others built their applications. This required good designs that supported a developer's needs, which had to be backed up with technical support staff. The firm also considered subsidizing the costs of widely used tools for developers, encouraging practices that helped PC users.

---

[6]This is a long story. The account in the text provides the basic outline, but does not provide much information about the alternatives, such as OS2, DR-DOS, and so on. See, e.g., Cusumano and Selby (1995).

[7]DOS became a layer within Windows 95, so old DOS users could face as few problems as possible when migrating their data and programs into the new operating system environment.

None of this arose solely through altruism. Helping a mass of developers also helped Microsoft. If a tool helped many developers, then the costs of its development were defrayed over a large base. The development of more applications for Windows 95 also would help Microsoft through its sales of operating systems.

Routine financial calculations stood at the center of Microsoft's actions. It gave away tools if it thought it recouped the investment with more developer actions or more valuable applications. It invested in designs if the returns looked financially strong. It invested in an organization to provide technical support because developers made the operating system more valuable for a greater range of applications.

The resulting operating system was quite an astonishing combination of old and new. Windows 95 was backward compatible with many applications from Windows 3.0, but the system included many features that were bigger, faster, more varied, more complex, and more efficient for many tasks. That embodied a promise for a high payoff. Most developers anticipated selling more applications, and Microsoft anticipated selling more operating systems. For that reason alone virtually every vendor acquiesced to Microsoft's design choices for most of the key standards.

That experience, along with related actions from Intel that had industry-wide benefits, fueled the view that platform leadership helped computing markets grow.[8] Yet a growing antipathy from the entangling quid pro quos that less accessible information and more restrictions on the use of technology embodied was holding the enthusiasm in check.

A Strategy for Pervasive Standards

Microsoft did not aspire to control all frontier technologies. Rather, its strategy stressed having an exclusive position as the provider of *pervasive* technologies on which applications were built. That exclusive commercial position was valuable to Microsoft for several reasons.

Obviously, it made life easier for Microsoft's own employees. Microsoft's application designers could contact other Microsoft employees to have their needs addressed. Microsoft also could retain the right to change

---

[8]See, e.g., the discussion in Gawer and Cusumano (2002) about "growing the pie," which features Intel's sponsorship prominently.

any feature if it yielded strategic benefits, and it could do so without coordinating with any other firm.

Indeed, outsiders frequently accused Microsoft of using its position to make its life easier, such as documenting for Microsoft's use, but not necessarily for any others, or not documenting code so they could alter it to their advantage. These accusations also could be exaggerated. For example, Allison (2006), who takes a developer's perspective, sees the merits of multiple viewpoints. When discussing why Microsoft did not document one part of the internal subsystems for Win32, he states:

> Why do this, one might ask? Well, the official reasoning is that it allows Microsoft to tune and modify the system call layer at will, improving performance and adding features without being forced to provide backward compatibility application binary interfaces. . . . The more nefarious reasoning is that it allows Microsoft applications to cheat, and call directly into the undocumented Win32 subsystem call interface to provide services that competing applications cannot. Several Microsoft applications were subsequently discovered to be doing just that, of course. . . . These days this is less of a problem, as there are several books that document this system call layer. . . . But it left a nasty taste in the mouths of many early Windows NT developers (myself included).[9]

While Microsoft's technological leadership position reinforced the value of the PC, its actions also shaped its ability to capture a larger fraction of the value from each PC sold if it reinforced the lack of substitutes for its operating system. For example, it contributed value to the PC through supporting new applications, growing user demand, or motivating more frequent purchases. It also improved its ability to capture a larger fraction of value by enhancing its bargaining position with developers, often through the inclusion of features into the operating system that substituted for another firm's, and for which the other firm had charged users.[10]

Microsoft protected assets important to making the standards by using intellectual property, such as patents, copyright, or trade secrets, and excluding others from imitating their actions. Microsoft also prevented others from

[9]Page 47 of Allison (2006).
[10]See Bresnahan (2003), and Henderson (2001).

gaining information about a standard's features, how it operated, and how it would change, necessitating that others negotiate with Microsoft to gain access to that information. These actions could and did bring about conflicts with others in the PC business, whose plans conflicted with Microsoft's.

As a practical matter, most application firms liked the improvements but objected to how the governance of the platform had changed around them. They perceived many entanglements, the use of too many carrots and sticks by Microsoft. What were the carrots? Those might be the tools Microsoft provided to developers to make Windows 95 easier to use, for example. What were the sticks? Those might be actions punishing unfriendly developers, such as withholding information about near-term changes, or merely not returning phone calls promptly. An alternative carrot or stick involved offering or withholding lucrative marketing deals or discounts to friendly or unfriendly firms.

Of course, one thing mattered above the others. If developers wanted to reach users of the PCs, they had to work with Microsoft. They had to call for support services, at a minimum to find out how to make the technical aspects of their applications work well with the operating system. Microsoft's management knew this—indeed, they had set it up this way deliberately. In circumstances where speed to market was valuable or margins were tight, offering relevant information sooner, in contrast to withholding it, could be a very effective incentive or punishment to inducing cooperation.[11]

Many vendors could perceive that they had become dependent on Microsoft's proprietary standards. Microsoft's technical staff held important information about how the APIs worked inside the operating system. This dependency arose at the beginning of product development, in the middle, and sometimes even just prior to launching a new product. It left developers vulnerable to getting held up at crucial moments in an urgent development process or marketing campaign. Microsoft's management recognized the situation too, and increasingly the use of technical support came along with reminders that only developers with friendly relationships with Microsoft got the best service.[12]

---

[11]See discussions in Gawer and Cusumano (2002), Bresnahan and Greenstein (1999), Gawer and Henderson (2007), Bresnahan (2003), and Henderson (2001) for illustrations of the range of such actions.

[12]Henderson (2001) stresses that this action was typically taken in context, as one of many ways for Microsoft to discourage other firms from taking action it deemed undesirable.

Dependency also came with a danger in the near future. Many software executives wondered if they could trust ambitious Microsoft employees with sensitive information. Executives at application firms who had seen the innovative features of prior software show up as features in later versions of Microsoft's products wondered if an employee's conversations with Microsoft's technical staff would contribute to seeding a future competitor. Years earlier the danger had seemed to be an exaggeration, but by early 1995 the experience was quite common and well known.

Adding to the distrust, Microsoft seemed to be able to expand its actions in ubiquitous ways. For instance, it could expand into a software market if its ambitious executives thought it was profitable to do. By the mid-1990s Microsoft had entered a wide range of product areas, such as network software, games, Encyclopedias (Encarta), and online services (MSN), as well as announcing its intent to produce a wider range of application software—most typically through self-development, but potentially also through purchase of small entrepreneurial firms. In fact, only the opposition of the antitrust division at the Department of Justice stopped Microsoft from buying Intuit, the leading developer of tax and accounting software.

The public discussion had become heated over these practices. SUN's CEO, Scott McNealy, for example, relished making public remarks using sharp language that denigrated Microsoft's lack of openness in comparison to his firm's. For example:

> We had openness. In other words, nobody should own the written and spoken language of computing . . . nobody owns English, French, or German. Now, Microsoft might disagree and think they ought to own the written and spoken language of computing and charge us all a $250 right-to-use license to speak English or Windows or what they happen to own.[13]

By 1995, virtually all computer industry participants were familiar with these practices. Microsoft retained control over information about the standards that composed its platform as part of a broader strategy to enhance its bargaining position with others, to deter entry, and to support its ability to generate revenue. Yet most developers tolerated it because some

[13]Segaller (1998), 235.

of them prospered. There also was no other avenue for selling PC software to the large number of buyers of IBM-compatible PCs.

Standard Protocols

Viewed broadly, the commercial Internet had comparable processes in place for making a standard bundle of protocols and altering those standards, but the details were quite different from the PC. For making standards and altering them, the bulk of activity took place in the Internet Engineering Task Force, or IETF. Whereas Microsoft unilaterally made decisions about standards, all such decisions in Internet standards emerged from consensus. In addition, the processes were much looser regarding establishing roadmaps and targets, and providing tools and assistance for others.

As chapters 2 and 3 discussed, the IETF had been established during the NSF era. It became part of the (not-for-profit) Internet Society after 1992, which was established during privatization. The IETF inherited a process for designing and endorsing protocol standards, still called Request for Comments (RFCs) from the earlier days.[14] The standards-making processes had not changed for the most part except in one respect described below, nor, ostensibly, had the technical skill of those involved in working groups. However, the number of participants had increased, which altered the composition of participation, involving more employees of profit-making companies.[15]

After 1992 the IETF differed from Microsoft in one important way. It had altered the assignment of authority at the top, devolving it from its older hierarchy in which the members of IAB had the final say over approval of proposals for standards. By the mid-1990s, such authority rested with the members of the Internet Engineering Steering Group (IESG), which was a larger group comprising different area heads. The area heads appointed/coordinated with working groups and tried to impose a semblance of structure on an otherwise loosely organized voluntary activity. In the mid-1990s many of the members of the IESG had been appointed by

---

[14]For a review of the process and how it has changed, documented as RFCs, see http://www.ietf.org/IETF-Standards-Process.html. Other places that explain drafting standards are RFC 2026 or RFC 1602.

[15]The IETF appoints working groups, and those have grown considerably over time. See, e.g., Abatte (1999), Russell (2006, 2014), or Simcoe (2006).

the very members of the IAB who had previously held authority. Uncertainty about the transition was largely gone by late 1994 and early 1995. As will be described below, routines had emerged.[16]

In contrast to Microsoft, the IETF produced nonproprietary standards. Like efforts in other industry-wide standard-setting organizations, the IETF asked workshop leaders to develop protocols and standards that did not use patents or other forms of proprietary technology, if possible.[17] Workshop leaders were discouraged from endorsing proprietary technologies unless the owner agreed to license those at reasonable and nondiscriminatory rates.[18]

Nothing in the commercial Internet contained subsidies after the NSF withdrew its support. Yet the IETF leadership did its best to invest in several actions to aid the process it governed. First, it tried to provide editorial guidance and support for the entire process. That resulted in remarkably clear and comprehensive documentation (particularly from some contributors who were not practiced at clarity and thoroughness). It also helped coordinate and sponsor *plugfests*, where vendors could test the interoperability of software (that could operate and be implemented). In principle, these fests were used to verify the existence of running code before advancing a proposal for an RFC to a final draft.

The Internet did not lack what programmers called "tools and libraries." These were partly a legacy of years of development with widespread university support. To be fair, while RFCs could be found in one central location, the same could not be said for many tools, which resided among many sites, dispersed across the Internet. In addition, the IETF leadership and many participants from some of the numerous new young firms in the commercial Internet continued to develop new protocols.

The situation for roadmaps and targets did not resemble commercial norms in the least. There was no figure comparable to Bill Gates at Microsoft

---

[16]See Russell (2006, 2014) or Simcoe (2006).

[17]Firms were required to disclose patent holdings if these were pertinent to the topic under discussion. For the present general guidelines, see https://datatracker.ietf.org/ipr/about/ and RFC 3979. Prior policies are largely spelled out in RFC 2026, and the anticipated processes and policies that pertained to the mid-1990s can be found in RFCs 1602 and 1310 (especially sections 5 and 6).

[18]The IETF leadership chose a position that allowed it to retain its inherited functioning processes. It also continued to do as many other standards organizations. It did not close the door on adopting a protocol that covered a private firm's patent, as long as that firm agreed to license at a reasonable and nondiscriminatory rate.

or Andy Grove at Intel, who stood at the center of the commercial Internet providing executive vision and discipline, or, for that matter, settling disputes between inconsistent visions. The IETF had limits. It was not the NSF. NSF had provided planning in the past; however, for all intents and purposes, those decisions were made and implemented in 1993 and 1994. NSF stepped away from planning after it privatized the backbone. By the norms of commercial computing, that left a void in planning as of 1994 and beyond.

Why So Little Centralization?

It would not have been odd to embed some coordination in processes for building Internet protocols. After all, that was the model in other successful commercial platforms. So why did the IETF take an approach at the outset of privatization that emphasized so much decentralization? As chapter 2 began to hint, if a rationale existed, it was simple: the membership—university computer scientists, equipment firm engineers, and many independent contractors with long-standing interests in the technology—wanted it that way, in their long-standing desire to avoid the centralized control endemic to AT&T and other established telecommunications carriers and contrasted with practices at international standardization efforts, such as OSI. Like OSI, the IETF encouraged enthusiastic participation from a wide variety of innovative contributors, but the composition of contributors differed sharply, weighting participation toward those who knew the workings of the Internet and had helped it in the recent past.

The result occurred gradually, and had been self-reinforcing. Enthusiastic supporters of the Internet volunteered their time to get the IETF established in the 1980s. Where they had choices they chose decentralized processes, which inspired enthusiastic participation from others. In addition, several parochial tugs and pulls inherited from the precommercial era coalesced into a unique set of processes and policies.

First and broadly, lack of centralization and looseness about roadmaps and targets was consistent with many other decisions made at the IETF and elsewhere. Beginning with the earliest conversations, subsequent legislation, and the final drafts of the NSF privatization plan, there had been plenty of opportunities to establish central institutions. Only in rare cases were those opportunities used for such a purpose, such as with the establishment of the domain name system. In large part, many participants in the NSF-sponsored Internet did not view centralization favorably.

The looseness about roadmaps also arose, in part, from the norms governing academic debate. That is, virtually no argument was settled (in principle), so that some contributor could make a proposal if it had technical merit. In other words, there was a preference for open-ended debate almost for its own sake. That accommodated proposals from many corners.

An open-ended process also was thought to accommodate the realities of developing a communications technology whose user base was geographically dispersed, where there were many administrators or intense users of the technology, each with a different experience that informed their contribution. It accumulated incremental advances in publicly documented ways, which far-flung contributors could independently access and review. As noted in earlier chapters, that had worked well in evolving applications that coordinated end-to-end processes with many contributors, such as e-mail. It also could accommodate a *swarm of standards*, that is, multiple proposals for potentially solving the same problem.[19]

While documenting decision making at intermediate and final stages was necessary to support open-ended debate, it also had another essential benefit: it gave public credit for individual effort.[20] The IETF's RFC process gave academics concrete results to which they could point for credit within their universities.[21] It was also useful because so many tools and contributions came voluntarily, and contributors needed to establish their historical credentials to gain rewards from prior accomplishments.

As in any large organization, there were multiple motives behind each practice, and despite all these efficacious reasons, numerous noneconomic motives also played a role. In particular, some participants expressed a strong distaste for the insular bureaucratic hierarchies that had historically shaped the flow of information and decision making in regulated communications markets.

---

[19] The term "swarm of standards" is due to Updegrove (2007).

[20] See Crocker (1993), Bradner (1999), or Simcoe (2006) for explanations about the roles of "informational" RFCs, which often served as a public documentation about a discussion for a new protocol or standard at an intermediate stage.

[21] Assigning credit was useful in the era when NSF funded improvements and academics needed to document their contributions to the NSF. It continued to have value later.

As discussed in chapter 2, there was tension between the decentralization of the IETF's protocol making (or upgrading) processes, which many participants preferred, and the appointment of the leadership at the IAB, which inherited its top-down and (largely) unchanging leadership from the legacy of TCP/IP's origins at DARPA. Privatization would necessarily have put pressure on this tension, pushing it toward more decentralization. This would have continued to grow throughout the mid-1990s, as new constituencies joined the conversation and brought a new set of views about the improvements needed to support commercial buyers.

As it happened, however, decentralization came to the leadership after 1992. A phrase from a 1992 speech by the IAB chair from 1981 to 1989, David Clark, encapsulates the transition. His phrase was:

> We reject: kings, presidents, and voting. We believe in: Rough consensus and running code.

Later many members shortened this to the alliterative credo, "rough consensus and running code."[22] For many participants after 1992 this became the slogan for the IETF.

A computer scientist by background and training, and one of the few elite cognoscenti of the Internet, Clark knew the boundary between the pragmatic and long-term ideal visions for the Internet. He also had a reputation for being a voice of reason during a chaotic debate. If that was not enough, he had a knack for being associated with catchy phrases at the boundary of technology and governance—for example, he had been one of the authors of the phrase, *end-to-end*. Catchiness aside, what did *rough consensus and running code* mean in practice?

Seen against a broad prospective, *rough consensus and running code* was meant to highlight the heretofore recognizable identity of the organization's shared sense of norms, and how the organization's participants chose among the various options for organizing its processes. In his overhead slides Clark referred to the trade-offs between processes. A standards organization could be flexible and responsive to current events, meeting unanticipated requirements. Or an organization could give slower and more deliberate consideration to various options. Clark referred to a firm

---

[22]See Russell (2006, 2014) for a full account of the developments behind this speech. It was delivered in July 1992 in Cambridge at an IETF meeting.

headquartered in New Jersey, which was a not-so-veiled reference to AT&T, whose corporate hierarchical practices were held in low esteem by many participants. At the time that Clark coined the phrase, he also contrasted the processes in the IETF and IAB with those of the OSI, which was more deliberative and much slower.

The phrase emerged during a crucial argument in the summer of 1992. A few members of the IAB were considering whether to coordinate a specific proposal (for upgrading the address system) with those behind the design of the OSI. This would have required making parts of TCP/IP and OSI designs compatible, and it would have required some coordination between the two efforts behind each standard. After long debate, this proposal, which was favored by some members of the IAB, was abandoned in the face of a general uproar from many participants in the IETF.[23] In other words, the IAB bowed to the wishes of the majority, even though the leadership favored an alternative course of action. It was in this talk that Clark declared that rough consensus was the preferred option over executive declaration from above.[24]

Ultimately, Clark's speech also was remembered because it occurred at the same time that the "wise old men" of the IAB agreed to a process for regularly turning over the leadership of the IAB. That solidified the preference for "bottom-up" processes in all aspects of the standardization processes for the Internet. That became the norms for the Internet Society, which became the oversight for the IETF.

That did not take long to become routine. By early 1995 the norm of open-endedness was embedded in the identity of the community. In their own materials the IETF leaders drew attention to decentralization and its emphasis on running code. This comes out clearly in Bradner (1999), for example. After summarizing many of the processes for newcomers, he states,

> In brief, the IETF operates in a bottom-up task creation mode and believes in "fly before you buy."

[23]Numerous reasons motivated the opposition. In addition to the concerns, noted in the text, about hierarchy and centralization of authority, there were technical objections and issues about melding the process. See Russell (2014).

[24]The strong emphasis of the contemporary debate on process above result, and on remaining independent of the OSI efforts rather than intertwined with them, led other contemporaries to label this a "religious war" among standardization efforts. See, e.g., Drake (1993).

The importance of preferences for open-endedness came with a large potential risk—namely, lack of coordination between the technical proposals of distinct groups. No participant wanted to see the growth of families of mutually incompatible protocols from distinct subgroups within the IETF. Yet such an outcome was not only technically possible, but also it was likely as the commercial Internet grew and participation at the IETF grew with it.

Rather than abandon the bottom-up processes for the sake of coordination, however, the IETF adopted a structure to accommodate decentralization. The costs of this process were explicitly placed on the shoulders of working groups and their area coordinators within the IESG. They were charged with the responsibility of identifying and coordinating development across distinct working groups with overlapping agendas, even requiring area coordinators to do so before assessing whether rough consensus had emerged for a proposal.[25]

Hence the IETF did not lack a planning process or de facto roadmap at a broad level. The collective efforts of the IESG at planning and assigning work between working groups provided the guidance for developments in the short run. They could only do that job if working groups documented their progress at every stage of decision making. Then a conversation with one of the members of the IESG could serve the same function as a roadmap, providing a member with a sense of where their efforts fit into the broader collection of ongoing work.

That solution worked as long as the community of researchers would share information about their technical inventions with each other through e-mail, postings in RFCs, and conversations at meetings. In other words, making accessible all documentation of decision making supported other principles of importance to the community.

In summary, by early 1995 the IETF had moved beyond its experiments with accommodating many points of view. It had established an organization that did not restrict participation or restrict access to its results. It remained blithely transparent in order to accommodate its unrestrictive participation rules. For many participants the transparency was a goal in

---

[25] Once again, the leadership at the IETF was aware of these requirements, and area directors (ADs) from the Internet Engineering Steering Group (IESG) were to have frequent contact with working group chairmen. See RFC 4677 (titled, *The Toa of the IETF: A Novice's Guide to the Internet Engineering Task Force*).

itself. Most of its progress became documented online, even at intermediate stages of development. In addition, it placed no restrictions on use of information after publication. Although nobody had any stated intent to foster innovation from the edges, these processes would have profound consequences for its occurrence.

Openness and Innovation

A few years later, as the Internet boom got underway, many enthusiasts for openness held it responsible for creating much innovation. What parts of these claims are myth and what claims stand up to scrutiny? The question cannot be addressed with a simple answer because the answer must be comparative. If openness had not existed, what was the alternative? Many innovations would have arisen with or without openness, and with almost any set of rules. A more nuanced question has to be asked: When did openness matter in comparison to a plausible alternative and why did it matter?

The remainder of this chapter offers evidence that begins to form the answer, and other chapters in the book will return to the question and complete it. In outline the remainder of this chapter says the following: Up until 1994, a skeptic had plenty of reason to think that openness played little role in fostering commercially important innovation. During the Internet gold rush, however, openness played a key role at two crucial and irreversible moments. It shaped outcomes in the fight between Microsoft and Netscape, and it shaped the relationship between Tim Berners-Lee and others at the IETF. Before getting to the heart of these two episodes, it is important to recognize their significance as counterexamples to a skeptical view.

The skeptical view had considerable merits. For example, though open processes had played a role in facilitating some of the entrepreneurial entry among carriers—for example, at PSINet or Netcom, as well as a plethora of equipment firms—it was possible to argue that this was a small factor in determining outcomes. Relatedly, it was plausible to argue that the supply conditions were a by-product of the academic origins of the Internet, and, as chapter 4 stressed, not unusual for inventions inside universities. That explanation also shifts emphasis to something other than openness, the core economic conditions that gave rise to the earliest entrepreneurs—namely, growth in demand for Internet services—in fostering incentives to innovate among these early entrepreneurs.

By early 1995, moreover, the potential drawbacks to openness were becoming more apparent. In early 1995, the discretion to make hardware and software upgrades resided with private parties. It left many unanswered questions about the future structure of operations. The NSF privatization was reaching its completion, which also raised budgetary uncertainty about long-term revenues from research and university clients, as well as private clients. The uncertainty in economic conditions did not encourage innovation from private firms, and firms with questions about the future saw no other large established firm in a leading position, ready to take a call and provide an answer.

Openness also did not help resolve other unaddressed questions about the near future. The IETF used nonproprietary standards, which eliminated points of differentiation. That potentially contributed to turning data carrier services and equipment design into a commodity service or product. Lack of coordination also cast uncertainty over the plans of every participant, and nobody had sufficient experience to forecast whether the commercial markets would be very profitable or not. None of the major carriers or equipment makers found it attractive to serve a market with so much potential uncertainty.

As it turned out, lack of a central planner was not a crucial gap at this moment. Carriers and equipment makers did not really have any alternative but to live with the openness. Experienced router and network equipment firms existed prior to privatization (for example, Cisco, IBM, 3Com, and many smaller firms), and they existed after as well. On the whole, in 1995 the Internet contained a healthy set of infrastructure operations built around TCP/IP-compatible operations. Market relations between carriers were functioning well, and data managed to find their way across all the networks without incident.

There was no magic to it. A skeptic would emphasize the basic economics at work. Existing firms stayed in the market after NSF withdrew support because they had spent and sunk investments to enter this market and they continued to see an opportunity to profit. Those were comparatively straightforward business calculations. Openness had little to do with them.

Openness also had little role at Microsoft, the most successful software firm at the time. Microsoft's process of using incentives and subsidies to encourage incrementally innovative applications had a couple seeming advantages over the openness of the Internet. The commercial Internet did not encourage anything with subsidies.

To be sure, this comparison was not a slam dunk. Microsoft provided tools for many applications and often subsidized their development. But the commercial Internet did not lack supplies of tools and libraries for sharing, often coming from university contributors and researchers with a wide variety of settings. The IETF also could accommodate an innovative commercial application, just as any platform leader would have.

A skeptic also could have argued one additional observation: Microsoft's organized platform appeared to have an innovative advantage over an open one. A large platform leader, such as Microsoft, had skills at organizing an upgrade requiring a *big push*, one that simultaneously altered the programming environment for many applications and that supported it with technical help. The upgrade to Windows 95 was an illustration of that innovative advantage. Nothing equivalent took place at the IETF, which tended to focus on incremental improvements on existing protocols, as developed by small teams of contributors to a working group. In short, before the commercial Internet had shown it could appeal to mass-market users, it was reasonable to argue that commercial platform leadership had an edge in pushing through big technically substantial projects into mass markets.

Despite merits of a skeptic's views, skepticism about openness is not fully persuasive in retrospect. Why? Openness turned out to have one important consequence for structural change. It permitted radical change to reach the market when it otherwise might have encountered roadblocks at private firms. However, this was less obvious until circumstances exposed it. The key features at the IETF were its lack of restriction on the development of new protocols that challenged established platforms, and the lack of restriction on access to the specifications for pervasive standards that challenged established platforms. Tim Berners-Lee's experience can illustrate this point.

How the Web Grew

The World Wide Web was first diffused through the initiatives of Tim Berners-Lee on shareware sites, starting in the early 1990s.[26] Initially,

---

[26] For the challenges and difficulties, see Berners-Lee and Fischetti (1999) and Gillies and Cailliau (2000).

Berners-Lee expected an individual installation to adopt software to support the three components of the web, the hypertext markup language (HTML), the hypertext transfer protocol (HTTP), and what eventually would be called the uniform resource locator (or URL), which Berners-Lee preferred to call the universal resource identifier (or URI).[27] Berners-Lee also diffused a browser, but very quickly the online community began to put forward better versions throughout 1992 and 1993. As discussed in chapter 4, this eventually led to Mosaic and Netscape.

Even before the web began to explode into large-scale use, Berners-Lee worried about how he would standardize his creation. He believed that standards would facilitate activities by others. By 1992, numerous installations had experience using the core technologies. In the summer of 1992, Berners-Lee took the initiative to start standardizing several aspects of the web within an IETF-sponsored subgroup.

From Berners-Lee's perspective a standards process had several benefits. It would permit the web to evolve in a unified way, that is, add new functionality without fragmenting into versions that could not interoperate. He also believed such standardization would contribute to making the web more pervasive, if users perceived less uncertainty about the management of its future.[28]

When he first approached the IETF, Berners-Lee naively assumed his experience would go well. He had running code, and he had followed Bradner's maxim, as stated earlier, approaching the IETF only after his code could fly. As he learned to his frustration, however, the existence of his running code and spreading adoption did not imply the emergence of a rapid consensus. The lack of centralization manifested in Berners-Lee's experience as an absence of decisive resolution.

Berners-Lee's proposals led to a contentious debate at the working group within the IETF. Problems in developing hypertext had generated intellectual interest for decades in computer science. Numerous camps for distinct theoretical and philosophical viewpoints had formed long ago. The existence of working software did not change viewpoints. Delibera-

---

[27] The URL is the term that emerged from the IETF deliberations. Berners-Lee preferred URI because it came closer to what he was trying to accomplish philosophically. Berners-Lee and Fishetti (1999), 62.

[28] This is a frequent theme in the first few chapters of Berners-Lee and Fischetti (1999), especially before the formation of the W3C.

tions became mired in many long-standing debates. About the meetings in 1992 through 1994 said Berners-Lee:

> Progress in the URI working group was slow, partly due to the number of endless philosophical rat holes down which technical conversations would disappear. When years later the URI working group had met twelve times and still failed to agree on a nine-page document, John Klensis, the then IETF Applications Area director, was to angrily disband it.[29]

By Berners-Lee's account, the debate became focused too often on issues he did not consider important, such as the meaning of "universal" when it is used as a label for a protocol. He gave in on several of these issues in the hope of realizing resolution, but he did not give in on anything that had to do with his design.

Almost certainly the debates partly reflected the social strains taking place at the IETF at the time. Berners-Lee was one of hundreds of comparatively new participants, and one with a particularly ambitious agenda.[30] While he also had the confidence that came with success diffusing his running code, his standing as a comparatively new participant was bound to interfere with persuading long-time acolytes.

Another issue initially clouded the debate. In 1992, Berners-Lee's employer, CERN, still retained rights to the code. Participants at the IETF clearly were concerned about that, and Berners-Lee could appreciate why. That issue was not settled until, at Berners-Lee's urging, CERN renounced all claims to intellectual property rights in web technologies in April 1993. After that, Berners-Lee pressed ahead, hoping CERN's act would lead to consensus. Yet, once again, consensus eluded the working group.

Eventually, in mid-1994, Berners-Lee followed two paths simultaneously. He both worked with the IETF and established another institution to support the web's standards. In effect, he decided to defer getting a consensus at the IETF, and, instead, he issued an informational RFC (RFC 1630) about what he had already designed. That effectively concluded the conversation in the short run. This RFC left too many issues unresolved to

---

[29] Berners-Lee and Fischetti (1999), 62.

[30] The IETF started to experience growing participation at this time. Bradner (1999) states there were 500 participants in the March 1992 meeting, 750 in the March 1994 meeting, 1,000 in the December 1994 meeting, and 2,000 by the December 1996 meeting.

serve as an effective standard—namely, a completely finished design for a protocol endorsed by the IETF.

At the same time Berners-Lee began working to establish the World Wide Web Consortium (W3C). In February of 1994, he had a meeting of minds with Michael Dertouzos at MIT. It altered Berners-Lee's vision for what type of institutional support for the web would help him achieve his goals. Berners-Lee established his consortium in mid-1994. By early 1995, his consortium was set up at MIT and in Europe, and he was able to elicit cooperation from many firms in the industry—in terms of both financial contributions and representation at consortium discussions. In short, Berners-Lee started on his way to standardizing the web in his own organization while bypassing existing processes at the IETF.

A brief comparison between the processes at the IETF and those adopted by Berners-Lee at the W3C shows what lesson Berners-Lee drew from his experience at the IETF. Berners-Lee stated that he had wanted a standardization process that worked more rapidly than the IETF, but otherwise shared many of its features, such as full documentation and no restrictions on how others used the standards.

In contrast to the IETF, the W3C would not be a bottom-up organization with independent initiatives, nor would it have unrestricted participation. Berners-Lee would act in a capacity to initiate and coordinate activities. To afford some of these, his consortium would charge companies for participating in efforts and for the right to keep up to date on developments. Notably, Berners-Lee retained the right to act decisively.

Rivalry played a surprisingly muted role in this situation. In spite of all these misunderstandings at the IETF, Berners-Lee continued to have cordial relationships with many active Internet pioneers and participants. Why was cordiality noteworthy? The establishment of the W3C removed the IETF from a position of technological leadership in the development of an important new infrastructure for Internet users and developers. And it rendered concrete what was commonly stated: IETF's leaders remained open to a variety of proposals to improve the Internet. They did not presume to be the exclusive institutional progenitor or technological source for all Internet-related activities.[31]

---

[31] Moreover, cordiality was notable because it was not an inevitable outcome. It stood in contrast to the rivalry and strained relationships between many IETF participants and other

To be sure, most initiatives ended up coming back to the IETF processes in one form or another because it was useful for them to do so. Protocol writers found it helpful to use and reuse existing processes. Indeed, Berners-Lee also returned to the IETF to eventually get the RFCs he had sought all along, just much later than he had initially aspired to, and much later than would have been useful.[32] Eventually the primary dispute between the IETF and W3C would be over minor issues, such as the boundaries of expertise between the two groups for niche topics.

This experience illustrates consequence from one aspect of openness, the lack of restrictions on use of information. The working group participants at the IETF treated the ideas behind the web as an object for philosophical debate, and (initially) the leaders treated the W3C with benign neglect, particularly in 1994. Neither action was helpful to the web, but none deterred it. More to the point, lack of control over the IETF standards effectively gave discretion to other individuals or organizations—in this case, Berners-Lee and the W3C—that were entrepreneurial enough to build on existing Internet protocols, even in ways that bypassed the existing process for making protocols and established new ones.

The Commercial Web and the PC

Tim Berners-Lee's experience with the IETF would contrast with events in the PC market, although that was not apparent at the outset. Microsoft's managers acted much like everyone else, incorrectly forecasting little technological and commercial success for the World Wide Web. Moreover, when Netscape first began, it was treated like any other application firm meeting a niche need. In early 1995, before Bill Gates changed his mind, Netscape was viewed as a firm making an application that helped raise demand for the PC platform. It was given access to software tools and to the usual technical information about Windows 3.0 and 3.1, as well as

---

organizations that claimed to design networking standards in the precommercial Internet, such as the OSI. See Drake (1993) and Russell (2006).

[32] Berners-Lee did return to the IETF for further refinements and upgrades. This included RFC 1738 in December of 1994 (a proposal for URL), RFC 1866 in 1995 (a standard for HTML), RFC 1945 in May 1996 (informational about HTTP), RFC 2068 in January 1997 (a proposal about HTTP), RFC 2396 in August 1998 (a draft standard about URIs), RFC 2616 in June 1999 (a draft standard for HTTP), and RFC 3986 in January 2005 (a standard for URIs).

Windows 95. Netscape's programmers would call for technical support, just like any other firm.

Events got more interesting in the spring of 1995. Bill Gates wrote "The Internet Tidal Wave" in May. As chronicled in the chapter 6, Gates's memo no longer cataloged Netscape as just an application. Not long after writing this memo, Gates tried to have Microsoft buy a stake in Netscape and gain a board seat. Those negotiations did not get very far.[33]

After further talks, the executives in Redmond concluded that Netscape would not cooperate on their terms, which led Microsoft to treat Netscape in as unfriendly a manner as it could in the summer of 1995, by denying it access to technical information and other marketing deals. Coming as late as these actions did for a product that had already been released, these actions only slowed Netscape down a little bit, and came nowhere close to crippling it.

The confrontation escalated from there. Over the next few years, as later chapters will describe in detail, Gates went to enormous and deliberate lengths to prevent Netscape's browser from becoming pervasive, particularly with new users. Microsoft put forward its own browser and undertook numerous defensive actions related to the distribution of browsers, such as making deals to prevent Netscape's browser from becoming a default setting at ISPs or in the products PC assemblers shipped.

A Conspiracy to Offer a Comparison

After the Internet had blossomed into a large market in the late 1990s, many of the most vocal defenders of Internet exceptionalism began to argue that open standards were superior to proprietary standards. These unqualified opinions were misleading at best or just plain wrong. There was no economic law then—just as there is none now—that makes platforms built on open standards superior to the others in the market, or vice versa. Both can succeed with meeting customer needs, depending on how they are designed, priced, and supported. Both will address many of the same incremental opportunities in much the same way and yield much the same outcomes.

---

[33]Cusumano and Yoffie (1998) provide a timeline and analysis of these events.

Historical circumstances rarely provide a clean comparison of the consequences from such distinct market and organizational structures, but in 1995 circumstances conspired to do so. Here were two markets and organizations that provided just such a comparison. Only a few months apart, the same technology, the web, diffused into two settings with distinct processes for making decisions. One was open while the other was proprietary. In both cases, initially the web received little help from established leaders, and that motivated actions that did not rely on the leader for much. In both cases, the leadership eventually recognized the error in their perceptions and began to take action.

There the similarities end. The IETF eventually came to an understanding with the W3C, Netscape, and all the complements built on top of it. In contrast, the first firm to develop a product for the web, Netscape, invited many other firms to build complements, and met with active resistance from Microsoft, the firm providing proprietary technological leadership. Microsoft did not want competition for its position of leadership from Berners-Lee, Netscape, or its partners.

Economic incentives accounted for the difference. Microsoft was intent on protecting its position as the exclusive firm to support pervasive standards in PCs, and it interfered with its aspirations to acquire a similar position in servers for business enterprises. In contrast, the IETF had a set of principles regarding equal access to information, transparency, and participation, and the organization stuck to those principles.

That comparison permits a summary of the key questions motivating this chapter: Did openness matter for the commercial Internet? Did openness shape the arrival of innovation from the edges?

It certainly did help to keep many longtime participants in the Internet motivated. Many participants preferred open institutions and processes for their own sake. Their participation helped keep the IETF vital. Openness could not help entrepreneurial firms raise revenue, or make payroll, but it did not stop inventive specialists from exploring many new application and content markets. It did enable participation and incremental innovation from a wide variety of contributors.

The experience of Tim Berners-Lee also helped those entrepreneurs. No policy at the IETF prevented him from taking initiatives, which he did, and to the benefit of others.

In contrast, the leader of the personal computing market, Microsoft, did not greet the emergence of the World Wide Web with glee. Microsoft actively tried to gain exclusive control over the deployment of pervasive standards.

The commercial development of the newly privatized Internet would have been different without an open organization at the IETF and W3C. While its enthusiastic proponents exaggerated the importance of openness, there was more than a grain of truth underneath the rhetoric. The commercial Internet would have encountered many more challenges without such an open structure to enable the growth of innovation from the edges.

8

Overcoming Two Conundrums

A good predictor of not finding an ISP is the presence of
hybrid corn seed.
—*Zvi Griliches, Paul M. Warbug Professor of Economics,
Harvard University*[1]

What does the spread of the Internet have in common with the spread
of hybrid corn seed? On the surface, there is not much similarity.
Each episode is drawn from rather different eras and distinct parts of the
economy. Below the surface of the merely superficial, however, the deep
insights of Zvi Griliches illuminate the hidden forces shaping both.

Griliches was an economic giant of the twentieth century, and his biography made his accomplishments even more impressive. Born in Lithua-
nia, the Nazi invasion shattered Griliches's youth, and in 1941 his family
was moved into Kovno, the Jewish Ghetto.[2] In 1944 he and his family were
interned near Dachau. A homeless orphan after liberation, Griliches immi-
grated to British Palestine, which then became the young state of Israel.
Lacking any formal education as a teenager, and largely self-taught, Griliches enrolled for a short stint in Israeli schools for young Holocaust

---

[1] Zvi Griliches, private conversation, December 1996. He stated this after being shown the
maps of the commercial dial-up ISP networks in the United States. This map is figure 8.1 in
this chapter. An account of this remark and its context can be found in Greenstein (2004).

[2] For summaries of his contribution to economics and personal reflections on Griliches's
contribution, see, e.g., Trajtenberg and Berndt (2001), 97. "There is something extremely rare,
indeed unique about Zvi's overall package of human qualities—that combination of paternal
warmth, intuitive understanding, ultimate wisdom, and cautious but firmly entrenched
optimism."

survivors. Soon he gained permission to attend university in the United States. He paid for his undergraduate education with an unlikely inheritance—selling land his parents had bought many years earlier in British Palestine to help the Zionist movement.

Aspiring to become an agricultural economist, Griliches began his undergraduate studies at the University of California, Berkeley. His brilliance quickly became recognized, and a few years later he began his doctoral studies at the University of Chicago. There he completed his widely influential dissertation, "Hybrid Corn: An Exploration in the Economics of Technological Change," in which he demonstrates how to statistically measure the determinants of the adoption and diffusion of the hybrid corn seed, a tour de force for the time.[3] Upon finishing, the University of Chicago's Department of Economics hired him as a faculty member. In 1969, Griliches moved to Harvard, where he remained for the rest of his life.

Griliches's dissertation was more than merely an impressive statistical exercise. Griliches chose hybrid corn for study because it was one example of the productive advances transforming agriculture in the local and national agricultural economy. In just a few decades, the entire agricultural economy had become dramatically more productive, squeezing a great deal more out of a great deal less. Prosperity had noticeably increased, giving sons and daughters much higher incomes than their parents. What had happened in hybrid corn, in other words, had happened across a large range of agriculture.

As unlikely as it seems on the surface, the economic forces that shaped hybrid corn seed were similar to those shaping the diffusion of the Internet. In both examples widespread economic growth could not arise until many market participants figured out how to make each innovation inexpensive and easy to deploy in a wide set of circumstances. Each innovation had to overcome the *adaptation conundrum*. To become useful on a large scale, the innovation needed to become valuable in nearly every circumstance—namely, in every location, with every supplier, and with every set of users.

Consider the adaptation conundrum overcome by hybrid corn. Existing seed became less expensive and more productive, allowing farmers to

---

[3]See, e.g., Trajtenberg and Berndt (2001), 93. "Griliches's work on the diffusion of hybrid corn (the first article, stemming from his PhD dissertation, was published in 1957), catapulted him to instant fame, and has since turned into a true 'classic.'"

redirect resources to other activities. Better seed resulted in more output (better corn per stalk) from all producers, and more output per input (land, labor, fertilizer) from any individual producer. That freed up spare time and resources for other activities. Fertilizers and pesticides eventually changed to accommodate a new scale and mix of crops. Crop failures became less likely, which altered the financial risks. Bigger equipment could be purchased for the more productive land. New uses were found for abundant and inexpensive corn. Seed vendors altered their inventories, carrying different supplies. Harvesting equipment designs evolved; therefore, the manufacturing stamps, tools, and dye changed too. Finally, new books about best practice were written, and educational practices were adjusted. Agricultural extension stations taught those methods, and they passed between farmers by word of mouth.

Said succinctly, numerous *work processes, organizational routines,* and *market relationships* were restructured to take advantage of new potential and new opportunities. No general economic law guaranteed whether and when such adaptation took place, or, for that matter, whether it succeeded at all. Widespread success required inventiveness from many market participants. The innovation had to be adapted to a multitude of circumstances faced by potential suppliers and buyers, and the hindrances and bottlenecks found in every nook and cranny of every region had to be overcome. Almost by definition, every inventive act took place at a unique point in a technology's development, and often the market circumstances were novel also.

As this chapter and the next will explain, the Internet would not spread and lead to economic growth until it too overcame the adaptation conundrum. Such growth involved inventive acts from many market participants—vendors and users, and their business partners and consultants.

The Internet and corn differ in one important respect. The Internet had to overcome an additional conundrum, the *circular conundrum.* In technically advanced communications networks, the circular conundrum arises because of the large number of economic actors providing technically interdependent services. Such interdependence makes them complements in demand, meaning that the maximum value of using any service cannot be achieved unless all the components and services are used together. The mere presence of complements in demand does not guarantee the coordinated supplier of all the components, however. If anything, collective fence sitting is the most common response to the circular conundrum—a response that manifests itself as cautious investment behavior by a group of erstwhile business partners and competitors.

Caution was common in 1994 and a real hindrance to the growth of the commercial Internet. A retailer might aspire to sell goods electronically, but would hesitate to spend for an inventive new website unless there were enough browser users it could reach. Or, a bulletin board firm might hesitate to provide Internet access in a novel location unless enough local businesses and users had computers equipped to handle the web. A computer consultant might delay in investing the time to learn HTML and adapt it to her client's needs unless she was sure enough clients had customers who would make use of electronic commerce. Or, a system administrator might pause before spending to install novel software to support browsers and gateways for electronic mail unless it were obvious that employees were going to use the new services. Each participant remained cautious, waiting for someone else to go first.

Starting in 1995 and accelerating thereafter, the US economy overcame the circular conundrum at the same time it overcame the adaptation conundrum. It is not possible to distinguish when one was overcome from when the other was overcome.

In the mid-1990s, there were several areas to observe triumphs over the two conundrums, but in this chapter, I focus on one key area, specifically, ISPs.[4] ISPs are a good illustration because they were an entirely new business, created for the commercial Internet. The most established firms in the ISP market, such as MCI, Sprint, and BBN, had fallen into the business after their involvement with the NSF. But the many more entrepreneurial firms that came from the edges of computing and communications, such as PSINet and UUNET, also played an essential role.

The behavior of ISPs in late 1996 motivated Griliches to make the quip quoted at the top of the chapter about the relationship between hybrid corn and ISPs. His observation occurred at a moment when the two conundrums had *not entirely* been overcome. There was virtually no Internet access in the places where corn grew, or, for that matter, in US counties where the cows and cotton outnumbered the local inhabitants. At that point, the commercial

---

[4] The next chapter focuses on another key area—providers of Internet and web services to business.

Internet aimed almost exclusively at rich technological enthusiasts in major urban areas. In two short years, however, the situation changed. It would become clear that technology enthusiasts would no longer be the sole users and, correspondingly, suppliers could reach rural areas. Commercial markets could supply the Internet nearly everywhere and in forms that appealed to a large number of nontechnical households and businesses.

Building and Adapting the Internet[5]

In 1994, it appeared as if there was only one known solution to the circular conundrum. It involved two risky steps, neither of which could occur quickly.

- First step: An important economic actor had to take on considerable risk by investing ahead of (a) others, (b) all other suppliers, and, crucially, (c) realized demand.
- Second step: An early mover had to motivate other vendors to follow with more investment.

Those two steps needed to occur before most mainstream suppliers would act. Only after others had taken the risks would the entire set of suppliers learn whether their biggest ambitions would be realized—namely, whether there would be enough revenue to pay back the collective expense from entering the market.

Before the Internet grew, however, most established firms believed only one type of economic actor could take that first step—a very large established firm that could financially handle a loss if a big risk failed, and that possessed the ability to bring others along with it. And only a few large established firms with recognizable brands could have played that role—namely, IBM, Intel, Microsoft, or AT&T, for example. Crucially, and each for different reasons, none of these firms had publicly backed the Internet as a technology for mass-market use prior to 1995, and, accordingly, many other firms hesitated to invest.

---

[5] The themes for this chapter have antecedents in research about the diffusion of general purpose technologies (e.g., Bresnahan and Trajtenberg 1995) and *coinvention* (e.g., Bresnahan and Greenstein 1997, 1999). Coinvention is the invention complementary to the general purpose technology, which makes it useful in a variety of settings. Coinvention can take place at user installations, vendor organizations, and the establishments of other participants in the economy around a general purpose technology. The themes in this chapter borrow extensively from writing about coinvention at ISPs (Greenstein 2000a, 2000b, 2001, 2005, 2008b, 2010b).

The conventional view turned out to be wrong because it remained blind to one other possibility—that a group of inventors and suppliers could collectively build a technology good enough to deliver value for many users. That too involved a slow two-step process, building first for technical enthusiasts and then later for general users.

As prior chapters have discussed, the potential to build for general users had eluded others. Events in the Internet illustrate why: Netscape sold an easy-to-use browser, building on tools developed by Tim Berners-Lee and operating on a network the NSF had just privatized. The multifaceted combination of the NSF's investments and privatization, many ISP's investments and delivery, and browsers built in the web led to a feasible network. And where the young Netscape led, many firms had to follow with real investment, anticipating enough demand for their services to justify the expenses they incurred.

There was more, as well. Between 1994 and 1995, a number of other young firms also began exploring new businesses built with web software, including Yahoo!, eBay, Amazon, Vermeer, and others. In addition, established firms began experimenting with web pages, including Sony, *Encyclopædia Britannica*, and others. With the release of the Netscape browser, and especially after the success of the Netscape IPO, numerous software entrepreneurs began making plans for new start-up businesses, and these plans did not depend on whether a large firm took action or not. In other words, the actions of AT&T, IBM, or Microsoft did not play a role.

As earlier chapters described, Netscape's and Microsoft's growing rivalry would eventually contribute to moving this entire market forward for a while. From the outset, both priced their browsers at an inexpensive point. At first Netscape allowed home users to download their browser for free and charged businesses to use a license. In comparison to typical enterprise software in most establishments, these charges were rather minimal.

The biggest expenses for ISPs were the human costs of installing the software and changing operating procedures, and those expenses were also much lower than typical. The Netscape browser was easy to install, and so were some of the basic tools for managing users. Netscape crowed about its compatibility with other TCP/IP and web software, encouraging users to install suites of such applications. Microsoft's Windows 95 also contributed to making it easier to go online. It included built-in TCP/IP compatibility, and, importantly, its networking software, Windows NT, eased the transition for many businesses.

After December 1995, prices sank even lower. Microsoft began pricing its browser at zero, bundling it with every operating system it sold. That made the browser nominally inexpensive, by definition, albeit, not any less burdensome to install. More important, Microsoft (1) began announcing plans to integrate its browser with its server software and other application software and (2) aggressively began to make it easier for businesses to use its browser. These events in browsers would have consequences for other parts of the young value chain for Internet services, because this crucial gateway to the Internet became seamless to users.

Why Internet Service Providers Mattered

To a user, there were two costs. The first were the hardware costs. The second involved the human costs, the hassles affiliated with learning how to use the software and adapt it to the unique needs of the user or business establishment. By 1996 installation costs became the principal hardware cost of adopting the Internet and World Wide Web. Installation meant establishing a connection with an ISP and adapting the connection to an existing PC or local area network (LAN).

The actions of ISPs played a significant role at this point. These were a new type of firm, and, after the browser firms, the most visible suppliers of the Internet and World Wide Web. Many aspects of the commercial Internet's value arose from the decisions of ISPs. These decisions determined how much many users valued the Internet, because many ISPs determined the appearance, packaging, and pricing of the initial Internet experience for many users.

By 1996, ISPs offered service in every major US city, and many large firms had begun building national networks. How did that happen? No dramatic technological invention lay behind these changes. Rather, a new and stable value chain emerged. It came about due to the interaction of three related inventions aimed squarely at the adaptation conundrum:

- Invention of a new pricing norm;
- Invention of a viable model for distributing Internet access over geographic space;
- Invention of new points of differentiation between ISPs.

Before discussing each of these in detail, consider why the overall market was so nurturing.

Markets for business access operated on straightforward principles. Sprint, PSINet, MCI, and plenty of other firms had figured out the value chain. Business establishments asked for either fixed-line access or dial-up access. Fixed-line access involved delivering Internet connections of various capacities in various locations while also interacting with an Internet gateway. Norms in that business followed administrative precedents set in the research network. Establishments controlled their data on one side of their own gateway, usually because the gateway lay at the end of a LAN. The ISPs controlled everything after the data was handed off from the gateway.

Fixed-line access involved figuring out how to get physical presence near customers. These challenges could be regulatory, as in gaining rights of way. The challenges also could be mundane, as in negotiating with various builders in order to snake underground lines throughout a city, which was expensive and not typically desirable. In either case, the challenges were not mysterious. ISPs knew what challenges needed attention in order to be in the business.

Dial-up access faced different challenges. The biggest puzzles were associated with serving unsophisticated users. Many, if not most, of the technological enthusiasts or wild ducks had adopted by 1995. After 1995 the users fit a different profile. They wanted a low-risk valuable service, one that was reliable, routine, and inexpensive. But attempts to reach unsophisticated users in the first half of the 1990s had made only marginal progress. Whereas AOL, CompuServe, Prodigy, and Genie had no more than several million users between them, PSINet and UUNET largely focused on business users and avoided home markets. NetCom and Spry did manage to build a customer base in the hundreds of thousands, but they were notable for their rarity as no other ISPs were getting the same scale of success. If there was a large untapped market, nobody was quite sure how to tap it.[6]

---

[6] The biggest problem was not with the technology per se. A number of other routine technical and business processes had begun to characterize the operations of ISPs. Technical practices improved. For a broader discussion of these and other technical issues, see Haigh (2008).

The invention and spread of the World Wide Web—namely, three spreading software tools, HTTP, HTML, and the URL, opened a new range of possibilities for nontechnical users. In addition, invention of the web enabled the growth of such a new potential market beyond e-mail, one that involved pictures and graphics. That potential was widely recognized among virtually every ISP by mid-1995. Nonetheless, it did not bring millions of users to the doors of ISPs. Somebody still had to show users that the technology did something useful and was worth paying for. In the meantime, ISPs had to price the service to cover their costs and appeal to users.

PRICING INTERNET ACCESS

Pricing had vexed firms for years. In the first half of the 1990s, most ISPs tried the same pricing norms governing bulletin boards. For bulletin boards the pricing structure of the majority of services involved a subscription charge (on a monthly or yearly basis) *and* an hourly fee for usage. Some prices for specific services were unlimited, while others had usage charges, and different firms experimented with different combinations.[7] For many applications, users could get online for "bursts" of time, which would reduce the total size of usage fees. Although it was cumbersome to log on and off, technical users did not feel hindered. E-mail, file transfer, and posting to listservs could accommodate these practices. But nontechnical users resisted these logging procedures as burdensome, and most did not think the benefits worth the hassles.

The emergence of faster and cheaper modems and large-scale modem banks with lower per-port costs opened the possibility for a different pricing norm, one that did not minimize the time users spent on the telephone communicating with a server. Modems allowed a user to move data over a digital phone line, at this time typically at a maximum speed of 14.4 and 28.8 kilobits per second. Modem banks allowed an ISP to handle multiple phone calls. The emergence of low-cost routines for accessing a massive number of phone lines also contributed to a new norm, because it enabled many ISPs to set up modem banks at a scale only rarely seen during the bulletin board era.

---

[7]Banks (2008) provides a long history of many of these experiments prior to the rise of the Internet.

That did not mean a successful solution was initially obvious to many vendors in 1995. Judging by the advertisements they used in *Boardwatch Magazine*, solutions varied widely. Some ISPs tried one thing, while others tried another, symptomatic that no consensus emerged right away.[8] Although there was a long-term trend toward more use of unlimited prices, the national ISPs also tried a variety of usage charges.

Two broad viewpoints emerged. One viewpoint paid close attention to user complaints about monitoring. Users remarked that surfing the World Wide Web was hypnotic. Users found it challenging to monitor time online. In addition, monitoring time online was nearly impossible with multiple users within one household. The ISPs with sympathy for these user complaints argued that unlimited usage for a fixed monthly price would be a feasible solution. A premium would cover the extra costs of the unlimited usage, though it was an open question how large that premium needed to be. These plans were commonly referred to as *flat rate* or *unlimited* plans.

An opposite viewpoint contrasted with the first one. Specifically, user complaints were transitory, and new users had to be "trained" to monitor their own time online. Supporters of this view pointed to cellular telephones and bulletin boards as examples. Cellular telephony was also beginning to grow, and pricing per minute had not deterred users. One up-and-coming bulletin board firm, AOL, had seemed to grow with such usage pricing as well. The ISPs that held to this view expressed confidence that usage prices would prevail, and they called for exploration of new combinations that might better suit surfing behavior by nontechnical users.

While the events that motivated these two viewpoints were new, the outlines behind them were not. The disagreement reflected a long-standing argument about the appropriate method for pricing telephone services. Each side could burnish its arguments with considerable experience from the past, and the argument could have continued indefinitely.

Although both sides recognized that the Internet might break with precedent, a competitive event settled the argument among ISPs, and a positive response from users reinforced the result. The key action came from AT&T, one of the established firms that could move a market. AT&T

---

[8]For example, the advertisements in *Boardwatch Magazine* showed such a variety. See Stranger and Greenstein (2006, 2007).

did move the market, in fact, but just not as AT&T's executives had expected.

Pricing at a New ISP

AT&T's Worldnet service was first aimed at business in late 1995 and then explicitly marketed at households in early 1996. Held in low regard by many technically oriented participants in the Internet, AT&T was not expected to succeed. When their success went well beyond expectations, it caught a lot of attention and framed a simple question: How was this possible? Although flat rate pricing was not solely responsible for AT&T's initial success, it was one of the unusual features of AT&T's service. Their success led other ISPs to consider imitating AT&T's *approach* to flat rate pricing.

Viewed as a potential competitor to virtually every ISP, the competitive response was swift and almost complete. Virtually all ISPs switched to unlimited usage except AOL and Microsoft Network (MSN). Why did AT&T's action induce such a swift response from all but these two? AT&T's strategy was aimed squarely at the nontechnical user at home, the same user community that all these firms were trying to court. AOL's holdout requires explanation, which in turn requires understanding AT&T's actions.

AT&T took a calculated business risk by choosing a design for its service that would not—indeed, could not—make a profit if it did not get widely adopted in many cities throughout the United States. The cost structure for AT&T placed challenging constraints on the network's design. AT&T aspired to make the service both national and inexpensive but could not meet those aspirations unless it achieved large scale in its operations. If it did achieve such scale, then its costs per user would be low, allowing AT&T to charge close to the lowest prices in the industry at that time. If it did not achieve such scale, then the costs would be too high, and the service would be unprofitable.

How would AT&T get so many users? AT&T's executives saw an opportunity to be among the first to offer home service that came from a branded and established national company, which appealed to certain users who did not trust young or unfamiliar firms. The executives compared AT&T with another potential entrant with similar credentials, IBM. Although IBM supported a worldwide service for business customers, the company had made it clear in 1994 that it did not aspire to provide service to the mass-market home user.

One part of AT&T's strategy was built on the path forged by MCI, Sprint, UNNET, and PSINet, which already had begun to demonstrate how to offer service as a national firm. A national firm needed a geographically dispersed set of investments because virtually all users preferred to access the Internet using local telephone calls. The US telephone universal service policy had long subsidized local landline household calls by charging greater prices for business and long-distance calls than for local calls, which were priced at a flat rate per month in almost every state, with the definition of *local* left to a state regulator. Typically *local* was defined over a radius of ten to fifteen miles, sometimes less in dense urban areas, such as Manhattan. Thus using local rates reduced household user expenses, thereby making the service more attractive.

If AT&T sought to provide service for an entire city, its management had to assemble a list of local phone numbers to permit all potential callers to have one or more options to make a local phone call. Providing national service meant assembling local numbers across many cities and states.[9]

As it turned out, with between four or five hundred phone numbers, AT&T, as well as any other ISP, could cover every major urban area of the United States—namely, any city with a population over fifty thousand inhabitants. Approximately 85 percent of the US population lived in such cities. In brief, with such a network AT&T could claim it had a national service.

A national network, however, involved more than phone numbers, which is where ISP service became expensive. Each phone number needed to be outfitted as a point-of-presence, or POP, a term borrowed from the NSFNET. The modem banks that handled the calls at POPs were one of the biggest expenses of an ISP.

Attracting nontechnical users was a strategic plan AT&T used to spread the expense of modem banks over a larger base of users. Their strategy bet that nontechnical users would *not* stay online nearly as long as experienced or technically oriented users—in effect, anywhere from twenty to thirty hours of time a month at most, and often a lot less. Because such light users did not all dial-in on the same day or at the same time of day,

---

[9] The US telephone network consisted of approximately 19,000 local telephone switches and each of those switches was affiliated with a single area code and multiple prefixes. For example, in the phone number 312-555-1212, the area code is 312 and the prefix 555. To offer dial-up Internet service in a city, AT&T had to compile a list of the local area codes and prefixes that covered the area, and then implement its service. Such information was readily available.

the equipment investment did not need to handle all calls at once. Rather, with light users, an ISP could serve a local area with modem bank capacity at anywhere from one-third to one-quarter the size of the total local service base.

More to the point, with such ratios, AT&T could offer the service at a low price. Their executives merely had to find the lowest price most ISPs offered at the time. The marketing department determined $20 per month, which generated revenue of $240 dollars per year per customer, which, in turn, was enough to cover the investment and operating cost of a POP with far less than one thousand customers.

Those cost and revenue scenarios made the service viable in many medium-sized cities. For example, a city of one hundred thousand inhabitants typically contained forty thousand households. If one-quarter of such households had personal computers at home (a plausible number for 1996), then there were ten thousand potential customers. To AT&T's marketing executives, gaining 10 percent market share in such a city seemed obtainable. And if that was obtainable in a town of one hundred thousand, then similar results seemed plausible in bigger cities, like Chicago, Atlanta, and Denver. It also meant that the financial risk of offering service in smaller cities was not too great, so AT&T targeted cities of fifty thousand inhabitants, even in isolated locations.

AT&T unveiled its home service and in a few months it signed up one million customers. This experience was stunning. It was the type of counterexample that attracted the attention of every ISP in the country. Alarmists among longtime Internet watchers wondered if AT&T, the firm many wild ducks resented and despised, would dominate home markets for Internet access. Virtually all small and medium ISPs quickly matched the $20 price and offered unlimited service as an option. Many tried to offer an additional option, usage pricing with some types of discounts, but over time many would drop the practice due to lack of customer interest.

The Response at AOL

Did AT&T's actions and its competitor's reactions settle the pricing norms for good? Not in the least. In early 1996 only two major ISPs, AOL and MSN, refused to change their pricing practices quickly. AOL was particularly interesting because it had one of the largest user bases in the country, so its hesitance received considerable attention.

Inheriting usage pricing from its long legacy as a bulletin board firm, AOL aspired to appeal to the nontechnical users with superior marketing, appealing page design, community building in moderated forums, and tailored content offerings, not just branding or technological prowess. Its existing pricing had worked well, covering the operating expenses. And a pricing change had not been part of its plans.

As ISPs converted to flat rate pricing, AOL's management found itself between a rock and a hard place. Multiple considerations hemmed in its options. If it did not change its pricing, AOL's management feared it would increasingly lose potential customers to other ISPs, especially national ones. Like other ISPs, AOL perceived the potential for growth by attracting new users over the next years, so choosing the wrong pricing could be a very costly mistake during the earliest moments when many new users came online. Yet, moving to flat rate pricing presented many immediate challenges. In 1996, AOL owned and managed its own facilities for providing access. A new pricing policy would undo years of fine tuning of capacity in multiple locales, which was designed to match historical (and tested) ratios between the number of local subscribers and the capacity needed to handle them.

This last observation was especially salient. AOL's users did not overuse modem capacity, because a large number avoided charges by logging in for short periods of time, thereby freeing up modem capacity. AOL's executives guessed (sensibly) that flat rate pricing would lead existing users to stay online longer than with usage prices. They also anticipated their capacity of phone numbers and modem banks in many locales would be inadequate, as would server capacity in some locations.

The competitive pressures were too much, however, and the potential loss of customers to MSN forced a change,[10] and AOL announced that it would match flat rate pricing, taking effect December 1, 1996. Capacity is-

---

[10] At the time MSN also did not have flat rate pricing. MSN's announcement that it would switch became the final catalyst for AOL to make the change. Steve Case, AOL CEO, reminisced many years after the change that AOL had studied the potential switch for quite some time, but had not acted on it because management could anticipate a difficult transition.

> It came to a head over a weekend as Microsoft announced they were offering MSN on a flat rate basis, and it was clear they were planning to steal a lot of market share from AOL. So I decided within hours of their announcement that we had to match them, and the company worked throughout a weekend so we could make an announcement.

sues did emerge in many locales, manifesting as busy signals, just as AOL's executives had feared.[11] These well-publicized troubles continued for many months, earning AOL a poor reputation among some users. The bad publicity induced further entry by other ISPs looking to acquire customers fleeing the busy phone lines. Ultimately, AOL survived the bad publicity through a series of new investments in facilities, new arrangement for content, and more intense marketing—that is, carpet bombing of trial CDs. That was not a foregone conclusion throughout most of early 1997.

This experience led AOL to alter many aspects of its business. It positioned itself as "the Internet and a whole lot more."[12] In the following year AOL sold off its facilities for access and contracted with others to manage them, while also acquiring the customers of CompuServe. While it became a software company primarily, its software became the most common gateway to the web in the United States in the late 1990s.

TENSIONS WITH THE PRICING MODEL

Throughout 1996, 1997, and 1998, ISPs experimented with hourly limits and high marginal pricing above the limit. These experiments largely failed, and those failures demonstrated how binding the unlimited contract became as a norm for pricing. The experiments responded to a stark problem: Many technical users, and even some nontechnical users, stayed online for more than twenty to thirty hours a month, ruining the key economics that allowed ISPs to share equipment across many users.

High usage could happen for a variety of reasons. For example, some technical users simply enjoyed being online for large lengths of time, surfing the growing Internet and web. Some users began to operate businesses from their homes, remaining online throughout the entire workday. Some users simply forgot to log off, leaving their computers running and tying up the telephone line supporting the connection to the PC. And some users grew more experienced and found a vast array of activities more attractive over time. The list of reasons went on and on.

See http://www.quora.com/AOL/How-did-AOL-make-the-decision-to-go-to-an-all-you-can-eat-pricing-strategy/, accessed November 2012.

[11] Less than three weeks later a company spokesman said seven million AOL customers in the United States were conducting 30 percent more daily online sessions, lasting an average of 20 percent longer. San Jose Mercury News (1996).

[12] See http://www.quora.com/AOL/How-did-AOL-make-the-decision-to-go-to-an-all-you-can-eat-pricing-strategy/, accessed November 2012.

Many ISPs tried to offer limited contracts in addition to their unlimited contracts, discounting the price (from the unlimited benchmark) in exchange for the limit. Most such limits were not particularly binding—involving monthly limits ranging from sixty to one hundred hours—unless the user remained online for hours at a time most days of the month. Some ISPs tried offering steep discounts for steep limits, such as $10 discounts for thirty hours a month. Yet few buyers took them, persisting with the slightly more expensive unlimited contracts.

A number of ISPs also included fine print that allowed them to automatically log off users after a large number of consecutive hours, or after their accounts remained inactive for a fixed period, such as thirty minutes. Because some customers were unaware of or did not read the fine print, they perceived such types of automatic logging off as poor service or unreliable equipment from the supplier. Consequently, many small ISPs hesitated to employ this approach.

A few ISPs deliberately adopted contracting policies that tried to move the costliest users by refusing to offer unlimited contracts and thereby forcing all users into hourly limits per month. Such limits imposed costs on only the most intensive users, which was a strategy to induce their most expensive customers to migrate to another vendor. If an ISP already had a strong customer base, the loss of a few intensive and costly users was perceived as a gain.

As in urban or high-density environments, limits also arose in settings without many suppliers, such as low-density environments. Some ISPs adopted limits because there was no substitute and this was the simplest way for them to limit the expensive user's activity. Because such actions were more common among ISPs in low-density environments, it suggested the practice could survive more easily in the face of less competition.

Despite all these experiments, the unlimited contract dominated transactions. One survey of pricing contracts in May 1996 found that nearly 75 percent of the ISPs offering 28K service (the maximum dial-up speed at the time) offered a limited plan in addition to their unlimited plan. That dropped to nearly 50 percent by August. By March 1997 it was 33 percent, 25 percent by January 1998, and less than 15 percent by January 1999.[13]

[13]See Stranger and Greenstein (2006, 2007).

Overall, why did unlimited prices become the norm? Once the market moved to that general practice, ISPs could not find many takers for the alternatives. Competitive forces kept matters oriented toward the user's preferences for unlimited capacity. Demand and competition forced suppliers to adapt, and ISPs had to figure out how to manage their businesses to support that preference.

Geographic Spreading

Not all ISPs were alike. Different firms came to different conclusions about how much territory to cover. Broadly speaking, ISPs could be divided into three groups, backbone providers, national access providers, and local access providers. Before 1996 it was unclear how these would differ. After the emergence of a pricing norm, all used the same basic economies of POPs. Nonetheless, these three types of firms behaved differently.

The first group—the backbone providers—was private national firms (that is, MCI, Sprint, UUNET, BBN), the largest carriers of data, and the followers of the NSF's original plans. In 1995 and 1996, all of them carried traffic from NSF's NAPs and the CIX. Any regional ISP could exchange traffic with them. This aspect of backbone behavior would begin to change in 1997, but not at this crucial moment, when the ISPs were trying to overcome the adaptation and circular conundrums. At this point, the backbone of the US Internet resembled a mesh, with every large firm both interconnecting with every other and exchanging traffic with smaller firms, just as NSF had conceived of it by fostering many NAPs.

The mesh carried from the backbone to the retail level. Many of these same national firms also provided retail ISP services to consumers or to other ISPs that rented rights to resell use of their modem banks. Not all took the same approach, but in a mesh it did not mater. Some of these firms owned their own fiber (for example, MCI) and some of them ran their backbones on fiber rented from others (for example, UUNET).

The next two groups, the national and local providers, were ISPs that ranged in size and scale from wholesale regional firms down to the local ISP handling a small number of dial-in customers. Many of the largest firms developed familiar brand names, such as EarthLink, Sprint, AT&T, IBM Global Network, AOL, and MindSpring. Other large firms included entrants or Internet insiders from the NSF, such as PSINet, Netcom, ANS, and GTE (which in 1997 acquired assets from BBN [Bolt, Beranek and

Newman] Planet) and others. Still others offered ISP services to consumers (for example, AOL and MSN), and might not own any facilities. They rented it from others (such as ANS), though users did not necessarily know this.

Market share at the retail level was skewed. A couple dozen of the largest firms accounted for 75 percent of market share nationally and a couple hundred for 90 percent of market share. In other words, the majority of these ISPs were small dial-ups covering a small regional area, but the majority of users employed national providers.[14]

A large number of small ISPs began to flood the market in 1996. The rapid growth of ISPs seemed almost magical to users with no BBS or Internet experience, as ISPs seemed to pop up instantly out of nowhere, and in every major city. For example, in May 1996 *Boardwatch* listed prices for just over two thousand ISPs. In August it listed prices for 2,934 ISPs. The proliferation of ISPs continued. In February 1997 *Boardwatch* listed prices for 3,535, in January 1998 for 4,167, and in January 1999 for 4,511. In each case, though, the magazine listed many more ISPs for whom they did not have price information. The highest reported number in *Boardwatch* was just over seven thousand in March 2000.[15] Half of these ISPs supported only one phone number, and the vast majority of the rest supported anywhere from two to six hundred numbers. The vast majority of ISPs offered unlimited service.

Coincident with this growth, Internet access became widespread. Notably, providing Internet access was feasible to almost anyone with technical skill, especially former BBS operators, many of whom wanted to open a POP in uncovered territory. Many entrepreneurs perceived that AT&T and AOL did not appeal to every user, and a local ISP could tailor its services to local customer needs. The economies of POPs allowed ISPs to survive with comparatively small customer bases, serving limited geographic customer bases. Many small ISPs ran their own network POPs and provided limited geographic coverage.

Also, many small ISPs could cover their costs on a small scale. Moreover, few barriers existed for an ISP. The standard server software for

---

[14] The National Telecommunications and Information Administration (NTIA) surveys do not begin to track broadband users until August 2000, when the survey finds that 4.4 percent of US households are broadband users (with 41.5 percent of households being Internet users).

[15] See, e.g., Downes and Greenstein (2002, 2007). Also see Stranger and Greenstein (2006).

supporting an ISP, Apache, was available without restriction, and the necessary technical know-how for getting started did not differ greatly from routine knowledge found at a firm performing computing services or bulletin board services prior to commercialization. Apache ran on Unix, which was increasingly becoming Linux, and many ISPs were operated by programmers who had the technical skills to manage this type of server.

The mesh of the backbone helped. Many small firms leased lines from larger ISPs, such as Sprint, or externally managed POPs through a third party, such as AT&T or MCI, in locations where they did not have coverage. This allowed them to offer national phone numbers to their local customers, which meant they were, in effect, competing with commercial online services with national coverage.

Figure 8.1 comes from fall of 1996. This was the map that prompted Zvi Griliches's remark about the Internet and hybrid corn, which was quoted at the outset of the chapter. There was never any issue about getting some service, even in the worse situation. A user could make a long-distance phone call and get service, but the effective cost was higher. In that sense most agricultural counties in the United States lacked local ISPs. As a rule of thumb, if corn, cotton, or cows dominated the county's economy in 1996 then the probability of finding an ISP in the local calling area was quite low.

Broadly speaking, therefore, the locations lacking local Internet access also were the poorest urban areas or the smallest and most remote rural populations. Some of these areas bore signs of permanent retardation of development, as in Appalachia or the Mississippi delta regions.[16] But more than poverty was at work in many locations. Rural areas often lacked a competitive supply of providers, and even when suppliers existed, they sometimes provided limited services or focused on specific segments, such as business users.[17]

The geographic spread of access changed, and it changed rapidly. A comparison of the fall of 1996 and 1998 captures these changes. In the fall of 1996, the entire commercial ISP network was estimated to be twelve thousand phone numbers for over three thousand ISPs. By the fall of 1998, the estimates were over sixty-five thousand phone numbers for just over six thousand

---

[16]See Strover, Oden, and Inagaki (2002). See also Strover (2001).
[17]See Nicholas (2000).

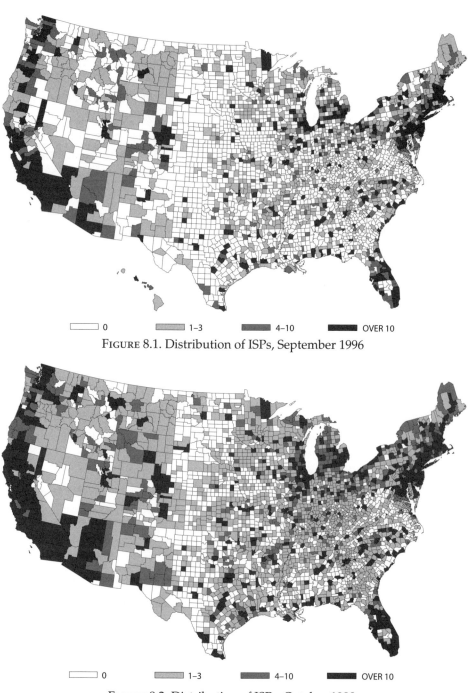

0   1–3   4–10   OVER 10

Figure 8.1. Distribution of ISPs, September 1996

0   1–3   4–10   OVER 10

Figure 8.2. Distribution of ISPs, October 1998

ISPs.[18] In addition, one estimate showed that in 1998 more than 92 percent of the US population had access through a local phone call to seven or more ISPs, and less than 5 percent did not have any access.[19] Almost certainly, these estimates are conservative. The actual percentage of the population without access to a competitive dial-up market was much lower than 5 percent.

Figure 8.2 shows the situation in 1998. While many ISPs had locations in all the major population centers, there were also some providers located in sparsely populated rural areas.[20] The commercial Internet had acquired the capacity to support the delivery of the Internet to half the households in the country, to virtually every medium and large business establishment, and to a large fraction of small businesses.

In 1996, national firms found it in their interest to offer service with somewhere between four and six hundred phone numbers and only in populations of fifty thousand or above. In contrast, the vast majority of the coverage in rural areas came from local ISPs. For rural counties with a population under fifty thousand, the providers were overwhelmingly local or regional.

In the fall of 1998, the equivalent figures for national firms were thirty thousand or lower, which indicates that some national firms had moved into slightly smaller areas and less dense geographic locations.[21] Additionally, many rural telephone cooperatives were opening Internet service. This followed long-standing traditions in small and rural cities to use collective quasi-public organizations to provide utility services that other private firms did not find profitable.

There was a dichotomy between the growth patterns of entrepreneurial firms that became national and those that became regional. National firms grew by starting with major cities across the country and then progressively moving to cities of smaller populations. Firms with a regional focus grew into geographically contiguous areas, seemingly regardless of urban or rural features.

The stark differences between figures 8.1 and 8.2 showed that ISPs had begun to invent a subtle solution to the adaptation conundrum. The arrangement borrowed from the practices that existed at bulletin boards and

[18] See Downes and Greenstein (1998).
[19] See Downes and Greenstein (2002).
[20] See Downes and Greenstein (2002) for a description of the dial-up market, or Downes and Greenstein (2007) for an analysis for why some areas had more entry than others.
[21] See Downes and Greenstein (2002).

the NSFNET, and, crucially, could be mastered by any technically oriented entrepreneur with the time to learn them. Involving a subtle combination of inventions at the POP level, changes to pricing, and alterations in operations to support inexpensive pricing, this solution built on the mesh and incorporated a response to local conditions, which put the ISP in a position to mediate between groups of local customers, their telephone companies, and the national backbone firms.

Experiments in Differentiation

By 1997 many users began to take flat rate pricing for granted. To attract users, ISPs had to respond to competitive pressure to offer flat rate pricing and something else users found appealing. For local ISPs especially, the volumes of customers generated revenue to cover costs but did not yield much profitability. These ISPs looked for additional revenue by offering additional services to their customers of ISP service.

A crucial question concerned how the user employed his or her browser. From an ISP's perspective, the question shaped the design of the opening home page—or, as it was subsequently labeled, *portal*—that users would see when they first clicked on their browser.[22] An ISP had three potential choices. Should it (1) design its own portal potentially at great expense, (2) default to another's portal, such as Excite or Yahoo!, or (3) leave the decision to a user altogether?

Different ISPs made distinct choices and learned different lessons about the trade-offs between these choices. For example, some ISPs maintained minimal home pages, which many marketed as a virtuous attempt to give users freedom to choose for themselves among Yahoo!, Excite, Lycos, and a myriad of other young portals then springing up. Of these, a portion succeeded with—or in some views, in spite of—this choice.

The choice AOL made was unique, and while it may seem savvy in retrospect, many Internet enthusiasts then regarded it as risky. Seeking to attract the nontechnical user, and building on its experience prior the rise of the Internet, AOL invested in a *walled garden*. This approach protected content and tailored it to users, or, in the eyes of technically sophisticated vendors, "spoon fed" content to users. As part of this strategy, AOL would

---

[22] For a review of technologies behind the browser and portal, and an analysis of the factors that shaped their evolution, see Haigh (2008).

merge with young firms or make deals with certain firms to feature their service or copyrighted content, making it easily accessible to users.[23] That left AOL controlling a large fraction of the user experience while sacrificing sophisticated users to other ISPs.

Yet AOL's strategy also continued activity it already had performed in the era of bulletin boards. Management thought that AOL's prior investments in community building would continue to have value as its users transitioned to using the Internet more frequently, and AOL further supplemented those actions with other practices that some of its largest rivals, such as CompuServe, did not pursue, such as using log-in names and e-mail addresses using natural language labels instead of combinations of letters and numbers.

Not all of the ISPs' choices succeeded. For example, CompuServe, Prodigy, and Genie all failed at an approach similar to AOL's. The success of AOL's campaign was frequently attributed to its aggressive marketing—particularly the "carpet bombing" of its disks in news inserts and other unlikely places,[24] which facilitated a trial use of its service in households across the United States.[25] As an interesting contrast, MSN attempted a similar marketing strategy, and, with the help of its marketing advantages and budgetary tolerance for operating losses, did not fail. Nevertheless, MSN was no better than a distant second to AOL in market share throughout the 1990s.

[23]See Elfenbein and Lerner (2003).

[24]The aggressive insertions began after Jan Brandt, chief marketing officer, had an inspiration at the local Blockbuster video rental store. Says Brandt:

> After a very long work week, I went into my local Blockbuster to rent some movies to help relax over the weekend. They had sample boxes filled with popcorn, small candies and coupons that they were giving away if you rented 3 movies. I took the box into work that Monday and we set out to get our disks inserted into these boxes. We got over a 3% response on this effort (for context, most insert programs like that would yield in the tenths of a percent). The dramatic success of this effort led to the acceleration of the alternative marketing programs we became known for where you'd find disks popping up in what seemed like unlikely places.

See http://www.quora.com/How-many-different-AOL-promo-discs-were-distributed, accessed November 2012.

[25]According to various recollections, this cost AOL approximately $35 per customer (Steve Case, CEO), with the firm logging in a new customer every six seconds (Jan Brandt, chief marketing officer). When AOL 4.0 was launched in 1998 AOL bought all the CD-ROMs produced on the planet for several weeks (Reggie Fairchild, product manager, AOL 4.0), yielding eight million additional users in a year. See http://www.quora.com/AOL-History /How-much-did-it-cost-AOL-to-distribute-all-those-CDs-back-in-the-1990s, accessed November 2012.

As a further example, in the mid- to late 1990s some cable companies believed they did not understand Internet users' requirements, so they ceded these decisions initially to others, such as, for example, @home, a new entrant that positioned its service for cable firms. Eventually, @home merged with Excite to gain access to the perceived advantage of owning a portal, a decision that was regretted later by several cable firms. When the cooperation between cable firms and @home/Excite ended, it produced a large amount of recrimination, and the transition was not smooth for users.[26]

Although this experiment was not financially successful for @home, the surviving firms—cable companies, in this case—learned valuable lessons about how to structure their ISP services. First, certain useful "investments" were recreated, such as geographic caching of content, and, second, certain "mistakes" were avoided, such as advertising. Cable companies depended on subscription revenue for access services thereafter.[27]

Many local ISPs sought to differentiate themselves from one another by offering additional services, such as hosting, web development, network services, high-speed access, and tailored content.[28] These services were in addition to e-mail, newsgroup service, or easy access to portal content, online account management, customer service, technical support, Internet training, and file space.[29]

Once again, ISPs in the major urban areas behaved differently from those in less dense settings. Table 8.1 shows the result of a survey for national, urban, and rural ISPs in 1998.[30] Virtually every ISP offered basic service, but the extras were far less common among small and/or rural ISPs. In general, a much lower percentage offered hosting, web development, network services, or high-speed services. In short, ISPs in the urban areas were more differentiated than those in the rural areas, and the larger ISPs also tended to be located more often in urban areas.

What lay behind the differences? ISPs approached the new opportunities with employees and entrepreneurs who possessed different skills, experiences, and commercial priorities. Some ISPs already had successful

---

[26]See, e.g., Rosston (2009).

[27]See, e.g., Rosston (2009) for an analysis of the changing views of cable firms about the source of value from controlling or not controlling a portal and ISP.

[28]See, e.g., Greenstein (2000b), O' Donnell (2001).

[29]For a review of these and related technologies, see Haigh (2008).

[30]These are a combination of the tables in Greenstein (2000a, 2000b).

PC businesses, or businesses offering network support services. Many of these investments could commit ISPs to offer a particular array of services, even before the full size of market demand was realized or the value of new commercial opportunities was fully known.

The ISPs also found themselves in widely different local circumstances. Areas differed in the number of ISPs, which led to very different local competitive pressure. In areas with multiple ISPs, not all came from the same background, leading to differences in approaches to differentiation. ISPs also could adopt different approaches to fostering long-term relationships with their customers, as well as anticipate different approaches to gaining revenue from such customers. Demand could vary over localities also, as some locales had many technical users and others had few.

An ISP's approach emerged out of combinations of these firm-specific and location-specific factors. Some ISPs would focus on specific customers, offering a cluster of services for that user base—for example, offering network support for small businesses in the area. Others tailored their services to a wide group of local customers—for example, offering hosting services to any household or small business that wanted to operate a web page. Some specialized in handholding activities, helping nontechnical customers walk through various stages of getting online, sending e-mail, and surfing. National ISPs most closely resembled their counterparts among urban local ISPs. As table 8.1 shows, national ISPs too had a higher propensity to offer additional services.

Most attempts at differentiation did not succeed at raising the price. At most, these helped attract customers or preserve market share. For example, small ISPs were largely unable to raise prices as the Internet improved. Many ISPs improved their own service in myriad ways, as did many complementors.[31] Yet such improvements were part of the standard package rather than vehicles for premium pricing.

An excellent illustration was the upgrade from 28K to 56K modems, which began in 1997 and accelerated in 1998. There were two price levels for a short time—with a higher premium for faster modem service, but by

---

[31] Most ISPs had adopted technologies to enable web pages to upload more quickly, either by improving dynamic web page allocation through caching or by making arrangements with Akamai for its service. In addition, browsers got better, and so did Apache, so every user's experience improved.

TABLE 8.1. Service lines of ISPs, 1998

Category definition	Most common service offered	ISPs, weighted by served territory	All ISPs	Small ISPs	Rural Small ISPs
Providing and servicing access through different channels	28.8, 56K, isdn, web TV, wireless access, T1, T3, DSL, frame relay, e-mail, domain registration, new groups, real audio, ftp, quake server, IRC, chat, video conferencing, cybersitter TM	28,967 (100%)	3,816 (100%)	2,089 (100%)	325 (100%)
Networking service and maintenance	Networking, intranet development, WAN, co-location server, network design, LAN equipment, network support, network service, disaster recovery, backup, database services, novell netware, SQL server	8,334 (28.8%)	789 (20.6%)	440 (21.1%)	36 (11.0%)
Website hosting	Web hosting, secure hosting, commercial site hosting, virtual ftp server, personal web space, web statistics, BBS access, catalog hosting	8,188 (28.2%)	792 (20.7%)	460 (22.0%)	45 (13.8%)
Web page development and servicing	Web consulting, active server, web design, java, perl, vrml, front page, secure server, firewalls, web business solutions, cybercash, shopping cart, Internet marketing, online marketing, electronic billing, database integration	13,809 (47.7%)	1,385 (36.3%)	757 (36.2%)	76 (23.3%)
High speed access	T3, DSL, xDSL, OC3, OC12, Access rate > 1,056K	15,846 (54.7%)	1,059 (27.8%)	514 (24.6%)	39 (12.0%)

Note: The category definitions give the most general aggregation of services, while the most common service offered provides self-described phrases for ISPs. Column 3 weights an ISP by the number of area codes it serves, while column 4 treats each ISP as a single unit. Column 5 examines a subset of column 4, small ISPs, defined as any ISP covering less than five area codes. Column 6 examines a subset of Column 5, small ISPs outside of the over five hundred urban counties, where urban is defined as a MSA by the 1990 census.

late 1998, the twenty-dollar price umbrella prevailed once again.[32] In other words, the primary gatekeepers for access did not capture a higher fraction of the value from improvements in the network's many components.

Although most ISPs could not raise prices, few saw any reason to lower them—especially if users were reluctant to give up e-mail addresses or other services to which they had grown accustomed. Accordingly, many ISPs adopted policies refusing to forward e-mail for former customers, as a way to make users reluctant to switch ISPs.

What else kept prices from falling more rapidly?[33] By continuing to invest in content inside their walled gardens ISPs such as AOL recognized the value of those gardens for their customers and endeavored to keep them from migrating elsewhere. Switching e-mail was costly, and AOL also invested in and facilitated community development with services, such as instant messaging and chat rooms. Once ensconced in these applications with a familiar group of friends, users were reluctant to leave AOL and comfortable communities. In addition, instant message users did not want to recreate their buddy lists for another platform.

Growing a New Source of Revenue

No single administrative agency could possibly have built and managed the commercial network that emerged after 1995. The shape, speed, growth, and use of the commercial Internet after 1995 were not foreseen within the government circles responsible for its birth. That was not due to any oversight or error, and it occurred in spite of comparatively benign motives from the overseers, as well as abundant advice from the best technical experts in the world.

The commercial network grew rapidly. Access fees generated most of the revenue during the first decade of the commercial Internet. The typical household spent more than three-quarters of its time online at free or

---

[32]Stranger and Greenstein (2006).

[33]The declines each year were no more (on average) than a dollar reduction for a monthly contract. See Stranger and Greenstein (2006) for estimates of price trends for non-AOL services. The Bureau of Labor Statistics began a price series for Internet access after December 1997. The series is dominated by the pricing of the largest firms (AOL in particular), so this series shows less than a half of 1 percent decline in prices between its inception in December 1997 and December 2002.

TABLE 8.2. Adjusted revenue for access markets, 1998–2003
(millions of dollars)

Year	1998	1999	2000	2001	2002	2003
Dial-up	5,499	8,966	12,345	13,751	14,093	14,173
DSL		228	1,245	2,822	4,316	6,954
Cable modem	138	274	903	2,600	4,117	7,372

ad-supported sites, devoting most of its Internet budget to access fees, not subscription fees.[34]

The US Census Bureau began tracking ISP revenue as a separate revenue category in 1998. Table 8.2 provides an adjusted summary of these reports.[35] Several sources suggest that between 60 percent and 75 percent of the revenue in table 8.2 came from households, depending on the year and access mode. The remainder comes from business users of Internet access. The growth in revenues in table 8.2—from $5.5 billion in 1998 to over $28 billion in 2003—is astonishing for an entirely new market, especially one that did not start growing quickly until after 1995. Broadband revenues constitute approximately half the total revenue over the eight years, beginning with less than 6 percent in 1999 and growing to half of the total revenue in 2003.

To say it simply, the adaptation and circular conundrum were overcome with remarkable alacrity. A range of foresighted and complementary investments came together in a short period—the newly privatized Internet and its mesh, the newly privatized browser in commercial form, a few intrepid websites and portals to organize the experience, and commercial ISPs with a digestible form of the service that generated revenue. Together these activities added up to a commercial system nobody could have forecast. The Internet became attractive to more than just technical users. Most astonishing of all, it became available almost everywhere in the United States.

[34]See Goldfarb (2004).
[35]For all the details see the appendix to Greenstein and McDevitt (2012).

9

Virulent Word of Mouse

The Internet is a telephone system that's gotten uppity.
—*Clifford Stoll*[1]

Electronic mail does not resemble Tupperware in any tangible dimension. Yet in 1995, Tim Draper saw a connection, and his flash of insight came at a propitious moment, when commercial motives would predominantly begin to shape the rate, direction, and tone of collective invention for Internet applications and infrastructure. Tim Draper had taken a circuitous path to this moment. In 1985 Draper formed a venture capital (VC) firm in Menlo Park, California, eventually partnering with John Fisher and Steve Jurvetson to form Draper, Fisher, and Jurvetson, or, DFJ, which specialized in funding entrepreneurs aspiring to start new firms. The company especially sought intrepid entrepreneurs who shot for the moon. Not a business for the faint of heart in practice, DFJ took *many* big risks on many big bets, so that the entire return did not depend on only a few eggs in one basket. In practice, however, usually only a few big winners emerged, and these generated large returns for the company's entire portfolio of investments.

In the summer of 1995, DFJ backed a start-up by two unknown entrepreneurs, Sabeer Bhatia and Jack Smith. The firm was called HoTMaiL, embedding HTML in the firm's name.[2] Bhatia and Smith did not reveal their business idea to DFJ right away. They were paranoid about venture capitalists—not of DFJ in particular, but of anyone and everyone.

---

[1] http://www.linuxjournal.com/article/2608, accessed October 2012.
[2] The name HoTMaiL emerged from the business plan. The name signified that the service was built on HTML, so it could be used anywhere on the web.

FIGURE 9.1 Tim Draper, founder and managing director, DFJ
(photo taken by Michael Soo; March 6, 2007)

FIGURE 9.2 Steve Jurvetson, founder and managing director, DFJ
(photo by Asa Mathat, March 6, 2014)

Bhatia and Smith had met while working at Apple Computer, and both later left to work at a start-up called FirePower Systems. The idea of HoT-MaiL came to them while they worked at FirePower. Aspiring to start a company, they could not e-mail back and forth without increasing the risk that their supervisor would see them discussing nonwork matters. They each had AOL e-mail, but that system also raised risks, because it relied on software on the desktop—that is, the software had to reside within the PC—and the office did not permit AOL software on its systems.[3] This restriction helped generate Smith's idea to design e-mail accounts that were accessible over the web, using any browser from any location.[4] Because both entrepreneurs believed that other Internet users faced the same problem that they themselves encountered at work, Bhatia and Smith thought that a general service of web-based e-mail would have wide appeal. They quickly developed a business plan.

Their paranoia and sense of urgency emerged after they hatched their plan. The two entrepreneurs correctly assumed that any technically skilled programmer familiar with the growing web could understand the plan, and, therefore, imitate it. The key idea was rather easy to copy once communicated to a knowledgeable listener, as would happen during a presentation to VCs. If Bhatia and Smith made the presentation but did not receive funding, then they would have given their idea to someone else who could copy it. In fact, they had more reason to be paranoid than they knew: other firms and inventors were independently pursuing similar ideas at the same time, though most of these efforts were not widely known.[5]

Bhatia and Smith decided to test the business savvy and trustworthiness of the VCs by using a fake business plan. They invented a Potemkin business.[6] If the two of them liked how the VCs reacted to their Potemkin business, then they would reveal their actual plan. The fake concerned an idea for a business that Bhatia and Smith had previously considered and rejected.[7]

Bhatia and Smith persevered in the face of twenty rejections, or in their view, twenty VCs to whom they would not reveal their true aspirations. At that point they reached DFJ and ran through the routine in front of Tim Draper and the intellectually peripatetic Steve Jurvetson. The VCs were not

[3] In time AOL would offer e-mail accounts that did not require downloading their software to the desktop, but at this point it was not available.

[4] For the long account, see Bronson (1998).

[5] The most widely publicized effort was undertaken by Lotus for its cc:mail service offering. It too involved using a web browser to access e-mail from any location. See InfoWorld (1995a, 1995b).

[6] Grigory Potemkin led the military conquest of Crimea, and allegedly created false villages to impress Catherine II and her entourage during her visit to Crimea in 1787. Accordingly, a Potemkin village refers to a village of false facades.

[7] The business concerned an Internet-based personal database they called JavaSoft.

impressed, but in Bhatia's view, Jurvetson did something no other VC had done. He asked the right questions about the Potemkin business. The two entrepreneurs indicated to each other that they were satisfied, as the VCs impatiently got ready to dismiss them if there was nothing else. At that point, Bhatia and Smith revealed their big idea for web-based e-mail, which struck a chord with the VCs. The conversation became animated. And somewhere in the ensuing cacophony, electronic mail met Tupperware.

Tim Draper thought back to a case he had seen in business school about Tupperware's marketing arrangement.[8] Tupperware had learned to inexpensively distribute and market its products by circumventing expensive retail distribution channels by working with homemakers, who acted as the sales force and were paid on commission. A representative would invite friends to a "Tupperware party." Friends would invite more friends, and so on. It involved no expensive retail outlets or ad campaigns, and it required minimal regular staff.

As Draper listened to the entrepreneurs, he thought about how e-mail could emulate Tupperware by circumventing standard distributional channels for computer software, and thereby cutting out a big potential expense while remaining very effective. What if a user of an e-mail service could invite another friend to use the same service, just as the Tupperware sales force could invite their friends? Draper voiced a way to implement it. He suggested placing the URL of the e-mail service in the footer of every electronic mail message, letting the social network of each user help spread the service. He suggested that the hyperlink at the bottom of every e-mail contain a message, "P.S. I love you. Get your free Web-based email at HoTMaiL." Clicking on the hyperlink would take the user to HoTMaiL's site to sign up for the service.

Initially Bhatia and Smith pushed back, liking neither the idea nor the specific phrasing. They had many reasons to resist. For example, the idea mixed elements from modular layers of the Internet by crossing the content of the specific electronic mail message with the language of the World

---

[8]Draper also thought of Tupperware in the context of chess strategy. One approach to chess strategy involves thinking multiple steps ahead. As Draper considered how one person would contact another in HoTMaiL, he began to think multiple steps ahead and envisioned that one user would contact another, who would then contact another, and so on. Tim Draper, private communication, August 2008.

Wide Web. Mixing modular layers stepped across a line that good programmers knew instinctively not to cross.

After many arguments the founders eventually relented, agreeing to include a link, but only if they dropped "P.S. I love you." That left the phrase "Get your free Web-based email at HoTMaiL" as a hot link on every e-mail. It took another day to strike the final deal after some brinkmanship over the ownership stakes. DFJ wanted 30 percent ownership for a $300,000 investment, while Bhatia and Smith wanted them to have 15 percent, effectively doubling the valuation of the company. The entrepreneurs eventually got the terms they wanted.

There was not much of a marketing budget for HoTMaiL, and all would learn quickly that it would not matter. As the service opened, it initially received uptake at addresses within the *edu* domain, with thousands of students signing up at universities. It then began to spread to other universities, and registration on the service mushroomed. Within a few weeks it had spread to India, reaching one hundred thousand Indian users three weeks after the first registration within that country. Less than six months into the launch, HoTMaiL had one million registered users, and by the following year, at the end of 1997, it had twelve million.

The rate of growth was astonishing, and even more astonishing was the cost. It had cost almost nothing to acquire new users. On December 29, 1997, a few days after reaching twelve million registrants, founders Sabeer Bhatia and Jack Smith sold the company to Microsoft for $400 million in Microsoft stock.[9] Bhatia became the new general manager of strategic business development for MSN.com, a position he stayed at for one year.

Two inventions occurred at that meeting with DFJ. HoTMaiL invented a business, and it would become one of many businesses oriented toward delivering a browser-oriented e-mail service.[10] A second invention emerged too, a method for acquiring new users for a new web service. Observers said HoTMaiL spread like a viral infection moving between people via a handshake,[11] so the process eventually went by several labels, among them

[9]Ransdell (1999).

[10]For example, DFJ was one investor in another successful web-based e-mail service, RocketMail, founded by Four11 Corporation, which competed directly with HoTMaiL. Managed with an internal firewall, RocketMail was acquired by Yahoo! in October 1997, after they passed on buying HoTMaiL. It eventually became the basis for Yahoo Mail. See Pelline (1997b).

[11]Greenstein (1999).

"viral marketing" and "word of mouse."[12] In the next half decade viral marketing showed up in thousands of entrepreneurial pitches.

A little myth making was invented that day as well. In popular imagination, HoTMaiL's invention emerged miraculously, as if out of the air. Its arrival and spread seemed especially fast to those who had not followed the development of the privatized Internet.

Looking more deeply, this was inventive specialization at work, and as part of a commercial network. A new application had simply employed existing infrastructure by working through a browser. Needing only to add some basic programming, the costs of developing the application were therefore low. Due to the modular structure, an inventive specialist could confine his or her effort and attention to the factors shaping an application, such as its features, operation, and marketing.

Inventive specialization was so powerful because so much lay behind the surface of what a user saw. An inventor could give the user a simple set of functions. As Brian Kahin, founding director, Harvard Information Infrastructure Project, said,[13]

> Digitization enables modularization with documented interfaces at one level while it also makes it possible to integrate functions, hide them from users, and make them look like a unified whole with no points of access other than a single user interface.

Demand conditions also had changed in a fundamental way. Privatization of the Internet had widened the set of potential users. No longer would inventive specialists depend on the assessment of administrators at universities, or the aesthetic preferences of the users from the Internet's academic community. What had replaced these preferences? That was an open question to contemporaries at the time. Nobody knew for certain what services nonacademic users would want, what services they would pay for, or how much they would pay for these new services.

Even the most optimistic venture capitalist did not forecast how inventive specialization would play out within commercial markets over the next half decade. Inventive specialists of all stripes would tap into a scale of demand far greater than any forecaster had dared utter at the outset of

---

[12] Greenstein (1999).
[13] Brian Kahin, private communication, October 4, 2013.

privatization. That would motivate an enormous and impatient explosion of economic activity.

A Boom at Its Adolescence

In his 1996 book *Only the Paranoid Survive*, the CEO of Intel, Andy Grove, remarked about the difficulty in foreseeing a fundamental change in business until those changes are right on top of the management.

> Most strategic inflexion points, instead of coming in with a bang, approach on little cat feet. They are often not clear until you can look at events in retrospect.[14]

The Internet had crept up on the computing market on little cat's feet, and the perception noticeably changed in 1995. The Internet market became vested with a degree of excitement and energy that insiders could sense. Netscape's founding and the release of its new browser began to generate excitement about the new era, but no doubts were left after Netscape's IPO in August 1995 and Microsoft's announcement in December 1995 that it would enter into making browsers as well. A considerable number of new businesses were launched in the ensuing year, further adding to the sense of anticipation and urgency.

Contemporaries called it a boom, which continued unabated for five years until the decline in traded prices for many Internet-related stocks began in the spring of 2000. Those prices rebounded for a short time, but subsequently reached a nadir in the fall of 2001 after the 9/11 World Trade Center terrorist attack sent much activity in the US economy into shock. After the fact, contemporaries called the decline a bust.

The boom coincided with something very real and substantive—namely, changes in Internet participation, both in its breadth and intensity. During this era the Internet became available for use in a variety of contexts, and many decision makers faced a choice about whether to make use of the

---

[14]Grove (1996). For a time Grove's phrase about little cat's feet was widely quoted. Where did it come from? It is borrowed from a Carl Sandburg poem about fog. "The fog comes / on little cat feet. / It sits looking / over harbor and city / on silent haunches / and then moves on." Grove would have been familiar with this poem from living on the peninsula of the San Francisco Bay Area. Almost every summer evening Pacific fog crawls over the hills west of Intel's headquarters and moves east on its way to the California Central Valley.

Internet or not. Unlike prior experience in universities and libraries, where users typically participated without personal expense, in the new era, participation was a commercial choice and a cost was attached to that participation. Many potential participants—households and businesses—chose to pay the price and participate, and some chose to invest heavily. The vast majority of these decisions were made after 1995 and, as will be discussed subsequently, only a select few of them were reversed after 2001.

Contemporaries needed an explanation for the increasing participation on the web. Several labels emerged. One of those labels, killer app, or killer application, eventually stuck. This label focused on the deployment of the browser and was a term borrowed from commercial computing. In personal computing a killer app delivered valuable functions and motivated a user to buy the application and all the complementary components (for example, a printer and PC). In the early history of computing, the killer apps had been word processors and spreadsheets.

By analogy the browser appeared to be the killer application of the web, just as electronic mail had been the killer app of the Internet prior to privatization. Many users were attracted to both applications, and their functionality motivated PC users to purchase modems, Internet-access service, and related software. For some non-PC users the suite of applications motivated them to purchase the PC and its affiliated complements. Thus, as will be discussed here, the killer app analogy captures a grain of truth about increased participation at home and in business.

Applications for the browser came from an entrant generically known as the dot-com, which led to the next label for this era, the dot-com boom. The label came from a feature of the domain name system for the Internet, which initially designated five types of domain names: gov, net, org, edu, and com.[15] Gov was for government entities and edu for educational institutions. Net, org, and com were designated for nonprofit and private entities, organizations, and networks. Com became the most popular by far among commercial firms, even for firms not based in the United States. The domain name, .com, had not received much attention prior to privatization because it had been reserved for commercial firms. In short, the

---

[15]Every country was assigned control over the allocation of domain names underneath its two-letter country code. The country code for the United States is US, but com, net, edu, gov, and org presume US sovereignty.

label, dot-com boom, also contained a grain of truth, as it stressed the commercial orientation of the many start-ups offering such changes.

Several popular labels stressed the macroscale of events, as entrepreneurs and established businesses engaged in a wide range of new thinking across many business activities—in back-office computing, home computing, and information retrieval activities in information-intensive industries, such as finance, warehousing logistics, news, entertainment, and more. Applications emerged for shopping for goods, planning for vacations, updating accounts, finding romantic companions, conducting transactions, experiencing erotic pleasures, investigating leisurely diversions, sharing experience with others, ticketing for traveling, understanding financial investing, and updating on the latest news. Thus because of the unprecedented nature of the rate of investment of new applications designed to enhance business processes, as well as investment in the infrastructure to support that growth, there was yet another grain of truth in labeling the Internet market as a macroscale of events.

Among such labels, entrepreneurs stressed the use of aggressive tactics in support of fostering these goods, such as viral marketing and the low expense for acquiring new users (as in HoTMaiL, for example). They also stressed maximum leverage of the existing Internet infrastructure for fast entry and quick growth. Deferring attempts to increase revenue until later, their emphasis focused on the strategies that aimed to gain users quickly. With prominent venture money to put such actions into practice, these strategies were sometimes labeled as "get big fast."[16] In the hands of the most enthusiastic advocates, get big fast was one example among many. It became interpreted in light of a broad principle: Internet business operated according to an unprecedented set of rules and norms, distinct from the fundamental benchmarks found in normal businesses up until that time. Those looking for a broad label called the entire movement "the new economy."

While founded on a substantive observation about investment behavior and strategies to support it, labels were nonetheless merely shorthand. Their meaning changed. One change was not profound. It resulted from competition between firms, and the broad pattern was familiar from other software markets. Something akin to an arms race between competitors emerged over features that appealed to users. This type of arms race arose

[16]Kirsch and Goldfarb (2008).

in browser markets, in many applications of electronic commerce to retailing, and in many applications of electronic commerce to publishing. This and other chapters will describe some of these arms races in detail. Technical insiders were acutely aware of the progress, and debated the market value of each technical advance. Insiders debated the strategic value of clustering different technical advances together in expensive and complex services, and, for example, compared that with the merits of removing expensive features to make a low-cost service appeal to a specific set of users. This type of arms race does not evolve in a linear direction, but, instead by fits and starts, as new proposals are tried, improved, or withdrawn. Winners emerge, losers leave, and during a boom the attention of insiders flits from one event to another.

If the new economy had involved only arms races, it would have been unusual for the scale of the market and number of participants, but not otherwise distinctive. A second change emerged, however, and it gave the boom its unusual flavor. The meaning of the new economy mutated over the course of the boom. The mutation had its origins in blurred boundaries between the (actual) substance of investment and the (as yet unrealized) forecast of its consequence. While early advocates for business in the commercial Internet were careful not to take the outcome for granted, later advocates eschewed such caution. They began to presume a large payoff was inevitable without questioning deeply the evidence for or against such a presumption.

This presumption was most evident in the strategies of many firms that aspired to get big fast. Often their business plan took a cavalier approach to generating revenue. Their business plan would aspire to grow an "installed base" of loyal users and generate revenue later, typically with unspecified plans for selling ads or charging loyal users a fee to retain service. It was as if generating the revenue was regarded as easy, while attracting loyal users required the greatest explanation.

Early on, a number of analysts for the new economy sprang up to help others navigate investing in and partnering with entrepreneurs. For example, one of the first systematic studies of the value chain for Internet services took place at Morgan Stanley, a Wall-Street-based investment firm with a wide range of clients. Morgan Stanley had managed the Netscape IPO and looked to step from that activity into leadership in a range of Internet investing. A forward-looking and ambitious analyst of software firms,

Mary Meeker, led the analysis. Along with her colleague, Chris DePuy, an engineer turned analyst of networking companies, they published an early and widely read study for investors called *The Internet Report*.[17] The report analyzed many firms with the ability to take advantage of the growing adoption of the web-based Internet. The report followed conventional norms for financial analysis, clarified the value chain and its leaders, and showed care about the links between investment and returns.

A new group of analysts and pundits also showed up and grabbed attention from the established line of analysts, such as Meeker and those similarly positioned, who were accustomed to speaking to a small group of professional investors. This new group did not have experience and considerable in-house investigative resources to build and enhance a reputation. Instead of aiming for the small audience of professional investors, the new group aspired to reach a new and growing audience—individual investors, hobbyists, entrepreneurs, and executives at existing firms who sought to understand the new economy. Analysts such as Henry Blodget appealed to this wider audience by speaking the language of the entrepreneurs and gaining notoriety for making predictions out of sync with the established analysts.[18] Many futurists, such as George Gilder,[19] also grabbed prominence, in this case, for offering a vision consistent with the enthusiasm of many entrepreneurs. As the Internet became a magnet for all manner of futurist, pundit, consultant, and analyst, the most enthusiastic advocates for the new economy found their spokesmen among a group that contemporaries called the *digerati*.[20] Later chapters will discuss their role at greater length.

Internet exceptionalism grew from these roots because it served the interest of entrepreneurs and many digerati, and it played to the hopes of many of them that they could succeed through emersion in the present setting. Internet exceptionalism argued that businesses based on web services

---

[17] Meeker and DePuy (1996).

[18] Blodget first received widespread attention in the fall of 1998 for forecasting the rise of Amazon's stock to (then an unheard of price of) $400. This is described in chapter 12.

[19] George Gilder writes on a wide set of topics, including information technology, for many prominent publications. This is described in chapter 12.

[20] The term combined digital and literati. The origin of the term predates the boom, arising first in 1992, and originally stressed writers that promoted their vision of digital technology. During the boom *digirati* took on additional meanings, denoting celebrity status among many involved in the dot-com boom. See, e.g., Markoff (1992), and Brockman (1996).

could develop quickly, using existing Internet infrastructure and new web tools. It also argued that Internet businesses would grow online businesses superior to those followed by established firms, once again, playing to the hopes of many entrepreneurs that established firm were encumbered by old ideas and existing ways of doing business. This view presumed that the business rules of established businesses were outmoded, obsolete, and destined to fail in confrontation with the best start-ups from the new economy. It also argued that executives in established firms had either outmoded views and inappropriate technology or organizational structures that prevented extending their business activities usefully into Internet-oriented activities.

Internet exceptionalism also began rejecting the conventional benchmarks of financial capitalism, such as referencing price/earnings ratios within a specific range. This presumption was, at best, grounded in the view that Internet start-ups would grow to extraordinary levels of revenue, replacing established firms. Accordingly, the financial value of leading publicly traded firms in the new economy began to rise far above levels that conventional analysis would support. During the boom the stocks for a number of firms benefited from this rise, including Cisco, Amazon, Netscape for a short while, Yahoo!, AOL, and many others.

The digerati began to use their own terms and vocabulary in sync with entrepreneurial ambitions. Presentations and business plans would stress their aspiration to "get big fast" through the use of processes affiliated with the new economy, such as viral marketing in the pursuit of "disruptive technology"[21] and as part of a "pure play"[22] in an act of "disintermediation."[23] A common public occurrence in this era had the digerati diagramming

---

[21] This term was first popularized in 1995 in Bower and Christensen (1995), then in an expanded description in Christensen (1997). The original publications offered a very specific mechanism—when a new technology with lower capabilities grows over time in functionality, eventually competing with firms who initially underestimated the potential for change. The term then mutated to encompass a much wider set of phenomena—almost any change with technical underpinnings that threatened to lower the value of services offered by an established firm, much more than analyzed within the original books.

[22] By this is meant the business provides only an Internet-oriented face to potential customers. These businesses leveraged other aspects of the Internet to achieve lower overhead expenses and then they competed with large brands.

[23] This term generally refers to removal of some firm or other commercial participant in a value chain in order to save cost. In the context of the times, this term often referred to, for example, Internet-enabled processes substituting travel agents with the use of online ticketing.

flows of economic activity that the Internet and web could support, usually arguing that the Internet would replace a flow of activities that previously had been accomplished entirely with tangible activities. Enormous numbers of entrepreneurs with these ambitions raised funds and aspired to implement their ideas in tangible processes. Entire conferences became devoted to these aspirations, and the trend acquired many of the trappings of a large social movement in which the members derided critics as outsiders who "did not get it."

Geography deserves a share of responsibility in fostering this movement. Participants in the commercial Internet shared their interests with one another, interacted with one another in a self-referential way, and, like normal humans, tended not to converse with skeptics or others that held contrary views. Enthusiasm for new Internet businesses was no different than the environmental movement or PC enthusiasts of an earlier era. The concentration of so many of these participants in a small number of places—Silicon Valley; Seattle; New York; Boston; Washington, DC; and the Research Triangle, North Carolina—positively reinforced one another's sense of belonging to something greater than themselves. To its participants the movement felt large enough to be self-sustaining, and in the absence of any large and visible shock, participants had every reason to continue their conversation.

Events eventually contradicted the premises underlying Internet exceptionalism, but the understanding that Internet exceptionalism was based on faulty logic and wildly optimistic expectations only emerged in retrospect. This revisionism eventually heaped ridicule on those who wasted resources under the guise of pursuing the new economy, but that was far down the road.[24] That retrospective bias should not shape our understanding of the phenomenon as it emerged.

Internet exceptionalism survived in the face of skeptical remarks from leaders with considerable authority and public stature. Here are two examples of skeptics who could not dent the tide. First, Andy Grove, president of Intel, continually (and incorrectly) publicly forecast that the end of the boom was near. He became known as the boy who cried wolf.[25] Before the bust his warnings had little public resonance. As another example,

---

[24] A particularly sardonic account of the wasted resource includes Kaplan (2002).
[25] See Heilemann (2001).

consider Carl Shapiro and Hal Varian—respectively, professor from the Haas School of Business, and dean of the Information School, both at University of California, Berkeley. They published a book in 1999 with Harvard Business School Press titled *Information Rules: A Strategic Guide to the Network Economy*. They openly criticized many new-economy philosophical tenets by arguing that mainstream economic models provided the basis for analytical insight. Addressing managers, they state in the introduction:

> The thesis of this book is that durable economics principles can guide you in today's frenetic business environment. Technology changes. Economic laws do not. If you are struggling to comprehend what the Internet means for you and your business, you can learn a great deal from the advent of the telephone system a hundred years ago.

The book became a best seller, and it is often credited with motivating many conservative business executives to take action. Yet in spite of wide circulation, as well as the authority of the opinions, it did not dent the overarching tide of enthusiasm for Internet exceptionalism among its supporters.

It was as if a fever had gripped many decision makers and entrepreneurs. To those not under its power this fever appeared like a lovesickness that clouded judgment. The warnings of authorities were treated selectively, like the wise musings of an older uncle whose insights about his generation seemed distant from the present. To those under its spell, the combination of resources and perception (as well as, perhaps, misperception) provided business owners, investors, and entrepreneurs with the courage and justification to take risky actions, to take the leap of faith needed at the start of a new entrepreneurial venture.

Seen on its own terms, the new economy philosophy offered a self-reinforcing system of beliefs. This system argued that investors traded effort in the short run for riches eventually, and the confident rhetoric reduced the perceived risk to entrepreneurial start-ups. Prior generations of entrepreneurs had faced stiff competition with existing firms that had many comparative advantages, such as established brands, operations, and investments, as well as loyal customers. Prior generations of start-ups had faced a steep challenge, trying to attract customers with their new service and operations. The new economy arguments argued that these challenges were less salient to the experience in the new economy. They convinced many investors to give money to start-ups—many of whom went public or sold out to existing firms. It also convinced many managers, engineers, and executives to change their careers in the hope of starting such firms, or joining one.

Later chapters will return to Internet exceptionalism in the context of describing particular application markets, such as the slow evolution of events leading to the dot-com bust, or the rise of advertising to support portals and search engines, and these examples will provide details about the decline of this system of beliefs. The remainder of the chapter turns to the real side of the economy and provides illustrations and outlines of three types of investment activities that were composed in the new economy:

1. Entrepreneurial entry;
2. Adoption of browser-based Internet services by homes;
3. Adoption of browser-based Internet services by businesses.

These three groups were big investors, but not the only investors. As that adoption accelerated it motivated two types of investment that worked with the increasing number of Internet users, translating it into routine and pervasive processes at a large scale. Those investments are the subject of the next chapter. In other words, two additional investors join the above three, and these two focused on:

4. Enhancement of business processes by existing businesses; and
5. Capital deepening in the infrastructure to support all these activities.

Although uncoordinated by any single entity, it was as if all five of these disparate economic actors simultaneously agreed to build the commercial Internet at a scale that would make it ubiquitous for mass markets, and would do so with a pervasive sense of urgency.

Entrepreneurial Entry and the Start-Up Boom

As the Internet built up, it began to take on a great size, one that quickly began to remind venture capitalists of the PC boom, which had been the largest previous entrepreneurial boom. Eventually the scope of aspirations exceeded any prior boom. The breadth of opportunity was too big for a brief race among several dozen firms to develop new components and related systems. There was open discussion about changing the entire chain of actions supporting the delivery of any valuable information-intensive activity, such as music, publishing, news, financial activities, and entertainment.

Who would meet the demand for these new services? Perceiving gaps between what was possible and what they and established firms could do, droves of entrepreneurial firms jumped into the fray. Particularly motivated by notions of Internet exceptionalism, many entrepreneurs sought to establish "pure-play" businesses, firms that operated solely over the Internet, and, in many cases, without physical presence.

Much of the entry was geographically concentrated. As ISPs sprouted in many locations, and as browsers began to diffuse, software entrants began exploring new businesses. Many of them were founded in the San Francisco Bay Area, and in the area along the peninsula known as Silicon Valley, named for the integrated circuit firms founded there generations earlier. This location became a focal point as a direct outgrowth of the entrepreneurial orientation of the venture-funded community, and where the preexisting labor market for technically skilled employees was becoming privy to the latest developments for the commercial web. These entrants included Yahoo!, HoTMaiL, Excite, eBay, Vermeer, and many others that anticipated building businesses on browser-based computing.[26]

The entrepreneurial movement at the outset extended beyond the San Francisco boundaries. For example, Bill Gates's memo of May 1995 titled "The Internet Tidal Wave" advises other executives to examine web pages by Lycos, Yahoo!, Oracle, Symantec, Borland, Adobe, Lotus, the *San Jose Mercury News*, Novell, Real Audio, Disney, Paramount, MCI, Sony, ESPN, and many other sites.[27] Although the first eight of these companies were located in the Bay Area, the rest were not.[28] Nevertheless, as the growth

---

[26] With twenty-twenty hindsight it is too easy to treat this outcome as obvious. For insights into the uncertain experience of an entrepreneur in this early era, see Ferguson (1999).

[27] See Gates (1995). At the end of the memo Gates provided a list of websites to give other executives examples of sites Gates found exemplar in various respects.

[28] As another illustration of the extent of geographic dispersion consider this example from a slightly later time, Meeker and DePuy (1996) highlights young Internet companies from California, such as Silicon Graphics, SUN, Cisco, Excite, Netcom, and Netscape, but

continued, the venture-based entrepreneurial community based near Silicon Valley became the major source of funding, and a majority of start-ups located there. Other prominent locations were Seattle, Boston, New York, and Washington, DC, but all were much smaller in scale.

The scale of entry was enormous, whether measured by the number of new businesses proposed and founded or by the amount of investment dedicated to this activity. There were, in fact, two phases to the growth. The first phase could be labeled the Internet gold rush, and it occurred between 1995 and 1997, when the first wave of enthusiastic entry into entrepreneurship began. Because the first wave of businesses had success in the IPO market and in selling out to larger firms, another wave began, which provided additional momentum, lasting from 1998 to the middle of 2000. This second wave included many of the examples that later became infamous for the descriptive phrase, "Too much money chasing too few good ideas."[29]

An examination of *funded* entrants provides a sense of timing of the boom, as well as some sense for the difference in scale. Figure 9.3 shows the amount of money that was funded to start-ups in ten areas of computing, communications, and software. The first eight had their fortunes tied directly to prospects in the Internet, while the latter two—wireless telecommunications and computer peripherals—provide comparisons with the wider market.[30]

---

also features plenty from all over the country, such as AOL, CompuServe, UUNET, Dell, Compaq, US Robotics, IBM, and others.

[29] Lerner and Gompers (2003).

[30] All data come from Venture Expert. Commercial communications (peak number: twenty-four funded start-ups in 1999) includes several categories of entrants from media, broadcasting, CATV, cable services, and pay TV. Data communications (peak of ninety-five funded start-ups in 2000) include communications processors, local area networks, wide area networks, protocol converters, modems, hubs, switches, and routers. Internet communications (peak of 114 in 1999) includes Internet access, Internet infrastructure, and Internet multimedia services. Electronic commerce technology (peak of seventy in 1999) includes a variety of Internet security software, e-commerce software, and e-commerce services. Internet software (peak of 107 in 1999) includes Internet system software, site development software, search software, web-service software, web language and web authoring tools. Fiber optics (peak of forty-nine in 2000) includes cables, couplers, and other systems related to fiber optics. Internet content (peak of 178 in 1999) includes products for businesses, consumers, retailing, publishing, agriculture, transportation, manufacturing, and recreation. Internet services (peak of twenty-four in 1999) include services for medical health, and services aimed at communications, education, reference, scientific, and legal services. Wireless services (peak of eighty-seven in 2000) include wireless services, paging services, and components. Computer peripherals

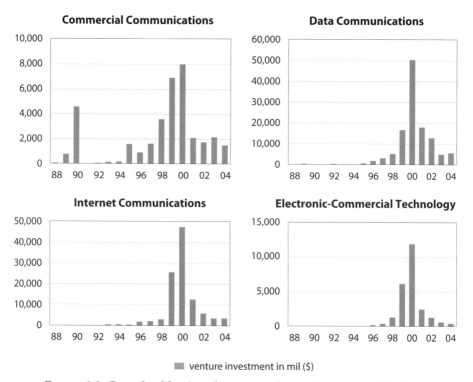

FIGURE 9.3. Growth of funding for venture-backed startups, 1988–2004

All the graphs show the same pattern—growth in and around 1995, followed by decline in and around 2001. Similarly, the scale of the peak years exceeds anything that had come before it, and generally the peak comes in 1999 or 2000.[31] This is so of any area, even those without direct relationship to the Internet. The non-Internet areas differ from those directly related to the Internet in only one respect, though they reach a peak in 1999 or 2000, many new start-ups continued to receive funding in periods past the peak. Examination of the number of funded entrants (instead of the amount of funding) provides a similar insight.

(peak at eleven in 2000) includes a myriad of products, including terminals, printers, I/O devices, hard-drive storage, and cards for PCs.

[31]Six of the eight Internet areas reach their peak number of entrants in 1999, while two reach their peak in 2000. However, all reach their peak in funding in 2000, which includes funding for firms founded prior to 2000. These data are in nominal terms, but adjusting for inflation would not change the insight.

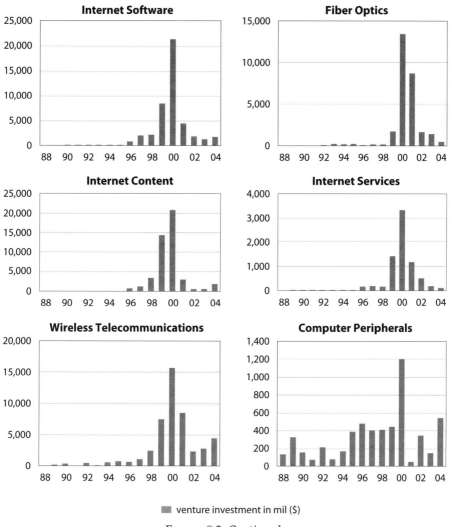

FIGURE 9.3. *Continued*

The magnitude of investments also obtained extraordinary levels during the peak. Investment in data communications exceeded $50 billion at its peak in 2000, and in Internet communications exceeded $45 billion. Internet software and Internet content each exceeded $20 billion at their peak. Wireless telecommunications exceeded $15 billion, fiber optics $13 billion, electronic-commercial technology $11 billion, and commercial communications $8 billion.

This only represents the funded entrants. By some estimates, these defined the tip of the iceberg. When less prominent businesses are included, one study estimates that less than 15 percent of the start-ups that sought funding during the boom followed get big fast approaches requiring large financial support, with only a tiny fraction subsequently having an IPO. Most had business ideas that did not require much funding.[32]

Although dot-com entrants covered a wide range of new businesses and used a wide set of models, three categories received special attention: (1) electronic commerce, (2) advertising-supported media, and (3) portals. Consider first *electronic commerce*. An entirely distinct group went into electronic commerce in various forms. Some sought to sell and distribute goods and services, such as books, travel services, or apparel. Others sought to sell subscriptions to services, such as the *New York Times* crossword puzzle or regular updates of industry news. Still others tried to assemble groups of buyers and sellers, either in open auctions or for more tailored matching purposes.

Ticket purchases illustrate the last trend. It did not take long to remove travel agents from the vast majority of trains, planes, autos, and hotel purchases. Web technology allowed users and vendors to directly deal with each other. A related innovation arrived quickly, and it might be called the inexpensive automated intermediary. After a firm set it up, a user (or purchaser) could easily query a database for seats or rooms (or just about any object). These services extended into many other areas, such as vacations, concerts, theaters, and restaurant reservations.

Another area of electronic commerce that assembled groups of buyers and sellers had a web presence but needed a substantial operational component to support it. Amazon.com was a leader in that category. Amazon began selling books online early in the history of household web use, and its experience is well known. Online offerings of CDs, toys, plane tickets, greeting cards, cheese, and tons of other merchandise followed quickly, often by other firms. These entrepreneurs deliberately mimicked the prac-

---

[32]See, for example, the analysis of 50K business plans from this era, as analyzed in Kirsch and Goldfarb (2008). They argue that a large number of businesses were founded outside a fast-growth strategy backed by a venture capitalist, and that a large percentage of these firms (close to half) survived just fine.

tices of catalogs, and minimized building physical facilities in most states. Thus they avoided legal obligations to pay sales taxes, which made their products cheaper in many states and municipalities than those bought in physical stores.[33]

These entrepreneurs generally attempted seven different approaches to starting a pure-play Internet firm.[34] Surveys of business plans[35] showed that many dot-com entrepreneurs listed more than one potential source of revenue. The most common revenue source listed was fee for service. Over three out of five (62 percent) had such a plan. Another popular source of revenue was advertising, with over a third relying on it (36 percent). Similar rates were found in the use of production (26 percent), subscription (25 percent), and commission (23 percent). Less common were businesses relying on markup (18 percent), and referrals (13 percent).[36]

Now consider *advertising-supported media*. Initially a large number of entrants went into advertising-supported websites or sites with no usage fees.[37] A number of sites covered directory and search activities, while others specialized in supporting conversations and information sharing for particular topics or groups.[38]

Much of the advertising-supported Internet initially resembled the related offline magazine industries, with users spreading themselves among a range of topics. Early surveys[39] showed that the most popular (after general portals and electronic mail) were community gatherings (for example,

---

[33]Why did political actors leave these local sales taxes uncollected, and not set up a system to do so? This is an interesting question about the political economy of the time. The nonaction implicitly subsidized online retailing as well as avoided local/federal jurisdictional disputes over collecting taxes.

[34]See Afuah and Tucci (2003).

[35]See as well, Goldfarb, Kirsch, and Miller (2007).

[36]*Fee for service.* This type of business charges for professional service in relation to use of it. *Advertising.* Especially used in media business, this online business attracts readers, and shows them banner ads, pop ups, etc., and receives fees for the ads. *Production.* A manufacturer sells directly over the Internet, which cuts out distribution expenses. *Subscription.* A company charges for use of a service for a certain period of time, such as month or year. *Commission-based.* A fee was imposed on a transaction by a third party, usually an intermediary. *Mark-up based.* Employed by resale sites acting as middlemen, a business charges a markup over wholesale cost. *Referral fees.* A company steers customers to another company, often on fee per click-through.

[37]See Goldfarb (2004).

[38]See Haigh (2008) for a discussion of this segment, and see Goldfarb, Kirsch, and Pfarrer (2005) for discussion of the variety of entrants.

[39]See Goldfarb (2004).

Geocities), financial information (Motely Fool), news (CNN.com), games (Boxerjam), streaming media (Real.com), sports (ESPN.com), technology (ZDNet), specialized portals (Women.com), music (MP3.com), weather (Weather.com), and so on.[40] Throughout the decade the list of categories continued to expand.

A tension emerged between start-ups that contracted for all their services using copyright licenses, and those who adopted pieces of the hacker ethic found among ISPs. Like the ISPs, even if they did not hold this attitude for ideological reasons, many small start-ups turned a blind eye to piracy of content among their users because it helped business. They had no incentive to police it, and many were too impatient to do so. This tension was largely held in check as long as larger firms who licensed their content, such as AOL, dominated commerce.

It was further held in check by a related important innovative offering called *portals*. Portals became some of the most popular websites among Internet users, accounting for the opening pages for most users, acting as a tool for organizing web surfing, and accounting for the highest share of an individual's time online. There were two approaches to providing portal services at first. One approach made it an extension of another service, and virtually all of these firms aimed their product at mainstream users. For example, Netscape and Microsoft made the opening web page a default setting on their browser, directing considerable traffic to netscape .com and msn.com, respectively. Both were far down in use to AOL, which made its opening page an extension of its dial-up Internet service and organized its contents in an easy-to-use proprietary format—a strategy that became known as a *walled garden*.

Another approach was of stand-alone portals, and these differed in their appeal to technical and nontechnical users. Most early (and successful) portals in the mid- to late 1990s provided directory services for the vast amount of content on the web. Yahoo, Lycos, Excite, and others took this approach. Yahoo grew into a vast organizer of content and a popular destination. Excite sold itself to @home as part of a strategy to help cable Internet users.[41]

---

[40] The remainder were chat, television, electronic cards, entertainment, directories, health information, maps, jobs, city guides, movies, genealogy, classifieds, and real estate.

[41] See the account of Rosston (2009).

During this time many firms offered alternatives to portals, focusing on searching the web, which chapter 13 will discuss. In the late 1990s several different firms offered popular search engines, including Inktomi and Alta Vista. In 1998 a newly founded firm, Google, entered with a new approach to searching—namely, by ranking web pages on the basis of the number of links to those pages and, eventually, by supporting itself with advertising. This turned out to be popular with users; after the turn of the millennium, Google continued to grow this business and eventually surpassed the early leading portal, Yahoo, in usage, revenue, and capitalized value. At this stage, however, many of these search engines were pieces of functionality for the portals, acting in the background.

Internet Adoption in Homes

Many households viewed the increase in the web's functionality as a good reason to acquire Internet access.[42] Not all households adopted right away. The different timing of adoption arose from a mix of factors. Prices for Internet access fell perceptibly in 1995 and 1996, but steadied thereafter.[43] Meanwhile, its availability from a local phone call spread into virtually every small urban area by 1997. Households also differed in their willingness to adopt due to their perceptions of how affordable and valuable they found it. As the Internet improved after 1995, with the entry of many new services, many households found the benefit worth the expense.

The Internet's adoption was closely linked to the PC's. The Internet was much easier to adopt if the PC already existed at a household. In that sense, the diffusion of the Internet depended heavily on the diffusion process of PCs prior to 1995, and, for similar reasons, the Internet's diffusion thereafter depended on the PC's subsequent diffusion. On top of this interdependence, within the class of PC users there were also differences in their willingness to experiment and the intensity of their use.[44]

---

[42] Any household was considered connected to the Internet if it had the capability of communicating with other entities via the physical structure of the Internet.

[43] The price drop coincided with the rush of new entrants into the market for ISPs. See Stranger and Greenstein (2007).

[44] For more on the diffusion of PCs, see Goolsbee and Klenow (1999), US Department of Agriculture (2000), or NTIA (1995, 1997, 1998, 2002).

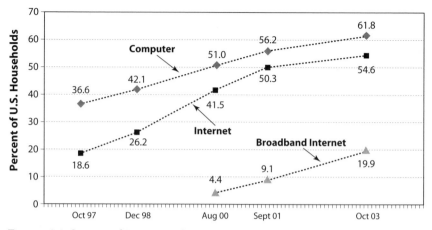

FIGURE 9.4. Survey of Internet adoption in US homes, 1997–2003 (NTIA 2004)

The importance of the PC and browser can be seen in US government surveys of Internet adoption. The government had completed a large-scale sampling of PC use across the country in 1995, the fourth such survey. At the beginning of 1995, just under 25 percent of US households had a computer, up a couple percentage points from the previous survey done a year earlier, and up from 15 percent of households in the fall of 1989.[45] The Internet was so new in 1995 that the government survey did not directly ask about its use until the next survey in the fall of 1997, when 36.6 percent of US households had a PC. In that survey just over 50 percent of the PC users, or 18.6 percent of households, had an Internet connection. Growth was rapid from then on, with 26.2 percent of households using the Internet in the fall of 1998, and 41.5 percent in the winter of 2000.[46] As of 2001, approximately 56.2 percent of American homes owned a PC, with Internet participation rates at 50.3 percent in 2001.[47] Over 80 percent of US households with an Internet connection used dial-up connections in 2001. This is illustrated in figure 9.4.

After triangulating from multiple sources to fill in many missing observations and estimate adoption in those years, Greenstein and McDevitt (2012) put household adoption at slightly higher levels, as shown in table 9.1.

[45] See NTIA (2000), figure 1, page 1.
[46] NTIA (2004).
[47] See NTIA (2002).

TABLE 9.1. Internet adoption, 1997–2003

Year	1997	1998	1999	2000	2001	2002	2003
Households (millions)	103.0	104.0	105.0	106.0	107.0	108.0	109.0
Internet adopters (millions)	19.1	27.2	35.5	44.0	53.8	56.7	59.5
Adopters (% of households)	18.6	26.2	33.8	41.5	50.2	52.5	54.6
Broadband (millions)	n.a.	n.a.	0.9	3.2	9.6	13.0	18.5
Dial-up (millions)	19.1	27.2	34.5	40.8	44.2	43.7	41.0

Source: Greenstein and McDevitt (2012).

By 2001, Internet usage correlated with higher household income, employment status, and educational attainment. Much of this disparity in Internet usage can be attributed to observable differences in education and income. For example, at the highest levels of income and education there were no significant differences in adoption and use across ethnicities.[48]

Since the vast majority (87.6 percent) of PC owners had home Internet access, the marginal Internet adopter looked similar to the marginal PC adopter. For households, therefore, PC demand had two distinct populations: (1) Those already owning a PC, and (2) those that were first-time purchasers of a PC. In the middle of the 1990s, two distinct Internet adoption patterns mirrored the two populations of PC demand. That pattern ceased to exist by the end of the period, when either existing PC adopters converted to the Internet, or households bought PCs and converted to the Internet. By 2001 to 2002, virtually all existing PC adopters had experience with the Internet at home.[49]

[48] With regard to age, the highest participation rates were among teenagers, while Americans in their prime working ages (twenty to fifty years of age) also were well connected (about 70 percent). Although there did not appear to be a gender gap in Internet usage, there did appear to be a significant gap in usage between two widely defined racial groups: (1) whites, Asian Americans, Pacific Islanders (approximately 70 percent); and (2) blacks and Hispanics (less than 40 percent).

[49] In his paper, Prince (2008) describes three main determinants of the "divide" in PC ownership. See also Goolsbee and Klenow (2002), where the role of local network effects in motivating early adoption is emphasized.

Quite a different set of factors, therefore, shaped later adopters than did those for earlier adopters. As the diffusion of the PC moved deeper into mainstream use, the marginal PC and Internet adopter became a household with low marginal value for PC quality, high start-up costs, significant price sensitivity, and potential difficulty in determining *when* (not necessarily *if*) to buy.[50]

The form of basic access at households also changed over time. Netscape tried building electronic mail functionality into its browser during 1995 and 1996. Many independent and small ISPs liked this function because it allowed them to offer electronic mail to their customers simply by supporting the browser. Many sophisticated users of basic services were satisfied with this option, or used one like that offered by HoTMaiL or Yahoo Mail. In 1998, AOL bought CompuServe,[51] and, with that merger and organic growth, by the end of 2000 AOL was the most widely adopted provider of Internet access in the United States.

Internet Adoption in Businesses

The diffusion of basic Internet connections to businesses had many of the same determinants as in households. Implementation for minimal applications, such as e-mail and browsing, was rather straightforward in the latter half of the 1990s. It involved a PC, a LAN or modem, a contract with an ISP, and some appropriate software. The presence of internal IT expertise at a larger business establishment permitted a wider range of implementations, including Lotus Notes and cc:mail, and eventually Microsoft Outlook and Exchange.

In 1995 it would not have been a spurious conjecture to assume that some industries would adopt basic access sooner than others. Firms that moved earliest were those in industries with a history of being more information intensive or making more intensive use of new IT developments in operations. The latter group would include research industries, where the Internet was already familiar. Heavy computer-technology-user

---

[50]For a general explanation of browser adoption strategies and their interplay with the diffusion to early and late adopters, see Bresnahan and Yin (2007).

[51]The deal was reached in the fall of 1997 and completed in February of 1998. The network services and infrastructure part of CompuServe was sold to Worldcom, while the Information Services part was sold to AOL. See Pelline (1997a).

industries included finance, utilities, electronic equipment, insurance, motor vehicles, petroleum refining, petroleum pipeline transport, printing and publishing, pulp and paper, railroads, steel, telephone communications, and tires.[52]

Such a forecast never faced a direct test because at that time no comprehensive survey equivalent to the surveys presented to households examined business use of the Internet. One of the earliest attempts to comprehensively measure national Internet adoption rates took place at the end of 2000 and confined attention to medium and large establishments.[53] These studies showed why it was essential to distinguish between two purposes for adopting, one simple and the other complex. The first purpose, here labeled *basic participation*, relates to activities such as e-mail and web browsing. This represents minimal use of the Internet for basic communications. The second purpose, here labeled *enhancement*, relates to investment in frontier Internet technologies linked to computing facilities. These latter applications were called e-commerce and involved complementary changes to (1) internal business computing processes, such as part procurement, or (2) customer-facing distribution channels, such as electronic retailing.

The economic costs and benefits of basic participation and enhancement were distinct. The determinants of the diffusion of each type of use differed, so adoption proceeded at separate and distinct paces.

Let's begin with basic participation. Adoption costs for basic participation were low, and at its smallest scale, were similar to households—involving simple $20 per month contracts. Basic participation was economically feasible in virtually any business in almost any location. Because nearly every business experienced some benefit from adoption, it was widespread and was almost a necessity for US business by the end of the millennium. Thus by the year 2000, adoption of the Internet for purposes of participation approached near saturation in most medium- and large-scale establishments in most industries. Hence, the forecast for information-intensive industries was wrong, by being too pessimistic about those firms

[52]See Cortada (1996) and Forman, Goldfarb, and Greenstein (2003 a, b).

[53]See Forman, Goldfarb, and Greenstein (2003 a, b). The US census also attempted to understand adoption, and took a different approach. It examined established businesses of all sizes—small, medium, and large—but only in manufacturing. See McElheran (2011).

that had not been information-intensive in the past. Virtually all firms in all industries adopted.[54]

The rate of adoption was remarkably fast in historical perspective. The closest historical analogue came from several software applications, which industry wisdom suggests were killer aps for PCs. In this sense, there was a large grain of truth to the claim of advocates of the new economy about the unprecedented nature of the rate of improvement. The diffusion of e-mail and the browser had few precedents except the diffusion of the spreadsheet (that is, Visicalc and Lotus 1-2-3), second-generation word processing (that is, WordPerfect), or electronic financial planning (that is, Quicken), which were some of the fastest-diffusing software applications.

E-mail played an important role in this experience, because basic service supported e-mail and browsing. As it turned out, the widespread diffusion of the Internet did render moot the advantage held by established firms, such as MCImail, or Lotus Notes.[55] Instead, it became an opportunity for the growth of web-based e-mail services, and at this time, Microsoft and Yahoo bought the two leaders of e-mail providers, HoTMaiL and Rocketmail, respectively. The widespread diffusion also made it particularly easy to operate e-mail software at the level of an establishment and connect servers between establishments using the Internet's gateway.[56] Coincident with this opportunity, Microsoft began selling Exchange server, bundling the client software, Outlook, for free. Outlook also included its calendar and contact manager and could be purchased as a part of the Office suite bundle. The firm also began pricing at discounts to convert an entire enterprise. It eventually became the dominant electronic mail provider in businesses.

There were good reasons the investments in basic participation occurred at the same time as investments in enhancement. Increasing participation increased the gains to enhancing business processes. This is a big topic, and the next chapter will discuss its characteristics.

---

[54] See Forman, Goldfarb, and Greenstein (2003 a, b). Medium and large establishments employ approximately two-thirds of the employment for the labor force, so this was substantial. However, this record was not replicated in many small establishments, which had a much more mixed set of outcomes, especially in rural areas.

[55] Its attempt to build an e-mail client software, cc:mail, did not make up for this problem.

[56] Todd Warren, private communication, June 2009.

The New Normal

The commercial Internet could not be built without simultaneous investments from many distinct participants—households, business, carriers, software developers, ISPs, retailers of all stripes, and more. Consistent with the rhetoric to support it, many different participants in the economy, in fact, simultaneously adopted the Internet and made investments to make it useful. Virtually all of it leveraged off the existing infrastructure in the network, and then extended its scale. An innovation that had lived outside of the perception of many was quickly becoming a mainstream activity.

That accumulation of investment began to accelerate in the mid- to late 1990s, as all participants saw how pervasive the commercial Internet had become, and all forecast it would become more pervasive. Investment by one type of participant raised the gains to investing by another, which accelerated the real economic incentive to continue to invest after adoption, which generated incentives for the laggards to become involved.

For those from the edges this situation represented the realization of a long-desired dream. For entrepreneurs and investors in their venture-funded businesses this represented an enormous potential market. Many perceived it as a once-in-a-lifetime opportunity to change the world. Students dropped out of college to found businesses. Engineers gave up stable work to take a chance on a fast-growing start-up. News outlets reported extensively and widely on such episodes, reinforcing the public perceptions that the zeitgeist had reached an unusual and unique point in history.

10

Capital Deepening and Complements

The universal reach and connectivity of the Internet were enabling access to information and transactions of all sorts for anyone with a browser and an Internet connection. Any business, by integrating its existing databases and applications with a Web front end, could now reach its customers, employees, suppliers and partners at any time of the day or night, no matter where they were. Businesses were thus able to engage in their core transactional activities in a much more productive and efficient way. And they could start very simply, initially just Web-enabling specific applications and databases.

—*Irving Wladawsky-Berger, first general manager for IBM Internet Division*[1]

IBM suffered unenviable circumstances at the outset of the commercial Internet boom. Although IBM had played an important role in the National Science Foundation Network (NSFNET) from 1987 to 1995, its participation had done little to alter the practices or perspective of IBM's top management. By the mid-1990s, IBM's mainframe business had declined significantly from its peak in the late 1980s, and the PC division had lost much market share over the same half decade. Perceiving IBM to be in a free fall, the board had removed the CEO. Then the board broke with precedent in hiring a new CEO from outside the firm in 1993. That is how Lou Gerstner Jr. came to IBM.

---

[1] See Wladawsky-Berger (2005).

FIGURE 10.1 Lou Gerstner, CEO IBM, 1993–2002
(photo by Kenneth C. Zirkel, 1995)

FIGURE 10.2 Irving Wladawsky-Berger, first general manager
for IBM Internet Division (date 2014)

Gerstner undertook a long-term review of every part of IBM, and after considerable study came to two key decisions: he chose not to break IBM into distinct business units for sale, and he decided to reorganize many of the existing business units around a service-oriented strategy that focused on helping clients to implement IT in more effective ways.[2] The strategy

---

[2]See Wladawsky-Berger, private communication, August 2010.

included some restructuring, such as—eventually—selling IBM's network-ing business and, instead, purchasing networking services from others. It also stressed investing in business services, especially those related to im-plementing all aspects of IT used in business operations. While IBM had done some of these activities for years, there was only one obvious prob-lem with this approach in 1995: IBM did not provide every service its cli-ents wanted. In particular, it had no services related to the Internet.[3]

L. L. Bean was one client who wanted such services. Long one of the world's largest catalog companies, the rapid rise of the commercial Inter-net had put numerous worries on the minds of its management. While the situation was not yet dire in 1995, the potential rise of electronic retailing threatened to take a large fraction of revenue in the near future. The man-agement also took seriously the boasting of Internet enthusiasts who fore-saw a transformed sales experience, selling directly in Internet users' homes. The new services were forecast to use faster and cheaper Internet technol-ogy, and do it with more vivid web pages than L. L. Bean could offer in the pages of its mailings.

The management at L. L. Bean sought to develop a strategy to develop its own electronic services, and meet the anticipated competition head on. L. L. Bean already knew how to fulfill an order if it came over the phone, but the company could not perform a comparable service over the web. The company needed the equivalent of a reliable and scalable electronic process, one that used the Internet, triggered the fulfillment process, and did so at a large scale. It also wanted to get this quickly and with as little money as possible, so it desired not to start from scratch. That meant it had to find a way to make the new front end for electronic retailing work with its existing order-fulfillment process.

Why did L. L. Bean turn to IBM, its longtime computer supplier, for a new approach? The management of IBM and L. L. Bean were tied together by a long working relationship, reinforced over many years. IBM had al-ways been more than just a supplier of computer hardware. It helped build reliable and scalable processes, and its employees had deep familiar-ity with L. L. Bean's needs and with standard industry practices. L. L. Bean also had little reason to go to the Internet enthusiasts with their entrepre-

---

[3] See Gerstner (2002) for an extensive description of the state of the company when Gerst-ner arrives, and the rationale for his approach to turning it around.

neurial ventures. Many of the entrepreneurs focused on establishing businesses that potentially competed with L. L. Bean. As one of the largest catalog retailers in the world with an established brand, L. L. Bean had little room for the experimentation of an unknown start-up. It needed to satisfy its customers as soon as possible, and it trusted IBM to do that with as few errors as possible.

As it turned out, IBM and L. L. Bean's experiments together came at a propitious moment for both. IBM's solutions gave L. L. Bean what it wanted, a way to maintain its existing order-fulfillment process for catalogs, and make it work with a new electronic retailing channel. It would make L. L. Bean one of early leaders among old-line catalog firms and give it a viable path to respond to the new entrants. As this chapter describes, IBM also got what it wanted. It learned a great deal from this situation and applied these lessons elsewhere. Using their expertise in their traditional strength, enterprise IT, and making it work with web technologies, IBM's employees learned how to create bridges between L. L. Bean's IT processes and a new web front end. They called this bridge middleware. IBM regarded it as a definable IT enterprise project, with many elements that had value in many settings, and where IBM provided all the pieces to adapt the mainframe system to the web and Internet.

A speech to the Internet Commerce Expo on April 9, 1997, by Irving Wladawsky-Berger, the first general manager for the IBM Internet Division, made clear how well the middleware solution had worked for both parties. It was less than two years after IBM initiated its new Internet strategy, and the talk was titled "E-Business and Killer Apps." Taking issue with the common definition of "killer app" Wladawsky-Berger said:

> If you mean one or two major applications that kill off the competition and leave a handful of IT firms with architectural control of this new era, you won't find them, and I doubt they will emerge in the future. But from the customer's point of view "killer" apps are appearing all over the place. These "killer" apps are the ones that help them do what they have always done . . . only faster and more efficiently, and with a global reach that two years ago was a dream.[4]

[4]See http://patrickweb.com/points_of_view/presentations/audio-and-text-transcripts/ice-los-angeles-1997/, accessed April 2013.

That set up the latter half of the speech, in which Wladawsky-Berger gave many examples in which IBM provided the middleware. Last of all, he mentioned L. L. Bean's experience over the 1996 Christmas shopping season.[5] In the speech L. L. Bean served as the poster child for successful adoption of electronic retailing by an established firm. Without revealing specific data, Wladawsky-Berger let it be known that traffic at the site had exceeded all expectations and forecasts.

IBM's first two years' experience with L. L. Bean illustrates a pattern that would be played out over many years as the commercial Internet began to grow. IBM emerged from its near-death experience with a healthy strategy and a lucrative line of services, and it did so by readopting the Internet to new circumstances. This strategy emerged because many of its clients—large enterprises—needed help integrating the commercial Internet into their businesses processes. Integration turned out to be productive, because it reused existing capital for new purposes instead of needing to build processes and operations from scratch. That approach led to a cheaper solution and in less time, and it preserved plenty of valuable processes these large enterprises had perfected in prior years. Hence, the buyer of IBM's services made out well, and so did IBM.[6] Understanding why illustrates many general lessons about the value of installing business processes related to the Internet.

There is one additional reason to examine IBM's experience. Events illustrate a larger economic logic to why the commercial Internet yielded productivity advance. First, as noted, the most common response among established firms contained many of the same elements, retrofitting of existing processes with new technology.

A second reason is more subtle. Retrofitting existing business processes did not happen in isolation of other investment in the economy; growing investment in large enterprises generated demand for a supply of complementary services. One type of service firm acted as an intermediary, helping a buyer improve its existing business processes and adapt many ele-

[5] While advertising the benefits of their standards to support secure transactions, other firms mentioned in this speech included the global engineering company of Asea, Brown, and Boveri; the transportation firm Caterpillar Incorporated; Japan Airlines; the Bank of Montreal; Smith Barney; Charles Schwab; MasterCard and Visa; the Swiss Federal Railway; Acxiom Corporation, among others.

[6] Reflecting that success, IBM's stock price rose from $14.12 at the end of the year in 1993 to $120.96 at the end of the year for 2001.

ments of new technology. A very different set of participants, data carriers, responded to that demand by investing in their operations, propelling the network to provide a large scale of activity. In turn, greater network capabilities enabled additional commercial investment in a virtuous cycle, which became self-reinforcing.

The Rebirth of IBM

When the commercial Internet began to take off, Gerstner appointed a task force, which concluded that IBM needed a new Internet division, and the new division should not be in the classic mold. It should not have a product and its own profit and loss statement, engage in product development, or compete in a race to develop new features. Rather, it should coordinate activities across divisions in IBM.[7] Why? Because, said Irving Wladawsky-Berger, who became head of the Internet division in late 1995, the "Internet touches on all parts of the company. . . . [You] cannot gather it together in one place."

The essence of IBM's strategy emerged in 1996, during his first year.[8] Wladawsky-Berger's team began talking with existing customers with whose business processes IBM's staff had gained deep familiarity. Many of these were the largest firms in the globe; many had recently bought mainframes and related applications from IBM. More to the point, many of their managers had heard the outsized claims of the new economy entrepreneurs and did not dismiss these claims as outsized. Many viewed their own firms as under threat and wanted IBM's help in developing a solid strategic response. In that sense the market opportunity fell into the lap of Wladawsky-Berger's team; many of IBM's longtime clients had a need and were willing to pay for substantial services that addressed it.

Wladawsky-Berger's team queried IBM's technical staff and sales force. The team discovered that while a large number of IBM experts were studying the right set of problems, they had not constructed prototypes

---

[7] Gerstner had Denny Welsh, head of the services division for IBM, organize a large task force. Wladawsky-Berger, private communication, August 2010. Also, see Wladawsky-Berger (2005). The independent division also avoided political issues affiliated with assigning the Internet strategy to one existing unit, which would have made it challenging to get other units to buy in to the organization's strategy. See Gerstner (2002).

[8] Interestingly, the strategy emerged at the same time as the removal of the 1956 IBM consent decree, which had forbidden IBM from entering some complementary markets, such as consulting service. CNET (1996).

that buyers wanted. In the recent past employees at IBM had developed network applications of, for example, news aggregation, yellow pages, hosted electronic commerce, and shopping sites. These prototypes addressed many of the potential issues Wladawsky-Berger's team heard from customers. Yet the vast majority of prototypes in IBM's laboratories used proprietary components and approaches, not Internet software and web protocols.[9] In short, IBM's prototypes had part of the vision right in a lab, but all of them implemented solutions that did not appeal to users. They were too cumbersome and far too expensive in comparison to what the web was making possible.[10]

At first Wladawsky-Berger's team concluded that these prototypes gave IBM no comparative advantage in developing solutions for clients. Any competent HTML programmer could design a web page as easily as IBM, after all. The first impression was misleading, however, and Wladawsky-Berger's views evolved as he came to appreciate that no other large supplier understood the buyer's business processes of large enterprises as well as IBM's staff did. IBM could do something unique; they could bring in programmers who had worked at their client in the past, and understood what the middleware needed to accomplish. That made IBM well placed to address the buyer's needs as well as preserve some of the existing processes.

IBM also could take on a role as a technological intermediary, aiding the client's move from its unique situation to a distant technical frontier. Why did IBM have a comparative advantage at that task? Because IBM's employees also had a vision of what the new technology could accomplish in a large enterprise, and they understood from their own prototypes what types of services could be built. IBM's employees also already had familiarity with IT-related issues in security, firewalls, and preservation of brand value. That knowledge could be very valuable if married to an effective vision about how to implement the new frontier using new Internet and web technologies.

[9] Wladawsky-Berger, private communication, August 2010.
[10] Also see Gerstner (2002) for an extensive discussion about the use of proprietary or nonproprietary technologies, and the attitudes he encountered when trying to move the firm to nonproprietary approaches.

IBM could get there if they made only one large change to their attitude about using open systems. Many years later, looking back on it, Wladawsky-Berger described that critical shift:

> IBM, like many large businesses, used to be very inward-looking, preferring to do everything by ourselves if at all possible. Embracing the Internet, its open standards, and overall inside-out approach turned out to be much more than a technology change for us. I think it had a very big impact on the overall culture in IBM, as it did in many other companies. It truly made us much more open—e.g., embracing new technology ideas from external communities, as we did with Apache, Linux, and Grid.

Principles for a strategy emerged comparatively quickly and employed these three elements:

- A vision of the future prototype that created value by delivering new services and meeting the client's need to match competitive threats;
- A commitment to adapt to and respect the client's existing business processes that already delivered value to the client's users;
- A preference for the open technologies of the Internet and web.

IBM had two early experiences that became canonical for the company and were referenced frequently. The introduction to this chapter gave an overview of the experience with L. L. Bean, which showed how the catalog firm opened new channels using web technology. The other example comes from United Parcel Service (UPS), which would replace some of its activities, and enhance them. Rather than merely match a competitive threat, this enhancement would create an entirely new service for users.

UPS operated one of the largest shipping services in the world, moving packages from almost any location to any other. UPS sought ways to use the web to help customers keep track of these shipments. As with any shipping company, UPS already tracked packages using internal processes, and used that information to correct routing problems when they emerged. UPS sought to make that information more readily available.

Once again, IBM's employees were quite familiar with the computing resources that supported internal processes. After all, IBM had installed the software to support such logistics. IBM's staff concluded that it was possible—indeed, not technically difficult—to attach a web server to the transactional system, which had a mainframe computer at its core, and support a website with standard Internet functionality. What would that site do? It would answer a query from a user about the location of a package, sending information directly from the mainframe to the user.

After it was installed many users went to the automated system repeatedly, watching their package as it passed through various checkpoints. This had not been possible previously with human operators, as it would have been prohibitively expensive. According to Wladawsky-Berger, users loved the insight into the operations. "People thought these were magical."

Both parties benefited from the deal. To IBM, it looked again like an IT enterprise project with middleware, where IBM provided all the pieces to adapt the mainframe system to the web. To UPS it looked like a cost saving measure because the website bypassed an operator. In addition, it offered a convenient way for the user to find information, enhancing the value of the company's services.

IBM found similar issues at many of their clients. Integrating aspects of traditional IT with the web became a large business for IBM. Because many firms in many industries use similar processes, IBM's solutions for L. L. Bean and UPS generalized to a variety of settings and processes. For example, developing an online presence was valuable for hotels needing to fill rooms, or large retailing firms eager to reach more customers. All made use of back-office computing in innovative ways, typically by integrating a web-based application with an existing mainframe-supported business process so that users could reach the process over the Internet. As Wladawsky-Berger summarized, "We discovered the strategy in the market place, what our (longtime) clients wanted and what others were not doing."[11]

Once the Internet division had articulated a strategy, the next step was to implement it inside IBM. In prior years that could have encountered major hindrances, but, as it turned out, virtually every IBM division manager cooperated with its execution. The "near-death" crisis at IBM in the early 1990s had helped soften the resistance to open technology, paving the way toward using open systems throughout IBM. Moreover, no divi-

---

[11] Wladawsky-Berger, private communication, August 2010.

sion manager wanted to oppose the CEO, who backed the new strategy and was prepared to implement it across the organization.[12]

Many division managers were persuaded that the new strategy was in their self-interest, because they saw that their divisions could receive more sales if they made their products and services compatible with TCP/IP and the web. Although such conversion could be an enormous task, the growth potential was also apparent. Accordingly, every IBM division began the engineering efforts to add designs that reflected the Internet strategy to existing products.

The tough times of the early 1990s thus became a hidden blessing during the implementation of the Internet strategy. It helped silence the loudest defenders—who had been quite vocal prior to Gerstner's appointment and even at the start of his tenure—of the older way, or the proprietary approaches inside IBM. The mainframe division had defended proprietary solutions, for example, but had suffered serious declines in revenues in the 1990s, and under Gerstner no longer held veto over firm strategy.[13]

As IBM gained one successful example after another, Wladawsky-Berger recognized early that IBM had a comparative advantage in providing large IT projects with these characteristics. Few other firms possessed the same combination of client relationships, intimate knowledge of existing processes, and familiarity with the prototypes of electronic commerce. Few other firms had sufficient staff to handle large and complex projects. This orientation also was consistent with the costumer-oriented strategy Gerstner was implementing throughout the company.[14] The strategy sustained itself throughout the latter part of the 1990s and beyond.

IBM's unique position fostered an additional strategic element—to provide intellectual leadership and associate IBM with that leadership. Despite the publicity that came with such leadership, IBM's near-death experience did hurt its reputation with financial analysts. Although IBM

[12]Wladawsky-Berger, private communication, August 2010. Also see Gerstner (2002) for a similar point.

[13]Perhaps one of the most prominent symbols of this change came from the experience of Ellen Hancock. In the early 1990s, Ellen Hancock, the networking division head, had staunchly defended selling exclusively proprietary equipment. However, Gerstner spun off the division, and Hancock moved on to other prominent executive positions in high-tech. Hancock left in 1995, prior to the development of the Internet strategy, so spinning off the network division appears to have been a propitious move, rather than one that fully anticipated the open Internet strategy. See Gerstner (2002).

[14]See Gerstner (2002).

did not face problems selling services in the boom atmosphere of the late 1990s, its approach did not impress many financial analysts at the time. To an analyst who subscribed to Internet exceptionalism, IBM appeared to be merely profiting from helping old firms stave off extinction for another day. The value of IBM's approach became widely appreciated only much later, after the collapse of the dot-coms. After 2001 IBM was still selling services to clients and did not suffer large drops in demand as a result of the dot-com bust.[15]

What overall lesson does this illustration provide? IBM found ways to recombine the new and old into a complementary whole rather than build new IT systems from scratch. It helped pioneer an approach to changing the face of selling on the web and the Internet, altered the value of electronic commerce, and eventually adjusted the conception of where the bulk of value lay. As such, it is also an example of a leading firm altering its previous conception and adopting the vision of those who brought innovation from the edges. It even made a business from explaining that vision to others and selling implementations of it.

Moreover, IBM's experience partly explains how and why the first wave of pure dot-com entrepreneurial businesses did not wholly—or even substantially—replace established large firms. As it turned out, a number of traditional business processes could be improved with complementary inputs from appropriate implementations of web-based technology. That altered business processes, and in ways that preserved value in existing brands, relationships with customer bases, operations and order fulfillment processes, and relationships with suppliers. More to the point, it gave established firms a potential pathway to competing with new entrants by taking advantage of declining costs in Internet access and by taking advantage of the potential for adding new capabilities affiliated with web-based technologies.

Demand for Enhanced Business Processes

IBM's experience illustrates the most important factor shaping business investment in the commercial Internet in the late 1990s—the economics of *business process innovations*. Indeed, it is not much of an exaggeration to say that a large part of the failure of Internet exceptionalism was due to

---

[15] Wladawsky-Berger, private communication, August 2010.

the blindness of many pure-play entrepreneurs to the unglamorous success of investing in business process innovations that worked well with existing business processes.

Business process innovations were easily misunderstood during the early stages of the commercial Internet. They were not the standard fare of undergraduate courses in economics or MBA courses in business development. Business process innovations involved both new processes and products, and the payout was generally not known with any certainty at the outset. Because important business process innovations in enterprise IT occurred on a large scale, they typically involved a range of investments, both in computing hardware and software, and in communications hardware and software. They also involved retraining employees and redesigning organizational architecture, such as its hierarchy, lines of control, compensation patterns, and oversight norms. Total costs and benefits varied, depending on circumstances and the resolution of unexpected problems that emerged.

A number of misunderstandings shaped common perceptions of business process innovations, and these in turn created confusion about how the Internet would yield productivity gains. For example, there was a myth that new IT hardware or software yielded the vast majority of productivity gains by themselves. In fact, business process innovations were not often readily interchangeable with older products or processes, meaning that the initial investment often did not generate a substantial productivity gain until after complementary investments, adaptations, and organizational changes. Many of these necessary changes were made long after the initial adoption. Hence, it was common for a business process innovation to have zero or negative returns in the short run before it yielded positive returns.

Among the functions altered by electronic commerce, for example, use of electronic retailing generated many changes to routine processes, such as altering customer/supplier interactions, and these took time to smooth out. That explains why adding electronic commerce to something as basic as parts supply yielded productivity gains eventually, but occasionally long after the initial rollout.

That observation relates to another common misunderstanding: the planning myth. Although the installation of any substantial business process innovation required planning—that is, administrative effort by an enterprise in advance of installation to coordinate complementary activities—such planning alone rarely ended the administrative tasks required to generate productivity gains. Administrative effort did not cease after installation, or even necessarily reach a routine set of procedures. Rather, planning continued throughout implementation and morphed into reacting to unexpected issues. Hiring and training personnel generated use of new hardware, software, and procedures. New users in new settings then noticed unanticipated problems, which generated new insight about unexpected issues.

Consider the example of adding web-enabled processes to the regular routines behind a simple business process, procurement of parts. Electronic methods made delivering the order more convenient, and it potentially made the billing process smoother, and it reduced the number of errors in the order due to misspellings or poor writing. But not all orders go according to plan, and poorly designed software could make adjusting an order more difficult when a component was out of stock, or weather interfered with shipping parts on schedule. The rise of unanticipated issues typically required considerable effort from users, because they had to tailor newly installed software, while simultaneously manage changes with multiple suppliers. If users were changing complex processes, then the challenges could be very difficult.[16]

That relates to a third common misunderstanding: the shrink-wrap myth. Installing business process innovations was not equivalent to installing shrink-wrap software for a PC that worked instantly or immediately after training staff. Instead, often necessary was *coinvention*, the post-adoption invention of complementary business processes and adaptations aimed at making adoption useful.[17] As in the first myth, the initial investment in IT was not sufficient for ensuring productivity gains. Those gains depended on later inventive activity, that is, whether employees in the adopting organization found new uses to take advantage of the new capabilities, and invented new processes for many unanticipated problems. Once again, many users failed to anticipate this inventive activity and retained the wrong staff, or did not employ the right consultant. This too could shape the immediate payoff. Until issues of coinvention were

---

[16]See McElheran (2011) and Bresnahan, Brynjolfsson, and Hitt (2002).
[17]See Bresnahan and Greenstein (1997). Also see Forman and Goldfarb (2006).

addressed, in many instances there was a strong potential for delayed, if any, payoff.[18]

Indeed, that problem was illustrated by the challenges of adding electronic commerce to consumer relationships. Catalog companies such as L. L. Bean had to change what they showed customers, but did not change the order-fulfillment process much. Order fulfillment involved tracking and billing, moving goods from warehouse to shipping, and, in the event of error, additional intervention. As it turned out, catalog companies had a comparatively easier experience adopting electronic commerce than did pure-play firms because their order fulfillment processes required less coinvention after the adoption of electronic commerce.[19]

Misunderstandings about the necessity of coinvention sometimes generated a fourth myth—namely, expectations that the entire cost of investment was incurred as monetary expense. In fact, nonmonetary costs—unexpected issues causing delay, hassles for employees, or foregone opportunities—comprised a significant risk of installing a business process innovation, and this was the most substantial issue established firms faced. Once again, this could create delays too.

The issues became particularly challenging when an enterprise could not shut down when installing the software. In such settings, issues had to be resolved and bugs removed as they appeared.[20] Moreover, interruptions to ongoing operations generated large opportunity costs in foregone services that could have been substantially mediated with internal resources (for example, development of middleware by in-house IT staff) for which there may be no market price or, for that matter, no potential for resale.[21]

---

[18] Delays arose from one of several different causes. For one, delays could arise because of the technical necessity to invest in one stage of a project only after another was completed—e.g., the client could not be modified until the servers worked as designed. For two, investments also could be nonconvex and lumpy, and not used in operations until entirely installed—e.g., all the wiring had to be installed before the communications routines could be tested. Third, as hinted in the planning myth, cognitive limits could cause delays—e.g., staff did not anticipate idiosyncratic issues until a new process was at their fingertips, and only after observing it did an issue emerge and receive attention. It often was challenging to forecast which of these would be most problematic in practice.

[19] Also see Hanson (2000).

[20] See Forman and Goldfarb (2006).

[21] Forman (2005).

A final myth sometimes arose in some organizations facing these issues, and that is the go-it-alone myth. Many organizations failed to recognize that they shared issues with many others, and they did not have to
face the growth of electronic commerce alone. As with other enterprise IT,
third-party consulting services could be hired on a short-term basis from
the local market and could attenuate these costs by sharing the learning.
The incentives around utilization and investment also could change considerably over time due to changes in the restructuring of the organization's hierarchy and operational practices, rendering old internal personnel staffing levels inappropriate for the evolving needs of the organization.
Once again, third party consulting services could fill those gaps.

The presence of coinvention had two key implications for the deployment of the Internet inside of enterprises. First, there was a visible relationship between investment in the Internet to enhance enterprise IT and
local conditions in a limited metropolitan geographic area. Large cities
had thicker labor markets for complementary services and specialized
skills, such as consultants who could program in both the language of
mainframes and the language of the web. The presence of those labor markets for technical talent, greater input sharing of complex IT processes,
and greater knowledge spillovers in cities increased the benefits to adoption of frontier technologies in big cities relative to other locations.[22]

Second, enterprises with existing IT facilities could expect lower coinvention costs than establishments without extensive operations, which
shaped costs around the time of adoption. Having more resources elsewhere in the organization meant access to lower-cost resources and loans
between an organization's projects. Programmers with IT experience
could reduce development costs if they were able to transfer lessons
learned from one project to another. Prior work on other IT projects could
create learning economies and spillovers that decreased the costs of adapting general purpose IT to organizational needs, reducing the importance
of external consultants and local spillovers. Existing support in firms for
PCs also made the transition easier, making support for Internet access
and the web an additional routine for the same staff.

In 1996 the technology was new and untested in a wide set of circumstances. Existing businesses needed something, but each faced different

---

[22] Forman, Goldfarb, and Greenstein (2005) provide extensive evidence for this statement.

economic circumstances that arose from differences in local output market conditions, quality of local infrastructure, labor market talent levels, quality of firm assets, and competitive conditions in output markets. In short, every business faced a different adaptation problem.

The Market for Coinventive Activity

There were many ways for a market to organize coinvention activity. Firms in need of coinvention could do it themselves or hire third parties to do it for them. Firms that supplied services to help users reduce the costs of coinvention could specialize in problems that many buyers shared. Such specialists could choose to supply problems common to an industry, a location, or an organizational activity. Being part of a crowd was the best situation for a buyer, as that crowd generally induced a considerable supply of services and allowed one coinvention experience to generate lessons for another. Being unique was more expensive for a buyer, as it left the buyer unable to take advantage of the services third parties offered.

As it played out, providing coinvention services in the late 1990s became an enormous business opportunity. The gap between the needs of business and the technical frontier, as defined by the potential gains from using the commercial Internet, was large and persistent. This gap created business opportunities for others to help existing firms advance from where they found themselves to where they aspired to go. Simply stated, many established businesses faced similar coinvention issues, and consequently innovated in similar ways. As illustrated above, IBM took advantage of this opportunity. It was not alone. Anderson Consulting (Accenture), Booz-Allen, and many others grew client bases under these conditions.

While many dot-com entrants received substantial public attention, many other companies began the process of upgrading their IT installations in order to implement enhancements and thereby increase their productivity from the web-enabled Internet. Because the costs of basic participation and enhancement were distinct, the second layer of business investment—enhancement—followed a trajectory distinct from basic participation.

Just as Wladawsky-Berger stated in his speech, there was no single "killer app" generating large investment in enhancement. Instead, the most complex and productive adaptations of the Internet followed the path laid out by most innovative IT enterprises. This was directed toward automating functional activity or business processes within an organization, such as bill collection, inventory replenishment, or point-of-sale tracking.[23] These activities were essential for operating an organization. Such rearrangement of functions had the potential to lead to, for example, the reorganization of supply chains in many specific markets over the long run.[24]

An additional factor accelerated investment in enhancement activity. The entry of entrepreneurial firms provided motivation for many existing firms to act. The rapid success of firms such as HoTMaiL and others fostered the perception that some entrepreneurial firms would succeed quickly in finding a competitive advantage against established businesses. The best chance for existing firms was to avoid losses. The fear of large losses motivated implementing quick change through large investment.[25] In addition, accelerated rates of replacement and upgrades of existing systems arose from several other factors: constant improvement in the quality of PCs, falling prices along the entire range of IT equipment,[26] general improvement in networking and the Internet, and the need to address potential Y2K issues.[27]

Enhancement of IT was not a minor activity in many firms and required deliberate change in large organizations. Even in the most adventurist organizations, these changes would not come without a large amount of analysis to legitimize any departure from refined and tested processes. The arrival of books, such as Shapiro and Varian (1999) or Hanson (2000), was often the earliest economic and marketing analysis of the Internet read by many American senior executives. Because they used a familiar language, and came from faculty at traditional universities, they influenced

---

[23] The investor in IT seeks the same process at lower cost or the same process at the same cost with improved features, such as lower error rates, more timely supply of inventory, or better real-time decision support for firms in rapidly changing market environments. Cortada (2003) argues that the appropriate model varies between industries and even within industries over different eras.

[24] Cortada (2003) argues that only three innovations have spurred such investments: the UPC code, EDI, and the Internet.

[25] Wladawsky-Berger, private communication, August 2010.

[26] The consumer price index for "Information technology, hardware and services" is dominated by quality adjustments in the price for personal computers. This price index dropped from 63.8 in 1995 to 21.3 in 2001, or a 66.6 percent decline. Subcomponents for PCs were only made public for a time that begins in 1998 and declines from 875.1 to 330.1 from 1998 to 2001, or by 62.2 percent.

[27] The Y2K problem arose in old mainframes that lacked the ability to update their dates after January 1, 2000. Many firms with such old systems replaced them and used that moment to upgrade all IT facilities.

thousands of companies that finally got online on the Internet in the latter part of the boom.

The experiences of lead users—pioneers who make investments in new technology in order to seek competitive advantage and achieve dramatic leaps in productivity—can illustrate these observations. A survey of lead users of enhancement at the end of 2000 showed the variety of industries the Internet affected.[28]

The two biggest lead adopters in using the Internet for enhancement were not a surprise. They came from two very different areas: management of companies and enterprises; and media, telecommunications, and data processing. The former represented the financial side of Internet use, including corporate headquarters for multidivisional firms, securities firms, and financial holding companies, all of which were longtime users of frontier computing. The latter included publishing firms, thus representing the change the Internet brought to media. It also included information and data processing services, an industry with firms such as AOL and other Internet-access providers. These too were frontier users.[29]

The second tier of lead users also represented a wide mix of industries that had a history of pushing out the frontier of computers. These were finance and insurance, professional and scientific services, utilities, and wholesale trade. The latter two included heavy use of sophisticated applications, which combined database software with communication technologies. The next tier of lead users included a large part of manufacturing, notably computer and electronic manufacturing, and printing and related support activities. Another important lead user of this category was oil and gas extraction, a longtime user of computation-intensive modeling. Lastly, many lead users employed logistical information for greater efficiency, such as water transportation, pipelines, motor vehicle and parts dealers, electronics and appliance stores, sporting goods, and nonstore retailers. The last four were leaders in consumer e-commerce.[30]

---

[28]See Forman, Goldfarb, and Greenstein (2003a, 2003b).

[29]Management of companies and enterprises is NAICS 55 in the North American Industry Classification (NAICS). Media, telecommunications, and data processing is NAICS 51. It also included information and data processing services, NAICS 514.

[30]Computer and electronic manufacturing refers to NAICS 334. Printing and related support activities refer to NAICS 323. The rest of the sentence refers to oil and gas extraction (NAICS 211), water transportation (NAICS 483), pipelines (NAICS 486), motor vehicle and parts dealers (NAICS 441), electronics and appliance stores (NAICS 443), sporting goods

The activities of lead adopters coincided with geographic variation in the propensity to adopt. Establishments in MSAs (metropolitan statistical areas) with more than one million people were nearly 50 percent more likely to adopt enhancement than MSAs with less than 250,000 people. The strong urban bias toward the adoption of advanced Internet applications resulted from the fact that lead-user industries tended to be located in urban areas. Related work suggests that small establishments in nonurban locations might have been unable to take advantage of Internet opportunities due to lack of thick labor markets for technical talent.[31]

Overall, the growth rates in real investment in computing equipment were extraordinarily high in the latter part of the 1990s. Investment in software reached 9.5 percent growth rates per year from 1990 through 1995, and 14.2 percent for 1995 through 2000. Computing equipment growth rates reached, respectively, 13.5 percent and 7.1 percent per year for the first and second half of the decade. Communications equipment reached 7.2 percent and 15.5 percent growth rates. All of these exceeded rates of growth in non-IT capital, which reached 6.8 percent and 4.9 percent per year over the same periods.[32] The productivity gains from this enhancement ultimately became one of the lasting legacies of this period's investment.

Economy-wide investment in IT continued to grow at high rates for all of the late 1990s. Investment in IT, pictured in figure 10.3, continued to grow at rates well above 20 percent a year. Market demand for new goods and services was as high as any participant had ever experienced. Suppliers of equipment, business software, and business services had never had it so good. Indeed, as it would turn out, the good times would last until the beginning of the new millennium.

Capital Deepening of the Network

Capital deepening refers to investment in existing processes, where that investment aims to increase the scale of existing activity or, at most, change it in incremental ways. Generally speaking, capital deepening lowers costs

---

(NAICS 451), and nonstore retailers (NAICS 454). Low adopters at the NAICS three-digit level also existed and would not have surprised any longtime observer of computing. These include transit and ground passenger transportation (NAICS 485), food services and drinking places (NAICS 722), social assistance (NAICS 624), and amusement (NAICS 713).

[31] See Forman, Goldfarb, and Greenstein (2008).

[32] For a review of studies of Internet investment by business, see Forman and Goldfarb (2006) and also Doms (2004).

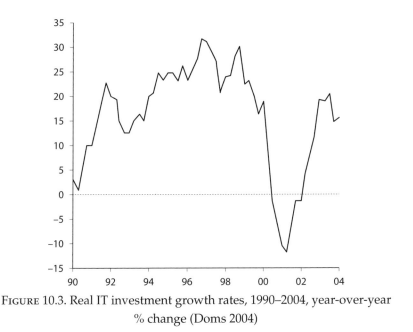

FIGURE 10.3. Real IT investment growth rates, 1990–2004, year-over-year % change (Doms 2004)

by preserving existing business processes while it increases scale. As it turned out, increases in business processes motivated investments that led to capital deepening in the network that supplied data.

Capital deepening in the network was essential for everyone, as it would permit doubling the scale of traffic handled by the network with *far* less than double the scale of investment. If the Internet would support a wide array of applications for a dispersed set of users, society also would need a tenfold and one-hundred-fold increase in traffic. That had to be available at *less* than a tenfold and one-hundred-fold increase in expense.

Although costs reductions in data carrier services were precisely the gains Stephen Wolff had envisioned when he initiated the privatization of the Internet backbone, there was little precedent to forecast the next generation of investment to achieve those gains. Growing demand certainly would motivate carriers to respond with investments that attempted to generate efficiencies. What would those investments look like? Would they be more of the same but on a larger scale? Would those investments require fundamental restructuring of the arrangement of the supply of services by infrastructure firms? Would new increases in traffic put enormous strains on the Internet's existing infrastructure?

The shadow of recent history hung over the open question. The network had been built for researchers sending e-mail and files, not households and business users sending web traffic. How would the privatized network handle the new type of traffic? Would more traffic merely lead to more investment in the same activity, or would it require a fundamental rethinking of the structure of processes supporting the network? There was no historical basis for addressing the question.

The first test of these concerns came early, as web-based traffic began to grow. Electronic mail had been the dominant application prior to the privatization of the Internet and invention of the web. It continued to be popular with adopters after 1995. All surveys showed all new Internet adopters making use of e-mail,[33] which generated the most Internet traffic in 1995. Lotus, Microsoft, HoTMaiL, and even Netscape provided widely used services. Yet no sensible observer expected this dominance to last. Everyone expected traffic affiliated with the web to overtake e-mail traffic. Indeed, in retrospect it was clear that it did by the middle of 1996.[34]

Capital deepening enabled the growth in web traffic. At the time traffic grew, it was quite challenging to get solid facts. In the latter part of the 1990s advocates for the new economy were fond of claiming that traffic doubled every year or at even faster rates. Firms who benefited from this assertion, such as WorldCom, also made similar claims and assertions.

This assertion was rarely supported by actual data or met with skeptical analysis from contemporaries. In retrospect, the facts seem not to support the most optimistic claims.[35] While traffic volumes doubled every few months in the early years (the early 1990s), this growth rate was an artifact of the low base from which it grew. Although traffic growth could vary across locations due to local influences, generally speaking, by the late 1990s traffic was growing at a rate of 50 percent per year.[36] Estimates can be seen in table 10.1.

After 1997, a structure began to take shape around this increasing traffic. It was part mesh and part hierarchical, using "tiers" to describe a hier-

---

[33] Clemente (1998).

[34] Estimates vary for when HTML traffic exceeded e-mail and file transfers and other traffic, but every estimate points to sometime in 1996. For example, see table 2 of Odlyzko (2003).

[35] Odlyzko (2003).

[36] See the ongoing discussion on http://www.dtc.umn.edu/mints/igrowth.html, accessed July 2012.

TABLE 10.1. US Internet traffic, 1990–2003, estimates at end of each year (in PetaBytes/month)

1990	0.001
1991	0.002
1992	0.004
1993	0.008
1994	0.016
1995	0.15
1996	1.5
1997	2.5 to 4
1998	5 to 8
1999	10 to 16
2000	20 to 35
2001	40 to 70
2002	80 to 140
2003	130 to 210

Source: Odlyzko (2003).

archy of suppliers.[37] The first group of backbone providers in the United States (MCI; Sprint; UUNET; Bolt, Beranek and Newman [BBN]) had been the largest carriers of data in the NSF network. In 1995 and 1996, any regional ISP could exchange traffic with them. At that time, the backbone of the US Internet resembled a "mesh," with every large firm both interconnecting with each other and exchanging traffic with smaller firms.[38] Some of these firms owned their own fiber (for example, MCI) and some of them ran their backbones on fiber rented from others (or example, UUNET).

A hierarchy began to take shape with tier 1 suppliers acting as national providers of backbone services who charged a fee to smaller firms to interconnect. The small firms were typically ISPs that ranged in size and scale from wholesale regional firms to local ISPs handling a small number of dial-in customers. Tier 1 firms did most of what became known as "transit" data services, passing data from one ISP to another ISP, or passing data

[37] See Friedan (2001, 2002).
[38] The term "mesh" first appeared in Besen et al. (2001).

from a content firm to a user. In general, money flowed from customers to ISPs, which treated their interconnection fees with backbone firms as a cost of doing business.

Tier 1 firms adopted a practice known as *peering*, which was a self-propagating way of reinforcing a tier 1 firm's status. Specifically, peering involved the removal of all monetary transfers at a point where two tier 1 providers exchanged traffic. Peering acknowledged the fruitlessness of exchanging money for bilateral data traffic flows of nearly equal magnitude at a peering point. Hence, it lowered transaction costs for the parties involved. However, because their location and features were endogenous, and large firms that denied peering to smaller firms would demand payment instead, many factors shaped negotiations. As a result, the practice became controversial. It was impossible to tell whether peering reflected a more efficient transaction for large-scale providers or reflected the market power of large suppliers, which smaller firms or non-tier-1 firms could not acquire.[39]

Another new feature of Internet infrastructure also began to emerge at this time. Most households received considerably more data (from content firms) than they sent out to others. Such asymmetric traffic put more strains on the network, which had to find ways to deliver large amounts of data to households quickly.

That asymmetry led to the rise of third-party caching services. Caching was an enhancement to the operations of the network backbone. For reasons explained in a moment, it accomplished what capital deepening would have been unable to accomplish except at a very high cost.

Starting in 1998 Akamai—a pioneering caching company—began to locate its servers within key points of an ISP's network, sometimes paying the ISP a nominal fee for the inconvenience, but most often paying nothing. Aspiring to reduce delays for users, content providers and other hosting companies then paid the caching companies to place copies of their content on such services in locations geographically close to users. Users were directed to the servers instead of the content provider's home site, and the data traveled a shorter distance, and thus the homes received faster response to queries.

---

[39]See Besen et al. (2001) and Laffont et al. (2001, 2003) for analysis of incentives to sign peering agreements.

Capital deepening in the backbone of the network would have been very expensive in the absence of caching services. Both ISP and the content firm benefited from caching, as this bypassed potential congestion in other parts of the network. In general, these became known as *overlays*, because they were not part of the original design of the noncommercial Internet.[40]

These changes raised an open question about whether the market for intermediate data transmission was still competitive. For much Internet service in urban areas, the answer appeared to be *yes*. ISPs could choose from multiple backbone providers and multiple deliverers of transit IP services, and many ISPs "multihomed" to get faster services from a variety of backbone providers. ISPs also had multiple options among cache and content delivery network (CDN) services. For Internet service outside of urban areas, the answer appeared to be *no*. ISPs did not have many options for "middle mile" transit services, and users did not have many options for access services. The high costs of supply made it difficult to change these conditions.[41]

Changes in National Policy

Capital deepening of the US data network would have occurred under almost any policy regime, but its rate was sensitive to the policy regime of the country. As it was, in many ways both large and small, the Federal Communications Commission (FCC) tried to foster the Internet's growth from 1992 through much of the decade.[42] At the same time, the statutory regime changed with the passage of the Telecommunications Act of 1996. It was the first major piece of federal legislation for telecommunications since the 1934 act that established the FCC. While the Telecom Act contained many complex features, several facets shaped the capital deepening over the next few years.[43]

The act did not impose a financial burden on the young commercial activity. ISPs did not have to pay the universal service fees that telephone

---

[40] For more on overlays, see Clark et al. (2006).

[41] See Strover (2001) or Downes and Greenstein (2002). A summary can be found in Greenstein and Prince (2006). Also see the discussion in the Federal Communications Commission (2010).

[42] Hundt (2000).

[43] This is discussed in more detail in Greenstein (2005).

companies had to pay. The act also exempted cable companies, and—because of the asymmetric burden placed on telephone companies—that legal exemption became especially important to regulators when cable companies began aspiring to convert their lines for carrying Internet traffic to homes.

Related, the act also contained provisions for the "E-rate program," which had both real and symbolic significance. The E-rate program, which was aimed at alleviating inequities in the provision of the Internet, was proposed as a funding scheme for bringing the Internet to disadvantaged users, particularly at schools and libraries. Although delayed by legal challenges, the E-rate program eventually raised over two billion dollars a year from long-distance telephone bills, and continued indefinitely. Closely identified with the ambitions of Vice President Al Gore, who had made fostering next-generation information technology a special interest, the E-rate program was labeled the "Gore tax" by opponents.[44]

Internet infrastructure received an additional implicit and explicit subsidy with the passage in October 1998 of the Internet Tax Freedom Act. It placed a federal moratorium on taxing the provision of Internet access. Unlike several other communications technologies, such as cellular telephony or landline telephony, Internet access was free from local attempts to tax the service (except those that were grandfathered in prior to October 1, 1998). The market's young status justified the law, according to supporters, who worried that excessive local taxation could deter growth for the new nationwide applications of electronic commerce in retailing.

Probably most important, the 1996 Telecom Act tried to encourage competition in telephony and data networks by formalizing national legal definitions for competitive local exchange companies (CLECs).[45] The new definition formalized a broad framework governing the access of CLECs to facilities from incumbent local exchange companies, or ILECs, which was the formal name for local telephone companies. These provisions were intended to advance competitive local telephony, but they also fostered the growth of CLECs, which supported ISP growth throughout the

---

[44]It survived several court challenges and regulatory lobbying efforts after its passage. This money was administered by the FCC. In 1998 this program was just getting under way.

[45]CLECs bore some resemblance to competitive access providers of the recent past. These were firms who connected with the existing telephone networks and offered services that competed with the telephone network.

United States.[46] This will be discussed in more detail in a later chapter about the telecom meltdown, and for now a simple statement will do: Eventually CLECs presented an acute issue for the intersection of US telephone and Internet policy. While the growth of CLECs supported growth of the Internet, an unintended subsidy had been built into the system, transferring money from telephone companies to CLECs. As it would turn out, these implicit subsidies would be removed in 1999.[47]

These policies mattered in another way. By 1998, many local telephone firms had begun basic Internet service. In addition, the long distance and data carrier AT&T emerged as the largest retail Internet provider to businesses; AT&T had already had a data carrier business with firms, but it grew larger when IBM sold the company its operation in 1997. Likewise, WorldCom was not far behind AT&T, having acquired UUNET and other firms. However, as a result of inheriting so many policies from competitive telephony, the independent dial-up Internet market had worked out a set of processes for doing business with local telephone companies. In many countries an independent dial-up industry never got off the ground, and government policies did not encourage it; in contrast, in the United States the government policies did get in the way, and many independent firms thrived.

Seen in retrospect, the growth of the dial-up network was quite an achievement. The national network grew without heavy-handed government intervention to make firms coordinate with one another. Symptoms of this achievement arose in many places: independent dial-up firms competed with large firms, and everyone interconnected; backbone providers (MCI,

---

[46] In his book recounting his years as FCC chairman between 2003 and 2007, Reed Hundt (2000) gives his staff at the FCC credit for interpreting the act in such a way as to foster growth of entry instead of protect incumbent telephone monopolies. Referring to how his agency implemented the 1996 act, he says (154–55):

> The conference committee compromises had produced a mountain of ambiguity that was generally tilted toward the local phone company's advantage. But under principles of statutory interpretation, we had broad authority to exercise our discretion in implementing the regulations. . . . The more our team studied the law the more we realized our decisions could determine the winners and losers in the new economy.

[47] This is described in more detail in chapter 12. A number of CLECs set up businesses to *receive* ISP calls from households but *send* very few, which effectively billed other telephone companies for "reciprocal compensation."

Sprint, and such) were the largest carriers of data, and many of these firms also provided retail ISP services to consumers while renting facilities to other ISPs, who rented rights to resell use of their modem banks; interconnection disputes also did not interfere with new entry. For example, Level 3, which had raised considerable funds, announced plans to enter at a national scale with a network architecture well suited to TCP/IP traffic, and began building its network from 1998 onward, and did not require government intervention to resolve interconnection issues.

Some restructuring did encounter roadblocks from policy makers, but it was rare, and arose only when consolidation threatened to eliminate competition. When MCI and UUNET became part of WorldCom in 1998, WorldCom became the largest backbone provider and a large reseller of national POPs to other firms. The divestiture of some Internet backbone became a condition for government approval of the MCI WorldCom merger. The proposed merger between Sprint and WorldCom also generated opposition. European regulators were the first to oppose it, and the US Department of Justice (DOJ) almost certainly would have opposed the merger, too, at least in part, but the merger was called off before official DOJ action. Relatedly, in late 1998, Bell Atlantic proposed a merger with GTE, forming Verizon. As condition for approval, GTE spun off the backbone as a separate entity, forming Genuity.

Viewed by the light of WorldCom's later accounting fraud, these government reviews appear to have been prescient. The government's actions helped to partially deconcentrate ownership of basic infrastructure assets and spread investment decisions into multiple hands. It did not allow a dominant firm to dictate terms of interconnection to any other, or impose their vision for the architecture on others. The US backbone, therefore, did not depend solely on the actions of a single firm, or on the (in)competence of that firm's management.

A Sense of Urgency

From the middle of the 1990s and onward for the next half decade, capital deepening extended far and wide throughout the network economy. Large enterprises, such as L. L. Bean and UPS, made investments aimed at developing new services, reducing costs, and responding to competitive threats. Network suppliers, such as WorldCom, MCI, and Level 3, made new investments aimed at carrying a large increase in traffic, enabling the new users to gain their productivity. Third parties, such as IBM, made a business of helping the investment work with existing equipment so it generated the maximum productivity advance. All of this investment extended the Internet into a vast array of business activities throughout the economy.

At a broad level, such a combination of expansion in sales, variety in approaches, and increasing standardization in operations was not unusual for a young entrepreneurial market. Yet to contemporaries the specific accomplishments appeared remarkable. The scale of investment was huge, and no contemporary communication network had ever been as entrepreneurial and expanded as fast.

Participants chose to act without spreading out the investment over time. This urgency arose for multiple reasons. For one, competitive pressures motivated actions sooner than later. Many established firms perceived a viable threat to revenue from entrepreneurial entrants, and, eventually, from their traditional competitors, who were making productive investments in electronic commerce. Second, growth of browser-based applications motivated more adoption of Internet access in homes and businesses, which generated more investment from suppliers of data services and in infrastructure to support it. Meeting this genuine growth in demand also motivated investments sooner rather than later.

The simultaneous growth of investment in all of these activities became self-reinforcing, which is an additional factor, and the most unusual one. Better infrastructure generated better services, which motivated new users, and new application development, deepening capital in every related process.

This positive reinforcement often went by another shorthand label, and was called a "network effect." In dry abstract terms a "network effect" arises if the value of participating in a community rises with the scale of participation in that community. In this instance, more participants wanted to join a whole array of complementary TCP/IP-based activities. Said another way, the simultaneity of capital deepening investment was symptomatic of many commercial firms facing the incentives to invest now (instead of later) to take advantage of the network effect they all experienced at the same time.

This positive reinforcement contributed to impatient investment, and, unrecognized by many at the time, connected the beginning of the boom to its later fate. As later chapters describe, in the latter part of the 1990s some investors took the positive reinforcement for granted, anticipating its appearance.

That anticipation could be either correct or incorrect. When correct, it allowed for additional investments in advance of use of the capacity. The positive experience in the first few years of the boom—1996, 1997, and 1998—largely rewarded those who took it for granted, or, what was equivalent, presumed an optimistic outcome. Many new services met with quick uptake and use.

That anticipated demand motivated many to continue investing into 1999 and 2000. While nobody planned for the Internet's investment boom to cease, it made no sense to plan for calm. The investments were urgent and required attention. Their inevitable and unavoidable end was something to worry about later. With all those taking each other's investment for granted, however, it was only a matter of time before somebody overshot their investments—either because they presumed too much about the actions of others or jumped out in front too quickly to gain a competitive advantage that never materialized, or let their optimism overrule good business sense.

Such overshooting was in the future, too far away to be a concern just yet. Contemporaries talked as if they were experiencing a once-in-a-lifetime event, and many acted accordingly. Their impatience was visible in a wide range of economic activities—in cavalier attitudes about equipment purchases, in stock valuations that presumed sales would grow exponentially higher in response to business investment, in the use of unethical competitive tactics that the purveyor presumed were too expensive to police. Managers at firms that had never been big players in IT faced issues they had never considered, and many chose to invest.

EXPLORATION AND RENEWAL

Chapters 11, 12, 13, and 14 analyze exploration, and related activities that encouraged or discouraged it. The chapters examine Microsoft during the browser wars, Wall Street analysts during the financial bubble, the entry of Google, and the growth of wireless Internet access.

TABLE 11.1. Selected notable events from chapters 11, 12, 13, 14

Year	Chapters	Notable Events
1994	13	Lou Montulli invents the cookie at Netscape
	13	Sergey Brin begins his graduate studies
1995	11	Bill Gates writes "Internet Tidal Wave"
	11	Netscape IPO and Windows 95 launched in same month
	13	Larry Page begins his graduate studies
1996	11	Microsoft begins pressuring partners not to support Netscape
	12	Greenspan makes speech about "Irrational Exuberance"
	12	Wave of new entrants marks start of dot-com boom
1997	14	FCC issues final draft of Part-15 rules for spectrum
	11	Jobs makes deal so IE becomes default browser for Apple
	11	Netscape and Microsoft reach near parity in browser features
1998	11	Senate hearings about Microsoft
	13	Google founded by Larry Page and Sergey Brin
	11	Netscape coalition collapses, AOL eventually buys Netscape
1999	12	Dot-com boom reaches greatest height
	12	Telecom meltdown begins after rule change for CLECs
	14	IEEE committee 802.11 issues design a & b, labeled "Wi-Fi"
2000	11	Judge Jackson issues judgment that finds against Microsoft
	12	NASDAQ reaches its peak in stock valuations of dot-coms
2001	14	Wi-Fi becomes available on Windows-based systems
	12	PSINet declares bankruptcy
	12	9/11 terrorist attacks on World Trade Center
	11	DOJ settles with Microsoft
2002	12	Internal accountant discovered fraud at WorldCom
	13	Google scales quality-weighted second price auction
	12	Economic decline reaches its nadir
2003	13	Google launches AdSense
	14	Intel launches Centrino

11

Bill Votes with a Veto

Bill Gates is an ingenious engineer, but I don't think he is
adept at business ethics. He has not yet come to realize
that the things he did (when Microsoft was smaller) he
should not have done when Microsoft was a monopoly.
—*Judge Thomas Penfield Jackson*[1]

The life of William Gates III has followed a unique arc. In the late 1970s
Gates founded Microsoft with his friend, Paul Allen. Allen left for
health reasons while the company was still young. Gates, along with college buddy Steve Ballmer, managed it for the next two and a half decades.
Gates finally retired from his full-time position in 2006. In the process he
became unbelievably wealthy—to the tune of $50 billion. Many of Gates's
associates also became extremely wealthy, Ballmer and Allen most notably. However, Gates's wealth outshines everyone's, making him comparable to only a small number of other business figures in history—robber
barons in popular speak—such as Carnegie, Rockefeller, Bell, and Ford.

Gates has not always seemed certain how to manage his unique status
in society and history. The social expectations, responsibilities, and worldly
public persona often required by the media, public, and social stratosphere
in which Gates lives were difficult for him to internalize and then project
to the public. During Gates's long tenure as CEO of Microsoft, a team of
public relations experts tried to cover this particular weakness by managing or modifying how Bill appeared to the public. Yet every so often a crack

---

[1] Quoted in Opinion for the United States Court of Appeals, 2001.

would appear in Gates's carefully crafted image. On occasion, one such public gaffe would illuminate the professional side of Gates's life.

In volume 3 of Robert Cringely's *Nerds 2.0.1,* a movie about the growth of the Internet, Cringely conducts an interview with Gates. During the time of the interview, Microsoft's fortunes were growing, but the federal antitrust case against Microsoft had not yet been filed. Gates is not feeling defensive and is relaxed, even when Cringely asks Gates if Microsoft is losing money in its browser strategy.

Gates pauses, smiles, and then, speaking with just a hint of dry humor, says, "Well, nobody ever accused Microsoft of not knowing how to make money." The smiling Gates then exhales in a little involuntary laugh, an introspective response to his own wit. There is nothing suave or planned about it—just a cross between a guffaw and a boyish giggle. After another pause, Gates provides an explanation of how Internet Explorer, or IE, helped the Windows business. The answer does substantively address the question, but it seems to dissolve in the revelation about the source. Gates is a socially awkward man who knows how to make money, and knows that he knows.

The Internet had not escaped Gates's notice. However, for a time he did not see how Microsoft—or any other software firm for that matter—could make money in the browser business or any other Internet application. Gates had maintained a consistent position throughout 1994 and early 1995. He regarded the Internet as a useful piece of functionality and an additional feature of server software. Microsoft needed the functionality in its servers to compete with Unix systems. He saw no reason for Microsoft to develop browsers or experiment with prototypes of Internet applications to sell to end users. But by the spring of 1995, Netscape's success had forced Gates to reconsider his assessment, and, as other chapters have mentioned, Microsoft's behavior thereafter appeared to be focused on winning the market share for his browser at any cost.

Why did Gates behave this way? Why did Microsoft's browser meet Netscape's browser head on in the marketplace? What did Microsoft do and why did it upset so many in the industry? Contemporary commentators began calling the confrontation *browser wars.* The browser wars were more than just an ephemeral competitive episode in the Internet ecosystem. The strategies of both firms touched every single major participant in the commercial Internet, and shaped their actions. The episode also illustrates an important policy issue: how a large powerful firm can discourage the blossoming of innovation from the edges when it possesses the ability and incentive to do so. In this instance, the government took action, and the legacy of that intervention mattered for years thereafter.

What Happened inside Microsoft

By 1995 Microsoft combined aspects of a publicly traded company with many of the trappings of a privately held one. Gates helped take Microsoft public and had always owned a significant fraction of the company.[2] Gates's ownership coincided with considerable personal authority. He sat at the center of every major decision within the firm, and he retained the right to review any employee's action.

Gates did not make money through commercializing one big invention, like Alexander Graham Bell. Rather, Microsoft made money by employing Gates's uncommon savvy in the art of software commercialization. Gates made countless little decisions. The strategic and financial benefits accumulated over years, occasionally becoming manifest in a few well-known events, such as the rollout of the Office suite and Windows 95. Gates repeatedly approached situations with the intent to outthink and out-execute others. In pursuit of that approach, he became a devoted student of computer industry business models and lessons learned from other markets.

Gates's approach was on full display in the key memo for the browser wars, "The Internet Tidal Wave," which, as prior chapters described, Gates wrote after a night of surfing, arranged by the skunk works within his firm. Few CEOs could have written a single-spaced eight-page document that (a) summarized fifteen years of strategic positioning, (b) provided technical detail of that strategy, and (c) repositioned the firm's priorities for the next epochal change. Gates had learned from the efforts to investigate browsers, and the memo showed that he grasped an impressive range of facts and theories.[3]

---

[2] By 2006 that percentage decreased to 10 percent when Gates stopped working in the firm day to day.

[3] As earlier chapters described, Ben Slivka wrote "The Web Is the Next Platform." The fourth and final draft is available at http://www.usdoj.gov/atr/cases/ms_exhibits.htm, exhibit 21. Gates's memo is exhibit 20.

The timing for the memo shaped Gates's analysis. Microsoft had set itself on a lucrative trajectory with Windows 95's development, whereby Microsoft aspired to realize its ambitions through a two-pronged approach: first, provide every piece of ubiquitous software for PCs; and second, prevent any other firm from offering the same degree of functionality. Together these assured Microsoft a unique position: a piece of revenue from every PC purchase. As discussed in prior chapters, Netscape's browser brought to life a version of Gates's biggest nightmare—namely, the possibility that enormous functionality could be delivered to users through alternative channels—the Internet, in this instance. That functionality would be a substitute for software Microsoft provided.

Multiple versions of this nightmare would eventually grab hold of Microsoft's strategic outlook. In one version, Netscape invited application developers today, and Netscape became an operating system tomorrow. In another version Netscape and related "middleware"—software that stood between the operating system and other applications—facilitated the entry of an operating system from another firm on PCs, or it facilitated entry of a range of new devices that accessed the Internet. In any of these versions, the strategic focus was the same; Netscape's presence and prosperity reduced the value of Microsoft's position on the value chain because it facilitated entry of substitutes.

While Microsoft's actions later appeared to outsiders to follow a relentless logic, things looked different inside Microsoft. Gates initially proceeded over many tense discussions in which Microsoft executives disagreed with the substance of his nightmare. For example, the launch of Windows 95 was going well by the spring of 1995, and, accordingly, many inside Microsoft could forecast high sales with confidence. In that light those in charge of marketing and distributing the operating system did not share Gates's vision of Netscape. They saw Netscape's entry as unexpectedly good for sales of Windows 95 and Microsoft's bottom line, because growth in Internet adoption would lead to more PC sales than originally forecast. In short, Netscape's success appeared to immediately help the sales of Microsoft's biggest product, Windows 95, not threaten it. (Indeed, this turned out to be a correct forecast of what the Internet and web did to PC sales over the next several years.) Employees with this vision took direct issue with the paranoia in Gates's strategy and saw Netscape as a gift, and they believed Microsoft should seek to encourage it to blossom.

Was Gates prophetic or paranoid to change his mind about browsers? Gates had been right in the past, steering the company into its unfathomable position of profitability, and in most parts of Microsoft Gates had earned the benefit of the doubt. That will partly explain why he was able to induce many actions, though many employees did not fully perceive the threat, even at Microsoft's largest and most profitable division.

He also could induce many actions because Gates had a comparatively free rein throughout the firm. Most employees did not perceive all that he did, or even part of it, unless it involved their own corner of the firm. Many employees looked only at their own division's behavior.

The first version of a browser, IE 1.0, actually arrived at Microsoft before the "Internet Tidal Wave" was written, because it came from actions taken by the earliest investigations into browsers and the Internet. Shipped with Windows 95 in August 1995 as an additional "plus pack," IE 1.0 was a mildly changed version of the browser licensed by Spyglass, the firm that licensed Mosaic for the University of Illinois.

The next key actions took place behind the scenes before IE 1.0 ever shipped. In June 1995, before Netscape's IPO and before the official release of Windows 95, Microsoft contacted Netscape. Their stated intent: they wanted to make an investment in the young firm and, in return, gain a board seat. In fact, Microsoft's discussions with Netscape had multiple motives. Firstly, to explore whether it was possible to gain control over Netscape's action through an inexpensive board seat or merger; secondly, to explore whether it was possible to gain insight into Netscape's strategic intent through mere conversation about the purchase of a board seat; and thirdly, to engage in a conversation and gain information that might help settle debates inside Microsoft's headquarters in Redmond, Washington, about whether any of Netscape's outsized aspirations conflicted with Microsoft's goals.[4] Eventually the first meeting turned into several, and those talks would evolve into discussions about Microsoft buying all of Netscape.

There was little publicly said about the talks until several years later, when the antitrust trial in 1999–2000 (discussed later in this chapter) shed light on them, and the lawyers for both sides fought over interpretations of the ambiguous notes taken at the meeting. The meetings and conversation did have lasting consequences because they altered the view that each

---

[4]See Cusumano and Yoffie (1998).

side took of the other. Netscape refused Microsoft's last offer for an acquisition, which Microsoft's management interpreted as a signal of their outsized aspirations. Microsoft's management believed their last offer had
been respectfully high, and no firm would turn it down except a firm who
intended to invade Microsoft's core market. In contrast, Netscape perceived Microsoft's offer for Netscape as much too low. Netscape's managers gained the impression that Microsoft did not understand the potential
size of the market opportunity for Internet software. They concluded that
Microsoft's market forecasts were either too pessimistic or misguided.

Whose perceptions were right and wrong? A couple months later, it did
not matter. On August 9, 1995, Netscape held its IPO. This event settled
many matters, both establishing Netscape as a publicly traded company
and providing the investment community with a public demonstration of
the potential for Internet firms. More to the point, the IPO settled any lin-
gering debates inside Netscape and Microsoft. The management at Netscape believed events had shown they had been correct to hold out. The
IPO suggested many investors had a very optimistic view of Netscape's
potential. After the IPO, inside Microsoft, Gates was no longer met with
any opposition to his view that Netscape's aspirations posed a threat, as
he continued to push for a coordinated set of actions across Microsoft.

Two Platforms and Two Positions

In August 1995 Microsoft released the first version of Windows 95. The
next key moment would come in early December 1995. To understand that
moment, it is essential to appreciate the strategic similarities and differences in the positions of Netscape and Microsoft. These differences would
translate into strategic advantages and disadvantages in their fight.

The strategic similarities arose from similar forecasts. Both Microsoft and
Netscape anticipated supporting developers who would write applications
for the platform, and both firms anticipated that developers would prefer to
write applications for the browser with the most users, and users would go
to the browser with the most functionality. Thus both firms anticipated
fighting to win a majority of users and developers. Both firms also had a
similar forecast for the near future, anticipating that the majority of new
users of browsers would arrive somewhere in the future. That forecast
translated into similar strategic stances—namely, both firms sought to gain

an edge in 1995 in anticipation of a competitive future in 1996 and 1997 and beyond. That forward-looking attitude would persist throughout the browser wars. Accordingly, from the fall of 1995 onward, every confrontation between Netscape and Microsoft took on extra importance for management, even in episodes where the short-term stakes appeared to be small.

The similarities ended there. Their different business interests would shape their actions in visible ways. Microsoft profited from selling PC software and server software. In contrast, Netscape sold browsers and a range of complementary products to help enterprises take advantage of the commercial web. It had no other revenue, nor any other business to support, though it had aspirations to grow many more.

As prior chapters have discussed, Netscape had moved first. It priced its browser with the intent to build its base of users. Netscape had employed an imaginative and genuinely novel pricing strategy. Calling it "free but not free," Netscape gave away its browser to home users, but sold commercial licenses to businesses. Throughout 1995 the free browsers achieved Netscape's goals, displacing Mosaic browsers already in use, and it began building word-of-mouth support for more adoption, while the licensing brought revenue into Netscape.

Netscape also faced a major strategic challenge: it needed partners. For Netscape to succeed, in addition to attracting programmers, many other software firms would have to help Netscape's platform. It also needed firms to aid in the adoption of browsers at businesses. Netscape intended to attract such firms by committing to the open standards of the Internet and web. Many of these firms already did business with Microsoft in one way or another, so Netscape had extra work to do. Attracting and supporting many business partners stretched the young firm from the outset and continued to stretch it over the next few years. Netscape had to invent its support processes, hire and train employees, and build operations from the ground up.

Microsoft faced a rather different set of strategic challenges. The late start framed many of these. Microsoft had to find a way to slow down the adoption of Netscape's browsers by developers and new users, and thereby give Microsoft sufficient time to develop a browser that matched Netscape's in functionality. In the short run that meant Microsoft had to find a way to convince developers that they should not exclusively cooperate with Netscape.

Throughout the fall of 1995 Bill Gates studied this situation and debated with his colleagues. From that debate came two fateful strategic choices: First, he chose a strategy that depended on his programming team's ability. They would have to build a browser at an extraordinarily fast pace, while keeping up with any new functionality available at Netscape. Second, Gates chose to financially subsidize the effort, hoping to turn the development race into a contest that stretched Netscape's resources, which played to Microsoft's superior financial strength. In short, Microsoft funded programmer time and personnel far in excess of the direct revenue generated in the short run.

This was a familiar playbook at Microsoft. Microsoft had become the largest software firm in the world because it was so good at out-executing and, when it helped other parts of its business, out-spending others. As the remainder of the chapter describes, in fact, Microsoft stuck with these two grand strategic principles over the course of the browser wars, and it certainly mattered.[5] This persistence also accounts for one of the biggest myths about the browser wars. Observing *only* these two actions, it is possible to conclude (incorrectly) that these actions—and *only* these actions— led Microsoft to win the browser wars. Relatedly, it is also possible to point to only these actions and conclude Microsoft did not deserve any legal troubles. That is a misleading inference based on incomplete observation. As described later, Microsoft's additional actions got them into trouble.

On December 7, 1995, Microsoft held a major press conference announcing their Internet strategy. Prior to that announcement, the executives at Microsoft used the preparation for the news conference as a "forcing function" to finalize their strategy.[6] The event received considerable notice in the national news. In industry circles each word from this event was parsed for deeper clues. One key announcement on that day got more attention than any other. Microsoft announced that it would not charge

---

[5]Notice that the logic also implies the opposite, which did come to pass. After the war ended Microsoft also reduced the speed of development and level of funding, illustrating that the fast execution was motivated by strategic considerations in a competitive race.

[6]A "forcing function" is an event that leads management to settle open matters, and sometimes the event is under the control of the management and sometimes not. See Cusumano and Yoffie (1998) for a lengthy description of this event, and an argument that Microsoft's management deliberately scheduled the news conference to make it serve as a forcing function.

any price for its browser. It went further, announcing that future browsers would be integrated into its operating system as a feature, ceasing to be an application in Microsoft's products.

Several things followed: First, an integrated browser could take advantage of the ubiquity of Microsoft's operating system. As long as the browser was displayed prominently and supported, it would have to be distributed to users—almost automatically—along with the Windows operating system, which was used by close to 90 percent of the user base among PCs at that time. Second, although IE was not as good as Netscape's browser at that point, a free and integrated browser would eventually motivate Netscape to give away its browser too, reducing Netscape's revenue. Third, and less obvious, Internet Explorer was made the default browser unless users made efforts to change it to something else, such as Netscape's browser. Finally, and perhaps most important, there was no longer any public doubt about Microsoft's intent and commitment.

One other dimension to Microsoft's actions was less appreciated at the time and became public only very slowly. Starting from the winter of 1996 Microsoft had begun to use an additional and broad tactic—namely, beginning to place pressure on every business partner—nearly every major firm in computing—to help it to push IE into widespread use and to prevent Netscape from gaining widespread use.[7]

Later it would be left to the court to decide why Microsoft had added this last tactic. In one view, Gates had not seen the progress he wanted in early 1996 and reacted in a panic. He had taken a risk and pushed beyond ethical limits. In another view, Gates was so focused on winning the browser wars that he lost sight of broader ethical and legal limits, and he simply misjudged where the line should be drawn by letting his self-interest interfere with his conversations with his legal team. A related third view stressed a feature of Gates's personality in competitive situations: his stubborn unwillingness to concede points to others. In this view Gates misunderstood the legal ramifications of his own actions and misinterpreted the complaints as merely sour grapes over Netscape's competitive misfortunes.

---

[7]The most succinct description of the allegations is in Tim Bresnahan's (2003) summary of the DOJ case and Henderson's (2001) declaration for the remedies portion of the trial. These stress control of information, control of interfaces, tying, bribing potential middleware suppliers, using control over original equipment manufacturers, and bribing and/or coercing other third parties. The chapter is necessarily a simplification.

Not all of this was known at the time, but information about the strategy leaked out over time. For example, almost a year and half after the Internet strategy news conference, in July 1997, *Jupiter Communications* published a retrospective analysis of Microsoft's Internet strategy, including analysis about the earliest moments in the browser wars. This article made public what others had inferred about Microsoft's behavior: it was pursuing a strategy of "embrace and extend." The strategy—allegedly based on an internal memo at Microsoft—was described succinctly:

Phase 1: Identify the market leader;
Phase 2: Emulate the market leader;
Phase 3: Steal the vision, provide a migration path;
Phase 4: Integrate, leverage, and erode.[8]

The quote reflected the popular view that Microsoft was focused on winning the browser war by matching any and all features found in its rival. It also reflected popular perceptions that Microsoft took a blunt and brazen approach.

Three Versions

Gates was a unique executive with an idiosyncratic approach to making strategic choices. His approach reflected a combination of technical smarts, personality traits, and acquired business sense. First, Gates liked technical topics for their own sake. For example, he taught himself to program and debug DEC's computers when he was a teenager. Second, Gates drew on an almost unique mix of drive, persistence, and patience when pursuing his goals. For example, he furiously drove himself to learn things he believed he needed to know, and he negotiated incessantly until he won the points he wanted, while, in contrast, he could wait eons for results from strategic investments. Third, and least well known, Gates used his authority inside his company to teach and conduct lengthy investigations. He would convey a view, address questions and consider them in light of the available facts, and, in many cases, argue back and forth with employees. Every longtime Microsoft executive had experienced these pop quizzes,

---

[8]Jupiter Communications (1997).

and, as a result, could talk intelligently about the firm's strategy as well as every one of the Microsoft's major competitors' strategies.

All three predilections shaped Microsoft's actions during a release of software. Gates arranged its product launches with the intent to learn from market experience. Many observers came to label this behavior a "three-version strategy." In the first version Microsoft experimented with features and learned about market demand. In the second, they responded to feedback by improving its features. In in the third, they put all the lessons together, often to produce a hit product. Prior to the browser wars, Gates had personally coordinated the execution and updating of the strategy many times.

The three-version strategy was well known by the time the browser wars began. Most commentators assumed Microsoft would continue to follow the three-version strategy in an attempt to reach parity with Netscape. Since version 1.0 came from the University of Illinois, that meant parity had to be achieved by version 4.0. Knowing that others would expect this behavior, Gates anticipated that developers would look at the gaps between the functionality of Netscape's and Microsoft's browser after the releases of 2.0 and 3.0. Others would expect the gaps to decline with each release. That set up the situation: Netscape and Microsoft raced to add features that impressed users and developers. Each firm added more features that users valued, such as a range of bookmark tools and editing tools. Each added shortcuts and tools for developers, making their activities easier, and expanding the range of what they could offer to users.

Although a race can benefit users by adding features, some aspects of this race were not benign. Both firms tried to introduce proprietary features into their browsers, making it harder for vendors and users to switch to alternatives. For example, both distributed editing tools that generated web pages that included proprietary extensions to HTML that only their browser could read, and which their rival could not. Each of these was a step toward multiple proprietary flavors of HTML, one from Microsoft and one from Netscape, in addition to the version that the World Wide Web Consortium supplied.

HTML did not become proprietary, however. Tim Berners-Lee announced his opposition to such proprietary features, and he announced that the World Wide Web Consortium would never endorse such features. A large number of developers listened to Berners-Lee and refused to use these features. Chastened, neither firm tried this tactic again.

In the service of this race one other tactic also gained prominence: buy what could not be developed quickly. This played to Microsoft's advantage in cash. For example, a start-up, Vermeer, had a well-developed authoring and editing tool, easy use, and was perfect for many new users. The founders decided in early 1996 that continuing as a stand-alone firm was less viable than merging with another. It made itself for sale, creating a bidding war between Microsoft and Netscape. Bidding eventually settled on $130 million. Netscape gave up, and Microsoft rebranded the software as FrontPage.[9]

The war did eventually unfold as forecast. Microsoft did catch up in three versions. IE 1.0 and 2.0 did not measure up to Netscape's browser, but 3.0, released in August 1996, closed the gap considerably. For all intents and purposes, 4.0, released almost a year later in September 1997, closed the gap entirely.

Moving Developers

Microsoft's strategy needed time. It needed time so the functionality of its browser could catch up to Netscape. It needed time so it could have a chance to gain new Internet users before they committed to another browser. This translated into a simple strategic imperative: Microsoft had to slow down user adoption of Netscape's browser. How would it do that?[10] In so many words, Microsoft could ask for the slowdown and buy it from business partners. Microsoft already did business with many industry participants, and many of them depended on maintaining good relationships with Microsoft. Nobody would refuse to take the call from Bill. Yet this course of action had an obvious drawback as well; many developers were not in a mood to do Microsoft any more favors.

Prior to the browser wars many developers respected and (begrudgingly) admired Gates for his achievements and quick mind. However, just

---

[9]See Ferguson (1999). Despite selling the firm to Microsoft, the sale did not stop Ferguson from devoting the last chapter of his book to an analysis of the competitive problems Microsoft's actions posed.

[10]This description is necessarily a shortened version of events. For a full recounting of the sequence of actions, see the court's Findings of Fact, especially pages 40–177. http://www.justice.gov/atr/cases/f3800/msjudgex.htm, accessed November 2012.

as many despised him for being rich and ungenerous and self-centered and unwilling to suffer fools among his employees and business partners. He also was accused of being far too willing to imitate another firm's good ideas without giving credit. Many also had walked away from negotiations with him with observations about his lack of social graces, his combativeness, and his unwillingness to yield a reasonable point to anyone else. Initially, many developers' contempt for Gates helped Netscape, because Netscape recruited employees who wanted to develop browser technology and applications, and who wanted to see that technology bypass Microsoft's products and APIs.[11]

Microsoft pressed ahead in 1996. Every important firm delivering Internet services received a phone call either from Bill or someone on his staff—all major ISPs, all PC manufacturers, all major Internet vendors, all major software firms, and all major consulting firms. Firms were offered deals to promote Microsoft's browser while simultaneously making it difficult for Netscape to distribute its browser. Many reached a deal with Microsoft in 1996 or 1997. A few examples of what happened at companies doing computer assembly can illustrate how and why.

Consider Dell Computer. Dell had positioned itself as a low-cost provider of PCs, and it profited from high volumes of sales to business users. It needed the full cooperation of its business partners, particularly Intel and Microsoft, to produce a wide range of designs at large scale. It also had received preferential pricing and promotional deals from Intel and Microsoft—as good as or better than any other deal in the business. Dell needed such pricing to continue with its strategy of being a low-cost provider of PCs.

Dell cooperated early and readily with Microsoft's demands. Without any fanfare, Dell stopped putting Netscape's browser on its systems even when users asked for it. Not coincidently, Dell continued to get its favored status. This capitulation was well known and became the status quo quite early in the browser wars.

Such protocol generated an embarrassing moment for Michael Dell, in a March 1998, Senate hearing. Senator Orrin Hatch asked Michael Dell why his company promised to give customers whatever they wanted and

[11] See Cusumano and Yoffie (1998).

yet did not offer a Netscape browser to customers. Dell offered an explanation that stressed his licensing agreements.[12] Hatch shot back:

> Could you explain why, when committee staff called Dell's 1-800 number, five different sales representatives—George, Brad, Jason, Bobby and Jeff—told them that Dell could not distribute Netscape because of Dell's licensing agreement with Microsoft?[13]

Michael Dell did not and could not provide a satisfying answer. His firm was doing well by cooperating with Microsoft.

Other firms that did not cooperate immediately suffered a painful route to cooperation. One firm, Compaq, having heard from many business customers who wanted Netscape browsers, featured it prominently. Unfortunately for Compaq, as a "reward" for listening to its consumers, Microsoft made an example of the company.

In 1996, for example, employees at Compaq removed the IE icon from shipped versions of computers. Their buyers were primarily businesses, and businesses had told them that they wanted the Netscape browser. Compaq removed IE in order to keep the icons less confusing and thus orient the computers toward the business needs of their buyers, while providing the applications users wanted. Microsoft believed Compaq had a business obligation to display IE, and it sent a letter to Compaq threatening to cut off its operating system license in sixty days if a removed IE icon was not put back on all new systems.[14]

Compaq capitulated quickly. At the time, it left everyone in the industry with the strong impression that Microsoft had chosen to make an example of Compaq. If nothing else, it also publicly demonstrated the draw-

---

[12] As quoted in McWilliams (1998), Michael Dell said,

> We negotiate vigorously with all of our vendors to obtain the best possible terms that we can for our own company and our customers and our shareholders. And based on the terms that we have negotiated . . . the incentives that have been put in place for us to sell one product or another are going to dictate our actions.

This answer is both true, and not, related to explaining why Michael Dell promised customers anything they wanted but acted differently than promised, maintaining an exclusive relationship with Microsoft, even when customers directly asked for Netscape.

[13] Quoted in Chandrasekaran (1998).

[14] Hardwick (1996). Or see the court's Findings of Fact, pages 99–101, http://www.justice.gov/atr/cases/f3800/msjudgex.htm, accessed November 2012.

backs to being a business partner that did not play by Microsoft's rules in all respects.[15] Why did it leave that impression? As was frequently pointed out in public forums, the actions were public, but what lay behind them were not public (and it remained that way until the antitrust trial). This was but one of several alleged strong-arm tactics that most computer company executives refused to discuss with news organizations for fear of retaliation from Microsoft.[16] Relatedly, no senior executive at Microsoft ever apologized, nor disavowed the action, nor did the firm ever give back any of the strategic gains it reaped from the action, which left the impression that the negotiating method was not an accident.

Despite the example Microsoft made of Compaq, the executive team at Microsoft decided to take further strict action with its business partners. Thereafter, Microsoft inserted clauses into operating system licenses that included but were not limited to restrictions on assemblers. Assemblers had to support an "out of the box" experience for users as they first fired up their systems, and it had to follow Microsoft's script.

That sounds innocuous, but it was not because Microsoft wanted something that its business partners did not want to do. For example, one contracting provision prevented original equipment manufacturers (OEMs) from adding help screens for users of the Netscape browser. That is not a misprint—help screens for Netscape were forbidden, even though that reduced the quality of the user experience and drove up OEM service expenses (OEMs fielded the phone calls from irate buyers who could not operate a browser).

The restrictions generated strong feelings. Consider this statement from an executive at Hewlett-Packard, who wanted to include a help screen on its PCs to help a user figure out how to use Netscape:

> We must have the ability to decide how our system is presented to our end users. If we had a choice of another supplier, based on your actions in this area, I assure you [that you (Microsoft)] would not be

---

[15] The dispute was (apparently) settled through a few phone calls, but only after the threatening letter had been sent, which makes one wonder how much of the public discussion was simply putting lipstick on a pig. Thereafter, the Netscape and IE icons appeared on both desktops for a short period, but Compaq renegotiated its contracts with others. See McCullagh (1999).

[16] See Chandrasekaran (1999).

our supplier of choice. I strongly urge you to have your executives review your decisions and to change this unacceptable policy.[17]

By what right did Gates have the ability to tell OEMs not to help its users? His lawyers had inserted the clause and the OEMs could not refuse, lest they lose all their business.

Gates pressed everywhere, even at Apple. The newly returned CEO, Steve Jobs,[18] cut a deal to make IE the default browser, which Jobs announced at MacWorld in Boston on August 6, 1997. Jobs received boos for this deal at the industry conference in which it was announced. But he preferred boos from his loyal buyers than the irritation of—and delays from—the provider of some of the Macintosh's valuable software applications.[19] Witness, once again, Redmond's negotiating leverage. It never actually delayed the delivery of any software for the Macintosh. In conversations with Jobs, Gates merely had to allude to the possibility, even though development inside Microsoft (in truth) proceeded apace.

Microsoft also turned its attention to firms providing Internet access. While Microsoft successfully engineered to have many firms providing Internet access support its browser, there was one firm it never had been able to push around, America Online (AOL). AOL showed what a firm needed to bargain successfully with Microsoft—something Gates wanted.

As earlier chapters described, for many users AOL acted as both Internet access firm and portal, and through aggressive marketing had started to become the largest ISP in the United States. In 1996 and 1997 AOL focused their marketing efforts on new users to the Internet, where they believed they could add the greatest number of users. Executives at AOL did not trust Gates. They considered Microsoft a competitor for new users, and there was merit to the perception. Microsoft's initiatives in MSN resembled AOL's, were designed to compete directly with AOL for the same

---

[17] After the introduction of these restrictions Hewlett-Packard sent a letter to Microsoft with the strongly worded lines. See also, United States v. Microsoft Corp., 84 F. Supp. 2d 9 (D.D.C. 1999), 210–15.

[18] He was the interim CEO at the time of this announcement.

[19] The deal also settled several patent disputes, gave Apple cash in exchange for stock, and committed to make Microsoft Office available for five years. After the announcement about the default browser, Jobs said to applause, "Since we believe in choice, we're going to be shipping other Internet browsers, as well, on the Macintosh, and the user can, of course, change their default should they choose to."

customers, and contained many features that imitated AOL's. When Microsoft called to make a deal, AOL pushed back and negotiated hard.

AOL controlled the default browser settings for its users, who themselves tended not to switch these defaults. Although AOL users were not frequent Internet users, AOL had made itself compatible with the Internet. Its defaults could move significant amounts of "browser usage share" for a large fraction of online users. AOL argued that these defaults would not change unless Microsoft gave in on the thing AOL wanted—the right to have AOL's branded icon on every desktop. The icon would link to directions that helped new users get online.[20]

Why was Microsoft in a position to trade position on the desktop? Once again, Bill has told Microsoft's lawyers to insert a clause into contracts with OEMs about how the operating system had to look when it first booted up for a new user. Such was the power of Microsoft's contract restrictions on assemblers. Microsoft could offer AOL the right to show up on a user's system after it booted up, even when the assembly was being performed by IBM, Dell, HP, and others.

Repeatedly Gates refused to make this deal with AOL, even though his browser division wanted it. He worried that his employees at MSN would view it as a broken promise to protect and promote MSN by giving it favorable placement on the desktop. Accordingly, AOL refused in return to make Internet Explorer the default browser for their users.

The standoff broke when AOL threatened to make a deal with Netscape in March 1996. Only when the Netscape deal neared completion did Microsoft budge.[21] Accordingly, AOL received the best deal of all. Along with hundreds of millions of dollars, it got the key item that Steve Case, CEO of AOL, had held out for. Case got a button on the desktop. No other ISP ever successfully managed to again get such a placement. In return, Microsoft moved enormous market share. Although it took a while to implement, by January 1998, over 90 percent of AOL's users—by then, the largest access provider in the United States—were using Internet Explorer.[22]

[20] Microsoft also made certain cash payments to AOL. See page 71, and pages 135–48, court's Findings of Fact, http://www.justice.gov/atr/cases/f3800/msjudgex.htm, accessed November 2012.

[21] Page 142, court's Findings of Fact, http://www.justice.gov/atr/cases/f3800/msjudgex.htm, accessed November 2012.

[22] Page 147, court's Findings of Fact, http://www.justice.gov/atr/cases/f3800/msjudgex.htm, accessed November 2012.

In the midst of these debates in Microsoft, Gates revealed that he fully understood these trade-offs. He wrote:

> We have had three options for how to use the "Windows Box": First, we can use it for the browser battle, recognizing that our core assets are at risk. Second, we could monetize the box, and sell the real estate to the highest bidder. Or third, we could use the box to sell and promote internal content assets. I recognize that, by choosing to do the first, we have leveled the playing field and reduced our opportunities for competitive advantage with MSN.[23]

Circling back to the main theme, these aggressive tactics and obsession with beating Netscape yielded high short-term costs—in terms of employee time, managerial attention, and reputation costs—and far exceeded the short-term benefits in terms of revenue. While many contemporary news outlets highlighted the drama of the confrontation, these actions could not be rationalized without recognizing the trade-off between short-term costs and Bill Gates's perceptions about long-term benefits for Microsoft. Gates authorized such an approach because he wanted users and developers not to work with anyone else other than Microsoft, regardless of what users or developers wanted.

More broadly, these examples illustrate how Gates made the browser wars a top priority, and expended costs far above any direct revenue affiliated with Internet-related businesses. Microsoft effectively pushed its browser out to all kinds of PCs, not just new versions of Windows, and it prevented Netscape's browser from becoming the default in widespread distribution. Microsoft made it difficult for Netscape to distribute its browser to the typical mass-market user, thereby slowing down Netscape's adoption.

Netscape had had to put up with something no mass-market application software firm ever had faced. Much of the adversity Netscape faced distributing its product had nothing to do with the products' merits and functionality. It had to do with reluctant business partners, and partially or fully closed distribution channels, none of which would have been reluctant or closed had Gates not worked so hard to achieve that outcome.

---

[23]Quoted from page 141 in court's Findings of Fact, http://www.justice.gov/atr/cases/f3800/msjudgex.htm, accessed November 2012.

From High-Flying Entrant to Collapse

Netscape aspired to become the primary commercial hub for developing browser applications and the primary window for the user experience of the growing World Wide Web. Yet as Gates had hoped, the competition continued throughout 1996 and 1997, and it stretched Netscape's resources and eroded its competitive position. Despite the stellar résumés and high-profile founders, any young firm taking on this role would face enormous challenges scaling their operations and executing its goals. Like any young firm, Netscape lacked routines grounded in years of experience. Flaws were bound to surface as they grew, and they did. Complaints began to surface about Netscape's overwhelmed support staff, and lack of returned phone calls from many employees.[24]

Marc Andreessen, Netscape's CTO and media-appointed wunderkind, did not make the situation any better by talking aggressively in public. His business inexperience showed. He satisfied every mid-twenty-year-old's desire to gain an adrenaline rush from bold quips quoted in major news outlets, but in doing so made the strategic situation worse. At one point, for example, he predicted that Windows would be reduced to a "poorly debugged set of device drivers." On other occasions he referred to Microsoft as the "beast from Redmond," "Godzilla," and "the Evil Empire." His quips were very entertaining for readers who despised Microsoft, and were therefore widely reported and repeatedly quoted.[25] To Microsoft employees, they came across as disrespectful, condescending, and combative. Although doubters were increasingly few in number, Andreessen's quotes also confirmed Bill's theory that Netscape wanted to bring down Microsoft.[26]

Most of these types of flaws are forgiven in young firms, and in a normal situation an inexperienced organization merely irons out their rough edges over time. In due time sober venture capitalists and experienced

---

[24]This is documented in some detail in the account of Cusumano and Yoffie (1998), as well as in the court's Findings of Fact, http://www.justice.gov/atr/cases/f3800/msjudgex.htm, accessed November 2012.

[25]See Chapman (2004), 189, for a short compilation of many of these quotes.

[26]This noisiness contrasts with a "stealth" strategy, in which a young firm publicly denies having aspirations to compete with an important firm, and denies have aspirations to become as important as the leading firms in its industry, in the hope of not generating defensive investments, so that the young firm can later surprise them in a more vulnerable position.

board members know how to quietly inch talented but mouthy founders out of their firms and bring in reliable managerial talent, or patiently teach an inexperienced executive to behave better. Netscape, however, faced a situation that did not permit room for forgiveness. Netscape found itself in a race to develop features with one of the world's most efficient developers of packaged software, and in a setting where Netscape faced a growing distributional disadvantage.

By the middle of 1997 the three-version strategy began to play out as Gates had hoped. Contemporaries began to predict that plenty of potential users would still be available and amenable to adopting IE 4.0. By mid-1998, plenty of households and businesses were just starting to use the Internet. To many of these new users IE 4.0 was just fine for their needs, and many tried it first because it was the default browser in the new PC they bought or the AOL account they used, and, as well, in plenty of other places.

The increasing realization that Microsoft had caught Netscape sucked the enthusiasm out of many developers who had committed time and energy to the Netscape browser. As Netscape's revenues declined in visible ways and as public support waned, Microsoft's success seemed inevitable to many observers. Finally, the Netscape coalition simply collapsed, with hundreds of developers each month switching exclusively to Microsoft and ceasing to add to and maintain their code for Netscape's browser.

In a short time, Netscape's value declined precipitously. Its market value effectively became reduced to the traffic attracted by its home page—which was still considerable by the norms of start-ups, but small by the heights the firm had previously obtained. The decline happened so quickly and irreversibly it was shocking to behold. Only three years earlier Netscape's IPO had symbolically given birth to the commercial Internet. Now it was a "destination site," kept alive by the inertial habits of many users who had made its website their default start page for surfing.

More indignities for Netscape followed. Seeing an opportunity to move traffic on Netscape's web portal to include different content and a different advertising network, AOL bought Netscape in November 1998, with the company exchanging at a value of more than four billion in overinflated stock.[27] The deal finished the following spring, effectively ending

---

[27]Junnarkar and Clark (1999). Also see pages 148–49, court's Findings of Fact, http://www.justice.gov/atr/cases/f3800/msjudgex.htm, accessed November 2012.

the existence of an independent browser firm, and nobody knew how long it would be before another arose.

It took a few years. By 2002 it was said that well over 95 percent of the browsers in use were from Microsoft. The code for alternative browsers remained moribund, and reemerged later as the Firefox browser.[28] It was as if the progeny could not resist the fight; in the middle of the next decade Firefox became a competitor to IE 6.0, the dominant descendant of IE 4.0.

Legal Problems[29]

Antitrust law includes many arcane details, but at a broad level it is straightforward. Antitrust law makes it illegal for a dominant firm to use its negotiating leverage to gain an advantage when it competes for a new market. Implementing that law accomplishes two goals at once: first, it encourages dominant firms to compete only with new or improved products and services; second, it discourages a dominant firm from using distributional restrictions on rivals or other advantages obtained through negotiating leverage with existing business partners. Discouraging firms from investing in the second encourages them to invest in the first, and that benefits everyone.

Here, Microsoft was at risk. Gates's priorities for browsers were no secret, and many of Microsoft's actions had received attention in the news. Many participants in PC and ISP markets suspected that Gates had talked to and put pressure on everyone. A few fights with business partners, such as the fight with Compaq, had made it into public knowledge. It was reasonable to wonder whether Gates *was* using Microsoft's negotiating leverage with a variety of market participants to avoid innovating without using that leverage.

---

[28] Near the end of the browser wars, Netscape had declared its code "open source." That invited suggestions from outsiders, though these did not arrive nearly fast enough to improve the browser dramatically. It also left the code in a general purpose license. After AOL lost interest in improving the browser, another group of ex-Netscape programmers and others coalesced around improving the code and starting an open source browser, which later became Firefox.

[29] This is necessarily a summary of a longer set of arguments. This section draws on a number of perspectives. See, e.g., Eisenach and Lenard (1999), Liebowitz and Margolis (2000), Evans et al. (2000), Evans (2002), Bresnahan (2003), Rubinfeld (2004), and Page and Lopatka (2007), not to mention the court's documents, as already cited.

In popular conversation two issues became intermingled. First, had Microsoft stepped over the line morally? Second, had they violated a legal definition, one founded on antitrust law? These questions were animated by the brazen way Microsoft had competed in the browser wars, fueling the sense that fouls hung in the air. Confusion characterized popular discussion.

Microsoft's bolting of IE to the operating system became a major source of confusion. It seemed to be technically unnecessary. The competing application could and did deliver similar functional performance without any bolting whatsoever. This action was raised frequently in popular conversation to illustrate Microsoft's unfair advantages.

Although brazen, this specific action was not a legal foul. It did users a favor by making the operating system better. For good reasons, no court or lawmaker ever has made it illegal to enhance a product while charging users nothing for the enhancement.

If there was a foul with IE, it lay in something simpler about its design. For example, Microsoft made it virtually impossible for users or suppliers to remove IE if they wanted to do. This was an unnecessarily restrictive design and a transparently self-serving departure from prior practice. Indeed, its triviality illustrates the point: no detail was too small. Microsoft would go the extra mile to limit user options and choice if Microsoft foresaw a benefit for itself.

Another illustration comes from the way Microsoft treated Java, a piece of middleware. Specifically, SUN Microsystems invented a computer language for networking, called Java, and wanted to do some experimentation with developers and users. Hyped well beyond any realistic possibility, Java attracted considerable attention from developers. Netscape was interested too, because Java could potentially improve the workings of their browser. Many developers attempted to write code for Java and test out its capability in applications that users valued. Unlike Netscape, SUN was an established firm with an experienced division for supporting developers, so developers expected to get the best of both worlds—frontier software and first-rate technical support.

Gates thought of Java's promise to developers to deliver services on the desktop in much the same way he thought of Netscape's browser. If circumstances were auspicious either one could facilitate entry of applications that substituted for applications in the existing value chain. In short, it could threaten the revenues of his core product. Gates did not want that bud to blossom, and he took deliberate actions to make it more challenging for developers to experiment with Java in ways SUN desired, even when such experiments had a strong chance of benefiting users.

After difficult negotiations Gates signed a contract with SUN, as if Microsoft intended to make Windows compatible with SUN's preferred version of Java. However, not long after the ink was dry, Microsoft took actions designed to confuse users and developers about what was possible with the Windows-compatible Java, inviting a public fight with SUN over some features Microsoft implemented, making it unclear what version of Java worked with Windows. That slowed down everyone's experiments.

Later, in the antitrust trial, there was a reductionist legal debate about details. Did Gates negotiate with SUN in bad faith? Lawyers for Microsoft also stated that it had the right to defend its business, and it was under no obligation to hurt itself.

Both arguments missed the key point—namely, that Microsoft's tactics seemed to cross a line about using technical complementarity to slow the distribution of software users valued. Gates's actions sowed fear, uncertainty, and doubt about whether Microsoft's and SUN's versions would work together. That did not help vendors and users experiment with Java. Every established firm, aspiring entrepreneur, and venture capitalist in the country watched these events and got the message. No experiment would be allowed to win or die on the technical merits if Gates didn't like where the experimentation might lead. If Gates could do something about it, he would. The promise of originality, technical potential, or user benefits did not matter. Only Gates's self-serving judgment did.

Such behavior violated common understanding of how the technical meritocracy operated in the computer market. As discussed in earlier chapters, the technical meritocracy was quite a familiar concept for many participants in the Internet, and part of that familiarity was inherited from the computer industry and part of it came from the experience in the precommercial Internet. In technical meritocracies every entrant had to have their chance to reach users, whether that supplier was an insider or outsider, established or entrepreneurial, big mouth or unknown. In markets the technical meritocracy played out in competition. Products and services were supposed to compete against one another on the merits. The market had to give users access to new products and services, and young firms had to have time to grow and experiment.

The US meritocracy did not grow and operate on its own, and this was the sticking point for Gates. Gates did not believe his leading firm had an obligation to nurture the technical meritocracy, to allow it to thrive, not if it came at the expense of his firm. It only had an obligation to be self-serving, and that trumped all else, including the meritocracy. Adding to that, even his firm's tactics used his market distributional strength as a tool, shaping the technical meritocracy to his preferences. As long as it stayed within the letter of contracting law, Gates asked, what could be wrong with that?

It would be imposing retrospective bias to characterize the actions of government antitrust prosecutors as if they knew the issues before investigating the actions. At first the legal case developed slowly. Government lawyers did not just come out and accuse Microsoft of committing anti-competitive fouls by restricting user choice and limiting distribution, or making it harder for rivals to reach consumers. Rather, in 1996 and throughout 1997, government lawyers raised questions about whether Microsoft was abiding by a settlement that the firm and the government had reached in 1994 over antitrust issues in Microsoft's contracts with assemblers.[30] The answers were unsatisfactory, and that kept the investigation alive. One case led to another.

The legal confrontation became unavoidable after a day in court in which Microsoft behaved as if it believed the government lawyers had no basis for raising additional legal issues. This defiance dared the government lawyers to investigate further and fight back, and, after considerable deliberation, they did. By the time Netscape's coalition began to collapse, the lawyers at the antitrust division in the Department of Justice believed they had enough material to bring a federal antitrust case. On May 18, 1998, Janet Reno, the US attorney general, announced that the Department of Justice was filing suit.

Microsoft's lawyers indicated that they believed they did not think they had done anything wrong, and they spoke as if they anticipated winning any courtroom confrontation. Popular opinion speculated that Gates welcomed this confrontation.

---

[30] A brief summary of the events leading to case can be found in Rubinfeld (2004).

The Trial[31]

The trial began in May 1998, and would last for many months, with the later appeals dragging into the next millennium. It involved many eye-opening revelations and spectacles. The first occurred at Gates's deposition, which had been recorded prior to the trial. Depositions are normally perfunctory, boring legal events. This was anything but that. Under the cold light of hard questions, the lead prosecutor, David Boies, reduced Gates to human proportions.

Boies made Gates sound unprepared for skeptical questions, as well as uncooperative and internally inconsistent. Gates denied his firm had market power, and he denied recalling e-mails that showed that he fully comprehended his negotiating advantages with business partners. Boies made it appear that Gates lived in his own self-serving world, effectively deploying market power against anything he regarded as a threat, no matter how far off in the future the threat lay, no matter what anyone else wanted, including his own users.[32]

During the actual trial, things became even worse for Microsoft. One subpoenaed e-mail after another revealed coarse and selfish language. The substance also did not help, as the e-mails exposed the defensive motives that characterized Microsoft's internal debates.

The prosecution eventually achieved its principal legal goal. It persuaded the presiding judge, Thomas Penfield Jackson, that management had both motive and ability to diminish the competitive process. As for motive, it possessed defensive intentions, and these had motivated the firm to take multiple actions to alter the competitive process in its favor and not compete on the merits. As for ability, it also possessed many levers to influence other firms in computing, and Gates had not hesitated to pull those levers.

Jackson's two rulings strongly favored the prosecution's view of events. The "Court's Finding of Facts," dated November 5, 1999, provided a coherent narrative of the many ways in which Microsoft had used its existing monopoly in operating systems to restrict the distribution of Netscape's products. The judge then encouraged the government and Microsoft

---

[31] For a narrative focused on the trial and its public face, see Auletta (2001), or Brinkley and Lohr (2000).

[32] See, e.g., the account in Chapman (2004), 178–86.

to negotiate. They did not reach resolution after many months of secret negotiations. Judge Jackson then issued his second judgment on April 3, 2000. In it Microsoft was found guilty of multiple antitrust violations. Before any hearings before Judge Jackson on remedies—the DOJ proposed breaking Microsoft into multiple firms—the case was appealed, as expected.[33]

All the publicity led to tons of collateral damage to Microsoft's and Gates's public image. News commentators wondered if the company's internal culture had any sense of restraint. Many prior business partners wondered whether their deals had been enacted in good faith. By association, it tainted many legitimate activities at Microsoft, reducing the value of years of brand building.

Microsoft's legal defense team next did what any good law team would— it attempted to reverse the judgment before an appellate court. The lawyers accomplished many of their goals, winning on some points and losing on others. More importantly, the court agreed to place some limits on the range of punishment Microsoft could receive.[34]

Yet by losing just a little, Gates lost a lot. The appellate court did not conclude that Microsoft's actions fell outside the domain of antitrust law. It did uphold the finding that Microsoft possessed market power and a monopoly. It did not exonerate Microsoft from accusations that it used its market power to restrict the distribution of products from rivals. It *did* find that established firms did not have free rein, even with underdeveloped products. The court said:

> It would be inimical to the purpose of the Sherman Act to allow monopolists free reign [*sic*] to squash nascent, albeit unproven, competitors at will—particularly in industries marked by rapid technological advance and frequent paradigm shifts.

This ruling had enormous consequences for the tone and texture of industry competition. Had Gates won all points at the trial or on appeal, then Gates would have been free to continue to authorize Microsoft to behave as

---

[33]See the website maintained by the Department of Justice, http://www.justice.gov/atr/cases/ms_index.htm, accessed November 2012.

[34]The appeals court decision came down on June 28, 2001. See http://www.justice.gov/atr/cases/f257900/257941.htm, accessed November 2012.

it had. In that case, other powerful executives in computing would have been tempted to adopt Gates's strategic playbook for limiting distribution and subverting the experimentation of others.

As for whether the trial undid the fouls in this particular event, however, ambiguity carried the day. Although Microsoft did not escape punishment altogether, it did avoid severe punishment. That occurred through a sequence of highly unlikely events.

Specifically, Judge Jackson had been all too aware of the attention the trial received in the news, and, showing poor judgment, gave long and frank interviews to reporters *during* the trial.[35] Although he embargoed those interviews while the trial continued, he allowed them to be published after it was over. The interviews made for entertaining reading, particularly because Jackson thought Gates and his colleagues needed to be taught a lesson, and he used colorful language to describe why. Judge Jackson compared Bill Gates to Napoleon Bonaparte for displaying arrogance from unalloyed success. He also remarked on the lack of maturity among the executives at Microsoft and compared their declarations of innocence and lack of repentance to what he had heard in a prior trial involving gangland killings.[36]

These quotes were published prior to the appeals court's final judgment, as the appeals court proceedings were ongoing. That violated longstanding practices at the court. In its June 2001, decision (which is another great read), the appellate court severely reprimanded Jackson for breaching protocol.[37] The reprimand showed some examples of quotes the appellate court found inappropriate. In addition to the remarks about Napoleon and gangsters, this long story from Judge Jackson to reporters came under severe rebuke:

---

[35] Two books resulted from those interviews, e.g., Brinkley and Lohr (2000), and Auletta (2001). These interviews are dealt with on pages 106–20 of the appeals court decision, and were treated quite harshly for giving the appearance of partiality. Opinion for the United States Court of Appeals, for the District of Columbia Circuit, June 28, 2001, http://www.justice.gov/atr/cases/f257900/257941.htm, accessed November 2012.

[36] See e.g., Brinkley and Lohr (2000) and Auletta (2001).

[37] Pages 106–20, Opinion for the United States Court of Appeals, for the District of Columbia Circuit, June 28, 2001, http://www.justice.gov/atr/cases/f257900/257941.htm, accessed November 2012.

He told the same reporters that "with what looks like Microsoft intransigence, a breakup is inevitable." . . . The Judge recited a "North Carolina mule trainer" story to explain his change in thinking from "[i]f it ain't broken, don't try to fix it" and "I just don't think that [restructuring the company] is something I want to try to do on my own" to ordering Microsoft broken in two:

He had a trained mule who could do all kinds of wonderful tricks. One day somebody asked him: "How do you do it? How do you train the mule to do all these amazing things?" "Well," he answered, "I'll show you." He took a 2-by-4 and whopped him upside the head. The mule was reeling and fell to his knees, and the trainer said: "You just have to get his attention." The Judge added: "I hope I've got Microsoft's attention."[38]

The appeals court also found some of the judge's reasoning less than adequate. It sent the open legal questions, including the determination of the eventual punishment, back to another judge.

This outcome was quite fortunate for Gates. No other judge had sat through Gates's deposition, nor had any other judge watched one Microsoft witness after another wilt under David Boies's questioning.

Another unexpected event then played a role. Although the Bush administration had no appetite to fight Microsoft's case further, initially it could not act on those predilections without inviting very bad publicity, as well as a revolt from the states' attorney generals who had signed on. However, the horror of the 9/11 terrorist attacks on the World Trade Center in New York City provided motivation and/or cover to redirect the priorities of the Justice Department. The new lead prosecutor negotiated a settlement with minimal bite, which Microsoft readily agreed to, and after some tussle, got the new judge to approve it.

The new judgment did one thing well: it appointed a technical committee and set up a process for review. That made it far more difficult for Microsoft to claim legality for questionable tactics and defer a trial, something Gates had done in the past. Now a court or a court-appointed

---

[38] The court is quoting from Brinkley and Lohr (2000), and others. See page 112, Opinion for the United States Court of Appeals, for the District of Columbia Circuit, June 28, 2001, http://www.justice.gov/atr/cases/f257900/257941.htm, accessed November 2012.

committee heard all complaints quickly. Even so, since the market had already moved on, and the Netscape coalition had effectively disbanded, there was not much to adjudicate. Ambiguity ruled the day.

Ambiguity also trailed Gates's career. He had become singularly associated with the questionable behavior at the center of the firm's legal problems. After the final court judgment, Gates gave up his CEO position and moved to a newly created position, chief software architect. Steve Ballmer became CEO. The reasons were never fully explained in public, but indications were that—after the finger pointing stopped—even Gates's friends in Microsoft thought this was a way for the firm to move forward, at least on a symbolic level. Yet Gates continued to be present and contribute to decisions at every strategic level, so a skeptic might reasonably wonder if the move accomplished much in practice.

The case left the news after 2001—except for periodic stories involving Ballmer settling every private antitrust case Microsoft faced within the United States. The private suits in the United States cost over $4 billion, a small fraction of Microsoft's cash on hand. Later, Microsoft faced another set of issues from the European Union, which increased the final bill and hassles, and the concerns of that administrative process seemed to continue almost indefinitely.

Finally, fulfilling the dystopian predictions of Microsoft's biggest critics, the case also faded from view due to Microsoft's actions. Without a competitive reason to continue to invest in the Internet, Gates showed he did not care much about it. Microsoft went back to its older strategic priorities and slowed or eliminated investments in the Internet. Accordingly, Microsoft failed to execute an Internet strategy that took advantage of its dominant position in browsers. Once so prominent, Microsoft's aspirations in the Internet faded from public view, largely unfulfilled.[39]

Resisting Innovation from the Edges

Microsoft's experience illustrates an inherent tension with self-governance of commercial markets undergoing creative destruction. Self-governance

[39] For more on why and how this occurred, see the summary offered by Bresnahan, Greenstein, and Henderson (2012), as well as the chronicling of the debates inside Microsoft offered by Bank (2001).

relies on restraint by those who possess the incentives and ability to alter the competitive conditions in their own favor. While some of the largest firms stand to gain from the successful blossoming of commercial markets spurred on by innovation from the edges, others can anticipate the potential losses, just as Microsoft did. As Microsoft's actions illustrate, such established firms tend not to sit by passively, and their actions do not necessarily support the competitive processes underlying entrepreneurial capitalism.

This example also illustrates a related issue: the losses to society from self-governance are not felt in events that occur, and, instead, are felt in events that never occur but could have. To understand why, consider whether Microsoft's decisions altered the economic impact of innovation from the edges.[40] Specifically, think about what would have happened had the web become a competitor to Microsoft instead of merely new functionality to sell more PCs, as it might have, had Netscape had access to less clogged distribution. In short, compare what actually did happen to what might have happened without fouls.

As a baseline, first recognize what did actually happen in a broad summary. Competition between platforms—one organized by Microsoft and one organized by Netscape—began petering out in late 1997, when Microsoft's fouls drew developers away from Netscape's browser and SUN's Java. Competition then collapsed in 1998 when developers abandoned Netscape's platform altogether. After this collapse, Microsoft slowed several of its Internet initiatives. After 2001 IE went years without another upgrade, and IE 6.0 became heavily criticized on developer forums. Developers were stuck, and many complained, but they had nowhere else to go.

For the sake of speculation, consider the possibility that the lack of aggressive tactics might have allowed competition to continue for an additional, yet modest, amount of time. Let that be just a couple more years, say, to the end of 1999 or middle of 2000, while the Internet continued to diffuse to new users, or until the dot-com bubble burst.

---

[40]One of the more hotly debate points from the trial focused on the losses from Microsoft's actions. The questions were never settled because the remedy phase of the trial never was conducted. See, e.g., Eisenach and Lenard (1999), Liebowitz and Margolis (2000), Evans et al. (2000), Evans (2002), Bresnahan (2003), Rubinfeld (2004), and Page and Lopatka (2007).

More competition would have yielded considerable gains. Users would have experienced what would have been invented had developers had a cooperative business partner, such as Netscape, for a little while longer, and a competitive rival, such as Microsoft, trying to keep pace. Since the late 1990s was an era of easy money and the biggest venture-capitalist-led entry boom in the history of computing, there would have been additional experimentation in the form of new entrepreneurial entrants. For example, an additional eighteen months would have generated at least two—perhaps three—more rounds of competitive browser upgrades and complementary inventions in security, search, identity protection, transactional automation, and other applications.

Users might have experienced what Microsoft would have done in a features race, had it possessed a sense of competitive urgency after 1998. More competitive urgency would have generated more innovative features out of Microsoft, especially in comparison to what its browser division did after competition ended.

Innovation from the edges did not blossom as much as it could have. At a crucial time some entrepreneurial purveyors of the technology were not able to experiment, or able to take advantage of unrestricted distribution channels. The lack of experimentation made the commercial Internet a different place than it could have been and prevented society from benefiting from the gains innovation from the edges could have yielded.

The broad lesson is sobering and applies to today's market as much as it did to these events in the 1990s. Creative destruction does not necessarily emerge on its own, nor automatically. Market events need not be either creative or destructive if the leading core firms act on their incentives, and use their abilities to control events for defensive purposes. Said another way, the process of creative destruction emerges only after the failure of an established firm's attempts at defensiveness. It is not enough that established firms need to perceive the threat as a real one. If they can merely block it with actions that alter distribution for a rival, then blocking can reduce incentive to respond by innovating.

This example also illustrates the broad lesson about what open platforms do better than proprietary platforms coming from established firms. Established firms will hesitate to cannibalize their own leading products and will tend to follow their own planning, trying to make greater returns on their existing sunk investments. In contrast, creative destruction led by entrepreneurial entry that appeals to users will pay no heed to an established firm's existing profitability, or to its planning, or to the vision or investments underlying it. Said another way, platforms led by entrepreneurs can be especially effective at creating and supporting new value for users when they become unexpectedly destructive in the eyes of an established firm.

12

Internet Exceptionalism Runs Rampant

> I have this vague feeling that, just as every generation
> thinks it invented sex, every generation thinks it created a
> new economy.
>
> *—Andy Grove, CEO, Intel*[1]

WebVan impatiently launched in June 1999 after incorporating in 1997, and eventually lost more than $800 million.[2] It proposed to revolutionize the grocery business by delivering groceries to households who ordered their groceries online. It recruited a well-known executive, George Sheehan, and gained financial backing from several big-name venture capitalists. It laid out an extensive plan to grow in major cities across the United States. It settled on a customer-friendly plan that would deliver groceries within thirty minutes of an order. It aspired to operate out of warehouses in less expensive locations, cutting out expensive retail space, so it could lower its costs enough to make it profitable to charge very low prices for groceries.

There were a few problems with this proposal, but the biggest was most apparent to anyone who had studied the business years earlier, when online grocery ordering and delivering had been tried on a small scale and had not yielded dramatic success. The logistics of delivering perishable products imposed large costs on operations. The prior experiences had not been flawed in any obvious way, and the previous generation of entrepreneurs

[1] Quoted in Heilemann (2001).
[2] Delgado (2001).

had executed reasonably well. Try as they might, WebVan's business was going to be more similar to prior attempts than different from them, despite being shinier, newer, and better publicized. WebVan could improve on the past in only incremental ways at most, by delivering the service at high scale in new facilities.

The economics could be stated in simple terms. WebVan incurred a large sunk cost to entering and incurred high fixed costs during operations. To justify the costs of those facilities and operations, WebVan had to generate large revenue over operating expense. Since the delivered groceries were generally priced at competitive levels and did not generate high margins, and delivery costs were high and did not command high prices, large revenue could be achieved only one way, through a high volume of orders. WebVan's viability, therefore, came down to a simple economic question in every locale: how many households in a geographic area wanted groceries delivered, and could it become very large?

There were good reasons to be skeptical. The experience of one of the earlier entrants, Peapod, was well known and illustrated the constraints. Peapod started a small-scale version of the grocery delivery business in the Chicago area by partnering with existing grocery stores.[3] They had operated this entrepreneurial business since 1989, improving it constantly, and had showed it was viable. Peapod's experience also illustrated the challenges. No amount of operational cleverness could reduce the delivery costs—gasoline, vehicle maintenance, a driver's time. It was expensive to send a van from a warehouse to a customer. No amount of clever marketing—online, in magazines, flyers on door posts, and even from the grocery store partner—could convince most users to pay much money for a delivery service, or use it at all.

The problem did not appear to be the software. It went to something for which no technical solution existed, to something innate in human behavior. Stated simply, users changed their shopping habits with reluctance.

That was so of even the savviest online users in the early 1990s. It was quite sensible, therefore, to expect later users to be more reluctant. After all, these were the most inexperienced online users. No amount of website genius could induce a new online user to break with old habits and do their shopping for groceries on a web page. No clever marketing tool could con-

[3]See Greenstein (2004).

vince many shoppers to trust the selection of bananas to someone else. Many shoppers wanted to examine the day's daily specials in person. Many wanted a tactile grocery experience, merely as a way to stretch their legs. Many parents with young children wanted an excuse to get out of a claustrophobic house to roam the aisles. All those simple factors prevented many households from making use of the online service.

None of WebVan's senior management had extensive experience in the grocery business, or in the online grocery business. It is not surprising, therefore, that WebVan's management convinced itself that it had something that had eluded previous pioneers. They proposed to build brand new warehouses to gain efficiencies from scale and reduce costs as low as they could go. They believed that the newer features of their well-funded web-based grocery service would generate high demand.

The financial vulnerability of the proposal was plain to see: it only could be viable if it achieved a scale of use that no prior pioneer in online groceries had ever come close to achieving. Expensive warehouses and fancy operations would be too expensive if not employed at full capacity. The costs of delivery trucks and drivers would be too high unless demand grew to a point that spread those costs over many customers. The entire cost structure for the business would not be—could not be—low enough unless the business generated a large set of customers to use the capacity at or near its maximum.

In normal times that type of vulnerability would have led investors to call for a cautious expansion plan, reining in the aspirations of the management. Investors might have asked for less cavalier uses of their money, requiring WebVan to, say, first experiment with different mixes of marketing and operational novelties in a friendly location, such as San Francisco, which had a technically sophisticated population spread around a dense urban location. Yet following the prevailing view, WebVan's management eschewed caution. It avoided cautious exploratory practices. WebVan's management opened in several cities *without* first testing the concept in one city for an extended period of time.[4]

What happened? Soon after starting it became obvious that WebVan did not differ that much from any of the pioneers. The online grocery

[4]At its peak it served ten cities: the San Francisco area, Dallas, San Diego, Los Angeles, Chicago, Seattle, Portland, Atlanta, Sacramento, and Orange County. It made plans to serve twenty-six but went bankrupt before those could be built.

business could generate some interest, but not nearly enough to gain the advantages of scale. WebVan could not make any of its financial goals. Not enough households wanted to use the service to have revenue cover operations expenses—namely, to make that business viable.

Looking back, by the norms of standard business practices, WebVan's impatient experiment cost its investors dearly.[5] A more conventional expansion plan—patient, systematic, and incremental—would have led to limited initial trials in a few cities, demonstrated the issues, and limited the downside losses from experimentation, or stretched out the losses longer to allow more time for learning.[6]

WebVan was far from the only example of managers who invested with impatience. This chapter will describe a few others. In retrospect these examples beg the question: What led otherwise sensible managers to act so impatiently and so imprudently? What persuaded otherwise rational investors to put their money behind ventures that behaved this way?

Prior chapters have suggested that some part of the impatience was inevitable. The commercial Internet could not be built without simultaneous investments from many distinct participants—households, businesses, carriers, software developers, ISPs, retailers of all stripes, and more. That juggernaut of investment began to accelerate in the late 1990s, as all participants perceived how pervasive the commercial Internet had become, and all forecast it would become more pervasive in more households and businesses.

Prior chapters have also hinted at what could go wrong with so much uncoordinated investment. Once started, that juggernaut could not instantly or gradually slow. Nobody coordinated it. It was left to each participant to be informed about the activities of the others, and that was impossible to do, so each participant became only partially informed about others. As it continued, it became inevitable that the rates of activities in one group of suppliers would not match one another. One commer-

---

[5] WebVan raised nearly $400 million in four venture rounds, and it raised an additional $430 million more in its IPO.

[6] Since WebVan was financed through equity, even if the concept had been proven unworkable after a couple trial cities it is rather doubtful the management would have returned any of the investor money. That still does not take away from the observation that their expansion plan departed from conventional practices, which are designed to learn lessons over time, and not put them into practice on the next implementation until they are shown to be profitable.

cial supplier continued to invest at a rapid rate while another slowed down, and one set of users continued to adopt at a rapid pace while another did not. After the fact it appeared as if more capacity was built for more adopters and users of the Internet than actually showed up. In layman's terms, the building boom overshot its target.

This chapter delves deeply into an additional cause: the near inevitability of overshooting when egged on by poorly conceived strategies. Overbuilding became a certainty because a flawed prevailing view emerged to justify an aggressive approach to building new firms, one that accelerated the amount of investment and reduced the degree of caution. The prevailing view supported a range of investments in the commercial Internet and did so with gusto and optimism. After the fact the buildup became known as the dot-com bubble, its ending as the dot-com bust, and the flawed prevailing view as Internet exceptionalism. This chapter provides details about how Internet exceptionalism distorted the direction of investment in the commercial Internet, wasting many of the fruits of innovation from the edges.

The Prevailing View behind the Dot-Com Boom

A prevailing view is not a scientific hypothesis in which a deep theory links premises to conclusions. It is a social construct, a by-product of countless conversations, each one assessing the planning process at many firms. These conversations occur between investors and analysts, business partners and customers. Over time, a prevailing view always emerges from this collective conversation, and it evolves, becoming refined with myriad adjustments. Every well-run firm in a market is cognizant of the prevailing view, and every analyst and firm uses it as benchmark, assessing where their strategy overlaps with others and where it differs.

A prevailing view changes in reaction to events that arise, grow, and settle in a disorganized way. Chance events refine these beliefs and understandings, twist them occasionally, and obscure the origins of assumptions. They coalesce into a collection of opinion, facts, alleged consequence, promised payoff, and narrative arcs with biographical triumphs and failures. Some logical fallacies can persist for a time, and so can underexamined assumptions and hypotheses.

Prevailing views can linger, and for multiple reasons. No law forces every market participant to test his/her views against hard evidence.

Conclusive statements can lack tangibility until hard numbers match revenue with operational costs. There is no requirement or norm that a single coherent document answers the many dimensions for assayers. No entrepreneurial participant must meet a requirement for full transparency, and many private firms can hide their financial results from public scrutiny. No law requires every single participant to explicate all of its positions for pundits, skeptics, and news reporters.

Initially the foundations for the prevailing view behind the dot-com bubble arose for sensible reasons grounded in observable experience. The fast diffusion of e-mail and web browsing in 1996 and 1997 was unusual for the speed with which mainstream users adopted it. The number of browser users reached an uncommonly high level in the United States, and across the globe, and by 1998 showed no signs of slowing. Some very visible entrants with new conceptions of business grew quickly alongside household and business adoption, such as Yahoo, Cisco, AOL, Netscape, and Amazon, so commentators further (correctly) pointed out that the new technology could become viable businesses at an extraordinarily fast rate. Some early entrepreneurial ventures—Vermeer, HoTMaiL, or ICQ— also achieved their commercial goals, merging with other leading firms, reaping returns on investment far in excess of normal outcomes. That too suggested (correctly) that some early movers had earned high returns for their investors.

The dot-com bubble emerged because the early experience supported optimism about 1999, 2000, and beyond. It suggested that viable business could be developed quickly, and, crucially, that a lucrative outcome could arise from an incautious approach to growing a business for users as quickly as possible, often deferring the generation of revenue to later. It presumed all the other elements of the economy would raise the value of adoption, enhancing the value of services, reinforcing further incentives to grow. Eventually the reasoning about the economic value of growing a new business became detached from grounded reasoning about what type of value the business actually created, how much revenue a new business could realistically expect, and what would be needed to cover operational expenses.

What led experienced and sensible entrepreneurs to throw out normal practices and invest with such incautious expansive plans? After the fact, it is challenging to make sense of the psychology of the times. Yet every explanation comes down to the same psychological mantra; these actions made no sense unless everybody believed the Internet made their business exceptional, that it would defy standard economic rules, gain many users in an extraordinarily short period of time, and then turn those users into a regular source of revenue in a profitable business with frictionless ease. No other rationale seems consistent with the facts.

What encouraged this view? It was tempting to fall back on cliché. It appeared as if some investors fell in love with these ventures, and their managers threw caution to the wind, as if hope triumphed over experience, dismissing tropes about the frailty of business success. Skewed social norms also encouraged an almost willful "misattribution bias," allowing entrepreneurs to believe commercial success largely grew out of their own efforts and had little connection to prior invention and investment in the Internet and the web. There also was a grain of truth in such cliché's. Building new businesses required the assent and enthusiasm of people who worked at these firms—entrepreneurs, programmers, managers, administrative assistants, and engineers. The pursuit of dreams could and did motivate extraordinary sacrifice, and in this moment of time, the prevailing view for the late 1990s informed many participants that it was time to pursue a once-in-a-lifetime opportunity. The promise gave purpose to work that often lacked it, such as routine programming, and motivated many talented people to change their careers and take risks.

The history of financial bubbles suggests a deeper explanation. Many investors questioned the relevance of traditional valuation processes for the rise of electronic commerce and advertising-supported online media. There were few observable and measureable activities, and most of the value for these firms lay in the future. The distance between the present activity and later value made these markets unlike a stable industry with a long historical record. Analysts of electronic commercial and advertising-supported media did not have sufficient records to construct models that predicted future revenue and costs. If certain factors changed—say, unemployment fell or the price of oil rose—analysts had no model to forecast the effects on demand and the cost of production. They had no finely calibrated model to predict the value of a firm under optimistic and pessimistic scenarios.

As a practical matter many analysts were left grasping for anything they could measure, such as web traffic. For example, small changes in the growth of traffic to a site—the number of visitors, the average length of stays, and any other aspect—would be seized on as informative. These analysts then had to layer heroic assumptions on top of such data, for example, presuming that more traffic at one point led to more advertising revenue at a later point.[7] These models were, at best, a shot in the dark, and only the most extreme outcome—such as little or no traffic to a website—could reject an optimistic thesis.

How did such shots in the dark take on the status of historical models? The history of financial bubbles also provides guidance. Investors need a prevailing view to explain and rationalize for participants why familiar long-term determinants of value ceased to determine firm investment and why familiar business risks did not apply with the same brutal force.[8] Internet exceptionalism offered that outlook.

Internet exceptionalism generally took on one of two forms. One form, common among technologists and engineers, stressed the unique technical basis for the Internet and saw it as a central, relegating any economic factor to a secondary effect. A second and related form, very common during the dot-com boom, believed that the Internet followed its own unique economic rules, having little in common with other important historical episodes. Economics mattered, or would matter eventually, but not for some time, and in the short run it certainly would not reflect the recognizable principles practiced only a few years earlier in non-Internet markets.[9] In either form, Internet exceptionalism forecast the replacement of existing non-Internet-related activities by the new entrepreneurial entities. Without specifying how it would happen precisely, there was a presumption that eventually revenue would appear as activities moved to the new and better Internet economy.

If there was a grain of truth to Internet exceptionalism, it arose in the recent experience with fast household and business adoption of browsers. It offered some basis for an optimistic forecast about the scale of sales in an Internet-based business. The strong rhetoric for the entrepreneur-led new

---

[7] For more of this view see, e.g., Rajgopal, Kotha, Venkatachalam (2000) and Demers and Lev (2001).

[8] Reinhart and Rogoff (2009).

[9] The latter attitude explains why many businesses could read Shapiro and Varian (1999) and its call for a return to traditional economic analysis, and, yet, hold its message at a distance.

economy built upon this optimism and went further, claiming a general trend of additional success for entrepreneurs in the majority of markets built around the web. Eventually the actual data caught up to this claim, but in 1997, 1998, and 1999 there was little to refute it. At that point, any investor could only speculate about a world characterized by pervasive adoption and use of the Internet, and what the world would resemble when many new firms served all those web surfers.

Cliché alone does not explain the phenomenon in its entirety for another reason, and this leads to a deeper inquiry. Investors did not apply brakes to the incautious actions of new ventures, as normally would have occurred. Sober and hard-nosed financial reasoning failed to limit the number of ill-conceived businesses. Financial markets failed to value an asset on the basis of the likely discounted sum of the revenues over costs, and, accordingly, failed to place brakes on imprudent investment. How did that happen? Answering that question is one of the goals of this chapter.

Timing had to play a role. Some risky investments made at the outset of any commercial gold rush will appear to be incautious later. It is not surprising that financial markets approved of some risky investments in 1996 and even 1997. Some risk leads to some return and some ruin. Some ruin could be excused due to the coincidence of the backbone's privatization and the growth of the World Wide Web, which generated considerable returns as well.

That explanation only goes so far, however. When discussing many investments in 1998 and 1999, events had gone well beyond the initial gold rush, and virtually all informed participants understood the key building blocks of technology. Financial analysts knew sufficient examples to illustrate how to make and build businesses using Internet technology, and, crucially, how not to. Yet the knowledge about what could go wrong did not stop the wave of investment.

Four explanations for this wave receive prominent attention in this chapter: the wisdom and grounded analysis of many seasoned industry experts became sidelined in favor of analysts that parroted Internet advocates; many financial advocates gave in to the prevailing view and also argued for Internet exceptionalism; enough investors followed this advice for a long enough time to set in motion enough demand to bid up prices for entrepreneurial firms, and far away from their long-term fundamental determinants; a number of institutional practices within financial markets in the United States suppressed information inconsistent with the prevailing optimistic view. In other words, this was a situation ripe to produce too much money chasing too few good deals.[10]

Cheerleaders

An examination of cheerleaders and financial institutions of Wall Street can help explain how a prevailing view can sustain itself. The actions of author and pundit George Gilder, a longtime and well-known commentator in conservative political circles, can begin to illustrate how the prevailing view began to take shape.

No law prevented a pundit from trying to shape the prevailing view about the sources of value in the future, and Gilder worked hard at becoming a recognized opinion shaper. That effort, by itself, put him in the same group with scores of others with similar ambitions. He wrote books,[11] and during the 1990s he published the "Gilder Technology Report" for subscribers. He differentiated himself by focusing particularly on broadband firms and activities taking advantage of abundant, pervasive, and inexpensive high-speed networking. At his peak Gilder had 75,000 subscribers, which generated $20 million in revenue.[12]

Nobody doubted his sincerity or integrity, as Gilder displayed an enthusiasm for his subject, clearly believed what he wrote, and invested his own money in the firms he liked.[13] Cynics publicly worried that Gilder merely played a role from which others profited and reached conclusions on the basis of many flawed and incautious observations. As Fred Hickey, editor of a newsletter called the *High-Tech Strategist*, said:

> If there was no George Gilder, the venture capitalists and investment bankers would've invented one. They needed some kind of pied piper to put the words on paper to justify the insanity of paying any price for anything that offered any kind of technical promise.[14]

Gilder acquired a distinct status somewhat by accident, as an unwitting result of crossing the line between pundit and investor. Ostensibly in order to be transparent, he began listing his own investments on the last page of

---

[10] See Gompers and Lerner (2003).
[11] See Gilder (1989).
[12] See Prince (2006), and Rivlin (2002).
[13] A reflection of these views can be found in, e.g., Gilder (2000).
[14] Rivlin (2002).

his newsletter, calling them his favorite firms.[15] Soon thereafter other observers noted that such a designation could move the stock prices of those
listed firms, and the movement often occurred whether or not any other
fundamental factor had come to light about that firm. Labeled the "Gilder
effect," other pundits and short-term investors began to pay attention to
Gilder's list, whether they agreed with him or not.

As the history of short-term financial bubbles suggests, once a person is
designated a prophet of price movements, such a prophet's pronounce-
ments could become self-fulfilling.[16] It was no surprise, therefore, that
self-interested investors learned to understand Gilder's well-documented
preferences and tendencies, and they made efforts to get the firms in
which they invested to tailor their appeal to his optimistic forecast about
networking's value. Firms with stakes in technology markets, especially
in networking, began to go to great lengths to influence Gilder's views,
paying his fees to give speeches to their clients, as much as $100,000 per
speech. Such firms hoped to use the opportunity to place a favored start-up
in front of Gilder, hoping for an endorsement of their favored entrepreneurial firm on his list.

After the dot-com bust a mini-industry of critics, perhaps motivated by
schadenfreude, began documenting the number of ways in which Gilder had
erred in his forecasts and analysis, as well as why he did.[17] Such observations
largely missed the point, that Gilder was a product of his time. Gilder, or any
cheerleader, could not have had such an inordinate influence without the
presence of a prevailing view that fostered a speculative financial bubble.[18]

Further illustration of this larger point comes from the experience of
Henry Blodget, who also acquired some of the same status, albeit from a
very unlikely path. After graduating from Yale, Blodget joined the corporate
finance training program at Prudential Securities in 1994 and next moved
to Oppenheimer and Company to do equity research. Blodget was young
and bold, blessed with an ability to write clear prose, and not colored by

---

[15]Gilder followed his own advice and eventually lost most of his wealth to the dot-com
bust. Rivlin (2002).

[16]This statement is necessarily a simplification of a vast literature. See, e.g., Reinhart and
Rogoff (2009).

[17]For popular press pieces with such themes, see, e.g., Prince (2006), and Rivlin (2002).

[18]For an analysis much closer to this observation, see Odlyzko (2010). He shows how
Gilder erred in his analysis of networking and stresses that investors *could have but did not* ask
sufficient skeptical questions before investing. See Odlyzko (2010).

association with an established line of analysts. He schooled himself in the new economy and made forecasts that gained attention. In his own words:

> In 1997, I recommended that my clients buy stock in a company called Yahoo; the stock finished the year up more than 500 percent. The next year, I put a $400-a-share price target on a controversial "online book-seller" called Amazon, worth about $240 a share at the time; within a month, the stock blasted through $400 en route to $600. You don't have to make too many calls like these before people start listening to you; I soon had a global audience keenly interested in whatever I said.[19]

Blodget was then offered a position at venerable Merrill Lynch, to which he moved. To longtime and established analysts, this represented a shocking departure from the norm—the ascension of a young child who had not paid his dues. For Merrill Lynch, this was merely an attempt to prevent clients from going elsewhere, an attempt to affiliate their brand with a newly minted analyst-turned-celebrity. It also illustrates just how quickly the established firms of Wall Street could and would jettison experienced and tempered analysts and those who used long-term fundamentals, replacing them with analysts who reflected the new prevailing view.

Blodget's job was ostensibly as an analyst, but after this appointment Blodget's role became similar to Gilder's—part pundit, part advisor, and part prophet of prices. From this post, and at the height of the bubble in 1998 and 1999, Blodget influenced the stocks of many firms. Many paid attention to him because they had to, and enormous efforts went into influencing his views. To be fair to him, also like Gilder, Blodget appears to have believed what he wrote. He invested his own money in the sector, losing it in the dot-com bust.[20] Indeed, Blodget eventually lost all credibility after the bust. He accepted a buyout offer from Merrill Lynch in 2001.[21]

---

[19] Blodget (2008).

[20] Eventually he lost a considerable fraction of his wealth during the dot-com crash. Blodget (2008) states:

> In the late 1990s, as stocks kept roaring higher, it got easier and easier to believe that something really was different. So, in early 2000, weeks before the bubble burst, I put a lot of money where my mouth was. Two years later, I had lost the equivalent of six high-end college educations.

[21] Later still Blodget was charged with securities fraud for stating public positions that contradicted private opinions documented in e-mails. He paid a fine and was barred from Wall Street analysis.

In a retrospective written many years after his time there, Blodget rationalizes his role by identifying the factors encouraging short-termism in all facets of the financial markets. According to this analysis, Wall Street firms lack institutional memory, because few money managers familiarize themselves with the history of prior bubbles and many have careers too short to recall prior bubbles, which happen only once every few decades. While that might have described Blodget's own biography, this argument can only go so far, as it did not apply to the senior management at any of the major firms, including those at which Blodget worked. Blodget's senior managers should have known about the need to limit downside risk and taken action to limit the downside risk to their firms from following a prevailing view with myopic features.

Perhaps this is why Blodget offers his second argument, that short-term pressures to ride a bull market overwhelm all other norms, such as valuing firms according to long-term fundamentals. To illustrate, Blodget tells three tales, each based on a real biography. In the first, an established money manager loses most of his investors for refusing to invest in high-tech stocks, which leads him to close the fund (just before the dot-com bust). In the second tale, a money manager gains considerable funds to invest because he does what the craziest clients want, only to lose it all in the bust. In the third tale, a reluctant money manager compromises between his traditional practices and the calls for more technology investments. That leads him to maintain a portfolio that loses considerable value after the bust, at which point he retires.[22] From these examples, Blodget argues that a perverse prevailing view will have its day, because no analyst or money manager can resist the pressure. These three stories together compose the "Blodget rationalization" for Wall Street's behavior.

There is a deeper answer to the Blodget rationalization, but it would require Blodget to explain why the skeptics did not speak when they normally do in financial markets. The answer involves the incentives of those who have information to aid the skeptics of the prevailing view, and it requires Blodget to condemn the behavior of his former bosses and senior colleagues. Said another way, Wall Street did not lack for seasoned experts in financial firms. Many of them, particularly the senior management at

---

[22] For review, see, e.g., http://www.pbs.org/now/politics/wallstreet.html, retrieved October 2012.

many of these firms, knew that the values of dot-coms departed from fundamental economic determinants. Why didn't they say so and authorize others to say so? Said simply, it would have cost them money. Many executives would have permitted craziness to continue as long as there was big money to be made.

During this time, self-serving rationalizations had captured the prevailing view within Wall Street, run amuck in managerial decisions, and no regulatory intervention corrected for this imbalance. Many aggressive Wall Street firms felt entitled to do whatever profited them, even if it meant undercutting others who sought to serve their clients honorably, and undercutting those who sought to serve society's long-term needs and public obligations. It was this type of behavior—exhibited at many firms and collectively making the whole much worse than the sum of its parts—that lay behind the inability of Wall Street to self-correct.

One contributing factor, of course, was the gullibility of investors and employees, which was fostered by the genuine technical complexity of the situation and the inherent absence of hard data to forecast future events.[23] Although lack of sophistication, by itself, helps explain some investor behavior, it cannot explain the dot-com financial bubble in its entirety. The presence of gullible investors, even in a large scale, is not sufficient to produce a bubble. A sufficiently large set of informed and sophisticated investors normally could have moved financial prices in the appropriate direction, profiting handsomely from outwitting the unsophisticated investor.

Yet sophisticated investors did not disappear in the late 1990s. Why did these participants not play their usual role?

First, there is a bias on Wall Street toward more activity, of any type. Many firms in the financial-services business profited from any activity, whether or not the investor ultimately profited. For example, many firms profited from fees for services supporting mergers, for related services, such as underwriting IPOs, and for investment services, such as arranging

---

[23] Andrew Odlyzko (2010), an expert in measuring networking traffic, identifies these factors as particularly salient in the late 1990s. 1. Innumeracy: Many lacked the ability to understand the implications of claims that traffic grew at such a fast rate, doubling every several months. 2. Misuse of basic engineering terms. Many investors measured capacity, not traffic. 3. Unchallenged inconsistencies: Many investors did not ask skeptical questions about different growth projections, with some predicting rates out of scale with each other.

to invest in growth funds consisting of entrepreneurial firms.[24] Such actors facilitated investment with *any* prevailing view.

How could that be permissible? Traditional US practices stressed caveat emptor, buyer beware, and placed the emphasis on buyers facing the onus of asking the right skeptical question. If the deals went through, the financial firms had little incentive to correct that view even if it was in error. In practice, many met the *letter* of their legal obligations by listing risks and potential issues, but few had any reason to meet the *spirit* of their obligations.

Second, many banking firms were less than fully forthcoming about their incentives to price IPOs properly. During the boom, many Wall Street firms gave access to early stock sales to privileged clients and then—either explicitly or implicitly—asked for quid pro quos, such as favorable public remarks or more banking business. This was known as *IPO spinning*, and the run-up in stock prices for IPOs from technology firms played a role in that behavior, making it especially easy to reward insiders.[25] Similarly, many firms also used laddering. That is, to purchase shares at a given price, investors also must agree to purchase additional shares at a higher price. Executed well, this guarantees higher prices for insiders who buy stock at low prices.[26] The profitability of spinning and laddering further muted any incentive for insiders to work with those who asked skeptical questions or make public information that corrected an error in a misguided prevailing view.

Third and finally, just plain self-serving unethical behavior gave financial firms incentives to arrange for IPOs, whether or not they made sense to investors. For example, many analysts worked at firms with conflicts of interest, facing pressure to make favorable remarks to keep some banking businesses at other parts of the firm.[27] That too underlay incentives not to correct an error in a prevailing view.

The misplaced incentive of many financial institutions provides an answer to Blodget's view. Merely because a dollar was on the line, firms in

---

[24] For a review of the evidence, see, e.g., Brau and Fawcett (2006), or Liu and Ritter (2010).
[25] See Liu and Ritter (2010). For a description of this behavior in the IPO for E-Toys, see Nocera (2013).
[26] Hao (2007).
[27] Reuter (2006).

the business of advising clients did not go out of their way to release information inconsistent with an overoptimistic prevailing view. Many skeptics held their tongue, or their questions about presumed future growth received little notice. It went on long enough to shape a majority of investment decisions. In this sense, Wall Street's reinforcement of the prevailing view contributed to the era, both accelerating the rate of investment and shaping its direction, though not necessarily for the better.

The Bust after the Boom

The dot-com bust, as it became known, can be viewed as either a systemic event or as a parochial one. As a systemic event it did not come suddenly or occur in a single moment in time. There was no singular epiphany or moment of revelation, or a single event that obviously caused later declining events. Rather, the first signs of the decline appeared in 1999, and a few participants recognized the canary in the coal mine. Only with the benefit of hindsight do those signs come to the foreground of a narrative explanation, and this chapter describes these signs in the description below.

As a parochial event many participants experienced the dot-com bust in much the same way a nearsighted surfer on an ocean wave experiences the feelings of ascent and decent as waves grow or decline or crash. The ascent started in the mid-1990s and generated unending adrenaline rushes unlike any employment experience of the past or any investment returns in near memory. Many experienced the descent from peak only after the spring of 2000, as financial markets began to decline and, with zigs down and up, reached a low point in 2002.

At a systemic level this bust was entirely a financial and business phenomenon, not a technical one. The Internet's engineering never failed. The Internet and the web continued to function properly and reliably, and users continued to make ample use of many valuable services, even after the bankruptcy of the largest backbone provider in the country, WorldCom, or the exit of some of the seeming leaders of the first era, such as Excite, or the entry of some of the leaders of up-and-coming firms, such as Google.

What caused the dot-com bust? It is quite common in popular discussion to frame this question around the timing of the peak, that is, the beginning of the decline. This common framing presumes that a trigger or spark caused the ascent to stop and reverse into a descent. This framing leads to what might be called "the fallacy of the last snowflake." Focusing on the date of the financial peak is similar to asking why a specific snowflake generated sufficient pressure to trigger an avalanche. Asking this question creates an unsatisfying approach to analyzing an avalanche. Why should the last snowflake take the blame? All the snow caused the avalanche, as did many other facets of the setting, such as water content of prior snowfalls, the topography of the mountain, and the location of trees. Focusing on that last snowflake takes away from assigning responsibility to all the other relevant factors.

Consider *all* the responsible factors that contributed to the dot-com bust, not just the last snowflake. The economic setting had been building to it for some time. First, as noted in earlier chapters, simultaneous investments in multiple sectors increased the value of other investments, as the network expanded and attracted more users. Overinvestment was inevitable in this setting, due to the lack of coordination between investments in so many facets of the Internet. The situation was ready for a change in the prevailing view that supported investment in the dot-com sector.

The first signs of overinvestment did not arise in the dot-com sector, as it happened. It arose in the building of the network infrastructure. Financial decline in this sector became known as the "telecom meltdown."

What happened? Firms had built backbone capacity to support far more traffic than anybody would need for many years.[28] Competitive local exchange companies, or CLECs, also had entered with abandon. While they supported local ISPs, CLECs were a child of a new deregulatory era in communications, as well as the implementation of the 1996

---

[28] As noted in Greenstein (2005, 40), "excessive" entry in infrastructure typically means some form of redundancy—two or more facilities serving the same geography. Some degree of overlap was inevitable at a national level because the Internet permitted data to take multiple pathways to accomplish the same tasks. Moreover, in most business ventures some "building ahead of demand is a calculated gamble," and the backbone business was no exception. Hogendorn (2011) goes on to show, however, that backbone firms faced fewer issues in building their physical infrastructure than in swaps and leases, the components that comprised virtual infrastructure. He also argues that much of the alleged overbuilding was a byproduct of double counting of leases.

Telecom Act, which laid out new competitive rules for interconnecting CLECs with the existing network.[29]

The key regulatory issues interested longtime telephone attorneys and activists, but these issues left many others confused or ill informed. In brief, the national billing system for telephony assumed that interconnecting firms made as many calls as they received. In the US compensation system, a firm paid for only one of these—the calls made, not those received.

The problems arose when the rules behind billing system met CLECs and CLECs met the Internet. If a CLEC received about as many calls as they sent, then no issue would have arisen. Taking advantage of the inter-carrier rules, however, a number of CLECs set up businesses to *receive* ISP calls from households but *send* very few, which effectively billed other telephone companies for "reciprocal compensation."

This strategy went unnoticed by regulators at first, and consequently, regulatory decisions for reciprocal compensation of CLECs encouraged CLEC entry, especially as the Internet grew in 1997 and 1998. The practice received attention as it grew, resulting in hearings at the FCC in 1998. The FCC passed a set of rules to do away with the practice in February 1999,[30] which made some CLEC business no longer viable.

In a short time the financial decline in stock prices hit firms in infrastructure markets particularly hard. Investors in CLECs and their business partners' firms, such as large-scale national ISPs, experienced declines in revenue unless they found other sources of revenue in the dot-com sector.

For many other participants in the Internet, the decline in CLECs was a distant event, and that perception illustrates the general challenges of the time. No single observer could easily grasp all the myriad forces at work. Behind the meltdown lay multiple complex causes, both commercial and regulatory, that enabled the meltdown to escape much public scrutiny. This lack of attention prevented it from serving as a warning for the majority of the Internet investment community.[31] The dot-com bust followed the telecom meltdown, as it had to, and, yet, it took many by surprise.

---

[29] For different interpretations, see Goldstein (2005), Greenstein (2005), or Goldfarb and Xiao (2011).

[30] FCC docket No. 99-38, Implementation of the Local Competition Provisions in the Telecommunications Act of 1996, Inter-Carrier Compensation for ISP-Bound Traffic, released February 26, 1999.

[31] See, e.g., Goldstein (2005).

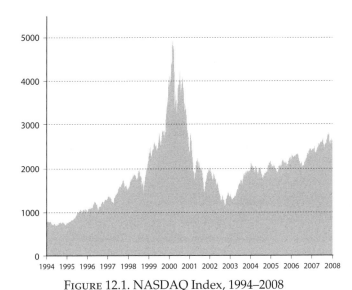

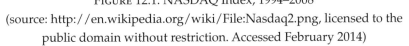

FIGURE 12.1. NASDAQ Index, 1994–2008
(source: http://en.wikipedia.org/wiki/File:Nasdaq2.png, licensed to the
public domain without restriction. Accessed February 2014)

The dot-com bust was not a sudden crisis but closer to a creeping realization, and one of diminished possibilities. For many participants the first
symptoms of decline became visible in the early spring of 2000. On March
10, 2000, the NASDAQ reached its peak.[32] It came down over several weeks,
taking a dive on April 4,[33] only to rebound again over the next few months.
Figure 16.1 illustrates this on the NASDAQ index, one of the important
stock exchanges for young and newly public Internet firms.

At first, proponents of the new economy began to characterize the private market as "hostile," and it delayed many IPOs. Those young firms
and their financial backers expected a rebound. Indeed, signs of the rebound showed up in the summer, bringing false temporary hope. Then

[32]On March 10, 2000, the NASDAQ composite index closed at 5,048 after reaching a peak
of 5,132 during the day.

[33]This is the day after the announcement of the Microsoft findings of fact. In circles critical
of the court's findings this coincidence of dates leads to the spurious conclusion that the
court's findings *caused* the dot-com bust. Such a conclusion is an illustration of the snowflake
fallacy. The dot-com bust was going to happen at some point because many factors caused
the overvaluation of stocks. The news on a particular day was, at best, a single snowflake, and,
at worse, merely a coincidence.

the decline returned, starting in the autumn of 2000. Skeptics of the new economy stressed the return to "normal," and virtually all technology IPOs ceased in the face of no demand to invest in dot-coms. Financial indexes reached their lowest point after the World Trade Center attacks on September 11, 2001, when travel by air shut down for several weeks across the country. Pervasive doubts about the future of economic activity and the war in Iraq and Afghanistan cast a pall of uncertainty over many investments for many months thereafter.[34]

These events led to an extraordinary loss in paper wealth. Stock market wealth, for example, reached bottom at $9.9 trillion in the third quarter of 2002. Overall, stock market wealth fell $8.3 trillion (or 46 percent) between its peak in the first quarter of 2000 and its trough in the third quarter of 2002.[35]

Many of the high-flying stocks of the late 1990s experienced declines, including Amazon, Cisco, and other firms in electronic commerce. Other firms in advertising-supported businesses, such as Yahoo, AOL, and many others, also saw their stock value decline.

Many of the most technically adept start-ups of the era—focused on fiber optics and high-speed landline facilities—suddenly found themselves without buyers for their products, or any buyers for their firms. The frontier had been successfully stretched and *it went too far*. So many of those start-ups succeeded in their technical goal, but did not get to sell their products because there was no demand.

The wake of the bust directly shaped investments in start-ups and fed back into the willingness to start firms. Few VCs could forecast when their existing investments could cash out, and many of them declined to fund new firms. Consequently, financing for Internet start-ups sharply declined after the bust, nearly stopping altogether in 2002.

That brings the discussion back to the most difficult systemic question: What were the systemic causes behind the timing of the general growth and the decline? Again eschewing the fallacy of the last snowflake, and

---

[34] In fact, the NASDAQ composite index reached its low almost a year later, closing at 1,108 on October 10, 2002.

[35] This comes from the flow of funds accounts, maintained by the Federal Reserve. These are available at www.federalreserve.gov/releases/z1.

taking a wider view, what fundamental economic factors changed between the fall of 1999 and the fall of 2000?

The first candidate is interest rates. Interest rates had been low throughout 1999, and that ended when the Federal Reserve chose to raise short-
term rates at the start of the new year. That factor alone would have led to
a decline in borrowing for financial investment, and as long-term rates
rose, a decline in the valuation of the future earnings of firms. The change
in interest rates did not precisely coincide with the change in the stock
market, but there was no reason for any coincidence of timing when Alan
Greenspan was chair of the Federal Reserve. He deliberately tried to
shroud the policies in the short run, and investors only gradually inferred
what those policies were, and as they did, they reacted.

Another contributing factor was the turn of the millennium, which exposed a false forecast about massive failures in installed mainframe computers. Known as the Y2K problem, many old mainframe systems found
at longtime users of enterprise IT contained programs that far outlived the
designer's expectations. These programs embedded a myopic error. The
impending year was coded as two digits—"00"—instead of four—"2000."
If left uncorrected, the programs with two digit expressions would ex-
press "January 1, 2000" as "January 1, 1900." Many of these issues could
be forecast in advance, and many enterprises undertook large infrastructure upgrades to avoid them. IT firms had sold networking and computing services to large enterprise buyers as part of a general package to
avoid problems with the expression of 2000. After there were minimal
computing problems with the transition to the new millennium, it was
almost inevitable that many of these budgets were going to decline. Consulting firms, hardware firms, and a wide variety of integrators for enterprises saw their businesses decline as well.[36]

The last (and, perhaps, ultimate) contributing factor came from the
performance of dot-com firms themselves. As the next chapter explains,
online advertising did not become effective right away, and, as a result,
did not generate enormous growth in revenues, as so many business
plans had assumed. Moreover, despite some success in firms such as

---

[36] That explanation is consistent with the general timing of the decline, albeit, it does not
explain why it occurred in March instead of February or April.

eBay, Amazon, and a variety of converts from catalog retailing, many of their cousins in electronic retailing did generate performances on anything close to the scale necessary to justify earlier impatient investments. The experience of WebVan, described earlier, was one such example. There were many others who were equally as impatient in their investment behavior, and some are described below. In this telling, the lack of performance in the Christmas season of 1999 would take special blame, as the poor results were reported in detail over the winter of 2000 for so many firms.[37]

Irrational Exuberance

A popular phrase emerged to describe the frenzied financial investment that had characterized the moments prior to the crash. That phrase came from the chairman of the Federal Reserve Board, Alan Greenspan. In December 5, 1996, he made remarks that contained the phrase "irrational exuberance."[38]

By the time of the bust, the phrase had taken on a new interpretation. Greenspan had focused on the challenges asset values posed for monetary policy, using the experience in Japan and the crisis in 1987 as illustrations. He had not aimed any remarks at the US technology sector.[39] After this speech the phrase took on a life of its own, and after the dot-com crash it acquired pejorative tones—as shorthand for business behavior that lacked common sense.

[37] Goldfarb, Kirsh, and Miller (2007), and Goldfarb, Kirsch and Pfarrer (2005), argue that the decline in stock values was attributable to poor reports from electronic commerce retailers in the just-completed Christmas season.

[38] It appeared in a speech given at the Annual Dinner and Francis Boyer Lecture of the American Enterprise Institute for Public Policy Research in Washington, DC.

[39] The original speech makes that clear:

> Clearly, sustained low inflation implies less uncertainty about the future, and lower risk premiums imply higher prices of stocks and other earning assets. We can see that in the inverse relationship exhibited by price/earnings ratios and the rate of inflation in the past. But how do we know when irrational exuberance has unduly escalated asset values, which then become subject to unexpected and prolonged contractions as they have in Japan over the past decade? And how do we factor that assessment into monetary policy?

See http://www.federalreserve.gov/boarddocs/speeches/1996/19961205.htm, accessed November 2012.

Perhaps the most frequently cited example of unbridled irrational exuberance came from a merger at end of the boom, the merger between Time Warner and AOL, the largest media firm in the United States and the largest Internet access firm, respectively. Justified by many anticipated synergies created by the merger, content firms at Time Warner were supposed to feed content to AOL's users, which then would give AOL excellent targeted advertising, and thereby gain the advantages of scale. In turn, this was supposed to raise the value of content from Time Warner, allowing them unprecedented opportunities to develop new content.

In hindsight, the merger looked like an obvious mistake, but nevertheless, the integration problems were so immediate and concrete it is a wonder nobody anticipated them.[40] Although the vision did not run into resistance among investors, its execution left plenty to be desired. In particular, financial incentives could not generate any cooperation out of Time Warner, which contained many established and successful magazines, and processes for generating stories and ads that had long successful histories.

Gains from combining the firms turned out to be a fantasy at worse, or an untested theory at best. Implementation never got close to the theory. Employees at both organizations were not enthusiastic about working with the other's employees, and many division managers guarded their autonomy, not perceiving any visible or short-run gains from cooperation. Lacking any reason or incentive to cooperate, most did not. Alleged synergies never arose, not even a little bit. Before management had time to develop long-term plans, the dot-com crash reduced advertising from many of AOL's partners. The decline in the US economy further reduced the value of many of Time Warner's businesses. That took the air out of further programs to generate new initiatives. Going forward the combined divisions continued their activities as if independent of one another.[41]

---

[40]See the critique in chapter 12, which benefits from hindsight: "January 2001: Merger of AOL and Time Warner," in Bruner (2005), 265–91.

[41]The financial value of the combined entities began to drop not long after the merger. Many years later the entire deal was taken apart at enormous loss to the participants. See the extensive description in chapter 12, "January 2001: Merger of AOL and Time Warner," in Bruner (2005).

Why did anyone think the merger of AOL and Time Warner was a good idea? There is really no good explanation for why the obvious challenges and risks were not anticipated. Blaming the prevailing view is the easiest explanation. Impatiently getting large was all that mattered, not carefully vetting the potential for raising revenue. The merger was consistent with the prevailing view at the point when crucial decisions were made, and the small set of executives responsible for it never got the message from any skeptic.

AOL and Time Warner were far from an isolated example of such managerial foolhardiness.[42] Additional poster children for irrational exuberance touched many high-profile firms, such as PSINet, which was still operated by its founder Bill Schrader more than a dozen years after its founding. Weakened by the telecom meltdown, the dot-com bust accelerated the decline of many infrastructure firms. Dot-com firms could no longer pay for access services and more. Eventually, PSINet faced financial difficulties that led to bankruptcy.

PSINet's bankruptcy, in June 2001, represented a comeuppance for Schrader, who had become one of the most vocal critics of the reluctance of telephone companies to invest in the Internet. By the end of the decade, the firm had become well known for its bold acquisitions, growing into one of the largest ISPs in the world. It was also well known for unbridled ambition—for example, purchasing the naming rights for the football stadium of the Baltimore Ravens.

The firm became the victim of two factors, a risky merger and leveraged debt. It merged with a large consulting firm, Internet consulting company Metamor Worldwide Inc., just before the dot-com bust. It was supposed to be a diversification, expanding PSINet into a business with a revenue flow distinct from its other lines of business.[43] In fact, it did not diversify at all against the bust. Metamor's revenue base declined rapidly during the dot-com bust, and at the same time as PSINet saw revenue decline in many of its retail ISP businesses.

Second, over many years PSINet had primarily financed expansion through debt, not equity. Rather quickly after the bust, therefore, it faced cash flow issues related to making interest payments, and eventually it

---

[42] A little subculture grew up around the most spectacular stories and declines, with websites devoted to collecting stories. See, e.g., Kaplan (2002).

[43] Bill Schrader, private communications, July 2008.

defaulted on these.[44] It is hard to fault PSINet's management for this choice, since bank loans appeared to be cheaper, and so many of its direct competitors and business partners used the same source of finance.

Nonetheless, to see the risk inherent in that choice, contrast PSINet's experience with Level(3), another infrastructure firm that also had expanded rapidly. Level(3) had financed itself through equity. While stockholders lost value after the bust, Level(3) neither had to declare bankruptcy nor cease operations because its interest (cash) payments were not as high. Instead, stockholders lost paper value. Stockholders were not happy, of course, but that is not the key point: at least their firm survived.

Other candidates for exuberance included WebVan, Pets.com, and JDS Uniphase, all of whom eventually filed for bankruptcy. These all appeared to be wasteful investments or excessive expansions made by faithful practitioners of the philosophy to "get big fast" who drove their firms off a cliff and wasted investor money. Each company was, in fact, a different variant of the illustration of impatient excess. As recounted earlier in the chapter, WebVan was the victim of impatient exploration, a flawed model unfurled too quickly.

In Pets.com the management committed a different type of mistake as a by-product of its impatience. It spent lavishly on publicity, especially its commercials involving a sock puppet, which became widely ridiculed. Its bankruptcy symbolized that no amount of advertising could make up for a poorly conceived business. As should have been apparent right from the outset, the shipping costs for large volumes of pet food rendered the service too expensive for a typical household, which could buy appropriate amounts from a local retailer. Once again, limited trials would have tested that theory and limited the downside losses.

JDS Uniphase, in contrast, had been successful for a time as one of the largest upstream suppliers of hardware components for a wide range of equipment. Yet after the crash it had few customers for its equipment and became a symbol of incautious expansion.

As with the other examples, it is hard to understand in retrospect how management made itself so vulnerable by expanding so quickly. As it turned out, the primary cause of its downfall was a classic textbook problem that any seasoned manager would have guarded against—namely, a

---

[44]See, e.g., Woolley (2001).

whipsaw effect, which sharply reduced their revenue as demand declined (and would have reduced revenue in any event). A whipsaw effect turns moderate demand downturns into big declines for upstream suppliers and is a risk for an upstream supplier facing a downstream buyer with volatile demand. It can arise when the upstream supplier faces more volatility than the downstream supplier because a downstream supplier may not recognize a decline in demand soon enough and, consequently, adjust to new demand by drawing down on (excessive) inventory holdings rather than placing new orders. As a result, the upstream supplier can see sharp declines in demand from moderate changes downstream.

Guarding against the whipsaw would not have been difficult for JDS Uniphase to do, and, indeed, other firms did guard against such actions. For example, in contrast to JDS Uniphase, Cisco had outsourced much of its upstream activity to others, which left Cisco holding many fewer assets when its revenue declined. After the dot-com bust, Cisco continued to operate with only one large layoff.[45]

Irrational exuberance also became a phrase for improper financial dealings in which the prevailing view enabled a firm to escape scrutiny (for a short while). For example, executives at WorldCom and Enron faced scandal as a result of accounting improprieties that came to light after the dot-com bust. First consider WorldCom, then Enron. Both will illustrate how impatient investors failed to ask skeptical questions, which allowed managerial impropriety to survive far longer than it should have.

WorldCom's bankruptcy, filed on July 22, 2002, also represented a comeuppance for a newcomer. The firm had expanded through merger to become the largest backbone provider in the United States and the second-largest long-distance telephone company.[46] It had swallowed up several viable businesses, including Metropolitan Fiber Company, which included UUNET, and the infrastructure division of CompuServe.[47]

---

[45] Cisco survived through one large layoff and, in effect, through transferring much of the risks of its expanding product line to its parts suppliers, typically Asian subcontractors, who were left holding inventories.

[46] Acquisitions included Advanced Communications Corp. (1992); Metromedia Communication Corp. (1993); Resurgens Communications Group (1993); IDB Communications Group, Inc. (1994); Williams Technology Group, Inc. (1995); and MFS Communications Company (1996), which included UUNET. Remarkably, after the Sprint merger was stopped, WorldCom attempted one more, the acquisition of Digex in June 2001.

[47] The online presence went to AOL, while the part of AOL, what was left of ANS (originally from IBM), was sent to WorldCom.

WorldCom had become so large that antitrust action had been deployed to limit the firm's actions. In February 1998, it completed its merger with MCI, the second-largest long-distance telephone company in the United States. The Department of Justice required WorldCom to spin off considerable backbone assets—those that were part of MCI—as a condition for the MCI merger. WorldCom's attempt to merge with Sprint, announced in October 1999, ran into so much opposition in Europe that the firm had to abandon the proposal, even before the US Department of Justice finished its review. It was abandoned in July 2000.

After the fact, these interventions by government antitrust regulators appeared especially sagacious. As it had turned out, WorldCom's management had been cooking its books, delaying the day that it had to represent its true financial state to outsiders.

On June 25, 2002, an internal auditor reported a newly discovered accounting fraud. WorldCom's CFO had reclassified assets as expense, giving WorldCom the appearance of being in a rosier financial condition than was true in practice. The ensuing trial exemplified the excess, as the CEO, Bernie Ebbers, seemed to rely heavily on his CFO for financial expertise. In trial he appeared to have little grasp of the underlying cost structure of the firm he had built.[48]

The comeuppance for Enron came at much the same time, and was especially dramatic. Its demise hurt investors, its employees, and a major national accounting firm, which had been intimidated into certifying financial rectitude even when Enron did not deserve it.[49]

The firm's experience became symbolic of business untethered from managerial competence, laced with charm and flamboyance that bordered on systematic deception. Although it was primarily an energy company, Enron had expanded into a range of prominent Internet businesses during the 1990s. It had a division that traded on contracts in backbone data exchanges, which had been the darling of scores of new-economy gurus. As came to light later, the trading had been a Potemkin village, nothing more

---

[48] News analysts speculated whether this was a feigned lack of understanding to escape culpability or evidence that he had been over his head, acting as cheerleader for a business he did not understand. See, e.g., Jeter (2003).

[49] These events reached epic levels for their incompetence, scale, and drama. See, e.g., Eichenwald (2005).

than a showpiece, mostly for reporters and the financial analysts, and no large-scale trading had ever taken place.[50]

It did appear to have real business aspirations behind the show. For example, the Enron Broadband Services group signed a deal with the video-rental chain firm Blockbuster for providing video on demand. That is not possible without real infrastructure, real pipes that deliver data at high volumes between points. Of course, the actual revenue from that deal was far in the future, while many of the costs were experienced early. Even in the face of those factors, however, and as it had done in other business units, Enron's accounting division could not resist bringing the revenue forward, giving the appearance that the project was profitable, as if the division had made its financial targets.[51]

These particular deceptions did not doom Enron as much as its practices for borrowing money. Its financial officers instituted a program of complex financial transactions that let it borrow money against future revenues without paying extra interest for the riskiness of the practice. Once investors uncovered the extent of the practice, it became clear that Enron had become addicted to living on borrowed money in excess of future revenue, and the company's financial position declined rapidly and irreversibly.[52]

Would the dot-com expansion have happened without Enron's deception? Yes, probably, but the absence of this particularly deceptive example might have dampened some of the false perception that the future had arrived so soon. That, in turn, would have reduced enthusiasm of the advocates for the prevailing view in the new economy, and the dot-com bust might have arrived sooner, wasting few resources for as long as it did.

These are but examples among scores that came to light after the dot-com bust. The decline of financial support for investments came as a shock to many with a parochial view of impatient investment. Such impatient investment was not sustainable without returns, and there were many signs

---

[50] The scale of the deception is rather remarkable, partly for its audacity. The division did nothing useful, nor was it profitable. Nobody really knew the truth until well after Enron imploded—not the reporters who profiled the firm during its rise in the 1990s, not the auditors, or stock analysts, or consultants. See, e.g., Eichenwald (2005).

[51] See http://phys.org/news68469936.html, accessed February 2014. Also see Eichenwald (2005), for a much more detailed explanation of the accounting, and how the firms systematically realized future revenue in its accounting prior to its actual collection.

[52] Eichenwald (2005).

that many would not experience such returns. In addition, the tales of deception, imprudence, and incompetence suggested unsound economic foundations, as if many investors had been duped. After so much scandal, the dot-com sector became tainted with suspicion, and the prevailing view supporting actions in the earlier era did as well.

Correcting Prevailing Views

Prevailing views don't arise, grow, or settle in an organized or orderly way. They involve a collection of opinions, unverified hypotheses, facts, alleged consequences, promised payoffs, narrative arcs with fragile foundations, and logical fallacies. More to the point, prevailing views lack tangibility. No single document declares its many dimensions for assayers. Instead, analysts compete to spot the flaws in general presumptions, which become visible during moments when an event exposes the gap between fact and fantasy. Lessons can become understood only after the facts falsify bogus premises, and analysts pour over traces of volatile economic events revealed within the shards of financial flotsam and jetsam.

In retrospect it is obvious that the prevailing view behind the dot-com bubble was flawed, and by the beginning of 2001 it had become inescapable. The news hit many participants like a hangover, as if economic fate had a sense of humor and favored jokes delivered with a sardonic tenor. It was a cruel joke, at best, to those who had sacrificed so much and worked so hard to build businesses that fundamentally relied on false premises and value propositions that could never become viable. It was a devastating punch in the gut to those who had identified with something they regarded as a greater purpose, and especially to those who had believed the promises to improve the world while building the commercial network.

For skeptics of Internet exceptionalism, in contrast, the bust appeared to be a well-deserved comeuppance. Internet exceptionalism made a challenging situation more economically wasteful than it had to be by rejecting decades of lessons about assessing financial risk and return. Because of the uncoordinated investment in the commercial Internet, some part of the bust, some degree of overshooting, was inevitable. In addition, because innovation from the edges generated many new economy opportunities that required experimentation and entrepreneurial energy to explore, it was inevitable that many investments would fail. Flawed and overly optimistic financial institutions, which were insufficiently supervised, were an additional factor, and it distorted behavior. It oriented toward selfish short-termism at the expense of investors and the economy as a whole.

The dot-com bust did not eliminate innovation from the edges, but it did reorient participants' and investors' understanding of it. After the turn of the millennium, the commercial Internet moved forward, with many participants chastened. Many survivors adopted a view grounded in actual user behavior, realistic assessments of the costs of supplier operations, and modest expectations about the costs of building a customer base for a web-based business.

13

The Paradox of the Prevailing View

We chose our system name, Google, because it is a common spelling of googol, or 10^{100} and fits well with our goal of building very large-scale search engines.
—*Sergey Brin and Lawrence Page, founders of Google*[1]

The National Science Foundation took a parent's credit for Sergey Brin's and Larry Page's success. The NSF's claim contained considerable merit because the NSF helped fund the fundamental research that eventually led Brin and Page to found Google.[2] Moreover, Google became the most profitable business in the first decade and a half of the commercial web.

It is useful to enumerate what NSF did and did not claim, and why. The NSF never claimed to have had perfect foresight, nor did it claim to sponsor the precise invention Brin and Page made. NSF only sponsored the general technical area in which Brin and Page worked. NSF's claims also fit the facts. When they began their studies at Stanford in 1994 and 1995, Brin and Page aspired to do precisely what NSF had sponsored them to do, get PhDs in computer science by making frontier inventions. Founding a company was not their primary goal at that point, nor was it an explicit goal, when the NSF first began to fund their work. Seen in retrospect,

---

[1] Page and Brin (1998).

[2] Thanks to Jeannette M. Wing, former assistant director of NSF's Computer and Information Science and Engineering (CISE) Division, for pointing out the connection between NSF and Google, and piquing my curiosity. See http://www.tvworldwide.com/events/pcast /100902/default.cfm, accessed July 2012. See http://www.nsf.gov/discoveries/disc_summ .jsp?cntn_id=100660&org=NSF, and also http://ilpubs.stanford.edu:8091/diglib/pub/proj ects.shtml, accessed July 2012.

FIGURE 13.1 Larry Page and Sergey Brin, cofounders of
Google (February 8, 2002)

however, there is no doubt the NSF funding played an essential role in helping Brin and Page make the inventions that led to Google.

Brin and Page did not have the same type or level of support from NSF, and this turned out to be a distinction without a difference. Brin arrived with a NSF fellowship, while Page arrived with a promise for tuition and stipend support from Stanford's computer science department.

Brin's NSF fellowship was quite difficult to get, and, therefore, prestigious. It provided full financial support for a graduate education, and it afforded the recipient enormous freedom in his studies.[3] Recipients of NSF fellowships, such as Brin, were given discretion to pursue any project. The money came with few strings attached other than a requirement that the students continue to enroll in their studies. As it turned out, Brin chose to work with Professor Terry Winograd.

In contrast, Page received a different deal, one that is more common for PhD students at elite research universities in the United States. His support came with a quid pro quo, in exchange for working as a research assistant for Professor Hector Garcia-Molina. As it happened, Garcia-Molina had promised NSF that he would do research on frontier issues in digital

[3]See http://www.google.com/about/company/facts/management/#sergey, and also http://www.nsfgrfp.org/why_apply/fellow_profiles/sergey_brin, accessed July 2012.

library science and train many graduate students in those issues. Garcia-Molina had made this promise in a grant application to NSF, which was written with Professor Terry Winograd. NSF had awarded the money to both Stanford professors as part of its Digital Library Initiative, NSF's giant enterprise that included, among other things, the goal to improve the science of large-scale information retrieval and storage.[4] Page could expect support as long as he remained in good standing. Good standing was earned by pursuing research on topics consistent with the scope of the NSF grant. In most cases earning good standing was the routine outcome from studiousness, perseverance, and disciplined work habits.

In practice, Brin and Page experienced virtually the same situation because Winograd and Garcia-Molina worked together and supervised a bevy of graduate students.[5] Brin and Page both had discretion to pursue new ideas. Brin's discretion came with no formal strings attached, but it did come with strong social norms of the technical meritocracy. He could expect that at some time near the end of his graduate school experience others within the computer science community would ask him to account for his time, and others would evaluate whether he performed well. Page's obligations came in conjunction with his work with his advisors, Winograd and Garcia-Molina. They also had to justify their actions in a final report, which would be made available within NSF the next time the researcher applied for funding. That report could play a material role in whether they received funding again. Once again, therefore, a researcher could expect to have to account for their actions within the computer science community at some later date, and they could expect to have their performance assessed by others.

These facts about the discretion of a couple of young graduate students are more than a pedantic detail. While Garcia-Molina and Winograd could not change the scope of the NSF-funded project, they retained discretion to change the precise details of a line of experiments if they perceived a new opportunity, and the opportunity was consistent with the goals of the initial proposal. Many developed countries fund R&D (Research and Development), but few give recipients such flexibility, as NSF does. In this case, it did matter, and it especially mattered for Larry Page's experience.

[4]See http://www.nsf.gov/discoveries/disc_summ.jsp?cntn_id=100660&org=NSF, and also http://ilpubs.stanford.edu:8091/diglib/pub/projects.shtml, accessed July 2012.
[5]Professor Hector Garcia-Molina, private communication, July 2012.

Professor Garcia-Molina and Winograd's original proposal to the NSF did not promise—*and could not have promised*—the specific idea Page eventually pursued.[6] The commercial web was quite young when Garcia-Molina and Winograd's proposal began in the fall of 1994.[7] The professors' proposal was written and evaluated even before the release of the first beta for the Netscape browser. By the start of his studies, however, the growing use of the web had accelerated and caught the attention of many, including Larry Page. He came into the lab one day and proposed to examine information on private web pages.[8] It was a conceptually interesting shift. Page shifted the focus from inventing tools to examine the digital content of libraries to inventing tools to examine the commercial web—similar tools, but a different setting. The supervisors recognized the potential scientific novelty of the proposal and let him go ahead and explore the possibility. That exact question had not been proposed in the NSF grant, because it could not have been asked. However, the professors knew they could authorize the change without worry.

A rigid system for funding science would have prevented both supervisors from allowing their students to address this new opportunity. NSF deserves credit for lacking such rigidity, for giving its researchers the discretion to pursue new opportunities related to those it had funded. It accommodates an unanticipated opportunity.

As it turned out, another member of the lab, Sergey Brin, eventually joined Page in the activity. What did Brin and Page develop? Using some advanced mathematics, they developed a method for measuring the links across websites by ranking a website more highly when other sites linked to it. Oversimplifying, the algorithm measured a web page's popularity. That ranking provided a better answer to queries seeking to find informative web pages. The technology was called a search engine, because it helped users search for useful information. Indeed, a search engine built around Page's invention was more informative than any other search en-

---

[6] Professor Hector Garcia-Molina, private communication, July 2012.

[7] The proposal has an official start date of September 1, 1994, and was written many months before, around the time of Netscape's founding. Professor Hector Garcia-Molina, private communication, July 2012. See also http://www.nsf.gov/awardsearch/showAward.do?AwardNumber=9411306, accessed July 2012.

[8] Professor Hector Garcia-Molina, private communication, July 2012.

gine at the time. Brin and Page called their algorithm Page-Rank,[9] in a play on words, referring both to web pages and Larry Page's last name.

Page-Rank led to Google, but not by a direct path. Page and Brin did not drop out of their studies right away, or quickly sacrifice their aspirations for a PhD. They took classes for two years, worked in the lab, and completed all the requirements for a PhD except the last one, writing a dissertation. They even took steps to making progress on that last requirement by making progress with implementing and refining their algorithm.[10] They implemented Page-Rank in a search engine they initially called Backrub, which became available on a server at Stanford. They wrote several papers about it.

The popularity of their search engine with campus users encouraged Brin and Page to seek some revenue in new licensees (which they would share with Stanford). Stanford took a patent out on Page-Rank and, following standard policies for the campus, licensed it to the inventor, Larry Page.[11]

Things did not go according to plan. Despite their proximity to Silicon Valley, at first these young entrepreneurs did not find any takers for their algorithm. That is not a misprint. Odd as it might seem in retrospect for an invention that eventually became the basis for a multi-billion-dollar company, Brin and Page were not able to find any existing firms who wanted to license Page-Rank. To say it simply, their invention did not stand out because they were merely a couple of smart kids trying to license an algorithm to revolutionize searching the Internet. In the middle to late 1990s there were a lot of smart kids claiming to be torchbearers for the next

[9] Page et al. (1999) and Page and Brin (2008).

[10] This originally could be accessed at www.google.stanford.edu. Professor Hector Garcia-Molina, private communication, July 2012. In fact, Page and Brin were not the only search engine inventors to have a similar insight. RankDex, established in 1996 by Robin (Yanhong) Li, also used an algorithmic approach to links between sites to rank relevance. See US patent 5,920,859. Li worked for Infoseek for a time, and went on to found the Chinese search engine Baidu. In addition, another pioneer for search engines at the time, Eric Brewer, was an assistant professor at UC Berkeley, and a participant in another NSF grant from the same program about digital libraries. Along with a graduate student, Paul Gauthier, he founded Inktomi, using a distinct approach to rank web pages. Dave Peterschmidt became CEO, with Brewer acting as the chief scientist and Gauthier as the chief technology officer.

[11] Larry Page and Stanford University were granted patent 6,285,999, with Page listed as the sole inventor, and Stanford as the assignee. The US patent database also includes several updates to the original filing.

revolution, and plenty of other approaches to search. Brin and Page did not look any more distinguished.

More to the point, Brin and Page happened to have the dumb luck to live in a geographic location, Silicon Valley, at a time of intense entrepreneurial activity. In most other universities and in many other technical eras they might have been big fish in small ponds, just not against that cacophony of activity in the valley in the mid- to late 1990s. The prototype built at Stanford worked well, but did little to convince others of the value of the algorithm. Everyone seemed to be a skeptic. The prevailing view dismissed their search engine and characterized its approach as not valuable.

Location did play a role in the next key event, however. Brin and Page found an angel investor in Andy Bechtolsheim, or, perhaps, it is more appropriate to say that Bechtolsheim found Brin and Page. Bechtolsheim had dropped out of his Stanford PhD studies many years earlier to become a cofounder of SUN Microsystems and over the years had retained a liking for the quixotic pursuits of PhD students. The timing was important. Had they stuck to their initial plan, both Brin and Page should have been doing the research to inform the writing of their dissertation. Instead, Bechtolsheim invested in the venture founded by Brin and Page, nurturing them through the next delicate steps of founding Google, which Page and Brin did in September 1998, just a few years after they showed up on the Stanford campus.

The new firm moved off the university's servers, establishing an office in a few rooms in a friend's house in Menlo Park, and set about scaling its search engine into something larger and more pervasive. At that point an observer could be forgiven for not seeing much that distinguished Google from the thousands of other start-ups at the time that aspired to profit from the growing web. The valley's VCs did not see them as anything special and did not regard a facile search engine as the first technical step on the path toward industry dominance or uncommon profitability.

This recounting of Google's origins touches the surface of the paradox of the prevailing view, the theme of this chapter. Every technology market has a prevailing view, and it helps guide collective behavior. The paradox of the prevailing view is this: While the prevailing view guides the activities of many firms in one technical and commercial direction, one consistent with the prevailing view, it also can simultaneously motivate others to pursue another technical and commercial direction, one that is inconsistent with the prevailing view. Said succinctly, the prevailing view tends to encourage the majority of innovation in a very specific direction, but—simultaneously and paradoxically—it can encourage something else, exploration of innovation aimed at activity that would alter the prevailing view.

When can the prevailing view play such distinct roles? It is likely to play these dual roles when the economic conditions tolerate a variety of business approaches, giving rise to exploration in many directions. For example, as this chapter will show, Google used an alternative set of principles for creating value than its near rivals. They had the opportunity to demonstrate their value because no single dominant view stopped them, either by acting as a gateway or slowing experimentation by raising frictions, or by outcompeting them before the technical meritocracy of the market went to work.

Advertising Supported Commerce

The importance of advertising arose from a fundamental feature of the web, its disorganization. Better said, users required help in navigating the material on so many web pages because Tim Berners-Lee had deliberately kept the web simple, embedding the web with minimal central control. Word of mouth, informal recommendations, and the links on web pages provided some guidance, but the scale of the number of pages found on the commercial web soon outran the functionality of those mechanisms.

The specific steps to succeed eluded many firms, however. Early on, some firms hoped to make money by charging directly for subscriptions to organized web-based information, much as indexed databases had done in the past, such as Lexis and Nexis. These efforts largely failed to generate much revenue.[12]

Attention largely turned to making money by one of two alternative routes. One approach was fundamentally technical. It oriented itself toward providing better technical solutions to finding information on the web. That led to various different engineered solutions to online searching that could be made profitable in two ways: by selling advertising to users, or by selling search results to firms who then licensed the search service.

---

[12]For a history of the variety of approaches, see Haigh (2008).

While this approach always yielded some revenue, especially for navigating internal corporate networks, the revenue from advertising approached a much larger potential scale, and so received much more attention from startups.[13]

The second approach looked for shared collective interests. It collected users in groups, showed them specialized content, and then showed them advertising. Many firms took this approach, assembling a wide variety of content and services, and the most successful among them grew into portals. Yahoo, AOL, MSN, and many other firms, aspired to become portals.[14]

Two aspects of advertising underlay the promise of value from portals: (1) better measurement of the results and (2) more precise targeting of the audience. In practice, inventors promised both but did not realize their promises over the late 1990s. In retrospect, these forecasts acted as if the new world would arrive faster and friction free, accusing the pessimists of being too unimaginative about how much could change in a half decade.

The problems became readily apparent with experience. And they began to shape investing at the beginning of the new millennium when enthusiasm for dot-com firms began to wane and investors asked the skeptical questions discussed in the prior chapter. In a stroke of good timing, Google's approach emerged around this time, and it improved upon measurement and targeting, while creating considerable value.

What was the promise of more precise targeting? The problem arose very early in the diffusion of the web, years before Google's founding. It can be understood through the history of the cookie.

The cookie originated with the ninth employee of Netscape, Lou Montulli. He was twenty-four years old in June 1994, just fresh out of college. Montulli called his tool a "cookie" to relate it to an earlier era of computing, when systems would exchange data back and forth in what programmers would call "magic cookies." While there were multiple technical ways to address the lack of history in a browser, the cookie sent information back and forth from a user's browser to a web site, letting the merchant know the user had returned, and letting the vendor store know small bits of information on the user's browser for repeated use. Users

---

[13]For a history of some of these attempts, see Haigh (2008).
[14]For a history of portals, see Haigh (2008).

could see it work too, and without having to change its settings, or, even without even being alerted to its operations. It saved users time and provided functionality for nontechnical users so they could complete their online transactions with greater ease.[15]

Microsoft's browser included cookies because Microsoft did not want its browser to be any less functional than Netscape's. With the two most widely used browsers holding identical functionality, the web-building community could depend on a ubiquitous and universal presence of cookies in all browsers. Third-party tracking of cookies built on top of that ubiquity. Although cookies had been designed to let one firm track one user at a time, nothing prevented one firm from placing ads on multiple sites and, through arrangements with the owners of those websites, tracking what users did as they moved from one site and another.

Third-party tracking was not one of Montulli's design goals, as it violated his notion of privacy. "We didn't want cookies to be used as a general tracking mechanism," said Montulli. Very soon many Internet technologists at the IETF thought so as well. Just as quickly firms that benefited from cookies began to defend third-party tracking. Attempts to regulate its use became opposed throughout the late 1990s.[16]

Cookies particularly benefited firms with large amounts of content— for example, Yahoo, which assembles a great deal of information in one site. They also benefited firms with the ability to track users across multiple sites, such as DoubleClick. Such a firm, in principle, could achieve a survey of a user's preferences by aggregating the insights made about one user across many properties. In principle, that permitted more effective targeting. Only a few years after the cookie was invented, Yahoo, AOL, and DoubleClick were well on the way to such an implementation, while making many deals to expand their offerings and match those of any other large site.

By the time Brin and Page founded Google, many of these firms had made progress but still faced difficult challenges matching their offerings

---

[15]Schwartz (2001).

[16]See Schwartz (2001). In addition, there are alternative methods for tracking user surfing, such as web bugs, though European Commission rules banned them, for example. See Goldfarb and Tucker (2011).

to users with accuracy. At the end of the decade rarely did ads match with any precision.[17] And that was so for both portals and specialty sites.

Reality fell short of the promise in one other aspect. The potential to place a "clickable/trackable ad" on a web page generated excitement.[18] Owners of a large amount of content could keep track of surfers and which ads they clicked on. Since advertising defied strict measurement in many other media, the advance of the web held the promise of measuring whether ad campaigns had direct effects on users or not. Although banner ads made money,[19] the vast majority were displayed to readers and sold in proportion to the number of times they were displayed, that is, they were priced on a "price-per-impression," not on any reliable measure of their impact on user behavior.[20] That left buyers and sellers with no certainty about the value of impressions, and it motivated sellers to find a better measure of impact.

Enter Google

Google eventually would improve on measurement and precision, but that was far from apparent in 1998 when Brin and Page founded the firm. At first Google offered its search service separately, with nothing else other than a bar for a user to input a keyword, just as it had appeared on the Stanford server. That generated a set of results, which the firm returned to the users. The design's simplicity gave it a distinctive look from the crowded portals, and that also drew attention to it as a specialized service.[21]

---

[17] As Haigh (2008) archly points out, both firms were quite far away from any finely grained targeting. Many of the ads sold in this era were sold at flat rates and with crude matching mechanisms, at best.

[18] Donaldson (2008).

[19] Although the history of the banner ad predates the growth of the web, its growth did not accelerate dramatically until the commercial web began to grow along with the browser. See Donaldson (2008). The BBS Prodigy appears to be among the first firms to deploy the equivalent to the click-through banner ad. http://nothingtohide.us/wp-content/uploads /2008/01/dd_unit-1_online_advertsing_history.pdf, accessed July 2012.

[20] Also see the skepticism in Haigh (2008).

[21] Marissa Mayer, vice president of search product and user experience, states that this design was a by-product of the limited HTML programming skills of the founders, and their desire for a fast-loading page. They decided to retain the simplicity after learning that many users expected more, and only came to understand the benefits of simplicity long after Google inserted the copyright notice at the bottom. See http://www.youtube.com/watch?v=so YKFWqVVzg, and http://alan.blog-city.com/an_evening_with_googles_marissa_mayer.htm.

Google was distinctive in another respect. The search engine declared its commercial neutrality with respect to advertising, which the founders believed made their search engine more user friendly. Hints of this neutrality could be found in the academic papers Brin and Page wrote when they were graduate students. Their first academic paper included an appendix with several paragraphs that described the potential conflicts between receiving compensation from advertisers and achieving a search result that best met user needs by avoiding any commercial influences on its search query answers. It included this declaration:

> we expect that advertising funded search engines will be inherently biased towards the advertisers and away from the needs of the consumers . . . [and] . . . we believe the issue of advertising causes enough mixed incentives that it is crucial to have a competitive search engine that is transparent and in the academic realm.[22]

In short, for many years Page and Brin did not focus on advertising. They had focused on attracting users with results that were relevant and quickly delivered. Speedy results became a well-known obsession of Larry Page. The focus on making search relevant to users—and doing so above all other considerations—could be called a strategic principle, but it is more accurate to call it an early outlook, a preference and inclination of the founders. It morphed into a strategic principle when the founders chose to retain it in spite of the short-run costs.[23]

In 1998, supply and demand did not seem to favor Google. Supply was high: Google was one of many search engines trying to find a licensee or buyer of its services.[24] Demand was low: The prevailing view at the leading portals did not see much value in search, and did not anticipate creating value from improving search. In the prevailing view, search engines helped match a few niche concerns with a few idiosyncratic web pages. That activity, at best, catered to a few niche tastes that the portal otherwise

---

[22]See appendix A, Page and Brin (1998). They identify several conflicts, stressing conflicts over the top listing, conflicts over the order in which results are listed, conflicts between the transparency of the decisions about how to order results and hiding favoritism, conflicts due to exclusion of companies with whom the sponsor has a conflict, and erosion of search engine incentives to improve quality when advertisers address user needs.

[23]Also see Schmidt, Rosenberg, and Eagle (2014), 78–81.

[24]Among the other prominent search engines at the time were AltaVista, Lycos, FindWhat, GoTo, Excite, Infoseek, RankDex, WebCrawler, Ask Jeeves, and Inktomi.

could not satisfy with its listing. Moreover, the search engine took the user away from the portal, because it sent users to the links uncovered by the search engine. It reduced the potential to sell advertising, and portals could do that more easily when users remained on their website. Encouraging users to leave portals was regarded as an undesirable feature for a portal. Accordingly, all portals included a search function, and it was not featured prominently.

Initially lacking any interest from licensees, Google made its engine available to any searcher with a query. Its market share of searches grew, and it began making a little revenue from showing simple display or banner ads—ads that displayed for a fixed period and did not tailor their content to the user—alongside the search results. These became distinguished from what soon became called the "organic listings"—namely, the results from the search engine.

Even at this early moment, Google honored the firm's commitment to make search results uninfluenced by advertising. At the outset the firm made a clear separation of ad from search results.

Google's approach differed from the prevailing view. Aside from differing with portals, Google also differed with experiments with "pay-to-list" strategies followed by others at the time.[25] Pay-to-list will be described more below, because it yielded lessons. Google did not win praise from analysts, since it attracted users but sacrificed revenue by not aggressively selling advertising, whereas other experiments, such as pay-to-list, focused explicitly on making more money.

Google's web page did have one other positive consequence: it advertised Google's capabilities to other portals, which occasionally rethought their contracts for search services. Google got its first big break when it found its first paying customer in June 2000, in a licensing deal with the web portal, Yahoo.[26] The deal also was not worth very much money to Yahoo, and at that stage, Yahoo primarily used search technologies as a

[25]GoTo's founders had taken out a patent on the pay-to-list method, receiving US patent 6,269,361, claiming to cover a broad class of paid-for-click advertising in a search engine. The claims were novel and legally untested but potentially could lead to a suit of any search engine that used anything similar. Google's approach to advertising at the time would have given them considerable merit to claim they were not infringing on these patents.

[26]This was not Google's first deal. Among Google's first deals was a deal to help search for Netscape's users. It had generated so much traffic, Google had to temporarily disable its site. See Schmidt, Rosenberg, and Eagle (2014), 84.

backup for queries that went beyond its own directories.[27] Nevertheless, the deal had great symbolic importance. Yahoo chose Google over Inktomi, the perceived leader in search at the time, which had provided search services for Yahoo during the prior two years.[28]

The arrangement was straightforward and similar to what Yahoo had done with Inktomi. Google provided the search service for Yahoo in exchange for a license fee. Yahoo sent queries to Google, while Google provided the answers.

This arrangement accomplished three things at once. First, it saved Yahoo from investing in search services, an activity Yahoo's management considered to be peripheral to its main services as a portal. Second, the deal gave Google revenue and legitimacy, which mattered to a young company founded by a couple of precocious graduate students. Third, it directed a large number of actual search queries to Google, which they could use to refine their algorithm.

The symbolic importance turned out to matter a great deal more than Google could have imagined. It also brought attention to Google, which soon signed similar deals with other firms, reaching 130 over the next two years.

Many years later, in multiple acts of Monday morning quarterbacking, commentators questioned why Yahoo and other portals chose Google over other alternative search engines available at the time. No single answer could be correct by itself. For one, there was no obvious early sign that these contracts would begin to lead to Google's dominance. The space appeared capable of supporting many firms racing to become technically better than the other.[29] Also, the contracts were short term and could be terminated if another leader emerged. Second, the deal contained considerable business sense in light of the prevailing view of the time. PageRank worked well at finding relevant answers, and it was fast, the result

---

[27] Google licensed the technology and also sold an undisclosed part of the company to Yahoo. See Hu (2000). Also see Angel (2002), 245. Yahoo continued to use Google until February 2004.

[28] New reports at the time stressed the symbolic importance of the change. Hu (2000).

[29] There had been considerable turnover in leadership over the prior half decade, involving the firms Excite, WebCrawler, Lycos, Infoseek, AltaVista, Ask Jeeves, and Inktomi, among others. See, e.g., Danny Sullivan's wistful recollections of search engines that had come and gone at Sullivan (2003). Also see the brief account of Mark Knowles at http://www.thehistory ofseo.com/The-Industry/Short_History_of_Early_Search_Engines.aspx.

of many improvements over the prior two years.[30] Many users lauded it in online discussion groups, and its growing use drew attention to its ability to satisfy users with unusual questions. Yahoo easily could justify its actions as in the interest of users with niche concerns.

In retrospect, one additional aspect deserves notice—the way Google masked its long-term aspirations by adopting what later became characterized as a "stealth strategy." At the outset it did not appear as if Google could substitute for any portal, because it specialized in one activity, while the portals had many additional lines of business, such as e-mail, hosting of groups, and basic news. Indeed, when asked about their aspirations, the firm's officer denied having any plans to expand the range of offered services.[31] Overall, therefore, Google appeared to pose no immediate competitive threat as a substitute, so existing players did not hesitate to cooperate with it.

Evolving into a Platform

Google's evolution into a platform for online advertising did not happen all at once. Like many young firms, Google's founders planned to improve in specific ways, but they also reacted to new opportunities and threats. Because their approach began with the unique perspective of finding relevant answers for users without regard to the commercial needs of advertisers, they sought to match, but not imitate precisely, the features of others. They adapted new ideas in ways consistent with their unique strategy and strategic principles.

Like any other firm, Google studied other firms that provided complementary and substitute services, and sought to learn from their mistakes and triumphs. Google learned from another start-up called GoTo.com, which offered pay-to-list to advertisers. GoTo.com—later called Overture, and much later bought by Yahoo—pioneered the idea of a word auction linked to a search engine.

---

[30] Very early Google began investing in large-scale arrangements of server hardware to support quick processing.

[31] Google initially denied in public that it had any ambitions to substitute for Yahoo's portal service. For example, in an April 2001, article, the following quote appeared. "The fact is that we have 130 customers that we power search for," said Omid Kordestani, Google's vice president of business development and sales. "They don't feel we're competing with them, and we're comfortable with that model. I use my favorite portals for sending e-mails, instant messaging, tracking stock portfolios—all these things Google isn't doing." Festa (2001).

At first GoTo/Overture implemented what became known as "playing for placement." It held a first-price auction for the right to list ads at the top of its searches, mixing those with the organic listings without informing users which were listings and which were ads. Overture's auction attracted attention from analysts and investors because it was novel.

Overture's management argued that vendors bid to provide relevant answers, so mixing bidding and organic listings helped users find what they wanted. That was a good sound bite when the experiment started. Closer scrutiny eventually revealed that the practical outcomes varied from this ideal. First, bidders manipulated the pricing of the first-price auction by gaming the system, that is, they bid a lot to show ads that users did not perceive as relevant. Second, advertisers could not measure the success of their ads. Those two factors led a search engine to an unsustainable strategy, collecting revenue in the short run while not measuring whether advertisers got any return on their ad.

The third related problem would lead to the downfall of pay-for-placement. Sites with deceptive motives annoyed many users, especially when the returned answers did not match their needs. This was especially apparent in the extreme case, when firms selling salacious or dubious services took advantage of users.[32] For example, simple requests or many other innocent phrases, could lead to unwanted material, or a poor user experience. After becoming annoyed many users did not return to the pay-for-placement services.

GoTo's management learned about auctioning from this experience and altered their business model. One day they announced that they would cease auctioning the listing. Instead, they auctioned off the ad next to a search result.

In the fall of 2001, two employees at Google learned from watching Overture's behavior, and sought to improve it.[33] Google implemented aspects of Overture's approach on its website, remaining consistent with Google's philosophy of giving users what they wanted. Google never changed its organic listings to reflect the needs of advertisers.

---

[32] The canonical example is the plumber who bids highest, gets the phone call, then bills a high amount merely for the visit before providing any service.

[33] Varian (2006) identifies the two employees as Salar Mamangar and Eric Veach.

Google identified the ads by listing them above and to the right, and identifying them as paid.[34] That was in keeping with its philosophy to be transparent and focus on the needs of users.

Google's next decision ran against the prevailing view, and it had tremendous implications. Google's auction designers eventually decided to use a second-price auction, not a first-price auction, for the right to have the first position, second position, and third position in the ads. A first-price auction requires bidders to pay what they bid, while a second-price auction requires the winner of the bid to pay the price bid by the next-highest bidder. While the first-priced auction was more intuitive and more familiar to potential ad buyers, Google's experience taught them that the second-price auction worked better. It helped stabilize the bidding behavior that determined prices.

How did the second-price auction stabilize bidding behavior? It addressed an issue that arises from running the same auction with the same bidders day after day. If the top bidder wins day after day, then it has an incentive to discover if it can still win the auction with a lower price that saves money. Google's auction designers observed that the highest bidder would win, and change its bid on a later occasion, shading its price, as if the bidder was trying to discover if they could have saved money by bidding less. Because the bidder would be returning for many sessions, they had strong incentives to save money on all their future bids. This type of behavior became known as "price exploration."

Price exploration made the whole auction less than the sum of its parts—namely, less than what the auction could have done for everyone. A sophisticated bidder could write a program to do the price search in an automated way. That worked well for one bidder, who would save money by searching for better prices. However, that exploration only worked if all the other bidders did not change their bidding behavior. If several bidders deployed an automated program to do the price search, then the auction might not settle on one set of prices. In other words, such exploratory bidding made prices less predictable day after day, and it frustrated bid-

---

[34] Did this implementation violate GoTo's patents? GoTo eventually would claim it did, though the merits of that claim are not obvious in retrospect. To avoid an extended lawsuit Google eventually settled out of court with Yahoo, which had acquired GoTo/Overture, selling a stake in Google to Yahoo. Yahoo sold its stake in Google after Google's IPO. Kuchinskas (2004).

ders, who wanted to manage ad campaigns with reasonable forecasts about the likely process and outcome.

In other words, the auction could run if one bidder explored the prices. It would become unstable if more than one did so.

How to stop such exploratory behavior? Google's team rediscovered a well-known principle in studies of auctions: bidders continually decreased the bid price until the bid just exceeded the price of the second-highest bid. The auctioneer could prevent exploration of pricing by announcing a second-price auction at the outset.[35]

Use of the second-price auction was an important invention, albeit easy to misunderstand and difficult to explain to bidders. Although confusing, it was technically easy to implement, and, importantly, like any digitized process, it could be automated and every auction could be tailored to the unique set of bidders for any keyword.

A third innovation had a technical dimension to it, but it was also largely aimed at improving the service: Google paid advertisers for user clicks, not impressions. That gave advertisers the ability to measure what consequence their ads generated, that is, whether a user clicked on the ad. It also promised advertisers they did not have to pay if the ad failed to attract any user clicks. Remarkably, this ideal had been discussed in online circles long before Google implemented it, but many firms had not bothered to implement it, even some of the very large firms. Google's implementation became the largest ever.[36]

It also created a problem, because the price of a pay-to-impression ad and pay-per-click ad should deliver equivalent value to users, even though seemingly different things are being valued.[37] As Google's chief economist, Hal Varian, later wrote, Google "wants to sell impressions, but the advertiser wants to buy clicks."[38] One hundred people might view an ad, but only five of them may click on it. That means if a buyer was willing to pay $10 for one hundred impressions, then it should be willing to pay $10 for five clicks.

---

[35] Simon Wilkie, private communication, September 2012. Also see the longer explanation in Hansen (2009) and Varian (2006).
[36] See Hansen (2009).
[37] Varian (2006; 2010).
[38] Varian (2010), 4.

The solution also was seemingly straightforward. Google needed an "exchange rate" between the two types of ads.[39] The most obvious "exchange rate" is the expected click-through rate for an ad. This exchange rate became the origins of a "quality ranking" inside Google's auctions.

At first Google used the history of clicking behavior of users who entered specific words (on which the advertiser bid) to generate the quality ranking. If users clicked on an ad then Google's system ranked its quality as higher. In practice, designing the quality ranking required considerable effort. Google experimented with better models of click-through rates over time.

A quality rating based on click-through rates broadly punished advertisers who showed ads that users did not click on. The mechanism and its importance can be illustrated by the experience of the ads coming from the sites with dubious motives. In an unweighted auction a user could get ads that did not meet their needs, annoying users. In Google's quality-weighted auction, in contrast, the quality ranking was low, and the dubious ads were disfavored. They could not bid their way to the top. Hence, a user avoided these annoyances, and most of these ads never appeared at all.[40]

As Google learned, paying for a click-through, by itself, does not generate appropriate incentives to economize on impressions. Excessive impressions impose costs on users. Advertisers had incentives to get free impressions by showing ads on unrelated queries—for example, showing a soda ad on a search for a restaurant.[41] That potentially allowed a soda company to gain a large number of impressions while paying for a few clicks.

Eventually Google formulated the ranking by mixing in other assessments of the landing page and other aspects of the site.[42] In this way Google's ranking lowered the price of ads for firms that advertised services

---

[39] Varian (2010), 4.

[40] Extremely low quality matches could be excluded while extremely good matches could be included. Through such a mechanism the pornography sites could be excluded from appearing on ads no matter how high they bid.

[41] This incentive is stressed by Schmidt, Rosenberg, and Eagle (2014), 70.

[42] Simon Wilkie, private communication, September 2012. See also the explanation from Hal Varian, chief economist at Google, available at http://www.youtube.com/watch?v=1v Wp2-QMOz0.

that were high-quality matches for keywords and raised the price of ads for poor matches.[43]

Google also took one more key step. It banned ads from pornographers, tobacco, and spirits. This was equivalent to giving these ads a quality of zero. Once again, it prevented these advertisers from buying a place in the ads, and reduced user annoyance.

Seen in broad perspective, quality ratings acquired a function with broad implications for ad auctions. They altered ads from being a negative feature of a search experience. Ads potentially became a positive feature, when the ad matched the needs of the user. That improved match bene-fited both user and advertiser and created value where there previously had not been as much.

Importantly, that positive experience was not followed by a negative one. By placing the ads off to the right many users simply ignored them, and that made the ads neither positive nor negative. Similarly, when Goo-gle started placing the ads at the top in boxes, users did not get annoyed if the ads were clearly marked.

Google's pervasiveness in 2002 and later enhanced the importance of quality ranking. As Google's approach to quality gained popularity with users and advertisers, a feedback loop developed, putting Google at the center of a virtuous cycle. Websites faced incentives to get higher quality rankings with Google, especially if they intended to bid in the ads. Conse-quently, websites began to tailor their designs to raise their quality score. That was an addition to the incentive they already faced to tailor their site to raise their ranking in Google's organic listings. Enhancement in one led to enhancement in the other.

Years later a myth developed about Google's success, viewing it solely as a technical achievement. There is a grain of truth in this myth. No other firm matched the quality ranking in the short run, because Google actu-ally had to invent some enormously difficult computer science to imple-ment it. The computer science of an automated quality-ranking algorithm

---

[43] The quality ranking stayed the same whether the ad appeared in the first, second, third, or fourth position, and, therefore, worked rather mechanically. Every bid came with a qual-ity, such as 1.1, 1.2, etc. Higher numbers represented higher quality. Hence, if two firms bid three dollars, the firm with a ranking of 1.1 would be treated as if it bid $3.30, while the firm with a bid of 1.2 would be treated as if it bid $3.60. The quality ranking rewarded better matches. Note that it could also punish firms for very poor matches. An extremely low qual-ity, such as 0.1 would be treated as $0.30.

for the *entire* web is extremely technically challenging and impossible for many organizations.[44]

Yet that is too narrow an understanding of how Google behaved. It ignores the broader context, and the nurturing features of the setting. Google's experience reflected yet another tale of a successful inventive specialist, and in this case, the specialist made the jump from an academic setting to a commercial one while continuing in its specialist activities. The founders had focused on addressing one problem and focused on doing it well. Like many other inventive specialists in the Internet, they took for granted the other functions of the network and the commercial web.

The prevailing view also served a nurturing role. Although Google invested against the tide of the prevailing view, it appeared to offer a complement to portals with minor value. It appeared to pose no threat as a substitute for the leading portals. Thus these leading firms initially were cooperative in sending traffic to Google.

Google accomplished something extraordinary in the long run. It became the rare case of a specialist that others in the ecosystem had to accommodate. Because its search algorithm could determine a high fraction of the traffic received at a website, many other participants in the commercial web began to modify their website in ways that favored the organic listings. Because Google's quality ranking generated a reaction from other participants on the web, other websites had to begin to pay attention to their quality. Their prosperity depended on how well their websites interacted with Google's ad services.

Extending the Auction

Google's leadership over advertising was further cemented in 2003 when Google began to offer one more service—namely, placing ads in designated places inside blogs, usually in little rectangle windows. This service,

---

[44]GoTo did not have anything equivalent to Page-Rank, so it lacked the ability to initially rank web pages for relevance as a basis for the quality ranking, and Google would not license Page-Rank to them. Goto only could employ a user's click-through experience, but that required sufficient data, which they lacked. After GoTo was sold to Yahoo, determining a quality ranking also became a priority at Yahoo. Simon Wilkie, private communication, September 2012.

known as AdSense, used an auction, but a different version of the mechanism.[45] Google split the money from the ads with the site showing the ad.

Once again, the computer science involved a number of technical challenges. Using automated linguistics as ways of identifying the content of sites,[46] AdSense involved entrepreneurial imagination that built an organization behind its service.

Google did not invent the computer science behind AdSense, nor did it imitate someone else's. Rather, Google bought Applied Semantics, a leading company in the area. After the purchase Google adapted to the processes at Applied Semantics, and renamed the service Google AdSense.[47]

The purchase was important from a competitive standpoint. Yahoo had worked closely with Applied Semantics, and Yahoo had no alternative partnership available after Google's purchase. Thus Google's competitive improvement came directly at the expense of its competitors. Moreover, Yahoo had no comparable auction to marry to such service, even if it invented one from scratch.

Google did not displace others overnight, and for a number of reasons. The early adopters were firms with a high fraction of their business online, such as eBay and Amazon. The auction met with considerable resistance among other firms, such as auto companies and packaged good providers, who would use web advertising to shape offline behavior. The process did not resemble ad purchases at newspapers or magazines, and it confused the marketing departments, who were accustomed to buying space at discount.

Google's key invention, the second-price quality-weighted auction, also met with resistance because it confused all but the most sophisticated ad buyer. It had to be experienced to be understood.

Scaling was also an issue for Google. The aforementioned features of the auction ended up determining many of features of Google as an organization as it tried to grow. Google could automate the processes behind the auction, such as the submission of bids and determination of ad placement. That automation enabled the auction to scale, that is, to grow

---

[45] AdSense uses a Vickery-Clark-Groves mechanism, which is a sealed-bid auction that charges a bidder the "harm" it causes others in the auction.

[46] Kawamoto and Olsen (2003).

[47] Kawamoto and Olsen (2003).

to the demand for its use without imposing additional costs on users or advertisers.

Other parts of the business did not scale, however; that is, they did not grow without additional cost. Google had to hire personnel to help ad buyers learn how to select appropriate keywords, bid appropriately, and mount a campaign. Google had to develop a sales department to explain the process and educate the ad buyer. It had to invest in tools to help buyers understand the value of its bids and manage large campaigns, and that required talented programmers. Google also had to invest in simulations of the auctions, so buyers could anticipate how to arrange large and complex campaigns that extended over thousands of keywords. Accordingly, as Google enjoyed increasing success in the market, Google, the organization behind the engine, began to hire thousands of new employees.

Advertiser resistance to the auction eventually declined for one principle reason: users returned to the keyword search. It offered an excellent way to reach them during their online session, and at the moment they asked a question. That permitted advertisers to target very specific users with very specific needs. It was an efficient process for matching a potential buyer with a potential supplier.

Google's rise solidified the irreversible movement away from the web's innocent roots and toward a pervasive commercialization of surfing. As every page became a potential poster for a relevant ad, every action took on an additional potential meaning as information about a user's preferences, or as a statistical indicator about how other like-minded surfers would behave next.

Summarizing, the economic model of ads and search had eluded others because it had been easy to misunderstand. The two sources—ads and organic listings—were substitutes in any given search, and that would have seemed to give incentives to the search engine to invest in hosting as many ads as possible.

Search services depend on repeated use, however. In many cases the user gets its answer from the organic listing and not the ad. A relevant organic listing is essential for attracting users to return to the site in the future. Something similar applies to ads. The likelihood that a user gets the answer from the ad rises with the quality and relevance of the ads.

Incentives for Improving

In a few short years, Google had transformed itself from its origins as an obscure firm with a graduate school project. The quality-weighted second-priced keyword position auction for ads had become a competitive advantage for Google, enabling it to create value that Yahoo or any other portal could not immediately match. Users came to Google with a question and got their answers from one of two sources, either the organic search results, or the ads. In the latter case Google got paid.

With no close substitute, a virtuous cycle emerged. Websites invested in features that raised their standing in organic listings. Ad buyers invested in their websites, which improved in quality. Users continued to use the search engine because it yielded relevant answers. Ad buyers only paid when users clicked on the ads, and gained experience about the value of ads.

That virtuous cycle generated strong incentives at Google to continue to simultaneously improve search and ad quality as complements to each other for purposes of attracting users to return.[48] Defensive motives—preventing users from ever going to another search engine—also provided incentives for continual improvements. Whatever the motivation, the result was the same: Google's management adopted a strategic principle consistent with continual improvement.[49]

With strong internal funding, Google began investing in a wide set of improvements. Some of these improvements benefited many users. For example, improvement included innovation in spell checking. Informed by many user misspellings, the search engine asked, "Did you mean . . . ?" Spell checking by itself nearly doubled traffic.[50]

Google went on to make innovations in news aggregation (that is, informed by user clicks on articles), filtering (that is, eliminating pornography with "safe search"), faster response (that is, due to large investments in server farms), and many more features. Eventually Google made

[48]This is one way to read the discussion in Schmidt, Rosenberg, and Eagle (2014), 80, which emphasizes attracting users in order to spur large volumes of users, and not let short-term revenue objectives overtake the long-term objective of attracting returning users.

[49]Schmidt, Rosenberg, and Eagle (2014) stress the organizational features at Google that supported continual improvement.

[50]See http://www.youtube.com/watch?v=soYKFWqVVzg, and http://alan.blog-city.com/an_evening_with_googles_marissa_mayer.htm.

investments in services that mimicked the broad-based offerings of portals, such as electronic mail and community support. All of these improvements were responses to the incentive to bring users back to search, and maintain the virtuous cycle.

Not all these incentives were unambiguous, however. The incentive to attract users placed Google in an unusual place when it came to online pornography. On the one hand it sought to reduce the influence of the pornographers in listings that annoyed its users. In addition, Google invested in tools for filtering pornography, meeting the needs of users who desired to avoid salacious material. Yet Google also accommodated the search terms, and did not filter pornography for a user who wanted it. Google helped users find websites that offered users what they wanted. In effect, the very tool that made it easier to filter away undesired photographs also enabled users to find any photograph, salacious ones included.[51]

The ambiguity of incentives fueled additional potential controversy. For example, Google faced incentives to take an expansive approach to fair use of online text. Fair use is a legal doctrine that permits a writer to quote copyrighted material verbatim for purposes of criticism, news reporting, teaching, and research, without the need for permission from or payment to the copyright holder. Not asking for permission was crucial for the search engine, as it quoted the most recent postings and content without transacting for it each time. Google faced no clear legal definition for how much of a website's article a search engine should quote. Google did not want to quote so much text that it filled up the page, since a well-designed listing of organic results would include more than one option. However, could it quote more than one or two sentences of text? What principles defined the limits? This question would remain open and haunt Google's actions as it expanded into more countries, where local firms could raise the issues within their legal system.

For related reasons, Google acquired a tense relationship with news and content sites. Google could move considerable traffic to those sites by making their content visible in its search engine. Yet a simple statement within the organic listing—a sports score of a recent event, a phone number for a business, or an address for a store, for example—could satisfy a

---

[51] See, in particular, Schmidt, Rosenberg, and Eagle (2014), 75–77, which emphasizes that the invention of safe search also generated additional tools for users.

user and obviate the need to chick through to the original site. This tension was inescapable. Google's prowess placed content sites in a dependent relationship with the pervasive search engine. Google was both the source of friendly referrals and a potential substitute. In the latter case Google was using the sites' own content.

The situation also gave Google incentives to turn a blind eye toward violations of copyright by users and hosting sites. For example, Google had incentives to satisfy the query of a user who turned its search toward illegally pirated software or music. Accordingly, it had incentives to evade responsibility for user action and place legal responsibility on the sites that hosted the pirated software or those users that looked for it. Not surprisingly, Google would be dogged by this tension as it grew bigger and spread to more countries.

Google's rise led many copyright holders to rue the decline of portals. Portals had incentives to contract for all their content, and, thus, stay within the bounds of copyright law, as interpreted by copyright holders signing a deal. The user orientation of Google gave it incentives to organize all of the web's content, whatever the user wanted, even its illicit content. In short order, Google's rise would be one of several factors enabling piracy to play a more prominent role in the web. The legal issues would persist for many years, as participants interpreted the many provisions of the Digital Millennium Copyright Act, which defined the legal liabilities of Internet intermediaries.[52]

By the middle of the decade the service had spread widely. "Ads by Google" became a common statement all over the web. Many small and large sites began using Google's ad services, paying only for clicks. It was convenient, especially for small and medium-sized businesses, and it generated enough revenue to support an inexpensive website. AdSense also helped change the ecosystem of the web. The long tail of an ad-supported web began to depend on it. Many niche sites, blogs, and aggregators of content expanded accordingly.

---

[52] The DMCA was passed in October 1998, as part of a broad initiative to coordinate copyright law around the world. For a description and explanation of the many provisions, see Nuechterlein and Weiser (2005).

What Was Accomplished?

As noted earlier, as Google grew, a myth arose that viewed its success solely through its technical accomplishments, as if the firm was merely an extension of Page-Rank, a lab project from a couple of graduate students that grew beyond its earliest aspirations. That myth interprets Google's accomplishments as an outgrowth of its technical prowess and deemphasizes how much of the firm's services evolved in response to commercial circumstances and incentives. It is very misleading.

Google's success was more than merely the sum of several technical inventions. It involved a complementary number of innovative commercial processes, which reflected the unique perspectives of its founders, as well as the discoveries of many employees within the organization, as they responded to challenges with deploying an auction for advertising. Once that was deployed, the firm responded to the economic incentives to bring users to the search engine and continually improve the service for more advertisers, which fueled a virtuous cycle between users, advertisers, and many web pages.

In some respects, therefore, at the outset Google's experience resembled other innovations from the edges. Google demonstrated a fresh perspective for a combination of a business process and new technical approaches, and these differed from those at the core of the industry. The prevailing view made it harder for Google to raise funds and get started, but entry was not blocked. Like many an entrepreneur before them, Google's founders were given the opportunity to implement their alternatives prototype, and scale it with customers.

There also was something different about Google's experience, and that difference illustrates how the commercial Internet had evolved by the late 1990s. Brin and Page were never truly outsiders. Google's founders had the luxury of a challenging but nurturing setting, with modest but initial financial backing from the National Science Foundation, and then backing from a sympathetic financial angel. Their university had experience with moving inventions to industry and had put in place policies to accommodate such movement, easing the transition for Brin and Page. Within a couple of years the founders also made deals with other industry players as they tried to grow their business and learn about resolving new challenges. The cooperation arose, in part, because existing players adopted a prevailing view that interpreted Google's services as a complement to theirs. Summarizing, Brin and Page had status as both insider and outsider, reflecting both the novelty of their invention and the familiar motif of their aspiration for commercialization, working with existing players while also pursuing a unique perspective.

That dual status also reflected the timing of Google's rise. It came at the end of the 1990s, at a crucial moment in the history of the prevailing view for businesses built on the commercial web, when a widely imitated entrepreneurial approach—the dot-com firm—began to show that it would not come close to realizing the most optimistic promises. Google walked into the scene at the same time the support for these dot-com firms declined. Google accomplished part of what prior participants had promised but had not delivered, achieving the first large-scale tailoring of advertising to the unique features of the web surfer.

Long after the dot-com bust, Google continued to experience success delivering and improving its service. As it encountered more challenges, and resolved them, it improved the Internet experience for the vast majority of users and advertisers, as well as their content-supplying web partners. This set Google on an extraordinary long run path, one in which Google's innovations would touch every participant in the commercial web.

14

The High Cost of a Cheap Lesson
in Wireless Access

[Economic experiments] . . . include experimentation with
new forms of economic organization as well as the better-
known historical experiments that have been responsible
for new products and new manufacturing technologies.
—*Nathan Rosenberg, 1992*[1]

In the late 1990s many industry developers were unsure whether any
design for wireless Internet access would ever become embodied in a
mass-market product. As it turned out, similar to other developments in
the commercial Internet, the crucial decisions behind wireless local area
networking—today called Wi-Fi—did not come to fruition by a simple or
straightforward path. Its birth arose from a series of experiments, and
these experiments involved decisions by several key industry executives,
principally Steve Jobs and Michael Dell. Those decisions built upon several other experiments by a committee of engineers, and a set of policy
makers at the Federal Communications Commission, which this chapter
explains. Although it may not be apparent at first glance, the economic
experiments that led to Wi-Fi contained many features found in other experiments that led to the commercial Internet.

The institutional details are generally underappreciated by all but insiders. The committee of engineers was sponsored by the IEEE (Institute
of Electrical and Electronics Engineers), which helped form many com-

[1] Rosenberg (1992), 181.

FIGURE 14.1 Michael Marcus and Vic Hayes, helped develop rules and standards for Wi-Fi (Photo by Gail Marcus, 2008)

mittees that endorsed standards for interoperable products, and these designs helped coordinate designs from multiple suppliers. The standard for what later became Wi-Fi came from Subcommittee 802.11, the eleventh subcommittee to explore issues within the domain of Committee 802. Committee 802 was formed in 1980 and explored standards for local area networking, while subcommittee 11 was formed in 1990 and explored standards for wireless data communications. The subcommittee designed a standard for how to send data between both antennae and receivers, and that became crucial for the birth of mass-market wireless Internet access over short distances, such as a hundred feet. The crucial design emerged in 1999, when the committee published Standard 802.11b, which altered some features not found in Standard 802.11a (changing the frequency of electromagnetic spectrum it used, among other things).[2] The draft of 802.11b eventually caught on.[3]

How did Steve Jobs become involved? Jobs had just returned as Apple's CEO in 1997, and he initiated a meeting with executives at Lucent,

[2]The subcommittee first proposed a standard in 1997 that received many beta users, but also failed to resolve many interoperability issues (among many issues). Learning from this experience, and viewing its efforts as racing against those of a private consortium—called HomeRF—the subcommittee rewrote the standard over the next two years. What came to be known as standard 802.11a was ratified in early 2000, just after 802.11b was ratified.

[3]Standard 802.11a was licensed for usage in Europe and Asia as well as North America, while for some time 802.11a was only licensed in North America. Liu (2001), or Kharif (2003).

who had supplied many key engineers to Subcommittee 802.11, including its leader, Vic Hayes. Lucent's wireless LAN management welcomed the phone call and initially viewed it as payback for all of its investment of time and personnel in the subcommittee.

Lucent got more than they bargained for. Lucent's management anticipated bargaining hard to become the dominant equipment supplier of the hardware to make wireless LANs operate within laptop personal computers. Apple was still a fraction of Lucent's size, so Lucent expected a certain amount of deference from Apple, though, that is not how it played out. Cees Links, from Lucent, attended the meeting and in a memoir about the growth of Wi-Fi (written much later), and he describes how it began awkwardly.[4] One side showed up in suits and ties, while the West Coast engineers showed up in more relaxed wear. Jobs did not show up at first, and nobody would start without him. After some awkward small talk, Jobs finally walked in late. From thereon he did the majority of the talking. Links began a planned slide presentation, and described it this way:

> Then Steve asked, "Are there any questions?" I tried to show a few slides: key wins, market positioning, product offering, value creation, etc. Presenting slides with Steve Jobs is actually quite easy: you put up the slide, and he will do the talking, not necessarily related to the slide: then he asks for the next slides.

Links goes on to describe a short dialogue between Jobs and the senior management team from Lucent. This is where the management made their pitch and where they had planned to bargain hard. In response Jobs described what he wanted. Links's description of the end of the meeting is the most revealing:

> Turning the conversation back to wireless LANs, [Jobs declares,] "We need the radio card for $50 and I want to sell at $99." Then Steve apologized; he had to leave. Standing up, he said "Hi!" and went. The room fell silent.

The silence was understandable. Up until that point none of the wireless local area networking producers had ever achieved that price point, or anything near it. This price level was regarded as quite an ambitious

---

[4]Lemstra, Hayes, and Groenewegen (2010), 129–31.

target by Lucent, or any other equipment supplier.[5] Steve Jobs, on the other hand, acted as if he was delivering the simple hard truths about making mass-market products, and, as he did often with his unique managerial style, expressed impatience with anyone who did not see the vision he regarded as obvious.

Later events favored Jobs's point of view. NCR/Lucent eventually achieved that price point, albeit only after negotiations continued with Apple throughout production, as Apple changed the product requirements.[6]

The Apple Airport—the first mass-market Wi-Fi product—debuted in July 1999 at a MacWorld convention in New York. As far as the insiders in subcommittee 802.11 were concerned, there was nothing technically new about it; it merely embedded the 802.11b design in a functioning product that Apple sold. However, it did something no prior wireless product had done: it was aimed at the mass market. It came in a branded product from Apple, Apple distributed the entire system, and the price and functionality—such as the data throughput speed—were good enough for a typical PC user.

That is not the whole story, and that is where Michael Dell entered the events. Lucent's cards for Apple laptops and the Apple Airport system did not serve those who had PCs from suppliers other than Apple. That still left a large part of the PC industry uncovered. Most PCs used a Windows operating system from Microsoft. As it happened, that market became first addressed at Dell Computer.[7]

Michael Dell, founder and CEO of Dell Computer, by then one of the largest PC providers in the world, heard about the announcement of the Apple Airport and called Lucent. According to the account from Cees Links, Dell was "furious" with them because Dell was not first to experiment with

---

[5] A $100 retail price would have been anything from one-fifth to one-tenth the price of equipment in the first half of the decade. A cost of $50 would require economies of scale in production and extensive use of standard components, as the production cost of cards was higher than $100 at the time of the meeting between Apple and Lucent. As described in Lemstra, Hayes, and Groenewegen (2010), 131, it required Lucent to put into the initial price some of the learning curve benefits it anticipated, which was a departure from existing practice.

[6] See Lemstra, Hayes, and Groenewegen (2010), 130, which describes changes in product requirements linked to "all-or-nothing type of negotiations."

[7] For an account see Lemstra, Hayes, and Groenewegen (2010), 131–32.

a product release.[8] Lucent executives had to remind Michael Dell that he had an opportunity to be in on discussions as early as 1992. However, Dell had decided in 1993 to stop the discussions because he concluded (incorrectly, as it turned out) that there was no market for the technology.[9]

The two parties subsequently came to a deal. Making a version for Dell became a priority thereafter, and making it compatible with Windows XP was the main challenge for the team at Lucent. Eventually Lucent would succeed at that as well. To do that Lucent and Microsoft cooperated in changing the design of Windows XP, and a new version was released in 2001. It supported 802.11b in all Windows-based systems. Just as with Apple, Lucent made a hardware card for an external slot in a PC.

Those first two projects established the mass market for laptop use, pioneering the technical issues affiliated with the challenges of the Apple and Windows operating systems. Both were investments in product designs embedding 802.11b, aimed at fostering sales as part of either Apple's or Dell's portfolio of products. In both examples, one pioneering firm, Lucent, would gain considerable sales from its position, and (in retrospect) would retain the position as a leading provider of equipment for several years.

The importance of those two experiments for the market's development is more readily apparent in retrospect than it was at the time. After those two projects, the consumer-oriented mass market for wireless Internet access took off, with a large number of other firms also entering into production. Those two projects served as the bridge between years of experimentation with prototype designs and the design and distribution of products for mass markets, showing other equipment firms that real money could be made if oriented toward the demand the pioneering firms perceived.

Looking more deeply behind events, a complete explanation requires understanding both technology and market institutions. This chapter must go inside a committee that few nonengineers ever have heard of, IEEE Committee 802.11. This committee developed a new standard and made the design available without restriction. As this chapter describes, the subcommittee designed a standard around a set of flexible govern-

---

[8] Lemstra, Hayes, and Groenewegen (2010), 131. Links says Michael Dell "was furious about the fact that he had been beaten by Apple."

[9] Lemstra, Hayes, and Groenewegen (2010), 131.

ment rules for the electromagnetic spectrum, the electromagnetic wavelengths invisible to the eye. Those rules were themselves an experiment. Such flexible rules had never been deployed by any government, or by the Federal Communications Commission, and this chapter must explain the sense in which the rules were novel. The key insight seems too simple to be so profound: flexible rules would enable commercial firms to put many options in front of users, and users would choose which applications gave them the most value. User choice in this market determined something unprecedented: few of the original use cases for the spectrum remained popular. Instead, the vast majority of use migrated to an application they liked more—namely, wireless Internet access.

That last observation takes steps toward the deeper economic lesson of this episode. Flexible rules allowed spectrum to move from low-value to higher-value activities. That sentence may seem obtuse at this point in the chapter, but it represents a profound shift in government policy for the spectrum. Policy makers did not intend to foster innovation from the edges, at least not explicitly, but that is what they ended up doing nonetheless.

Adopting Rules for the Spectrum

The story of Wi-Fi begins in the early 1980s in the Federal Communications Commission, which is based in Washington, DC. As is typically the case in Washington, DC, a simple proposal does not get far until sensible voices of all ideological stripes see the wisdom in it, albeit each may see something different in it.

Like every other government, until the 1990s the United States government had a very restrictive system for allocating the spectrum. Governed by the 1934 Communication Act, the law gave the Federal Communications Commission (FCC) authority to license or bar companies from using the spectrum. Known as allocation through "command-and-control," the FCC allocated each unique wavelength to a particular firm for a specific purpose, such as radio, television, and mobile telephony. This system was first adopted in order to minimize one user interfering with another. At one time it was thought that interference was a primary concern in all uses of spectrum. Hence, a central government administration could allocate rights to use spectrum, as well as determine other technical details, such as power over frequencies, which prevented one user's activity from stepping on top of another.

To put it in very human terms, until the 1990s the owner and the purpose for the spectrum were determined far in advance by expert committees comprised of engineers, whose deliberations were approved of by the FCC. Spectrum was given to specific firms and for very specific purposes. These choices had the force of statute behind them and could not be undone except by the FCC. The choices committees made were rarely reversed, and only in exceptional circumstances.[10]

Circumscribing use eliminated many economic experiments before any ever got started. Why bother with an experiment if it would require moving spectrum from one use to another that command-and-control would not approve? For many years that begged a question: If market participants had had the ability to decide how to employ the spectrum for a range of economic experiments, would they come to a different conclusion about how to deploy it? If it were possible, would spectrum move from a use with low value to one with high value?

Once again, it is possible to put a very human face on that question. In the early 1980s, one employee at the FCC, Michael Marcus, asked this question about the spectrum for short-range uses.[11] The question was rather pointed in the context of short-range uses, because one short-range application was less likely to interfere with another. Distance (or low power) prevented equipment in one location from interfering with another only a few dozen feet away. Moreover, in some of the primary short-range applications—for example, garage door openers, baby monitors, and wireless handsets—households used the spectrum infrequently, perhaps only a few times a day. Why would the FCC have to worry about interference if a user could transmit a signal no more than one hundred feet? Perhaps neighbors could work out the issues themselves, or perhaps simple technical solutions could be found (such as automated selection among multiple channels). The FCC could just leave market participants to find those solutions. Why would the FCC have to designate the licensee,

---

[10]Perhaps the best-known reversal occurred during the design of the broadcasting standard for color television. The Korean War delayed the deployment of the first approved design, and the after the war it was reconsidered, leading to deployment of a technically superior design from another designer.

[11]Marcus (2009).

an owner and designer, when plenty of firms could supply such equipment? More to the point, why would the FCC want the administrative burden of licensing hundreds of firms who made use of the spectrum in thousands of places?

Initially Marcus received a warm reception from those who had sympathy for free-market ideology. They saw an opportunity to make use of markets. The recent election of the Reagan administration had installed many commissioners with such sympathies. A task force was appointed and began to consider how such a system would work.

The initiative made it from blackboard to implementation in May 1985. FCC chairman Mark Fowler managed to pass the first civil use of unlicensed spectrum. Wireless telephone handsets were the first uses.[12] After that initial success, adherents to the established system raised many questions, momentum stalled, and only minor changes were made for many years. After many years another set of commissioners determined the priorities in the agency. Eventually backlash inside the FCC bureaucracy became powerful again, especially among those who did not see any merit to departing from command-and-control mechanisms. Marcus then became a target of deliberate efforts aimed to make him leave the FCC; he received terrible employee reviews and was hounded out of his job.[13]

After the 1992 election the Clinton administration installed commissioners who had a taste for reform. Giving the spectrum to users appealed to those who wanted to experiment with new forms of government, such as diffusing discretion to users and small manufacturers. Reed Hundt, the new chair of the FCC, felt he had a mandate for action, and he took it in many different areas, including spectrum policy. He foresaw information and communication technologies as a bridge toward a revolution in new services and productivity growth.[14]

The FCC took up Marcus's proposal again, and this time pushed through changes to enable new applications. By late April 1996 the FCC took the legal step to allow the change. The FCC initiated a "Notice for Proposed Rule Making" to make available a small amount of unlicensed spectrum for what became known as Unlicensed National Information Infrastructure (U-NII) devices. It was understood from the FCC's order that

---

[12]Marcus (2009).
[13]Marcus (2009).
[14]Hundt (2000).

the commission anticipated "short range, high-speed wireless digital communications" and devices that supported "the creation of new wireless local area networks ('LANs') and . . . facilitate wireless access to the National Information Infrastructure ('NII')."[15] Beyond that, however, little else was specified about the design or application of the spectrum. After deliberating over that summer, the commission made the spectrum available. The order that emerged on January 9, 1997, stated, "we are adopting the minimum technical rules necessary to prevent interference to other services and to ensure that the spectrum is used efficiently."[16]

Taking a minimal approach was, in fact, the key administrative innovation, though that was not apparent to all observers at the time. Traditional defenders of command-and-control regarded the allocation, known as the Part 15 rules, as "garbage spectrum," a throwaway to uses with low value, and a symbolic salvo in an ideological battle. The standard use cases used for reference—as mentioned, garage door openers, wireless handsets, and baby monitors—were also thought to be low value in comparison to radio, television, and mobile telephony. Perhaps a business case could be made for use in a warehouse, but this was not regarded as particularly valuable.[17] More to the point, forecasts about mass market wireless access to Internet data services did not play a central role in the design of these rules, or tip sides in the ideological fights in favor or against aspects of these rules. These rules issued as the commercial Internet began, and connection between these commercial events was distant. Use of euphemisms like the "National Information Infrastructure," as quoted above, was symptomatic of that distance.

Something crucial was embedded in the Part 15 rules, however. Consistent with Mike Marcus's original proposals, the spectrum did not have tight restrictions on its purpose—that is, the FCC did not control how the spectrum was used, or the purpose to which it was put. Any application was acceptable as long as it did not interfere with other activities outside the band. Even different applications could use the same spectrum.

---

[15]See the review of FCC policies found on http://www.cybertelecom.org/broadband/wifi.htm, accessed May 2007. Subsequent clarifications and rules aligned the spectrum in the United States with similar policies elsewhere.

[16]See the review found on http://www.cybertelecom.org/broadband/wifi.htm, accessed May 2007.

[17]See the discussion in Marcus (2009).

Related, the spectrum did not get designated to a single owner, and the FCC did not choose the equipment makers. Equipment makers were free to design their products in response to what they learned about its value from experimenting with its use. The spectrum was released with a few minor usage cases in mind, but the rules were made flexible enough to accommodate additional invention of new uses.

Standard Committees and Their Designs

The FCC has the force of law behind its actions. In contrast, any standard emerging from discussions at an IEEE committee was not legally binding on industry participants, and, accordingly, it was called a "voluntary standard." The committees did their work in the hope that such a design could act as a focal point for an interoperable design. In the best case, firms would embed the design in their products, such as wireless routers and receivers, and these would become interoperable as result. Firms could differentiate along other dimensions, such as other aspects of product design, brand, or distribution.

Committee 802 was formed in the early 1980s, before the privatization of the Internet was ever proposed. By the late 1980s the committee was well known among computing and electronics engineers because it had helped design and diffuse the Ethernet standard for local area networks.[18] By the late 1980s the 802 committee had become a victim of its success, and it had grown larger, establishing subcommittees for many areas, ostensibly to extend the range of uses for Ethernet.

Subcommittee 802.11 was established in 1990. Like all subcommittees of this broad family of committees, it concerned itself with a specific topic, in this case, designs for interoperability standards to enable wireless data traffic over short ranges—ostensibly doing with wireless technology what a local area network did with wires. A close look at the engineering suggests, however, that this label was mere window dressing for otherwise complex deliberations. For example, while "wireless local area networking" accurately described the aspirations for users, for suppliers the technical issues in this area hardly had any connection to the technical issues in

---

[18]See Burg (2001) for analysis of the growth of a local area network market and activities in Committee 802.

existing local area networking. As it would turn out, due to the very different error-correction issues, the software for a wireless local area network would end up bearing only a slight resemblance to that for a wired local area network, and contained many important technical differences.[19]

At first the committee did not get very far, lacking any clear direction. But then a new chair was appointed, Vic Hayes. Hayes was a technologist with a visionary outlook, a cheerful demeanor, and, more importantly, the patience to see his vision to realization. Hayes first developed prototypes of wireless technologies for National Cash Register, or NCR. At the time it was a subdivision of AT&T, which would later become Lucent (and later it was a division of Agere Systems). In that capacity Hayes first developed prototypes for wireless terminals for stockbrokers. Other applications for the technology were forecast, such as easy rearrangement of retail space.[20] From this experience he had a steady and flexible vision of the value of a standard that many component vendors could use to make interoperable equipment.

Other potential applications for this standard came up in the earliest meetings. One of the earliest prototypes had been a wireless local area network for a university campus.[21] Another was short-range wireless Ethernet in warehouses with complex logistical operations. Several firms had built expensive prototypes of these devices but had not found many buyers, or otherwise experienced very limited commercial response. Indeed, throughout the first half of the 1990s, as the 802.11 committee met and continued to do its work, pioneering firms continued their experiments with different uses and generated little interest among potential buyers, who regarded these prototypes as expensive in comparison to their usefulness.[22]

As with most such committees, Hayes tried to involve members who brought appropriate technical expertise and who represented the views of most of the major suppliers of equipment in which this standard would be embedded. At first, therefore, the group was comprised of enthusiastic designers focused on the needs of big users with potential warehousing applications (for example, FedEx, United Parcel Service, Wal-Mart, Sears, and Boeing), where the application's value did not seem specious. Al-

---

[19]See chapters 2, 3, and 4 of Lemstra, Hayes, and Groenewegen (2010).
[20]See Kharif (2003).
[21]See the description of Hills (2005), who began developing the equivalent of a Wi-Fi network for the Carnegie Mellon campus in Pittsburgh, starting in 1993.
[22]Also see chapters 2, 3, and 4 of Lemstra, Hayes, and Groenewegen (2010).

though it is obvious in retrospect, notably absent from the earliest meetings were representatives of many of the suppliers of valuable equipment a decade later, such as firms from electronics and computing.

Those firms would not be absent for too long. Several related efforts, such as HomeRF and Bluetooth, were founded in 1998. The former was organized by firms such as Motorola and Siemens, and at its peak involved over a hundred companies before it disbanded.[23] The latter was established by Ericsson, Sony-Ericsson, IBM, Intel, Toshiba, and Nokia, and currently still exists; today it involves thousands of firms. It focused on very short-range uses—under a few feet, and, as such, tended to have a set of applications distinct from Wi-Fi. Subsequent events would change the predominant use case, as economic experiments showed participants that high market value lay in a different configuration of technology, operations, and pricing than had originally been envisioned.[24]

Embedding the Design in Products

Wi-Fi did not emerge from a set of prespecified designs and classified stages. Economic experiments played a role in shaping that path, as pioneering firms took actions in response to the actions of the standard committee. As defined at the start of the chapter, economic experiments involved more than just new designs. They also involved new forms of economic organization and new products and new manufacturing technologies.

As it turned out, these experiments with Wi-Fi by Apple and Dell, described in the introduction, generated a response from many buyers, who also began to experiment. Users began deploying this equipment in a variety of settings, campuses, buildings, public parks, and coffee shops. Unsurprisingly, other vendors tried to meet this demand as well. Around the same time as the publication of 802.11b, firms that had helped pioneer the standard—including 3Com, Aironet (now a division of Cisco), Harris Semiconductor (now Intersil), Lucent (now Agere), Nokia, and Symbol Technologies—formed the Wireless Ethernet Compatibility Alliance (WECA). WECA

---

[23] HomeRF did not generate the enthusiastic sales that those who designed it predicted—even though the designers considered it technically superior to the alternatives. For speculation about why HomeRF failed, see, e.g., http://www.cazitech.com/HomeRF_Archives.htm, accessed in November 2010.

[24] See Rosenberg (1996).

branded the new technology "Wi-Fi," which was a marketing ploy for the mass market, since WECA's members believed that "802.11b" was a much less appealing label.[25] They aimed to nurture what enthusiasts were doing and broaden it into sales to a broader base of users.

WECA also arranged to perform testing for conformance to the standard, such as certifying interoperability of antennae and receivers made by different firms. This is valuable when the set of vendors becomes large and heterogeneous, as it helps maintain maximum service for users with little effort on their part. In brief, while the IEEE committee designed the standard, a different body (of similar firms) performed conformance testing.

Events then took on a momentum of their own. Technical successes became widely publicized. Numerous businesses became users of Wi-Fi and began directed experiments supporting what became known as *hot spots*, which was an innovative business idea. A hot spot is a data transmission mediated by a third party for local use in a public space or on a retail premise. A hot spot in a public space could be free, it could be installed by a homeowner, or it could be maintained by a building association for all building residences. It could be supported by the café or by a restaurant or by a library trying to serve its local user base. Or, it could be subscription based, with short-term or long-term contracts between users and providers. The latter became common at Starbucks, for example, which subcontracted with T-Mobile to provide the service throughout its cafés.

Hot spots were similar to, but outside of, the original set of use-cases for the standard. Since nothing precluded this unanticipated use from growing, grow it did. It grew in business buildings, in homes, in public parks, and in a wide variety of settings, eventually causing the firms behind HomeRF to give up. The growing use of Wi-Fi raised numerous unexpected issues about interference, privacy, and appropriation of the signals of neighbors. Nevertheless, these issues did not slow Wi-Fi's growing popularity.[26] Websites sprouted up to give users, especially travelers,

---

[25]The choice of the label "Wi-Fi" resembled "Hi-Fi" or high fidelity, a term commonly used to describe high quality and expensive musical components. The label was meant to signal high quality transmission. Yet 802.11b actually has little to do with music or fidelity, and "Wi-Fi" is a made-up phrase.

[26]In high-density settings it was possible for there to be interference among the channels, or interference with other users of the unlicensed spectrum reserved by the FCC, such as cordless telephones. The diffusion of so many devices also raised questions about norms for paying for access in apartment buildings, from neighbors, and others. See Sandvig (2004).

directions to the nearest hot spot. As demand grew, suppliers gladly met it. As in a classic network bandwagon, the growing number of users attracted more suppliers and vice versa.

Collective invention played its familiar role. Economic experiments among a community of participants led to many new insights that accumulated over time. While several pioneering firms took important steps in initiating market development, no single firm was responsible for all the economic experiments that eventually altered the state of knowledge about how to best operate equipment using IEEE Standard 802.11b. Rather, many firms responded to user demand, demonstrations of new applications with tangible market experience, and the lessons accumulated.

In this way, Wi-Fi became an industry-wide platform. All participants took actions using standards that invited activity from complementary component providers. In this instance of Wi-Fi equipment, the presence of a standard, related institutions for conformance, and the universal participation of virtually all the industry, encouraged experiments in antennae and receiver design, as well as in deployment of final equipment in new operational modes (such as a hot spot). Because Wi-Fi deployed at an industry-wide level, experimenters could presume (safely) that other complements would make use of the same design, which led each experiment to specialize on narrow issues and specific issues of interest to the experimenter.

Interplay

Later events in the development of Wi-Fi illustrate how a firm can invest in building on an economic experiment. Reacting to the experiment that generated Wi-Fi, Intel created Centrino, a large program that would install wireless capability in its notebook computers. It was officially launched in March 2003.

As with many aspects of growth in wireless access, the Centrino program is easy to misunderstand. Centrino was much less obvious to Intel in advance than it was in retrospect. It too was an experiment, just on a very large scale.

At the turn of the millennium Intel's strategic plans were responding to multiple market forces. While demand for desktop and notebook computers had grown along with the Internet in the 1990s, Intel's marketing department forecast an imminent slowdown in the share of desktop.sales, as well as increasing engineering challenges supplying faster chips. More worrisome, Intel had branded itself as a firm that always marketed better and faster microchips, while it was no longer clear that demand for bigger and faster would arise across all segments of computing. Notebook users valued mobility, for example, and that placed value on distinct attributes, such as longer battery life, less energy-intensive chips, physically smaller storage, more compact designs, less weight, and less heat. Even by the late 1990s many mobile users had shown a willingness to give up improvements in bigger and faster microprocessors in order to get improvements on these other attributes.

In 2001, in response to a number of initiatives and studies, Intel's management decided it was time to change priorities. Labeling this a "left turn," the company chose to embed a Wi-Fi connection in all notebooks that used Intel microprocessors.[27] This was easier said than done. The choice *not only* involved redesigning the Intel microprocessor, Intel's core product, stressing lower power and lower processing speeds, but it also involved redesigning the motherboard for desktop PCs and notebooks, adding antennae and supporting chips. Intel made a number of reference designs and made them widely available at low cost.

Intel's management hoped that its endorsement would increase demand for wireless capabilities within notebooks by, among other things, reducing weight and size while offering users simplicity and technical assurances in a standardized function. The firm also anticipated that its branding would help sell notebooks using Intel chips and motherboard designs instead of using microchips from Advanced Micro Devices (AMD). Furthermore, antenna and router equipment makers anticipated that a standardized format for wireless notebooks might help raise demand for their goods.

The redesign brought one concrete benefit to users—namely, it eliminated the need for an external card for the notebook, which was usually supplied by a firm other than Intel and installed by users or original equipment manufacturers (OEMs) in an expansion slot. Intel hoped for additional benefits for users, such as more reliability in wireless functionality, fewer set-up difficulties, longer-lived batteries due to less need for heat reduction, and thinner notebook designs due to smaller cooling units.

---

[27] For a full account see Burgelman (2007).

Seeking to inform users about all those changes, Intel adopted "Centrino" as a label, and it initiated a program to certify compliance.

Intel's management further worried that wireless notebooks would not be used widely enough to merit their investment in Centrino, so Intel's management considered exploring activities far outside of its core product, microprocessors. These exploratory actions were not far outside its philosophical approach to managing the demand for microprocessors. Intel long ago made a distinction between managing its first job, making microprocessors, and managing anything that helped it sell more microprocessors, which was often given the label "Job 2."[28] For example, the company launched a program to change the demand for the wireless feature of notebooks. As part of Job 2, Intel eventually certified fifteen thousand additional hot spots in hotels, airports, and other public places by the time Centrino launched.[29]

As another example of Job 2, Intel made motherboard designs available to others. The firm had crept into the motherboard business slowly over the prior decade as it initiated a variety of improvements to the designs of computers using its microprocessors. Years earlier, the firm had designed prototypes of these motherboards and by the time it announced the Centrino program, it was making some motherboards, branding them, and encouraging many of its business partners to make similar designs. The wireless capabilities of a notebook had not been the focus on these earlier programs, so the announcement of the Centrino program represented a shift in strategic aims and direction for the Intel programs affiliated with motherboards.[30]

This latter program illustrates one of the interesting conflicts that emerged in Wi-Fi's development. Intel's motherboard designs could increase the efficiencies of computers, but that benefit was not welcomed by every OEM that assembled PCs or other industry players. Firms such as Texas Instruments and Intersil had lobbied earlier for different designs for the 802.11g upgrade, investing heavily in the efforts at Committee 802.11. Neither of them had intended to help Intel's business, and neither of them

---

[28] Gawer and Cusumano (2002).

[29] Burgelman (2007).

[30] For history and analysis of why management chose to invest heavily in some complementary technologies and not others, see, e.g., Gawer and Cusumano (2002), and Gawer and Henderson (2007).

wanted to see Intel increase its influence over the designs that were deployed to most users.

Moreover, Intel's designs eliminated some differences between OEMs and other component providers. Many of these firms resented both losing control over their designs and losing the ability to strategically differentiate their own designs. At the same time, other OEMs liked the Intel design, since it allowed the firms to concentrate on other facets of their business. That competitive rivalry eventually generated cooperation from every small OEM, especially after Intel initiated marketing programs for Centrino. These programs were especially necessary to induce cooperation from many big OEMs.

Intel ran into several unanticipated crises, such as insufficient parts for the preferred design and a trademark dispute over the use of its preferred symbol for the program. However, the biggest and most important resistance came from the largest distributor of PCs, Dell Computer, one of the earliest firms to get the market started. Dell insisted on selling its own branded Wi-Fi products, buying internal cards from others that handled Wi-Fi, bypassing Intel altogether. Dell branded its solution and had grown a good side business from its pioneering efforts. It did not want to give that away to Intel.

Despite Dell's resistance, the cooperation from antenna makers and (importantly) users helped Intel reach its goals. By embedding the standards in its products, Intel made Wi-Fi, or rather Centrino, easy to use, which proved popular with many users. (Indeed, eventually this success would induce reluctant cooperation from Dell.)

The Centrino example illustrates the array of deliberate firm activities taken during a short period that built on top of learning from an earlier undirected economic experiment. The activities in IEEE Committee 802.11 ended up affecting the activities of many other firms, such as equipment manufacturers, laptop makers, chip makers, and coffee shops, which then shaped new activities in Committee 802.11 as well.

This example also illustrates that economic experiments can—and do—happen in spite of overt conflict between firms. Those firms may be either direct competitors or participants in a value chain with diverging interests. Conflict arises, as it did here, when all can forecast that the success of one firm's experiment adversely affects the business fortunes of another.

Experiments and Creating Value

What do we learn from the evolution of Wi-Fi? The growth of wireless access illustrates many of the elements underlying economic experiments, and, interestingly, these elements were present with the experiments that took place in dial-up access. It also illustrates the errors of many economic myths, and we start with those.

First consider the myth that new market opportunities evolved organically, independently generated by market incentives. Market incentives eventually played a role, but the historical facts suggest a nuanced reading of their role. In this instance a committee of engineers, many employed at industry suppliers, and not all of them participating with the same motive, met for years and designed a standard for a market in which products designed around proprietary standards had not appealed to many users. That involved collaborative ideation and iteration. Only after the emergence of a standard did recognizable profit-making activity emerge. Incentives worked indirectly, creating the shadow of future market events on collective action.

Second, incentives also did shape market actions, but not all innovative outcomes. There was a potential disconnect between those who incurred the costs of experimentation and those who learned from it. The disconnection occurred as an unintended by-product of deliberate experiments.

Where did incentives matter directly? By helping market participants learn about the nature of demand in quickly evolving environments, companies tried to position their offerings and pricing structures. Such lessons increased value for the experimenter by generating more revenue through improvement of an existing service, enhancing profits from lowering operation costs or avoiding higher investment expenses, or enhancing pricing power through targeting services to customers better than rivals. In general, many of these benefits could not be measured. If they could be measured—even partially—the private value could be measured in terms of the additional revenue contributed to a firm's business and/or the additional cost savings it generated.[31]

---

[31] Filtering between noise and cause is a key challenge in such experiments. See Thomke (2003a) for approaches for designing experiments so they can be measured in settings where firms control many of the key aspects of the experiment.

Revenue might have increased through altering pricing practices. For example, the acceptable pricing norm for hourly caps changed over time, as ISPs learned about the reaction of different customer segments to distinct menus of choices. Similarly, Wi-Fi prices in many hot spots reflected carrier perception about what the market demand could support.

Pricing experiments often coincided with experiments regarding the range of services offered. During the mid- to late 1990s, for example, virtually all ISPs experimented with changes to the standard bundle offered, such as default e-mail memory, instant messaging support, and hosting services in which the ISP maintained web pages for clients. Most Wi-Fi hot spots, in contrast, did not alter the standard bundle much, restricting access to one simple function. While ISPs experimented with performing services complementary to access, such as hosting services, networking services, and web design consultations, most Wi-Fi hot spots retained their status as stand-alone services.

Learning oriented toward cost reduction resembled learning oriented toward enhanced revenue. For instance, as dial-up ISPs learned from one another about the efficient deployment of 56K modems, those who deployed it found they could charge a modest price premium for faster service (approximately five dollars), but that that premium disappeared in less than a year, after the modems became more common.[32] Similarly, many Wi-Fi hot-spot providers initially charged for access but later found competition reducing their ability to price the service. Instead, Wi-Fi merely became an element of service for a location, often at no charge at all. While that might have led to better customer retention for a café, and eventually manifest as greater sales or higher firm prices, it would have been difficult to attribute a specific change in price or volume to only that investment in Wi-Fi.

More broadly, events in wireless access illustrate that incentives generate action, but others benefit. Pioneers reacted to incentives and expended costly resources on economic experiments. Those costs involved personnel taking time and effort. They also could involve real resources to build prototypes. In some circumstances, however, learning was cheap to an entrepreneur when others took pioneering action. In most circumstances

---

[32] See Stranger and Greenstein (2007).

an inexpensive lesson to a later beneficiary came at a high expense to a pioneer, such as a failed business. Succinctly, accounting for industry-wide costs, cheap lessons came at a high cost.

Industry-Wide Benefits

Events in Wi-Fi can be understood with reference to a traditional economic concept called a "learning externality." A learning externality arises when one party learns from the experiment of another but does not take part in the experiment and does not compensate those who incurred the costs from the experiment. Learning externalities were pervasive during the growth of the commercial Internet, and this example illustrates a widely pervasive phenomenon.

Looking back on the experiment in Wi-Fi and other access markets, at least two externalities shaped the experience with learning. There was an information externality *between* firms, as when one firm's directed experiment taught another firm a lesson, or a set of actions interacted in an experiment and taught every industry participant a lesson. There were also information externalities *over time*, as when the lessons of prior experiments generated lessons on which further experiments were built. The example of Wi-Fi shows that these two externalities were pervasive, as well as difficult to distinguish from one another.

Many of these learning externalities were *positive*, that is, one market participant benefited from the actions of another.[33] These positive externalities took one of two forms. In one case, what worked for one firm became known and imitated by others. For example, success from an experiment at one hot spot in one location in 2001 implied it might be profitable in another location with similar features. Alternatively, what did not work for one firm becomes known and, therefore, avoided. For example, the difficulties with the first design for 802.11 become known from experiences in 1997, leading equipment firms to save money by delaying building plans until a more suitable design emerged.

---

[33] In standard economic parlance, if it were possible to anticipate the benefit and to write a contract over its measured levels, the beneficiary would have *paid* for the benefit.

Intertemporal externalities also were common. For example, lessons about how to avoid commercial failure could be as valuable to observers as those who employed them. These valuable lessons often emerged this way, and it is easy to see why. The firm whose failure illustrated the lesson for others rarely, if ever, did so for the purpose of teaching others, and almost never under contract with the others who (later) gained the benefit of the lessons learned from the failure. For example, AOL learned from the experiments of many prior ISPs who altered their pricing or product lines, but did not arrange the rest of their product offerings in an appealing fashion. Similarly, many hot-spot developers of Wi-Fi learned from the pricing experience of others who did not get their pricing right.

Which externalities operated quickly and which operated slowly? The answer emerges by distinguishing among four distinct types of lessons that led to positive externalities. The first were *market lessons*. These pertained to norms and patterns of market-based actions, such as how to write a contract that users found acceptable, and how to price services, and so on. Second, *technical lessons* pertained to the design of a piece of equipment—for example, knowing how to configure Wi-Fi so that it worked in the type of space/location at all times that fit the supplier's needs. Third, *heuristic lessons* combined technical knowledge with either market or operational knowledge about how employees behaved in firms and how customers reacted to firm behavior. For example, knowing how to deploy Wi-Fi for a maximal set of users was such a heuristic lesson. Fourth, *complex lessons* were marketing and operational lessons that involved many functions inside an organization—for example, knowing how to integrate the use of Wi-Fi into a wide variety of other offerings. These four types of lessons spread at different rates.

Consider market and technical lessons. In 1999 the market and technical lessons about Wi-Fi were often rather trivial for an ISP to learn. Generally, these technical skills were common among those who operated bulletin boards, computers, ISPs, or related equipment. Most local and national ISPs already had procedures in place to, for example, implement billing, publicize their services to local users, or address user service calls. Doing so for Wi-Fi in a coffee shop or restaurant was easy. Although the market actions changed, these were relatively easy to execute within existing organizational procedures, and the contracts were easy to draw up.

Technical and market lessons tended to spread easily for another reason: they tended to become codified quickly.[34] For example, most equipment suppliers in competitive markets would not consider selling equipment if information about it were not codified because most buyers demanded it in contracts as a condition of purchase. Related, vendors of equipment also would have developed a set of marketing parameters for their buyers, which guided them toward best-practice deployment.

Others lessons pertained to heuristic knowledge about how to operate that equipment efficiently, and these too spread comparatively quickly. For example, lessons about how to manage a Wi-Fi router at peak usage levels was not known initially after a new piece of equipment became available for use, but such lessons would be learned through trial and error. As it turned out, those lessons spread to different coffee shops through a variety of mechanisms—administrators in key locations coordinated it (for example, at Starbucks), franchises communicated with one another (for example, at McDonalds), bulletin boards emerged to support different types of user groups, and the Wi-Fi association invested in support activities as well.

Several factors affected the speed at which heuristic lessons spread, and, as a result, these could spread quickly or slowly. On the one hand, some heuristic lessons spread slowly because, as sources of potential competitive advantage, the firms that first discovered them guarded them. For example, firms guarded their strategies for how to deploy equipment efficiently, and they may also have guarded information that indicated details about their future designs. On the other hand, some firms, such as equipment providers, had strong incentives to spread lessons, since their spread contributed to further sales. Such tension was inherent in the diffusion of Wi-Fi, for example. Intel's program to further fund development of certification of hot spots is another illustration.

The similarity between vendor organizations also shaped spreading of lessons. Most dial-up ISPs used similar software tools for monitoring users, particularly after these showed up in the discussion boards at an

---

[34] In this context, "codified" refers to an idea put in a structured format that another technically trained individual can understand without having the author present—e.g., words, mathematical formulas, plans, pictures, or professional drawings. See, e.g., the discussion in Nelson (2007).

open source project, such as Apache, the most popular web server. The community effectively coordinated many innovative efforts for dial-up ISPs in the mid- to late 1990s, by sharing multiple upgrades and fixes to the source code among ISPs. By supporting similar technology, operations, and heuristics, the designs embedded in standards in many organizations also contributed to sharing of lessons. For instance, organizations, such as the Internet Engineering Task Force (IETF) and the World Wide Web Consortium (W3C) facilitated the movement of lessons. Seen from this perspective, the 802.11 committee for Wi-Fi and WECA helped the lessons spread quickly.

The other side of the same coin is variance in idiosyncratic factors, which could slow the codification of such heuristic lessons. One community of users may differ from another. For example, though peak ISP usage occurs around the same time of day in different locations, surfing behavior varied according to gender, family status, age, education, and income of the members of the household. The sum of these varied across cities, and even from one vendor to another within the same city. Such variety interfered with finding commonalities in, for example, marketing strategies for a new feature across locations or vendors.

Complex lessons spread slowly. In part this was due to the lengthy investigations by firms seeking to lower cost or generate extra revenue. They often were interdependent, where one operational goal reinforced the other, or associated with unique firm features, such as scale. Almost by definition, these lessons resisted immediate codification and moved slowly from firm to firm. For example, management at one hotel chain would not lightly discuss with other hotel chains which type of customer showed a willingness to pay for Wi-Fi. This is not surprising, since firms often hesitated to share information about what sort of costly activities built customer retention most effectively—for example, did users have greater willingness to pay incrementally for access or as a standard part of their contract?

That does not means complex business lessons never spread. Rather, they spread with more effort and at greater cost. In general, they spread more slowly. Even while technical information and market lessons moved quickly between locations and firms, the ability of a firm to prevent direct rivals from imitating its business actions immediately slowed others. Some complex lessons also did not tend to spread to others, at least for a short time.

Economic Experiments in a Complex World

Stepping back from events, it is possible to see that policy makers did not foresee—indeed, could not have foreseen—the consequences of their flexible spectrum policies. Flexibility unleashed two complementary economic processes: movement of value and learning from experimentation.

The spectrum moved from low-value to higher-value activities as it became embedded in different products. Users bought Wi-Fi products instead of garage door openers and baby monitors. In comparison with the old command-and-control rules for allocating spectrum, which often fixed the application, the movement between uses occurred quickly. Users made their choices, and suppliers followed demand. More to the point, it occurred much more quickly than it would have occurred if government managers had retained the right to approve of a change in application.

Flexibility also enabled the firms to learn from experimentation. There were few restrictions on how accumulated lessons got used and by whom. Technical, operational, and heuristic lessons spread quickly, while some complex lessons did not spread at all. That allowed the spectrum to move between different users for Wi-Fi, such as between users who deployed Wi-Fi in business spaces and homes and those who deployed it in public spaces, such as café's and airports. Suppliers learned from one another's experiments, and moved to supply Wi-Fi wherever they could capture some of the created value. In comparison with the old command-and-control rules for allocating spectrum, which often fixed the identity of the seller who embedded the spectrum in products, this movement between uses occurred quickly.

Said simply, the flexible rules allowed lessons from experience in the market to spread quickly and widely. Accumulated lessons were built on the experience of other mistakes and triumphs. Almost by definition, the knowledge pool contained more lessons than any single firm could have learned on its own.

Accumulated knowledge also exhibited a mismatch between cost and benefit. Those who paid for lessons were not necessarily those who used them most profitably. As it typically turned out, many firms taught others lessons, and that had little to do with the original motives. Pioneers conducted the earliest experiments, and the timing of investment was determined by concerns that later participants did not—indeed, could not—influence. Only later, the most important lessons for value became known, creating the potential for regret over an earlier experiment that could have benefited others.

That last observation raises another question: What motivated a manager to pay for an experiment in the first place? Surely nobody was trying to do a favor for an unknown later participant in the market, so why conduct a lesson at all? While some lessons were conducted for the gains they generated for a firm, sometimes it seemed as if economic incentives did not drive a trial. Other inducements mattered just as much—the itch of curiosity, or the sporting thrill from doing something before others. Similarly, why did anyone let a lesson spread? Sometimes competitive pressures induced firms to learn from one another. Yet it also seemed as if lessons spread for reasons far less weighty than the market consequences, as when a manager boasted to a friend about inventing a clever enhancement, or about earning customer kudos for solving a common problem in a novel way.

Regardless of the reasons, the experience in wireless spectrum illustrates the benefits to enabling experiments by market participants. Expensive lessons appeared cheap to later borrowers, although no accountant would (or could) have recorded their value in a ledger, and both users and suppliers benefited.

EPILOGUE

15

Enabling Innovation from the Edges

As it developed, the Internet would have seemed ill suited for a commercial life later. The NSF managed an Internet that lacked market-oriented focusing devices and/or economic inducement mechanisms—namely, a setting that induces market actors to direct efforts toward the most valuable innovative outcomes. There were contracts for carrier services between government buyers and commercial suppliers, for example, but no general market orientation toward the pricing of the exchange of traffic between carriers. The applications were not for sale, nor did anybody design the applications with mass-market use in mind. They developed inside research laboratories that met the needs of a niche researcher and student community. This community desired technically advanced functionality and tolerated considerable imperfections to achieve those advances. That hardly seemed like the propitious beginning for a new transformative mass-market communications network.

Looking back on these events through a wide lens, it is now possible to ask and answer one of the core questions of this book: why did the privatization of the Internet—turning into a private asset a network designed to suit the needs of researchers and students—unleash a wide and profound set of economic outcomes as it grew into a widely used commercial network? How and why did the commercialization of the Internet bring about structural change? Why was this structural change coincident with an economic boom? The answer involves innovation from the edges—multiple perspectives originating from multiple places in an industry with little or no concentrated decision making. Innovation from the edges played an important role in all the key events:

- *Multiple perspectives.* The commercialization was shaped by a diversity of viewpoints. The design of the Internet met the needs of several different groups who funded it and who participated in its design. The commercialization of the network enabled participation from entrepreneurs with a variety of perceptions about the value of the economic opportunity, and with a variety of perceptions about how best to build businesses to address those opportunities. The opportunities also were larger than any single firm could pursue or would have pursued, so a variety of approaches thrived for a sustained time period.
- *Originating from multiple places.* Resources from many locations were directed toward building the commercial Internet. These were researchers in laboratories, administrators in a variety of organizations, students at universities, engineers at equipment-making firms, and suppliers of complementary services, to name a few. A set of institutions was adopted to encourage inventions arising from many participants—both before and after privatization of the Internet. The commercial network also accommodated applications from multiple participants in many locations. Especially after privatization and the invention of the web, commercial efforts extended the scope of the network far away from what any single firm would have pursued had it performed R&D by itself.
- *Lack of concentrated decision-making power.* A number of factors enabled dispersed decision making. Authority for technical improvements was not centralized within one firm or organization. No single entity or decision maker coordinated the Internet for an extended time with a single economic interest as motive. Even the standardization committees developed unrestricted access to their designs and did not restrict their uses. These same committees also maintained processes that did not restrict who could contribute additional improvements. Especially after privatization, competitive markets fostered commercial activities by more than one firm, and virtually every opportunity, from the largest to many small applications, received attention from many suppliers.

This book also has highlighted the many ways in which innovation from the edges encouraged exploratory activity. Demand for new value created different opinions about the appropriate actions to take. Not every participant perceived the value of the opportunities in the same terms, or possessed the same set of assets for exploiting the opportunities. Decentralized decision making was better at permitting a variety of experimentation than a central decision-making process. There were minimal barriers coming from the limitations affiliated with departing from the prevailing view, competing with an established firm, or approaching an opportunity that others had not perceived. All these factors reinforced one another, and the sum total of all this market activity addressed uncertainty about value by innovating much faster and with greater success than any single organization ever could have.

More concretely, innovation from the edges helps tell the economic story of how the Internet got built and why. It helps explain how the commercial Internet had an unexpectedly large impact as it became widely available and adopted as a commercial service. That explanation addresses one of this book's motivating puzzles: "Unexpected" and "large impact" and "innovative" does not usually happen at the same time. Here is a summary of the answer:

The economic explanation starts with the privatization of the network. As chapters 2, 3, and 4 described, prior to privatization, the creators of the Internet and web had sufficient time to refine their inventions, accumulate suggestions from many corners, and routinize processes for delivering services to users. Institutional support for the Internet was also close to routine, as the IETF was a functioning organization, designed to enable the accumulation and evolution of new functionality. The World Wide Web Consortium, though a new organization at the outset of privatization, governed a set of technologies that had already been tested and refined in a wide set of circumstances. As described in chapter 7, neither the IETF nor the World Wide Web Consortium restricted how technology could be used or who could use it. Both organizations eventually made all information available to any taker—albeit, with early access given to participants at the IETF, or to consortium members at the W3C. That helped to support a wide potential breadth of businesses after privatization, and many of these came from edges.

Very quickly after privatization, participants in commercial markets found new opportunities for the Internet and web. As chapters 4 and 6 stressed, many of these opportunities came as a surprise, and it caused a rush of economic activity. As chapter 6 explained, large parts of the economy would benefit from the commercialization of the Internet and the web, and had not acted in advance of its deployment. In part, this was due to the origins of the Internet and web, as a working prototype inside of universities and laboratories, one generated outside of commercial markets. In part, this was due to the behavior of the leading firms in communications, who had focused their attention elsewhere, and in part, as chapter 7 explained, the value chain behind the commercial Internet and web did not resemble existing value chains, and established players did not recognize how it would behave. Moreover, as chapter 5 analyzed in detail, in part, this was because bulletin board systems had helped grow firms who could enter as ISPs, and these firms held a special status within the industry as outsiders. Soon the opportunities extended to households and especially to businesses, touching virtually any process in which computing played an important role. At first this was not recognized, and BBSs were the best-placed private actors to see the opportunity.

Once the prototypes for the entire system were demonstrated, especially as embodied in the operations of a Netscape browser, innovative firms from many parts of the economy perceived many areas in which the Internet and web could apply—back-office enterprise information technology, customer-facing information technology, and operations-enhancing enterprise computing. That reaction occurred at households trying web-based applications, ISPs and access providers selling subscriptions and data services, entrepreneurial entrants growing web-based businesses, established firms modifying existing operations, and more firms with perceptions from the edges. The rush of entry into supplying web-based applications reflected a real economic opportunity for many entrepreneurs and established firms, simultaneously perceived by many of them. Contemporaries called that a gold rush, and, indeed, as chapter 6 explained, initially it resembled one.

The boom in investment and entrepreneurial entry persisted; many reasons account for that persistence, and these were distinct from the factors that started the gold rush. As chapter 7 stressed, the commercial Internet and web had a supporting value chain behind it, and those institutions had been built over a long time and would sustain more than just a transition of the technology out of the university and into commercial use. Those institutions possessed all the attributes affiliated with a successful commercial value chain. That enabled the support of value creation over a long period. One additional feature of the experience sprung from the openness of value chain: it permitted radical change to reach the market when it otherwise might have encountered roadblocks at private firms.

Unlike the initial rush, however, this radical change came about due to more entrants than just the earliest entrants that made discoveries of value. Chapters 8, 9, and 10 analyzed how that new opportunity provided potential value to a distributed set of participants. It provided new value in a dispersed set of circumstances across the economy—financial transactions, retailing and wholesaling, and logistics. That was a large-scale commercial opportunity, and it generated a concomitant scale of investment, again, coming from many edges of the economy, as well as from its core established firms.

Each participant's actions simultaneously raised the value of the other, and positively reinforced the economic incentive of the other to continue to invest. That was a symptom of the presence of a network effect at an economy-wide level, and by itself, would have generated a greater scale of investment. Moreover, in many settings the activities of one set of participants taught others lessons that they could use, so the simultaneous activities of so much experimentation at a large scale also increased the extent of learning. The breadth and number of opportunities in the late 1990s extended across virtually every sector of the economy, which meant that every important actor in the economy was investing in the Internet at virtually the same time. That placed enormous strains on the ability of firms and labor to supply inputs and services. The symptoms of impatience were everywhere and manifested themselves as resource shortages in IT labor markets and entrepreneurial managerial markets.

Said succinctly, the factors that started the boom differed from the factors that sustained it. A network effect manifested as a virtuous cycle in the late 1990s. That it is distinct from a gold rush—namely, the factors that catalyzed investment in the middle of the 1990s.

All the impatient activity encouraged another important feature of the economic situation, the seemingly high tolerance for economic experiments, many of these coming from the edges. Part of that tolerance was unsurprising in light of the scale of the new opportunity and in light of the background of many of the entrepreneurs—many had come from computing, where technological races were common. The late 1990s were extraordinary because the experimentation involved such an extensive list of participants and continued for so long. Many questions remained open about the value of different aspects of the Internet in the long run. Firms that initially explored approaches to creating value immediately after privatization continued to have incentive to explore new opportunities to create value several years later. Technically oriented entrepreneurialism thrived, and perceptions that had been regarded as from the edges were taken seriously by firms that had previously ignored such views. It made for strange bedfellows. Firms that had little economic relationship to one another prior to the Internet's deployment found themselves making deals and basing growth projections on those deals. Entrepreneurs began to talk with each of these firms, and established firms had to assign managers to follow developments that they had previously ignored to make thorough assessments.

The contrast between chapters 8 and 11 illustrates another lesson. These chapters highlighted how two established firms, IBM and Microsoft, profited from the commercial Internet and web. IBM eventually sold more services as a technological intermediary, while the commercial Internet and web raised the value of the PC value chain, described in chapter 7, and into which Microsoft sold its products. Their similarities ended there. As chapter 11 described, Microsoft also sought to control the value chain that emerged and cement its exclusive position. That led it to put up resistance to the emergence of alternative platforms, and it led to one of the dramatic confrontations of the era, between platforms built around Netscape's browser and Microsoft's.

For a time, especially near the end of the boom in growth, Internet exceptionalism became the prevailing view, a point stressed in chapter 12. This philosophy defied the economic archetypes of business history and boldly rejected traditional approaches to building and valuing businesses. This view partly arose as a product of the impatience of the era and the confusing nature of the new opportunities. Yet that alone does not explain how this perspective overwhelmed the voices of most experienced entrepreneurs and investors and analysts, such as those who had experienced technology-led prior booms in PCs and client-server networks. Internet exceptionalism was reinforced by a financial sector that reaped enormous short-term profits from encouraging the activity consistent with Internet exceptionalism, and because those with a skeptical view could not gain influential positions. Many participants overinvested or invested in directions whose merits eventually proved fleeting, and for some participants, the ideology of Internet exceptionalism lost creditability only long after the end of the boom.

The narrative of the Internet's evolution did not end with the dot-com crash. As chapters 13 and 14 describe, in, respectively, search engines and wireless local Internet access, the factors that shaped the next wave of investment would resemble those that shaped the first wave, while also differing from it. Further exploration took on an air of renewal in light of the lessons of prior experience. Thus the origins of the Internet, its privatization, and it diffusion into private use, connected to the next wave of investment by commercial actors. As it turned out, the creation of value from search engines built on the interplay between advances made in a university by a couple of graduate students and its commercialization, while the advances made in wireless Internet access resulted from the interplay among government policy for spectrum, the design of a standardization committee, and the aspirations of many private firms. As with prior episodes of commercialization of innovation, markets remained open to a variety of perspectives and contained institutions that permitted value to migrate to its highest value.

It added up to a remarkable set of events, one of the greatest episodes of technologically led growth in the two-hundred-year history of American capitalism. The growth and deployment of the Internet was unexpected, innovative, and impactful. It is not an exaggeration to say the deployment of the commercial Internet changed the way everyone lives, works, and plays, changing US economic activity in irreversible ways. Most astonishing of all, it brought about these changes at an extraordinarily fast pace.

Economic Archetypes

If Internet exceptionalism does not provide a valid explanation for events, then what should replace it? This book has argued that many well-known economic archetypes shaped the emergence of innovation from the edges. The rate, direction, and contour of events could not be understood without placing commercialization at the center of the explanation. Moreover, the economic forces that did matter for the Internet were not unique to the Internet. All of these archetypes had appeared in other technology markets, and, more specifically, other computing and communications markets.

A list of many key economic archetypes is provided below. No single economic archetype was solely responsible for the economic experience affiliated with the deployment of the privatization of the Internet, or with the experience with commercialization. A summary of important economic archetypes can illustrate the point:

- *Competitive core encouraged competitive complementary markets.* Backbone markets were competitive because, as explained in chapter 3, the privatization of the NSF backbone created competitive conditions. Chapters 5 and 8 discussed how competitive backbone markets helped grow competitive complementary markets in access for complementary infrastructure markets, such as ISPs. Those conditions enabled quick and low-cost entry of ISPs in many locations, which facilitated creating a large national network to support commercial applications.
- *A killer app could be a catalyst for adoption and investment.* The application with the highest value for the early Internet was e-mail, a point made repeatedly in chapters 2 and 3. The most valuable application for the privatized Internet was the web browser, a point first raised in chapter 4 and followed in many later chapters. The demonstration of the browser-based Internet motivated additional adoption by businesses and households. It also motivated the development of new applications that shared digitized pictures, digitized sound, and eventually digitized video. In other words, the web was the killer app of the privatized Internet.
- *Economic experiments in the marketplace generated valuable lessons about coinvention.* The privatization of the Internet motivated a number of ISPs to experiment with developing the access business and applying it to new areas and unserved applications, an observation central to chapters 5 and 8. The deployment of the browser-based World Wide Web motivated a number of programmers and entrepreneurs to start new firms that applied the browser in new applications, an observation central to chapter 9. The actions of entrepreneurs collectively amounted to a large economic experiment in

learning how to adapt the Internet to user needs in a variety of locations and commercial settings. As chapter 10 observed, established firms also incurred coinvention expenses as they adapted the Internet to their business needs.

- *Network effects in demand accelerated investment in all parts of the value chain.* The value of participating in the TCP/IP network—as either a supplier or a user—rose as the number of participants increased. Chapters 8, 9, and 10 explained how increasing household use, business use, and the provision of networking services reinforced the economic gains from investing in Internet markets. This was a network effect at an economy-wide level, and it shaped the activity of every participant. It increased incentives to invest sooner rather than later. It pushed many firms to invest simultaneously, exacerbating the boom.

- *Platform governance shaped the character of contributions from the periphery.* Different types of platform governance have different strengths and weaknesses; this was the key observation of the analysis in chapter 7. Well-managed modular platforms, such as the IETF's management of TCP/IP, supported many contributors and inventive specialists. Well-managed proprietary platforms, such as Microsoft's Windows, also could efficiently manage contributions from many specialized application developers. Open platforms, such as TCP/IP, allowed technical change to come from many contributors by making information accessible and from not restricting what got built for the platform, while proprietary platforms resisted changes that reduced the value captured by a platform leader. That led the open platform to support radical change that the proprietary platform resisted, and it led a well-managed proprietary platform to be superior at implementing a large coordinated improvement in the platform.

- *Creative destruction had many commercial determinants.* Just as Joseph Schumpeter wrote many decades earlier, creative destruction involved more than just the mere invention of new techniques or new technical knowledge, it also involved the creation of distinct new processes for delivering commercial services. Creative destruction also involved new combinations of business processes for organizations that support new services. This theme appeared throughout chapters 8, 9, and 10. The market-based setting of the late 1990s favored the commercialization of innovation, involving a wide variety of firms with distinct approaches to addressing the market opportunities.

- *No established firm willingly encouraged creative destruction against itself.* No established firm knowingly agreed to reduce its own value by letting another firm provide a substitute or cannibalize a product or service. No established firm planned for all contingencies and market events, and, therefore, planned to support the entire range of commercial services and applications enabled by new technology. Thus lack of cannibalization and lack of planning made it likely that established firms did less than market entrants in taking actions that fostered creative destruction. This theme arose with special salience in chapter 9, when discussing how IBM had failed to anticipate the commercial web, and how it responded to entrepreneurial entry with new services. It also arose in chapters 7 and 11, when discussing how Microsoft failed to anticipate the commercial Internet and web, and how it behaved during the browser wars by attempting to protect its lucrative position in the value chain for PCs.
- *The presence of monopoly and the exercise of market power discouraged innovation from the edges.* As chapter 3 discussed, IBM tried to control the privatized Internet backbone as a monopoly, while chapter 11 discussed how Microsoft resisted threats to reduce the value of its monopoly control over personal computer operating systems, and if federal prosecutors had not intervened, they might have pushed even further. Every instance of opposition to innovation from the edges came from established firms who had reasons to resist the competitive outcomes.
- *Unrestricted markets supported technological competition between distinct perceptions.* The history of the Internet contains several crucial moments when competition between organizations with distinct perceptions supported distinct approaches to creating market value. As described in chapters 2 and 3, in the early 1990s PSINet and UUNET were entrepreneurs with a distinct viewpoint about how the Internet would create value, and they invested more aggressively in the data-carrier business than many established firms. In

the middle of the 1990s, as chapters 4 and 7 stressed, Microsoft failed to make aggressive investments in supporting web technology, and Netscape, a start-up with a distinct viewpoint about how to create value, challenged it by trying to grow the browser-based market for new applications. As chapter 13 highlighted, at the end of the 1990s many of the earliest portals failed to anticipate the importance of search, and Google, a young firm with a distinct approach to generating search results, grew a business that supported an advertising-based model of search. In other words, entry into markets fostered technological competition, not as a contest between similar firms with similar visions, but, rather, as the result of unrestricted market entry by young firms competing with a different perception about how to create value.

There was nothing inevitable about innovation from the edges. Some economic behavior encouraged it, but not all did. One important aspect of the historical experience was the way events reinforced one another at a market-wide level. For example, lack of concentrated decision making and dispersed technical leadership fostered a variety of inventions, contributed to greater competitive conduct from more suppliers, and nurtured a great variety of economic experiments. The Internet platform fostered decentralized, independent decisions, which nurtured a variety of inventive specialists and, as it happened, enabled the invention of a killer app that spawned even more follow-on innovation. Each of these actions made the other more valuable and encouraged many actors to take a small action that reinforced the direction of change.

Three surprising observations emerge from this summary at this point. The first has to do with the symbiosis between several coordinated collective efforts—in particular, the design of standards—and the emergence of innovation from the edges. For example, the design of TCP/IP came from a very coordinated process, and that enabled inventive specialists. Upgrading TCP/IP in the IETF was much more of a collective effort, and with the additional investments in applications, it evolved into something no single designer could have imagined. As another example, the initial design of the World Wide Web also came from a single vision. It too became something bigger than any one individual could have imagined, especially once it grew into a large platform upon which others built their applications. Lastly, Wi-Fi also initially emerged from a coordinated collective effort at designing a standard. It too evolved into a range of valuable applications no individual could have designed in advance, building on a range of experiments by wireless access providers.

The second surprising observation has to do with the lack of coordination behind creative destruction. There was no invisible hand automatically guaranteeing that market events would become either creative or destructive. On the one hand, events were consistent with the classic Schumpeterian framework: entrepreneurial outsiders innovated, and existing firms innovated in response to entrepreneurial innovation from outsiders. Yet that is too simple a characterization. The same events that motivated innovative behavior also motivated defensive resistance and attempts to control competitive events. The process of creative destruction emerged only after the failure of attempts at defensiveness by established firms and failures in the attempts to control competitive processes. Competition triumphed if it became overwhelming, involving a wave of entrants and the sum of many actions. In short, creative destruction emerged endogenously because established firms were ineffective at manipulating the competitive process to slow down entry.

Another surprising observation about frictions emerges from this summary. During the deployment of the commercial Internet, low frictions shaped exploratory activities, and that affected multiple participants simultaneously. A friction refers to two related activities: the nonmonetary cost of designing and setting up procedures to deliver a new service or innovative product, and the nonmonetary cost of executing a set of proscribed processes and procedures for delivering services to users—specifically, the nonmonetary costs of employing personnel to gain technical knowledge and the hassles of addressing and managing delays, lost output, and other events for which no secondary market exists. In other words, low frictions encouraged innovation.

Why did low frictions matter? They helped make it cheaper to learn in markets when the most valuable direction of change remained unknown. By experimenting in markets, value creation emerged from novel combinations of demand-fulfillment and operations from multiple vendors combining their complementary services in new ways for mass users. That led to insight that no expert could cull easily from an experiment in a lab or an interview of a few survey takers.

More to the point, low frictions supported creative destruction many entrepreneurs led. Low frictions helped reduce the maddeningly difficult activities of establishing new firms at early stages, speeding up the emergence of a Schumpeterian wave. Any reasonably thorough case study of the processes behind entrepreneurially led innovation at the time emphasized the frustration, confusion, and utter plethora of loose ends an entrepreneurial enterprise experienced, even one with ample funding and adequate managerial experience. A very similar set of observations shaped established firms engaged in exploratory activity. Low frictions behind exploratory activity allowed economic archetypes to work devastatingly quickly, at a large scale across many firms at nearly the same time. That helped propel entrepreneurial activity into a catalyst for innovation from established firms.

Government Policy

Internet exceptionalism also overlooks the role of government policy, or merely mischaracterizes its importance. The US government alone could not have created the commercial Internet, nor could the commercial Internet have arisen in the absence of sagacious policy. The government's interaction with commercial firms played a crucial role in the development and growth of the commercial Internet. Policy either shaped incentives or placed bounds on the range of outcomes. Sometimes these policies were a matter of choice, reflecting the preferences, wisdom, or foolishness of those in positions of governance. Sometimes the policies were adopted with foresight and the intent to shape the Internet. Other times the policies grew out of unrelated concerns and issues and were adopted for reasons only loosely connected to their consequences for the Internet's growth.

Policies for moving federally funded technology from universities to private ownership played an enormous role in setting the stage for the Internet's commercialization. This theme appeared in many chapters, such as chapters 3, 4, 7, 13, and 14, which, respectively, discussed the growth of the backbone, the web, ISPs, Google, and Wi-Fi. Many chapters, especially chapters 5, 8, and 11, referred to one or more elements of the US government's competition policy for monopolies, and, once again, events cannot be understood properly without understanding how competition policy shaped outcomes. Sometimes the effect of policy was subtler. As chapters

5 and 8 stressed, some policies for the first amendment protected BBSs, and de facto acted as commercial policy to encourage ISPs.

To illustrate the broad point consider how several important policies shaped events prior to privatization:

- *Policies mediated the tension that arose when university technologies moved into commercial markets.* One policy decision mattered more than any other—the decision to privatize the NSF backbone, as chapters 2 and 3 described. Closely related was the decision to support nonexclusive interconnection through NAPs. Seen with the benefit of hindsight, those who initiated and managed the privatization of the Internet had some notion that procompetitive interconnection policies could lead to good outcomes, but they did not foresee all the effects that would result. The licensing policies of universities also played a role. Sometimes they led universities to assert property rights, as chapter 4 described, and, though done with good intentions, these could interfere with moving invention into commercial firms, such as taken by the University of Illinois during the commercialization of the browser. Sometimes the policies were light-handed, as chapter 13 described, and fostered use of university patents by private firms founded by former students and professors. Such policies ended up fostering the growth of Google.

- *Limiting the uses of the research-oriented Internet reduced the range of inventions for the early Internet.* The NSF's managers focused the Internet on the needs of their niche user communities—students, faculty, university administrators, and researchers. As chapter 3 observed, this had salutary effects and also distorted later events. Due to restrictions on participation and acceptable uses, many commercial applications for the Internet were unexplored prior to privatization. There was no possibility for tailoring new products and services to every potential new set of users outside of universities and research settings. Restrictions had an important impact on the applications built prior to privatization, and the large unmet potential available to commercial firms after privatization. The lack of working prototypes of commercial applications for the Internet also played a role in fostering misunderstanding about the potential for new opportunities in the Internet after privatization, as chapters 4 and 6 documented.

- *Government actors selectively intervened in network design at early moments.* The NSF and DOD played a crucial role in starting and sponsoring organizations that managed and standardized the operations of the Internet, such as helping to establish the IETF, an observation made in chapters 2, 3, and 7. Yet government employees did not have exclusive influence on design choices, nor did they assert a dominating voice. Most of those decisions were left to the Internet community. That discretion fostered the growth of independent Internet governance.
- *Pragmatic government policies nurtured institutions for the long run.* The NSF's managers foresaw the need to establish a standards organization to maintain the life of the TCP/IP platform. As chapters 3 and 7 stressed, government managers aimed to have the community survive past the era of exclusive government stewardship. NSF allowed standards development to embody academic preferences for a technical meritocracy, unrestricted participation, and unlimited access to the results. Those policies fostered unrestricted entry as the commercial Internet grew and helped to give discretion to a wide set of innovators.

Government policy continued to play a role after privatization, and no single statement can characterize government policy, nor did postprivatization government policy arise as a fully coordinated attempt to foster the Internet. Perhaps more surprisingly, despite the absence of explicit coordination across policies, many of the commercial policies tilted in the same general direction: toward increasing competitiveness, fostering more entrepreneurial entry, and reducing the role for a dominant decision maker in commercial markets. All of those encouraged innovation from the edges. This general tendency is evident in specific policies, including:

- *Common carrier policies encouraged competition in communications networks.* US policies for telephony evolved in an era when a single firm dominated, and this theme emerged in chapters 2, 5, 8, and 14. Computer II or federal policy for customer premise equipment continued to evolve after AT&T's divestiture. They applied to local telephone companies during and after the privatization of the Internet and encouraged competitive markets in complementary services and equipment with importance to the Internet, such as modems, personal computers, local area networks, and plenty of software applications. The key elements would differ from one example to another, but the general principle applied: regulations limited the ability of carriers for voice and data to alter their service for different types of traffic and loads from distinct complementary business services. Said another way, regulations prevented carriers from having any incentive or ability to refuse service, hold up complementary services, or discriminate their pricing and menu of services offered to different complementary firms.

- *Antitrust and regulatory policy protected and enabled entrepreneurs.* A range of competitive policies in the United States preserved the potential entry of entrepreneurial firms in computing and information services. Some were the outgrowth of policies to limit the reach of the monopoly phone provider, which chapters 2 and 8 described. Some of these were the outgrowth of other concerns, such as First Amendment rights to protect free speech, which protected a BBS with salacious or seemingly unsavory content from censorship, which chapters 5 and 8 described. Some resulted from standard antitrust concerns with the blockading of distribution by established firms, and this observation was crucial for understanding the origins of the competition policies described in chapter 11, which covered the browser wars.

- *Antitrust policy fostered less consolidated decision making.* Several chapters—notably 2, 8, and 11—discussed many antitrust decisions that moved toward less consolidation—for example, the breakup of AT&T, the continuing monitoring of local telephone firms after divestiture, and the review of the merger to prevent consolidation of communications markets, such as that attempted by WorldCom. These policies encouraged dispersed decision making, reduced the potential that a single prevailing view determined outcomes, and raised the potential for a variety of perspectives to shape the Internet.

- *Antitrust policy remained present when the name of the dominant firm changed.* The list of dominant firms changed, but not the concerns about dominance. Before the privatization of the Internet the concerns about dominance focused on AT&T and IBM, as chapter 2 stressed. At a later time those concerns focused on WorldCom, Microsoft, and AOL, as chapters 8, 9, 10, and 11 stressed. As many chapters discussed, antitrust policy played an essential role in limiting unfettered governance of key assets by a dominant firm. Such concepts also were applied broadly. A leading software firm, Microsoft, chose to respond with aggressive actions toward Netscape, a firm Microsoft viewed as a competitive threat to its lucrative platform. As chapter 11 described, the US government made a crucial decision when it chose to intervene in browser markets in order to limit anticompetitive behavior. It not only shaped events in those markets, it also made a statement that antitrust could be used to protect distribution of commercial innovation.

- *FCC policy could enable the migration of assets from low-value to high-value use.* By permitting ISPs to interconnect with the phone system, assets designed for one use, such as voice telephony, found value in another use, such as transferring data to support Internet applications. Chapters 5 and 8 showed that processes designed for one purpose, such as a BBS service, later served another, such as dial-up ISP service. Chapter 14 showed that designs aimed at one need, such as wireless transfer of data for baby monitors and garage door openers, served alternative needs, such as wireless Internet access in enclosed spaces. In some cases, such as the development of wireless access, new forms of property rights were salutary for developments.

- *Many policies encouraged innovation from the edges, even though this was not their primary or intended purpose.* As chapters 5 and 8 described, the FCC imposed Computer II on telephone companies to encourage growth in information services, and this was implemented long before the Internet privatized, and the prior decisions were reaffirmed to support growth of the commercial Internet rather than recreated anew. As another example from those chapters, the First Amendment protected a set of bulletin board firms in the pornography market, helping to provide a set of iconoclastic entrepreneurs for the young ISP market. And as another from chapter 14, the spectrum was available for the development of wireless Internet access, though the policies that made it available had a long and tortured political history and came into being for reasons only loosely connected to the rise of the commercial Internet.

Once again, nothing about these policies was inevitable. The backbone of the Internet almost became captured by IBM during privatization, as chapter 3 described, but this undesirable outcome was avoided due to the actions of several entrepreneurs, who established CIX. It also was avoided due to the modification of the NSF charter, which required congressional action. Several antitrust lawsuits pushed against the tide of consolidation, but none of these—AT&T, IBM, Microsoft, or even WorldCom—had a preordained outcome, as chapters 9, 10, and 11 stressed. Telephone monopolies could have interfered with the growth of the ISP industry, but rules prevented that from occurring, as chapters 5 and 8 stressed. Government policy makers had to decide to pursue these legal cases, and do so competently.

Policy also could lower frictions—in the sense that government policy could minimize or eliminate an entrepreneur's need to "ask for permission" of either a large dominant firm or an overbearing government regulator. This was especially evident in discussions about ISPs in chapters 5 and 8. If an ISP interacted with a telephone company that held to minimal government regulations, such as Computer II, then the ISP's entry could not be delayed. That permitted a private firm to pursue new commercial directions and new opportunities for creating value without giving advanced notice to any other firm or government decision maker. Another example arose in chapters 3, 7, and 14, when discussing standards. If a new entrant conformed to existing standards, such as those defined by the IETF, or comply with rules, as defined by the FCC's Part 15 rules, then it could move forward with its commercial aims. Thereafter these firms could focus on their commercial aims.

In a related sense not all government policy had salutary consequences. There were some examples of frictions caused by government policy or by the confusion in formulating policy. The privatization of the Internet became delayed by confusion about government policy for privatizing assets, and only after those plans were issued in 1994 could private actors move forward with certainty. As another example, the change in compensation for competitive local exchange providers in 1999 had a key role in fostering the competitive crash in telephony. Finally, as chapter 14 described, the FCC took a long time to designate some spectrum as unlicensed for short-range uses. The timing of those decisions shaped the timing of commercial experiments in wireless applications.

These observations lead to a surprising conclusion. Government actors are inherently limited; at most, policy can solve a specific issue, and suggest a direction, and not plan or mandate a long path for product development. And it was not the standard mantra of regulatory and antitrust policy to lower frictions, and only in a few circumstances—such as the formulation of Computer II—did government policy come close to framing the policies as aiming to foster entry from outsiders and entrepreneurs. Yet, in retrospect, it appears as if many policies aimed at reducing frictions for innovation from the edges, as if many policy makers made small moves in the same direction, and the policies sprung from a nearly unified vision and a persistent and coordinated policy effort, albeit, implemented and executed in flits and spurts.

How could such coordination arise over time, or across such a wide set of government policies and economics episodes? That brings this summary to the role of influential institutions.

Influential Institutions

Internet exceptionalism is deficient in one other respect. It does not orient analysis toward the role of influential institutions—that is, practices and social norms that shaped behavior and outcomes. Despite arising from noneconomic origins, many had an important role in economic outcomes, giving them similar impulses, embedding events with tendencies toward similar directions. As with economic archetypes and government policy, no single influential institution caused the economic experience of the late 1990s. Yet durable institutions last a long time and operate on multiple events, giving them that sense of coordination.

As illustration, here is a short list of several crucial institutions:

- *Democratization of standards development.* TCP/IP incubated in DARPA and was a centralized and top-down standardization effort. In the 1990s the IETF began to control more of the standardization efforts for new protocols. The computer science community favored nonhierarchical practices, and was notable for what they were *not*:

beholden to the managerial auspices of AT&T or IBM or any other dominant firm, such as Intel, Microsoft, or Cisco. This was an important observation in chapters 2, 3, and 7. Participants preferred not to have a single dominant view control development. Multiple viewpoints were encouraged, and information about outcomes was not restricted to a small number. Similar observations could be made about other crucial standards organizations, such as the IEEE and World Wide Web Consortium.

- *Respecting transparency.* Transparency was considered an unalloyed good feature of institutions that developed standards. The transparency of processes at the IETF, World Wide Web Consortium, and the IEEE reduced frictions with using standards. Respect for transparency facilitated the development of processes for disseminating information to any participant. As chapters 2 and 7 described, transparent processes allowed participants—ISPs, equipment firms, content firms, and big buyers of networking software—to know that change was imminent and to adjust their plans accordingly. That process helped develop an Internet platform with many interdependent decision makers, on which many other specialized firms built their business.

- *Embodying norms that respected independent decision making.* Academic norms shaped rules for making information accessible to all comers at the IETF and placed no restrictions on use. As chapters 3 and 7 stressed, these norms presumed a technical meritocracy would select among options invented by specialists, who had the discretion to address problems as they saw fit. Innovative activity was given the discretion to pursue any direction it desired. Once again, similar observations held for the IEEE and the World Wide Web Consortium. There was a pervasive attitude to enable others to build their prototypes and try to distribute them in the market.

- *Pursuit of purposeful idealism motivated action.* There were many examples of events where the pursuit of an ideal played an essential role. Perhaps no better example illustrates the role of purposeful idealism than the actions of Tim Berners-Lee, who chose to make the pieces of the World Wide Web available as shareware without restriction. As chapters 4 and 7 discussed, a few years after making the shareware available, he chose to establish a consortium to govern the evolution of the web and coordinate its improvement. At no point did he pursue diffusion through a more conventional commercial business strategy from which he could have profited directly. A second example comes from privatization of the Internet. It got the industry off to a competitive start, in part, due to the actions of honest policy wonks. As chapter 3 described, policies favoring competitive interconnection reflected the idealism of a large community, which sought to foster a new communications medium. A third example came from the attempt to release unlicensed spectrum, as chapter 14 described. The fights within the Federal Communications Commission reflected distinct ideologies about ideal policy. The spectrum was released once all political parties found something to like in the program and agreed that unlicensed spectrum put their reformist ideals into practice.

- *Impatient entrepreneurship became the new normal.* As chapters 6, 9, and 12 emphasized, considerable innovation activity was commercialized by entrepreneurs, funded by US venture capitalists, with IPOs that passed through Wall Street's financial firms. It oriented enormous sums of investment toward developing many applications for the commercial network. It also resulted in many entrepreneurial firms pursuing their strategies with impatient actions that appeared imprudent in retrospect. At the time, very few questioned the impatience. It is possible to use standard economic reasoning to partially explain behavior in the financial institutions, stressing self-dealing and a number of Wall Street practices that benefited insiders. It is more difficult to explain how so many participants willingly abandoned the standard tools of financial assessment and invested in growing entrepreneurial ventures with thin economic foundations. Yet for a short time it became acceptable and normal to act this way, and many adherents resisted calls to return to prior more prudent norms of business behavior.

The sum of these observations leads to a surprising conclusion. Innovation from the edges emerged under the encouragement of several institutions embedded in US commercial markets and government policy conversations. It was not as if one single invisible hand guided every actor, or the price system coordinated innovative decisions, as in classical economic thinking. Rather, many norms and institutions encouraged innovation from the edges, and inside a variety of myriad economic decisions and policy debates.

General Lessons for Economic Growth

This book has stressed that competition fostered growth in a range of economic activity related to the commercial Internet. This conclusion contrasts with the usual economic argument for more competition, and the contrasting implications deserve attention. The default arguments for more competition stress the direct gains to users from more suppliers, such as lower prices and more customer orientation in nonprice activities. While those benefits did arise in the commercial Internet—for example, more ISPs lowered prices for Internet access—the experience in this instance highlights an additional benefit that comes with competitive decision making. Decentralized decision making fostered a diversity of innovative viewpoints.

One benefit from diversity could be labeled "better benchmarking." Benchmarking was very valuable when trying to discern whether an established firm overcommitted to a single technological forecast. That type of error was likely when executives grew out of touch with frontier developments due to unquestioned hierarchical norms inside their organization. The lack of investment in the Internet by established firms in communications markets, such as AT&T or the Baby Bells, could serve as one such example. Bill Gates's error in not anticipating the Internet served as another illustration. Gates would not have changed his view had there not been a firm with a distinct commercial outlook directly confronting his plans for capturing value from a value chain. In other words, diversity of innovative approaches gave observers a point of comparison, which helped managers and outsider investors discern whether a particular firm made a good choice, particularly where there was greater uncertainty about the source of value or the right strategy.

The book also highlights a trade-off between uniformity and diversity, most explicitly in the discussions about standards. Standards performed two distinct functions. First, they produced technical uniformity in some aspects of a design. That reduced variety, by definition. Most standards committees did not pursue that goal with the expectation that a new design for a standard by itself marked the end the story. Most committees did it in the service of a second function, to enable variety of additional actions from commercial participants. Many standards could help specialists invent in one corner of a technical universe without worrying about the other layers. Almost paradoxically, therefore, standards could play a positive role by establishing uniformity in the service of diversity.

Another trade-off between diversity and uniformity emerged from discussions about learning and exploration, when there are a variety of viewpoints about the source of value. When value remained unknown, and could not be quickly or inexpensively uncovered in a laboratory, then experience with markets could contribute to understanding how to deploy and implement new innovation in operating businesses. As the experience in ISPs and wireless access markets illustrated, diversity of approaches generated a range of different lessons, and as many firms experimented, firms learned lessons from observing one another. Summarizing, more diversity fostered a greater variety of different lessons, and the accumulated pool of industry common knowledge became richer and more vital for all participants, and bigger than any single organization could have generated by itself.

In the case of the Internet, low frictions, decentralization, and a diversity of views allowed for an especially potent impact from more entry and competition, enhanced as it was by innovation from the edges. Sampling from a variety of perspectives encouraged the appearance of new or previously unimagined combinations of business activities, or, the coordination of complementary actions that fell outside of those established firms supported. Many inventive specialists discovered how to apply the Internet and the web to applications that had previously only been imagined. Other explorations opened up genuinely new opportunities no research had explored in a lab. Some of those discoveries were unreachable with prior prototypes, and the Internet enabled them by lowering costs or by allowing someone to explore a new combination of technology. The combination of low friction and high decentralization unleashed a particularly potent variety of approaches to market-based learning.

These observations also inform a sense in which the commercialization of the Internet was exceptional. Because innovation from the edges played such a large role, competitive markets reinforced the impact of drawing innovation from a variety of suppliers, both entrepreneurs and established firms. Experimenting with a variety of innovations in all parts of the economy, the whole had greater economic impact than the sum of the impact from any its parts.

That observation should not deter a reader of this book from walking away with one major theme, however. In every case, the key question should not be: how is the Internet different from all other technologies, and why does that make Internet economics exceptional? Instead, inquiries should start by asking: why does the commercialization of the Internet resemble the commercialization of other technologies? The key lessons are learned if the question is: how and why did the operations of economic archetypes, the adoption of government policies, and the influence of institutions encourage or discourage innovation from the edges? Addressing those two key questions provides the crucial insight for understanding why outcomes acquired their specific economic characteristics and contours.

Acknowledgments

Before I began this project I did not know if I would have the courage to go forward without knowing where the key questions would lead. I know now where my courage came from: a large community of friends and colleagues and family.

No chapter came exclusively from my solitary hand. I must thank numerous collaborators with whom I have had the privilege to write articles and essays over the years. These efforts informed all the chapters in this book. That includes Angelique Augereau, Tim Bresnahan, Lorrie Cranor, Paul David, Tom Downes, Chris Forman, Avi Goldfarb, Rebecca Henderson, Michael Mazzeo, Ryan McDevitt, Frank Nagle, Jeff Prince, Greg Rosston, Marc Rysman, Pablo Spiller, Greg Stranger, Catherine Tucker, and Victor Stango. Relatedly, a number of editors motivated me to write those articles. I would like to thank William Aspray, Michael Baye, Ernst Berndt, Amar Bhidé, Sherrie Bolin, Erik Brynjolfsson, Carl Cargill, Wes Cohen, Benjamin Compaine, Paul Ceruzzi, Lorrie Cranor, Mike Cusumano, Maryann Feldman, Barbara Fraumeni, Annabelle Gawer, Sharon Gillett, Bronwyn Hall, Rebecca Henderson, Chuck Hulten, Adam Jaffe, Steve Kahl, Brian Kahin, Josh Lerner, Al Link, Franco Malerba, Sumit Majumdar, Robin Mansell, Richard Newell, Martin Peitz, Nathan Rosenberg, Brian Silverman, Scott Stern, Ingo Vogelsang, Joel Waldfogel, Phil Weiser, and Steve Wildman.

Many friends suffered through the reading of half-baked and partially completed chapters, and they deserve praise for their inspiration, comments, and suggestions. In addition to my coauthors and editors, I wish to thank Ranna Rozenfeld, Ajay Agrawal, Jon Aronson, Ashish Arora, Jonathan

Baker, Carliss Baldwin, Ernst Berndt, David Besanko, Marjory Blumenthal, Pablo Boczkowski, Jen Brown, David Burstein, Maja Butovich, Martin Campbell-Kelly, Robert Cannon, KC Claffy, Iain Cockburn, Linda Cohen, Wes Cohen, Jim Cortada, Michael Cusumano, James Dana, Leemore Dafny, Paul David, Mark Doms, David Dranove, Roberto Fontana, Alfonso Gambardella, Mark Greenstein, Renee Greenstein, Zvi Griliches, Tom Haigh, Eszter Hargittai, Tom Hazlett, Igal Hendel, John Horrigan, David Hounshell, Tom Hubbard, Marco Iansiti, Benjamin Jones, Karim Lakhani, Kevin Maney, Sarit Markovich, Kristina McElheran, Therese McGuire, Joel Mokyr, Aviv Nevo, Roger Noll, Robert Porter, John Quarterman, William Rogerson, Nathan Rosenberg, Richard Rosenbloom, Andrew Russell, Mark Satterthwaite, Christian Sandvig, Scott Savage, Alicia Shems, Tim Simcoe, Marvin Sirbu, Jim Speta, Kathy Spier, Daniel Spulber, Scott Stern, Manuel Trajtenberg, Ann Velenchik, Joel Waldfogel, Scott Wallsten, David Warsh, Philip Webre, Kevin Werbach, Joel West, Jody Weverka, Phil Weverka, Larry White, Simon Wilkie, Oliver Williamson, David Yoffie, Chris Yoo, and the wonderful readers at Larry Bernstein's Chicago Book Club. Please forgive any oversight if I have forgotten to mention someone. Please accept my gratitude.

Special thanks must go to those who did editorial work on drafts of articles that informed this book. Over many years the IEEE provided a space for working out some of my ideas in columns for the membership. Thanks to Molly Gamborg, Marie English, Kristine Kelly, Janet Wilson, and Jenny Fererro for their comments and suggestions. Alicia Shems copyedited the first draft of every chapter of this book. She is a wonder, and I owe her a tremendous amount of gratitude. Tim Bresnahan, Chris Forman, and Avi Goldfarb read an early draft and provided numerous comments and valuable observations. Kristina McElheran took her red pen to half of the later drafts. I wish I could write as well as she wants me to. Adam Greenstein and Hannah Weverka examined the penultimate draft, and made many excellent suggestions. Dawn Hall copyedited the final manuscript with her extraordinary eye for detail. They deserve a huge thank you.

Over the years I have benefited from the feedback of many audiences and lunchtime companions, too numerous to enumerate. I must single out and thank hundreds of students at Kellogg School of Management, Northwestern University, who have suffered through pieces of this material in the classroom. Special thanks go to audiences at the Telecommunications Policy Research Conference, Silicon Flatirons, and the National Bureau of Economic Research, where early drafts of papers have been presented. I am grateful to the Searle Center for sponsoring a book reading, and I am especially grateful to all who attended that event. It meant a great deal to me. Seth Ditchik of Princeton University Press reviewed many aspects of the project, and arranged for many anonymous reviewers. I tried to listen to these reviewers and respond, and I hope those reviewers understand how much I appreciate their suggestions and feedback.

A number of people gave their time for an interview. They deserve thanks for sharing their insights and making events real to me with their memories. Gratitude goes to Tim Berners-Lee, Scott Bradner, Robert Cannon, David Clark, Gordon Cook, David Crocker, Barbara Dooley, Tim Draper, Dale Hatfield, Victor Hayes, Brian Kahin, William C. Lowe, Scott Marcus, Bill McCarthy, Michael Nelson, Barbara O'Keefe, Craig Partridge, John Quarterman, William Schrader, Ben Slivka, Marvin Theimer, Hal Varian, Todd Warren, Ted Weverka, Phil Weiser, Jeannette M. Wing, Terry Winograd, Irving Wladawsky-Berger, and Stephen Wolff. Special thanks to Dale Hatfield for familiarizing me with the phrase, "Innovation from the Edges." More special thanks go to the participants on Robert Cannon's Cybertelecom listserv for educating me. I never had to interview anyone on that listserv because—sans any question from me—they often ended up providing the answers I sought.

Gratitude goes to the organizations that funded pieces of this work. Throughout the process I have been grateful to my employers, the Economics Department at the University of Illinois, and the Management and Strategy Department at the Kellogg School of Management, Northwestern University, for providing a nurturing home for research and writing. My employer also funded projects that fed into this book. At the University of Illinois I received support from the Institute for Government and Public Affairs. At Northwestern University I received support from the dean's office of the Kellogg School of Management, the Searle Center for Law Regulation and Economic Growth, and the Institute for Public Research. The National Science Foundation and Council on Library Resources supported this research at a very early stage in the middle of the 1990s, when I first began examining the economics of communications infrastructure. I hope they appreciate what a catalytic role that early funding played in my thinking. Robert Strom at the Ewing Marion Kauffman Foundation acted as the catalyst for starting the writing of this book, when he funded a brief respite from teaching. The project took a great deal longer to complete than anticipated, so I needed funding to find the time to finish it. For that I am grateful to the Technology Operations and Management group at the Harvard Business School for their hospitality and support. I also thank the Berkman Center for Internet and Society, Harvard University, and the Center for Digital Business, Sloan School of Management, MIT, for their hospitality during that final period of writing.

I wish to thank all the research assistance I have received over the years on projects related to chapters in this book. Gratitude goes to Guy Arie, Angelique Augereau, Howard Berkson, Oded Bizan, Helen Connolly, Holly Gill, Brittany Jackel, Kristina McElheran, Jordan McDole, Mian Dai, Tam Le, Heather Radach, Alex Risman, and Benjamin Rothschild. Special thanks go to Northbrook Gymnastics Training Center for offering a table and chair from which to watch my children grow up; it also turned out to be a quiet location for writing a couple hours every Saturday.

Despite so much help, mistakes are inevitable in a project of this scale and scope. I must take responsibility for all remaining errors.

Last and not least, my family deserves enormous gratitude. They have lived with this project for a long time and watched me push aside other matters in order to engage with it. At last they can stop asking when it will be finished. Thank you Mom, Dad, Betty, Irv, Mark, Renee, Jody, Phil, David, Barbara, Debby, Charley, Ellen, Milford, Jon, and Jill. Special heart-felt thanks go to Barbara, Eli, Ilana, Rebecca, Noah, and Ranna. You deserve a big hug.

References

Abbate, Janet. 1999. *Inventing the Internet*. Cambridge, MA: MIT Press.

Afuah, Allan, and Christopher L. Tucci. 2003. *Internet Business Models and Strategies: Text and Cases*. 2nd ed. New York: McGraw-Hill.

Agre, Phil. 2000. "Who Invented 'Invented'?: Tracing the Real Story of the 'Al Gore Invented the Internet' Hoax." http://web.archive.org/web/20040603092645/commons.somewhere.com/rre/2000/RRE.Al.Gore.and.the.Intel.html, accessed January 2015.

Aiken, Robert, Hans-Werner Braun, and Peter Ford. 1992. "NSF Implementation Plan for Interim NREN." *Journal on High Speed Networking* 2: 1–25.

Allen, Robert C. 1983. "Collective Invention." *Journal of Economic Behavior and Organizations* 4 (1): 1–24.

Allison, Jeremy. 2006. "A Tale of Two Standards." In *Open Sources 2.0: The Continuing Evolution*, edited by Chris DiBona, Danese Cooper, and Mark Stone. Sebastopol, CA: O'Reilly Media.

Angel, Karen. 2002. *Inside Yahoo!: Reinvention and the Road Ahead*. New York: John Wiley and Sons.

Aspray, William, ed. 2004. *Chasing Moore's Law: Information Technology Policy in the United States*. Raleigh, NC: SciTech Publishing.

Aspray, William, and Martin Campbell-Kelly. 2004. *Computer: A History of the Information Machine*. Boulder, CO: Westview Press.

Aspray, William, and B. O. Williams. 1994. "Arming American Scientists: NSF and the Provision of Scientific Computing Facilities for Universities, 1950–1973." *IEEE Annals of the History of Computing* 16 (4): 60–74.

Auletta, Ken. 2001. *World War 3.0: Microsoft and Its Enemies*. New York: Random House.

Bank, David. 2001. *Breaking Windows: How Bill Gates Fumbled the Future of Microsoft*. London: Free Press.

Banks, Michael. 2008. *On the Way to the Web: The Secret History of the Internet and Its Founders*. Berkeley, CA: Apress.

Bauer, Johannes M. 2005. "Unbundling Policy in the United States: Players, Outcomes, and Effects." *Communications and Strategies* 57: 59–82.

———. 2006. "Broadband in the United States." In *Global Broadband Battles: Why the US and Europe Lag While Asia Leads*, edited by Martin Fransman, 133–63. Stanford, CA: Stanford Business Books.

Beaty, Randolph, and Jay Ritter. 1986. "Investment Banking, Reputation, and the Underpricing of Initial Public Offering." *Journal of Financial Economics* 15 (1): 213–32.

Behlendorf, Brian. 1999. "Open Source as a Business Strategy." In *Open Sources: Voices from the Open Source Revolution*, edited by Chris DiBona, Sam Ockman, and Mark Stone. Sebastopol, CA: O'Reilly Media.

Benklar, Yachai. 2002. "Some Economics of Wireless Communications." *Harvard Journal of Law and Technology* 16 (1): 25–83.

Berners-Lee, Tim, with Mark Fischetti. 1999. *Weaving the Web: The Original Design and Ultimate Destiny of the World Wide Web.* New York: HarperBusiness.

Besen, Stanley, Paul Milgrom, Bridger Mitchell, and Padmanabhan Srinagesh. 2001. "Advances in Routing Technologies and Internet Peering Agreements." *American Economic Review* (May): 292–96.

Besen, Stanley, Jeffrey S. Spigel, and Padmanabhan Srinagesh. 2002. "Evaluating the Competitive Effects of Mergers of Internet Backbone Providers." *ACM Transactions on Internet Technology* 2 (3): 187–204.

Blodget, Henry. 2008. "Why Wall Street Always Blows It." *The Atlantic.* http://www.theatlantic.com/magazine/archive/2008/12/why-wall-street-always-blows-it/307147/2/, accessed October 2012.

Blumenthal, Marjory S., and David D. Clark. 2001. "Rethinking the Design of the Internet: The End-to-End Arguments vs. the Brave New World." In *Communications Policy in Transition: The Internet and Beyond*, edited by Benjamin Compaine and Shane Greenstein, 91–139. Cambridge, MA: MIT Press.

Boardwatch. [1996–99]. *Directory of Internet Service Providers.* Littleton, CO.

Bower, Joseph L., and Clayton M. Christensen. 1995. "Disruptive Technologies: Catching the Wave." *Harvard Business Review* (January–February).

Bradner. Scott. 1999. "The Internet Engineering Task Force." In *Open Sources: Voices from the Open Source Revolution*, edited by Chris DiBona, Sam Ockman, and Mark Stone, 47–52. Sebastopol, CA: O'Reilly Media.

Brau, James, and Stanley Fawcett. 2006. "Initial Public Offerings: An Analysis of Theory and Practice." *Journal of Finance* 61 (1): 399–436.

Bresnahan, Timothy. 1999. "New Modes of Competition and the Future Structure of the Computer Industry." In *Competition, Innovation, and the Microsoft Monopoly: Antitrust in the Digital Marketplace.* The Progress and Freedom Foundation, Kluwer Press.

———. 2003. "The Economics of the Microsoft Antitrust Case." http://www.stanford.edu/~tbres/research.htm, accessed July 2006.

Bresnahan, Timothy, Erik Brynjolfsson, and Lorin Hitt. 2002. "Information Technology, Work Organization, and the Demand for Skilled Labor: Firm-Level Evidence." *Journal of Economics* 117 (February): 339–76.

Bresnahan, Timothy, and Shane Greenstein. 1997. "Technical Progress and Co-Invention in Computing and in the Use of Computers." *Brookings Papers on Economics Activity: Microeconomics*, 1–78.

———. 1999. "Technological Competition and the Structure of the Computer Industry." *Journal of Industrial Economics* (March): 1–40.

Bresnahan, Timothy, Shane Greenstein, and Rebecca Henderson. 2012. "Schumpeterian Economies and Diseconomies of Scope: Illustrations from the Histories of IBM and Microsoft." In *The Rate and Direction of Inventive Activity Revisited*, edited by Josh Lerner and Scott Stern, 203–76. Chicago: University of Chicago Press.

Bresnahan, Timothy, and Manuel Trajtenberg. 1995. "General Purpose Technologies: 'Engines of Growth'?" *Journal of Econometrics*, special issue, 65 (1): 83–108.

Bresnahan, Timothy, and Pai-ling Yin. 2007. "Setting Standards in Markets: Browser Wars." In *Standards and Public Policy*, edited by Shane Greenstein and Victor Stango. Cambridge: Cambridge University Press.

Brinkley, Joel, and Steve Lohr. 2000. *US v. Microsoft: The Inside Story of the Landmark Case*. New York: McGraw-Hill.

Brockman, John. 1996. *Digerati: Encounters with the Cyber Elite*. San Francisco: Hardwired.

Bronson, Po. 1998. *The Nudist on the Late Shift*. New York: Random House.

Bruner, Robert F. 2005. *Deals from Hell: M & A Lessons That Rise above the Ashes*. Hoboken, NJ: John Wiley and Sons.

Burg, Urs von. 2001. *The Triumph of Ethernet: Technological Communities and the Battle for the LAN Standard*. Stanford, CA: Stanford University Press.

Burgelman, Robert A. 2007. "Intel Centrino in 2007: A New Platform Strategy for Growth." Stanford Case, SM-156.

Campbell-Kelly, Martin, and Daniel D. Garcia-Swartz. 2013. "The History of the Internet: The Missing Narratives." *Journal of Information Technology* 28: 18–33.

Cannon, Robert. 2001. "Where Internet Service Providers and Telephone Companies Compete: A Guide to the Computer Inquiries, Enhanced Service Providers, and Information Service Providers." In *Communications Policy in Transition: The Internet and Beyond*, edited by Benjamin Compaine and Shane Greenstein. Cambridge, MA: MIT Press.

Cassidy, Mike. 2011. "Internet Pioneer Paul Baran Showed Silicon Valley How to Do Business." *Mercury News*, March 28. http://www.mercurynews.com/business/ci_17719914?nclick_check=1, accessed May 12, 2011.

Castells, Manuel. 2001. *The Internet Galaxy*. Oxford: Oxford University Press.

Cerf, Vint. 2005. "Vint Cerf Speaking Out on Internet Neutrality." *Circle ID*, November 5. http://www.circleid.com/posts/vint_cerf_speaking_out_on_internet_neutrality/, accessed August 2009.

Ceruzzi, Paul. [2006]. 2008. "The Internet before Commercialization." In *The Internet and American Business*, edited by William Aspray and Paul Ceruzzi, 9–44. Cambridge, MA: MIT Press.

Chandrasekaran, Rajiv. 1998. "Competitors, Senators Assail Gates at Hearing." *Washington Post*. March 4.

———. 1999. "Jabs at Company Figure into Trial." washingtonpost.com. http://www.washingtonpost.com/wp-srv/business/longterm/microsoft/stories/1999/jabs012799.htm.

Chapman, Merrill R. 2004. *In Search of Stupidity: Over 20 Years of High Tech Marketing Disasters*. Berkeley, CA: Apress; New York: Springer-Verlag.

Christensen, Clayton. 1997. *Innovator's Dilemma*. Boston: Harvard Business School Press.

Clark, David. 1988. "The Design Philosophy of the DARPA Internet Protocols." *Computer Communications Review* 18 (4): 106–14.

———. 1992. A Cloudy Crystal Ball—Visions of the Future, Given at the 24th Internet Engineering Task Force. http://xys.ccert.edu.cn/reference/future_ietf_92.pdf.

Clark, David, William Lehr, Steve Bauer, Peyman Faratin, Rahul Sami, and John Wroclawski. 2006. "Overlay Networks and the Future of the Internet." *Communications and Strategies* 63 (3rd quarter): 1–21.

Clemente, Peter C. 1998. *State of the Net: The New Frontier*. New York: McGraw-Hill.

CNET. 1996. "IBM Freed of Antitrust Regulation," July 2. http://news.cnet.com /IBM-freed-of-antitrust-regulation/2100-1023_3-279396.html, accessed February 2014.

Coffman, K. G., and Andrew Odlyzko. 1998. "The Size and Growth Rate of the Internet." *First Monday*. http://firstmonday.org/ojs/index.php/fm/article /view/620/541, accessed February 2014.

———. 2006. "Internet Growth: Is There a Moore's Law for Data Traffic?" In *Handbook of Massive Data Sets*, edited by James Abello, Panos M. Pardalos, and Mauricio G. C. Resende, 47–93. Boston: Kluwer.

Cohen, Linda R., and Roger G. Noll, eds. 1991. *The Technology Pork Barrel*. Washington, DC: Brookings Institution.

Coll, Steve. 1986. *Deal of the Century*. New York: Simon and Schuster.

Cook, Gordon. 1992–94. The Cook Report on the Internet. www.cookreport. com, accessed July 2008.

Cortada, James W. 1996. *Information Technology as Business History: Issues in the History and Management of Computers*. Westport, CT: Greenwood Press.

———. 2003. *The Digital Hand: How Computers Changed the Work of American Manufacturing, Transportation, and Retail Industries*. Oxford: Oxford University Press.

Crandall, Robert. 2005. *Competition and Chaos: U.S. Telecommunications since the 1996 Telecom Act*. Washington, DC: Brookings Institution Press.

Cringely, Robert X. 1998a. *Nerds 2.0.1: A Brief History of the Internet*. PBS Home Video. Distributed by Warner Home Video, Burbank, CA.

———. 1998b. "Who Really Invented the MultiProtocol Router, and Why Should We Care?" December 10. http://www.pbs.org/cringely/pulpit/1998 /pulpit_19981210_000593.html, accessed August 2009.

Crocker, David. 1993. "Making Standards the IETF Way." *Standards View* 1 (1): 1–15. Also available at http://bbiw.net/musings.html.

———. 2006. "Thoughts on the Future of the Internet." BBC4 Radio, Today Programme. Mimeo. http://www.bbiw.net/recent.html, downloaded August 2008.

———. 2008. "A Personal View: The Impact of Email Work Done at the RAND in the Mid-1970s." Mimeo. http://www.bbiw.net/recent.html, downloaded August 2008.

Cronin, Blaise. 2006. "Eros Unbounded: Pornography and the Internet." In *The Internet and American Business*, edited by William Aspray and Paul Ceruzzi, 491–538. Cambridge, MA: MIT Press.

Cusumano, Michael. 2012. "Platforms versus Products: Observations from the Literature and History." In *History and Strategy*. Vol. 29 of *Advances in Strategic Management*, edited by Michael A. Cusumano, Steven Kahl, and Brian S. Silverman. Bingley, UK: Emerald.

Cusumano, Michael, and Richard Selby. 1995. *Microsoft Secrets: How the World's Most Powerful Software Company Creates Technology, Shapes Markets, and Manages People*. New York: Simon and Schuster.

Cusumano, Michael, and David Yoffie. 1998. *Competing on Internet Time: Lessons from Netscape and Its Battle with Microsoft*. New York: Free Press.

David, Paul, and Shane Greenstein. 1990. "The Economics of Compatibility of Standards: A Survey." *Economics of Innovation and New Technology* 1: 3–41.

Delgado, Ray. 2001. "WebVan Goes Under, Online Grocer Goes Under—$830 Million Lost, 2000 Workers Fired." *San Francisco Chronicle*, July 9. http://www.sfgate.com/news/article/Webvan-goes-under-Online-grocer-shuts-down-2901586.php#page-1, accessed October 2013.

Demers, Elizabeth, and Baruch Lev. 2001. "A Rude Awakening: Internet Shakeout in 2000." *Review of Accounting Studies* 6: 331–59.

DiBona, Chris, Danese Cooper, and Mark Stone. 2006. *Open Sources 2.0: The Continuing Evolution*. Sebastopol, CA: O'Reilly Media.

Doms, Mark. 2004. "The Boom and Bust in Information Technology Investment." *Federal Reserve Bank of San Francisco Economic Review* (February): 20–34.

Donaldson, Dean. 2008. *Internet Advertising History: Flash by Name, Cookies by Nature*. Bournemouth Media School, London, UK, page 10. http://nothingtohide.us/wp-content/uploads/2008/01/dd_unit-1_online_advertsing_history.pdf, accessed July 2012.

Downes, Tom, and Shane Greenstein. 1998. "Do Commercial ISPs Provide Universal Access?" In *Competition, Regulation, and Convergence: Current Trends in Telecommunications Policy Research*, edited by Sharon Gillett and Ingo Vogelsang, 195–212. Mahwah, NJ: Lawrence Erlbaum.

———. 2002. "Universal Access and Local Commercial Internet Markets." *Research Policy* 31: 1035–52.

———. 2007. "Understanding Why Universal Service Obligations May Be Unnecessary: The Private Development of Local Internet Access Markets." *Journal of Urban Economics* 62 (1): 2–26.

Drake, William. 1993. "The Internet Religious War." *Telecommunications Policy* (December): 643.

Economides, Nicholas. 2005. "The Economics of Internet Backbone." In *Handbook of Telecommunications Economics*, vol. 2, edited by Martin Cave, Sumit Majumdar, and Ingo Vogelsang. Boston: Elsevier.

Edwards, Paul N. 1997. *The Closed World: Computers and the Politics of Discourse in Cold War America*. Cambridge, MA: MIT Press.

Eichenwald, Kurt. 2005. *Conspiracy of Fools*. New York: Broadway Books.

Eisenach, Jeffrey, and Thomas Lenard. 1999. *Competition, Innovation, and the Microsoft Monopoly: Antitrust in the Digital Marketplace*. Boston: Kluwer Academic.

Eisner, James, and Tracy Waldon. 2001. "The Demand for Bandwidth: Second Telephone Lines and On-Line Services." *Information Economics and Policy* 13 (3): 301–9.

Elfenbein, Dan, and Josh Lerner. 2003. "Ownership and Control Rights in Internet Portal Alliances, 1995–1999." *RAND Journal of Economics* 32 (2): 356–69.

Evans, David, ed. 2002. *Microsoft, Antitrust, and the New Economy*. Boston: Kluwer Academic.

Evans, David, Franklin Fisher, Daniel Rubinfeld, and Richard Schmalensee. 2000. *Did Microsoft Harm Consumers? Two Opposing Views*. Washington, DC: AEI Press.

Faulhaber, Gerald, and David Farber. 2003. "Spectrum Management: Property Rights, Markets, and the Commons." In *Rethinking Rights and Regulations*, edited by Lorrie Faith Cranor and Steven Wildman, 193–226. Cambridge, MA: MIT Press.

Federal Communications Commission. 2010. "National Broadband Plan, Connecting America." http://www.broadband.gov/.

Ferguson, Charles. 1999. *High Stakes, No Prisoners: A Winner's Tale of Greed and Glory in the Internet Wars*. New York: Times Business.

Festa, Paul. 2001. "Is Google Ogling Yahoo's Crown?" CNET News, April 10. http://news.cnet.com/Is-Google-ogling-Yahoos-crown/2100-1023_3-2556 01.html.

Flamm, Ken. 1988. *Creating the Computer: Government, Industry, and High Technology*. Washington, DC: Brookings Institution Press.

Forman, Chris. 2005. "The Corporate Digital Divide: Determinants of Internet Adoption." *Management Science* 51 (4): 641–54.

Forman, Chris, and Avi Goldfarb. 2006. "Diffusion of Information and Communications Technology to Business." In *Economics and Information Systems*, vol. 1, edited by T. Hendershott. Amsterdam: Elsevier.

Forman, Chris, Avi Goldfarb, and Shane Greenstein. 2003a. "The Geographic Dispersion of Commercial Internet Use." In *Rethinking Rights and Regulations: Institutional Responses to New Communication Technologies*, edited by Lorrie Faith Cranor and Steven Wildman, 113–45. Cambridge, MA: MIT Press.

———. 2003b. "Which Industries Use the Internet?" In *Organizing the New Industrial Economy*, edited by Michael Baye, 47–72. Amsterdam: Elsevier.

———. 2005. "How Did Location Affect Adoption of the Commercial Internet? Global Village vs. Urban Leadership." *Journal of Urban Economics* 58 (3): 389–420.

———. 2008. "Understanding Inputs into Innovation: Do Cities Substitute for Internal Firm Resources?" *Journal of Economics and Management Strategy* 17 (2): 295–316.

Frana, Philip L. 2004. "Before the Web There Was Gopher." *IEEE Annals of the History of Computing* 26 (1): 20–41.

Frazer, Karen. 1995. *Building the NSFNet: A Partnership in High Speed Networking*. ftp://nic.merit.edu/nsfnet/final.report/.index.html.

Friedan, Robert. 2001. "The Potential for Scrutiny of Internet Peering Policies in Multilateral Forums." In *Communications Policy in Transition: The Internet and Beyond*, edited by Benjamin Compaine and Shane Greenstein, 159–94. Cambridge, MA: MIT Press.

———. 2002. "Revenge of the Bellheads: How the Netheads Lost Control of the Internet." *Telecommunications Policy* 26 (7–8): 425–44.

Frischmann, Brett. 2012. *Infrastructure: The Social Value of Shared Resources*. New York: Oxford University Press.

Gabel, David, and Florence Kwan. 2001. "Accessibility of Broadband Communication Services by Various Segments of the American Population." In *Communications Policy in Transition: The Internet and Beyond*, edited by Benjamin Compaine and Shane Greenstein, 295–320. Cambridge, MA: MIT Press.

Gates, William. 1995. "The Internet Tidal Wave," May 20. Internal Microsoft memo. Redmond, Washington. http://www.usdoj.gov/atr/cases/ms_exhibits.htm, government exhibit 20.

Gawer, Annabelle, and Michael Cusumano. 2002. *Platform Leadership: How Intel, Microsoft, and Cisco Drive Industry Innovation*. Boston: Harvard Business School Press.

Gawer, Annabelle, and Rebecca Henderson. 2007. "Platform Owner Entry and Innovation in Complementary Markets: Evidence from Intel." *Journal of Economics and Management Strategy* 16 (1): 1–34.

Gerstner, Louis V., Jr. 2002. *Who Says Elephants Can't Dance?* New York: HarperBusiness.

Gilder, George. 1989. *Microcosm: The Quantum Revolution in Economics and Technology*. New York: Touchstone.

———. 2000. *Telecosm: How Infinite Bandwidth Will Revolutionize Our World*. New York: Free Press.

Gillies, James, and Robert Cailliau. 2000. *How the Web Was Born*. Oxford: Oxford University Press.

Goldfarb, Avi. 2004. "Concentration in Advertising-Supported Online Markets: An Empirical Approach." *Economics of Innovation and New Technology* 13 (6): 581–94.

Goldfarb, Avi, and Catherine Tucker. 2011. "Privacy Regulation and Online Advertising." *Management Science* 57 (1): 57–71.

Goldfarb, Avi, and Mo Xiao. 2011. "Who Thinks about the Competition? Managerial Ability and Strategic Entry in US Local Telephone Markets." *American Economic Review* 101 (7): 3130–61.

Goldfarb, Brent, David Kirsch, and David Miller. 2007. "Was There Too Little Entry during the Dot Com Era?" *Journal of Financial Economics* 86 (1): 100–144.

Goldfarb, Brent D., David Kirsch, and Michael D. Pfarrer. 2005. "Searching for Ghosts: Business Survival, Unmeasured Entrepreneurial Activity, and Private Equity Investment in the Dot-Com Era." Robert H. Smith School Research Paper No. RHS 06-027. Available at SSRN: http://ssrn.com/abstract=825687.

Goldsmith, Jack, and Tim Wu. 2006. *Who Controls the Internet? Illusions of a Borderless World*. Oxford: Oxford University Press.

Goldstein, Fred R. 2005. *The Great Telecom Meltdown*. Boston: Artech House.

Gompers, Paul, and Josh Lerner. 2003. *The Venture Capital Cycle*. Cambridge, MA: MIT Press.

Goolsbee, Austan, and Peter Klenow. 1999. "Evidence on Learning and Network Externalities in the Diffusion of Home Computers." Working Paper No. 7329. National Bureau of Economic Research, Cambridge, MA.

Gorman, Sean P., and Edward J. Malecki. 2000. "The Networks of the Internet: An Analysis of Provider Networks in the USA." *Telecommunications Policy* 24 (2): 113–34.

Greenstein, Shane. 1999. "Virulent Word of Mouse." *IEEE Micro* 19 (6): 6–8.

———. 2000a. "Building and Delivering the Virtual World: Commercializing Services for Internet Access." *Journal of Industrial Economics* 48 (4): 391–411.

———. 2000b. "Empirical Evidence on Commercial Internet Access Providers' Propensity to Offer New Services." In *The Internet Upheaval: Raising Questions and Seeking Answers in Communications Policy*, edited by Ingo Vogelsang and Benjamin Compaine, 253–76. Cambridge, MA: MIT Press.

———. 2001. "Commercialization of the Internet: The Interaction of Public Policy and Private Actions." In *Innovation Policy and the Economy*, edited by Adam Jaffe, Josh Lerner, and Scott Stern, Cambridge, MA: MIT Press.

———. 2004. "The Salad Days of Online Shopping." In *Diamonds Are Forever, Computers Are Not: Economic and Strategic Management in Computing Markets*. London: Imperial College Press.

———. 2005. "The Economic Geography of Internet Infrastructure in the United States." In *Handbook of Telecommunications Economics*, vol. 2, edited by Martin Cave, Sumit Majumdar, and Ingo Vogelsang Boston: Elsevier.

———. 2008a. "Economic Experiments and Industry Know-How in Internet Access Markets." In *Innovation Policy and the Economy*, vol. 8, edited by Adam Jaffe, Josh Lerner, and Scott Stern, 59–109. Cambridge, MA: MIT Press.

———. 2008b. "The Evolution of Market Structure for Internet Access in the United States." In *The Commercialization of the Internet and Its Impact on American Business*, edited by William Aspray and Paul Ceruzzi, 47–104. Cambridge, MA: MIT Press.

———. 2010a. "The Emergence of the Internet: Collective Invention and Wild Ducks." *Industrial and Corporate Change* 19 (5): 1521–62.

———. 2010b. "Innovative Conduct in U.S. Commercial Computing and Internet Markets." In *Handbook of the Economics of Innovation*, edited by Bronwyn Hall and Nathan Rosenberg, 477–538. Burlington, VT: Academic Press.

Greenstein, Shane, and Michele Devereux. 2009. "The Crisis at Encyclopædia Britannica." Kellogg Case No. KEL251-PDF-ENG, Kellogg School of Management, Northwestern University.

Greenstein, Shane, and Michael Mazzeo. 2006. "The Role of Differentiation Strategy in Local Telecommunication Entry and Market Evolution, 1999–2002." *Journal of Industrial Economics* 54 (3): 323–50.

Greenstein, Shane, and Ryan McDevitt. 2012. "The Broadband Bonus: Estimating Broadband Internet's Economic Value." *Telecommunications Policy* 35: 617–32

Greenstein, Shane, and Frank Nagel. 2014. "Digital Dark Matter and the Economic Contribution of Apache." *Research Policy* 43: 623–31.

Greenstein, Shane, and Jeff Prince. 2006. "The Diffusion of the Internet and the Geography of the Digital Divide." In *Oxford Handbook on ICTs*, edited by Robin Mansell, Danny Quah, and Roger Silverstone. Oxford: Oxford University Press.

Greenstein, Shane, and Mark Rysman. 2006. "Coordination Costs and Standard Setting: Lessons from 56K." In *Standards and Public Policy*, edited by Shane Greenstein and Victor Stango. Cambridge: Cambridge University Press.

Grove, Andrew 1996. *Only the Paranoid Survive*. New York: Random House.

Grubesic, Tony H., and Alan T. Murray. 2002. "Constructing the Divide: Spatial Disparities in Broadband Access." *Papers in Regional Science* 81 (2): 197–221.

Hafner, Katie, and Matthew Lyon. 1998. *Where the Wizards Stay Up Late: The Origins of the Internet*. New York: Simon and Schuster.

Haigh, Thomas. 2008. "The Web's Missing Links: Search Engines and Portals." In *The Internet and American Business*, edited by William Aspray and Paul E. Ceruzzi, 159–200. Cambridge, MA: MIT Press.

Hansen, Jacob. 2009. "The Economics of Search Engines—Search, Ad Auctions, and Game Theory." Master's thesis, Copenhagen Business School, Applied Economics and Finance. http://avmediasearch.eu/public/files/jacob_hansen.pdf.

Hanson, Ward. 2000. *Principles of Internet Marketing*. Cincinnati, OH: South-Western College Publications.

Hao, Qing. 2007. "Laddering in Initial Public Offerings." *Journal of Financial Economics* 85: 102–22.

Hardwick, Don. 1996. Group Manager, OEM Sales Div., Microsoft Corp., to Celeste Dunn, Vice President, Consumer Software Business Unit, Compaq, June 6. http://www.usdoj.gov/atr/cases/exhibits/650.pdf, accessed July 2012.

Hauben, Michael, and Ronda Hauben. 1997. *Netizens: On the History and Impact of the Usenet and the Internet*. Piscataway, NJ: Wiley—IEEE Computer Society.

Heilemann, John. 2001. "Andy Grove's Rational Exuberance." Wired, June. http://www.wired.com/wired/archive/9.06/intel.html?pg=4&topic=&topic_set=, accessed August 2012.

Henderson, Rebecca. 2001. "Declaration of Rebecca Henderson." http://www.justice.gov/atr/cases/f219100/219129.htm, accessed November 2012.

Henry, D., and D. Dalton. 2002. Information Technology Industries in the New Economy. In U.S. Department of Commerce, Digital Economy. http://www.esa.doc.gov/reports.cfm, chapter 3.

Hills, Alex. 2005. "Smart Wi-Fi." *Scientific American*, October.

Hippel, Eric von. 1988. *The Sources of Innovation*. New York: Oxford University Press.

Hogendorn, Christiaan. 2005. "Regulating Vertical Integration in Broadband: Open Access versus Common Carriage." *Review of Network Economics* 4 (1).

———. 2011. "Excessive(?) Entry of National Telecoms Networks, 1990–2001." *Telecommunications Policy* 35 (11): 920–32.

Hu, Jim. 2000. "Yahoo Sheds Inktomi for New Search Technology." CNET News, June. http://news.cnet.com/Yahoo-sheds-Inktomi-for-new-search-technology/2100-1023_3-242392.html.

Hundt, Reed. 2000. *You Say You Want a Revolution: A Story of Information Age Politics*. New Haven, CT: Yale University Press.

Hussain, Farooq. 2003a. "CIX Router Timeline." http://www.farooqhussain.org/projects/CIX%20Router%20Timeline_0905.pdf, accessed July 2009.

———. 2003b. "Historic Role of the Commercial Internet eXchange Router and Its Impact on the Development of the Internet eXchange Points [IXCs]."

http://www.farooqhussain.org/projects/cixrouter19912001/index_html, accessed July 2007.

———. 2003c. "The Internet and the Router." http://www.farooqhussain.org /projects/peeringarchiv/0471215929.pdf/file_view, accessed May 2009.

InfoWorld. 1995a. "cc:Mail Users Will Get E-mail through Web," October 2, p. 12. http://books.google.com/books?id=XDoEAAAAMBAJ&pg=PA12#v=one page&q&f=false, accessed August 2012.

InfoWorld. 1995b. "Lotus cc:Mail to Get Better Server, Mobile Access," February 6, p. 8. http://books.google.com/books?id=sToEAAAAMBAJ&pg=PA8#v= onepage&q&f=false, accessed August 2012.

Ingram, Paul, Hayagreeva Rao, and Brian S. Silverman. 2012. "History in Strategy Research: What, Why, and How?" In *History and Strategy*. Vol. 29 of *Advances in Strategic Management*, edited by Michael A. Cusumano, Steven Kahl, and Brian S. Silverman. Bingley, UK: Emerald.

Jeter, Lynne. 2003. *Disconnected: Deceit and Betrayal at WorldCom*. Hoboken, NJ: John Wiley and Sons.

Junnarkar, Sandeep, and Tim Clark. 1999. "AOL Buys Netscape for $4.2 Billion." http://news.cnet.com/2100-1023-218360.html.

Jupiter Communications. 1997. Microsoft Internet Strategy Report: Implications for Technology and Developers. www.jup.com, July. Deborah Coplin, Peter Dushkin, Ross Rubin.

Kahin, Brian. 1992. *Building Information Infrastructure: Issues in the Development of the National Research and Education Network*. Cambridge, MA: McGraw-Hill Primis.

———. 1997. "The U.S. National Information Infrastructure Initiative: The Market, the Web, and the Virtual Project." In *National Information Infrastructure Initiatives, Vision, and Policy Design*, edited by Brian Kahin and Ernest Wilson, 150–89. Cambridge, MA: MIT Press.

Kahl, Steven, Joanne Yates, and Greg Liegel. 2012. "Audience Structure and the Failure of Institutional Entrepreneurship." In *History and Strategy*. Vol. 29 of *Advances in Strategic Management*, edited by Michael A. Cusumano, Steven Kahl, and Brian S. Silverman. Bingley, UK: Emerald.

Kaplan, Philip J. 2002. *F'd Companies: Spectacular Dot-Com Flameouts*. New York: Simon and Schuster.

Kawamoto, Dawn, and Stefanie Olsen. 2003. CNET News, April 23. "Google Snaps Up Applied Semantics." http://news.cnet.com/2100-1032-998114.html, accessed July 2012.

Kende, Michael. 2000. "The Digital Handshake: Connecting Internet Backbones." Working Paper No. 32. Washington, DC: Federal Communications Commission, Office of Planning and Policy.

Kenney, Martin. 2003. "The Growth and Development of the Internet in the United States." In *The Global Internet Economy*, edited by Bruce Kogut. Cambridge, MA: MIT Press.

Kesan, Jay P., and Rajiv C. Shah. 2001. "Fool Us Once, Shame on You—Fool Us Twice, Shame on Us: What We Can Learn from the Privatizations of the Internet Backbone Network and the Domain Name System." *Washington University Law Quarterly* 79: 89–220.

———. 2004. "Deconstructing Code." *Illinois Public Law and Legal Theory Research Papers Series*, Research Paper No. 04-22. September 29.

Kharif, Olga. 2003. "Paving the Airwaves for Wi-Fi." *Business Week*, April 1.

Kirsch, David, and Brent Goldfarb. 2008. "Small Ideas, Big Ideas, Bad Ideas, Good Ideas: 'Get Big Fast' and Dot Com Venture Creation." In *The Internet and American Business*, edited by William Aspray and Paul Ceruzzi. Cambridge, MA: MIT Press.

Krol, Ed. 1987. "Hitchhiker's Guide to the Internet." August 25. http://www.textfiles.com/internet/hitchhik.gui, accessed March 2015.

———. 1992. *The Whole Internet: User's Guide and Catalog*. Sebastopol, CA: O'Reilly and Associates.

———. 1994. *The Whole Internet: User's Guide and Catalog*, 2nd ed. Sebastopol, CA: O'Reilly and Associates.

Kuchinskas, Susan. 2004. "Yahoo and Google Settle." InternetNews.com, August 9. http://www.internetnews.com/bus-news/article.php/3392781.

Laffont, Jean-Jacque, Scott Marcus, Patrick Rey, and Jean Tirole. 2001. "Internet Peering." *American Economic Review, Papers and Proceedings* 91: 287–92.

———. 2003. "Internet Interconnection and the Off-Net Pricing Principle." *Rand Journal of Economics* 34 (2): 370–90.

Leblebici, Huseyin. 2012. "The Evolution of Alternative Business Models and the Legitimization of Universal Credit Card Industry: Exploring the Contested Terrain Where History and Strategy Meet." In *History and Strategy*. Vol. 29 of *Advances in Strategic Management*, edited by Michael A. Cusumano, Steven Kahl, and Brian S. Silverman. Bingley, UK: Emerald.

Leiner, Barry, Vinton Cerf, David Clark, Robert Kahn, Leonard Kleinrock, Daniel Lynch, Jon Postel, Larry Roberts, and Stephen Wolff. 2003. *A Brief History of the Internet, Version 3.32*. Last revised December 10, 2003. http://www.isoc.org/internet/history/brief.shtml.

Lemstra, Wolter, Vic Hayes, and John Groenewegen. 2010. *The Innovation Journey of Wi-Fi: The Road to Global Success*. Cambridge: Cambridge University Press.

Lerner, Josh, and Paul Gompers. 2003. "Short-Term America Revisited? Boom and Bust in the Venture Capital Industry and the Impact on Innovation." In *Innovation Policy and the Economy*, edited by Adam Jaffe, Josh Lerner, and Scott Stern, Cambridge, MA: MIT Press.

Lessig, Lawrence. 1999. *Code and Other Laws of Cyberspace*. New York: Basic Books.

Liebowitz, Stan, and Stephen Margolis. 2000. *Winners, Losers, and Microsoft*. Oakland, CA: Independent Institute.

Liu, Bob. 2001. "Is New Standard for 802.11 Out of Luck?" Internetnews, November 4. http://www.internetnews.com/wireless/article.php/10692_923821, accessed April 2007.

Liu, Xiaoding, and Jay R. Ritter. 2010. "The Economic Consequences of IPO Spinning." *Review of Financial Studies* 23 (5): 2024–59.

Mandelbaum, R., and P. A. Mandelbaum. 1992. "The Strategic Future of Mid-Level Networks." In *Building Information Infrastructure: Issues in the Development of the National Research and Education Network*, edited by Brian Kahin, 59–118. Cambridge, MA: McGraw-Hill Primis.

Maney, Kevin. 2003. *The Maverick and His Machine: Thomas Watson, Sr., and the Making of IBM*. New York: John Wiley and Sons.

Marcus, J. Scott. 1999. *Designing Wide Area Networks and Internetworks: A Practical Guide*. Reading, MA: Addison-Wesley.

Marcus, Michael. 2009. "Wi-Fi and Bluetooth: The Path from Carter and Reagan-Era Faith in Deregulation to Widespread Products Impacting Our World." *INFO* 11 (5): 19–35.

Marine, April, Susan Kilpatrick, Vivian Neou, and Carol Ward. 1993. *Internet: Getting Started*. Englewood Cliffs, NJ: PTR Prentice Hall.

Markoff, John. 1992. "Business Technology: Pools of Memory, Waves of Dispute." New York Times, January 29. http://www.nytimes.com/1992/01/29/business/business-technology-pools-of-memory-waves-of-dispute.html, accessed August 2012.

———. 2005. *What the Dormouse Said: How the Sixties Counterculture Shaped the Personal Computer Industry*. New York: Viking Penguin.

McCullagh, Declan. 1999. "Compaq: It Was All a Big Mix-Up." Wired, February 16. http://www.wired.com/politics/law/news/1999/02/17938.

———. 2000. "The Mother of Gore's Invention." Wired News, October 17. http://web.archive.org/web/20040603002249/http://www.wired.com/news/print/0,1294,39301,00.html, accessed January 16, 2015.

McElheran, Kristina S. 2011. "Do Market Leaders Lead in Business Process Innovation? The Case(s) of E-Business Adoption." Harvard Business School Working Paper No. 10-104.

McMillan, Robert. 2000. "Apache Power." *Linux Magazine*, April 15. http://www.linux-mag.com/id/472/, accessed September 2013.

McWilliams, Brian. 1998. "Software Execs Trade Barbs in Senate Hearings." PCWorld, March 4. http://www.pcworld.com/article/6148/software_execs_trade_barbs_in_senate_hearings.html.

Meeker, Mary, and Chris DePuy. 1996. *The Internet Report*. New York: HarperBusiness.

Meyer, Peter. 2003. "Episodes of Collective Invention." US Bureau of Labor Statistics Working Paper No. 368. Available at SSRN: http://ssrn.com/abstract=466880, downloaded August 2008.

Mockus, Audris, Roy T. Fielding, and James D. Herbsleb. 2005. "Two Case Studies of Open Source Software Development: Apache and Mozilla." In *Perspectives on Free and Open Source Software*, edited by Joseph Feller. Cambridge, MA: MIT Press.

Mosier, Steve. 2004. "Telecommunications and Computers: A Tale of Convergence." In *Chasing Moore's Law: Information Technology Policy in the United States*, edited by William Aspray, 29–54. Raleigh, NC: SciTech Publishing.

Mowery, D. C., and T. S. Simcoe. 2002. "The Origins and Evolution of the Internet." In *Technological Innovation and Economic Performance*, edited by R. Nelson, B. Steil, and D. Victor. Princeton, NJ: Princeton University Press.

Mueller, Milton. 2004. *Ruling the Root: Internet Governance and the Taming of Cyberspace*. Cambridge, MA: MIT Press.

National Research Council of the National Academies. 2003. *Innovation in Information Technology*. Washington, DC: National Academy Press.

National Telecommunications and Information Administration (NTIA). 1995. "Falling through the Net: A Survey of the 'Have Nots' in Rural and Urban America." http://www.ntia.doc.gov/reports.html.

———. 1997. "Falling through the Net: Defining the Digital Divide." http://www.ntia.doc.gov/reports.html.

———. 1998. "Falling through the Net II: New Data on the Digital Divide." http://www.ntia.doc.gov/reports.html.

———. 2000. "Falling through the Net: Toward Digital Inclusion." http://www.ntia.doc.gov/report/2000/falling-through-net-toward-digital-inclusion.

———. 2002. "A Nation Online: How Americans Are Expanding Their Use of the Internet." http://www.ntia.doc.gov/reports.html.

———. 2004. "A Nation Online: Entering the Broadband Age." http://www.ntia.doc.gov/reports.html.

Nelson, Richard. 2007. "On the Evolution of Human Know-How." Mimeo, Columbia University.

New Paradigm Resources Group. 2000. *CLEC Report*, Chicago, Illinois.

Nicholas, Kyle. 2000. "Stronger Than Barbed Wire: How Geo-Policy Barriers Construct Rural Internet Access." In *Communications Policy and Information Technology: Promises, Problems, Prospects*, edited by Lorrie Faith Cranor and Shane Greenstein, 299–316. Cambridge, MA: MIT Press.

Noam, Eli. 2001. *Interconnecting the Network of Networks*. Cambridge, MA: MIT Press.

Nocera, Joe. 2013. "Rigging the IPO Game." *New York Times*, March 9. http://www.nytimes.com/2013/03/10/opinion/sunday/nocera-rigging-the-ipo-game.html?_r=0, accessed February 2014.

Noll, G. Roger, and Bruce M. Owen. 1989. "The Anticompetitive Uses of Regulation: United States v. AT&T (1982)." In *The Antitrust Revolution*, edited by John E. Kwoka Jr. and Lawrence J. White. Glenview, IL: Scott, Foresman.

Norberg, Arthur, Judy O'Neill, and Kerry Freedman. 1996. *Transforming Computer Technology: Information Processing for the Pentagon, 1962–1986*. Baltimore: Johns Hopkins University Press.

Nuechterlein, Jonathan E., and Philip J. Weiser. 2005. *Digital Crossroads: American Telecommunications Policy in the Internet Age*. Cambridge, MA: MIT Press.

Odlyzko, Andrew. 2001. "Internet Growth: Myth and Reality, Use and Abuse." *Journal of Computer Resource Management* 102 (Spring): 23–27.

———. 2003. "Internet Traffic Growth: Sources and Implications." In *Optical Transmission Systems and Equipment for WDM Networking II*, edited by B. B. Dingel, W. Weiershausen, A. K. Dutta, and K.-I. Sato. *Proceedings SPIE* 5247: 1–15.

———. 2010. "Bubbles, Gullibility, and Other Challenges for Economics, Psychology, Sociology, and Information Sciences." *First Monday*, September 15. http://firstmonday.org/htbin/cgiwrap/bin/ojs/index.php/fm/article/viewArticle/3142/2603Results, accessed October 2012.

O'Donnell, Shawn. 2001. "Broadband Architectures, ISP Business Plans, and Open Access." In *Communications Policy in Transition: The Internet and Beyond*, edited by Benjamin Compaine and Shane Greenstein. Cambridge, MA: MIT Press.

OECD. 2000. Local Access Pricing and E-Commerce, July.

Owen, Bruce. 2002. "Broadband Mysteries." In *Broadband: Should We Regulate High-Speed Internet Access?*, edited by Robert W. Crandall and James H. Alleman, 9–38. Washington, DC: AEI-Brookings Center for Regulatory Studies.

Oxman, Jason. 1999. "The FCC and the Unregulation of the Internet." Working Paper 31. Washington, DC: Federal Communications Commission, Office of Planning and Policy.

Page, Lawrence, and Sergey Brin. 1998. "The Anatomy of a Large-Scale Hypertextual Web Search Engine." http://ilpubs.stanford.edu:8090/361/1/1998-8.pdf, accessed July 2012.

———. 2008. "The Anatomy of a Large-Scale Hypertextual Web Search Engine." Comput. Netw. ISDN Syst. (Netherlands), Computer Networks and ISDN Systems 30 (1–7): 107–17, 0169-7552 Elsevier, http://ilpubs.stanford.edu:8090/361/1/1998-8.pdf, accessed July 2012.

Page, Lawrence, Sergey Brin, Rajeev Motwani, and Terry Winograd. 1999 [dated January 29, 1998, last updated November 11, 1999]. *The PageRank Citation Ranking: Bringing Order to the Web.* Technical Report. Stanford InfoLab. http://ilpubs.stanford.edu:8090/422/1/1999-66.pdf.

Page, William, and John Lopatka. 2007. *The Microsoft Case: Antitrust, High Technology, and Consumer Welfare.* Chicago: University of Chicago Press.

Paltridge, Sam. 2006. "Internet Traffic Exchange: Market Developments and Measurement of Growth." Working Paper on Telecommunication and Information Service Policies. OECD, Paris.

Partridge, Craig. 2008. "The Technical Development of Internet Email." *IEEE Annals of the History of the Computing* 3 (2): 3-29.

Pelline, Jeff. 1997a. "WorldCom, AOL in Deal for CompuServe." CNET, September. http://news.cnet.com/WorldCom,-AOL-in-deal-for-CompuServe/2100-1001_3-203012.html.

———. 1997b. "Yahoo Buys Four11 for Free Email." CNET News, October 8. http://news.cnet.com/Yahoo-buys-Four11-for-free-email/2100-1023_3-204033.html?tag=mncol;txt, accessed August 2012.

Price, Lee, with George McKittrick. 2002. "Setting the Stage: The New Economy Endures Despite Reduced IT Investment." In chapter 1, Digital Economy 2002, Department of Commerce. http://www.esa.doc.gov/reports.cfm.

Prince, J. 2008. "Repeat Purchase Amid Rapid Quality Improvement: Structural Estimation of Demand for Personal Computers." *Journal of Economics and Management Strategy* 17 (1): 1–33.

Prince, Marcelo. 2006. "Where Are They Now: George Gilder." *Wall Street Journal*, May 8.

Quarterman, John S. 1990. *The Matrix: Computer Networks and Conferencing Systems Worldwide.* Bedford, MA: Digital Press.

Rajgopal, Shivaram, Suresh Kotha, and Mohan Venkatachalam. 2000. "The Relevance of Web Traffic for Stock Prices of Internet Firms." EFA 0304. Available at SSRN: http://ssrn.com/abstract=207989.

Ransdell, Eric. 1999. "Network Effects." *Fast Company.* http://www.fastcompany.com/magazine/27/neteffects.html.

Reinhart, Carmen, and Ken Rogoff. 2009. *This Time Is Different: Eight Centuries of Financial Folly*. Princeton, NJ: Princeton University Press.

Reuter, Jonathan. 2006. "Are IPO Allocations for Sale? Evidence from Mutual Funds." *Journal of Finance* 60: 2289–324.

Rich, Ben R., and Leo Janos. 1994. *Skunk Works: A Personal Memoir of My Years at Lockheed*. Boston: Back Bay Books.

Ritter, Jay. 1991. "The Long Run Performance of Initial Public Offerings." *Journal of Finance* 46 (1): 3–27.

Rivlin, Gary. 2002. "The Madness of King George." *Wired*, July.

Roland, Alex, with Philip Shiman. 2002. *Strategic Computing: DARPA and the Quest for Machine Intelligence, 1983–1993*. Cambridge, MA: MIT Press.

Rosenberg, Nathan. 1977. "The Direction of Technological Change: Inducement Mechanisms and Focusing Devices." In Perspectives on Technology. Cambridge: Cambridge University Press.

———. 1992. "Economic Experiments." *Industrial and Corporate Change* 1 (1): 181–203.

———. 1996. "Uncertainty and Technology Change." In *The Mosaic of Economic Growth*, edited by Ralph Landau, Timothy Taylor, and Gavin Wright, 334–56. Stanford, CA: Stanford University Press.

Rosenbloom Richard, and Michael A. Cusumano. 1987. "Technological Pioneering and Competitive Advantage: The Birth of the VCR Industry." *California Management Review* 29 (4): 51–76.

Rosston, Greg. 2009. "The Rise and Fall of Third Party High-Speed Access." *Information and Economic Policy* 21 (1): 21–33.

Rubinfeld, Daniel. 2004. "Maintenance of Monopoly: US vs. Microsoft (2001)." In *The Antitrust Revolution*, 4th ed., edited by John Kwoka and Larry White. New York: Oxford University Press.

Russell, Andrew L. 2006. "Rough Consensus and Running Code and the Internet-OSI Standards War." *IEEE Annals of the History of Computing* (July–September): 48–61.

———. 2014. *Open Standards and the Digital Age: History, Ideology, and Networks*. New York: Cambridge University Press.

Saltzer, Jerome H., David P. Reed, and David D. Clark. 1984. "End-to-End Arguments in System Design." *ACM Transactions on Computer Systems* 2 (4): 277–88. An earlier version appeared in the *Second International Conference on Distributed Computing Systems* (April 1981), 509–12.

San Jose Mercury News. 1996. "Flat-Rate Pricing Keeps AOL's Lines Busy," December 20. http://chronicle.augusta.com/stories/1996/12/20/tec_201508.shtml, accessed November 2012.

Sandvig, Christian. 2004. "An Initial Assessment of Cooperative Action in Wi-Fi Networking." *Telecommunications Policy* 28 (7/8): 579–602.

———. 2007. "Wireless Play and Unexpected Innovation." Working Paper, University of Illinois. http://www.spcomm.uiuc.edu/csandvig/research/.

Sandvig, Christian, David Young, and Sascha Meinrath. 2004. "Hidden Interfaces in Ownerless Networks." Paper Presented to the 32nd Annual Telecommunications Policy Research Conference (TPRC) on Communication, Infor-

mation, and Internet Policy, Arlington, Virginia. http://www.spcomm.uiuc
.edu/csandvig/research/.

Schmidt, Eric, Jonathan Rosenberg, and Alan Eagle. 2014. *How Google Works.*
New York: Grand Central Publishing.

Schneider, Karen G. 1996. *The Internet Access Cookbook.* New York: Neal-Schuman
Publishers.

Schwartz, John. 2001. "See Giving Web a Memory Cost Its Users Privacy." *New
York Times,* September 4. http://www.nytimes.com/2001/09/04/business
/giving-web-a-memory-cost-its-users-privacy.html?pagewanted=1, accessed
July 2012.

Segaller, Stephen. 1998. *Nerds 2.0.1: A Brief History of the Internet.* New York: TV
Books.

Shapiro, Carl, and Hal Varian. 1999. *Information Rules: A Strategic Guide to the
Network Economy.* Boston: Harvard Business School Press.

Shiman, Daniel, and Jessica Rosenworcel. 2002. "Assessing the Effectiveness
of Section 271 Five Years after the Telecommunications Act of 1996." In
*Communications Policy and Information Technology: Promises, Problems, and
Prospects,* edited by Lorrie Faith Cranor and Shane Greenstein. Cambridge,
MA: MIT Press.

Sidak Gregory. 2003. "The Failure of Good Intentions: The WorldCom Fraud
and the Collapse of American Telecommunications after Deregulation."
Yale Journal of Regulation 20: 207–67.

Siegler, M. G. 2010. "More on AOL's Disk Strategy." *Tech Crunch.* http://tech
crunch.com/2010/12/28/aol-floppy-disk/, accessed February 2014.

Simcoe, Timothy. 2006. "Delay and *de jure* Standardization: Exploring the Slowdown in Internet Standards Development." In *Standards and Public Policy,*
edited by Shane Greenstein and Victor Stango. Cambridge: Cambridge University Press.

Sink, Eric. 2007. "Memoirs from the Browser Wars." http://biztech.ericsink
.com/Browser_Wars.html, accessed March 2007.

Stern, Scott. 2004. "Do Scientists Pay to Be Scientists?" *Management Science* 50
(6): 835–53.

———. 2005. "Economic Experiments: The Role of Entrepreneurship in Economic Prosperity." In *Understanding Entrepreneurship: A Research and Policy
Report.* Kaufman Foundation. http://research.kauffman.org/cwp/Show
Property/web/CacheRepository/Documents/Research__Policy_Singles
.pdf.

Stranger, Gregory, and Shane Greenstein. 2006. "Pricing at the On-Ramp for
the Internet: Price Indices for ISPs in the 1990s." In *Essays in Memory of Zvi
Griliches,* edited by Ernst Berndt, Chuck Hulten, and Manuel Trajtenberg.
Chicago: University of Chicago Press.

———. 2007. "Pricing in the Shadow of Firm Turnover: ISPs in the 1990s."
International Journal of Industrial Organization 26 (3): 625–42.

Strover, Sharon. 2001. "Rural Internet Connectivity." *Telecommunications Policy*
25 (5): 331–47.

Strover, Sharon, Michael Oden, and Nobuya Inagaki. 2002. "Telecommunications and Rural Economies: Findings from the Appalachian Region." In

Communication Policy and Information Technology: Promises, Problems, Prospects, edited by Lorrie Faith Cranor and Shane Greenstein. Cambridge, MA: MIT Press.

Sullivan, Danny. 2003. "Where Are They Now? Search Engines That We've Known and Loved." *Search Engine Watch*, March 3. http://searchengine watch.com/article/2064954/Where-Are-They-Now-Search-Engines-Weve -Known-Loved.

Swisher, Kara. 1998. *aol.com: How Steve Case Beat Bill Gates, Nailed the Netheads, and Made Millions in the War for the Web*. New York: Random House.

Temin, Peter, and Louis Galambos. 1987. *The Fall of the Bell System*. Cambridge: Cambridge University Press.

Thomke, Stephen. 2003a. *Experimentation Matters: Unlocking the Potential of New Technologies for Innovation*. Boston: Harvard Business School Press.

———. 2003b. "R&D Comes to Services: Bank of America's Pathbreaking Experiments." *Harvard Business Review* 81 (4).

Trajtenberg, Manuel, and Ernst Berndt. 2001. "In Memoriam: Zvi Griliches (1930–1999)." *Journal of Economic and Social Measurement* 27 (3–4): 93–97.

Turner, Fred. 2006. *From Counterculture to Cyber-Culture*. Chicago: University of Chicago Press.

United States Court of Appeals. 2001. For the District of Columbia Circuit, June 28. http://www.justice.gov/atr/cases/f257900/257941.htm, accessed November 2012.

Updegrove, A. 2007. "Product Evolution and Standards Swarms." http:// consortiuminfo.org/blog/blog/php?ID=45, January 31.

US Department of Agriculture. 2000. "Advanced Telecommunications in Rural America, The Challenge of Bringing Broadband Communications to All of America." http://www.ntia.doc.gov/reports/ruralbb42600.pdf.

US Department of Commerce. 2005. Statistical Abstract of the United States, 125th ed.

Varian, Hal R. 2006. "The Economics of Internet Search." *Rivista di Politica Economica* (November–December): 177–191.

———. 2010. "Richard T. Ely Lecture: Computer Mediated Transaction." *American Economic Review: Papers and Proceedings* 100: 1–10.

Waldrop, Mitchell. 2001. *The Dream Machine: J.C.R. Licklider and the Revolution That Made Computing Personal*. New York: Penguin.

Watson, Thomas J., Jr. 1963. *A Business and Its Beliefs: The Ideas That Helped Build IBM*. New York: McGraw-Hill.

Werbach, Kevin. 1997. *A Digital Tornado: The Internet and Telecommunications Policy*. FCC, Office of Planning and Policy Working Paper 29, March.

West, Joel. 2007. "The Economic Realities of Open Standards: Black, White, and Many Shades of Gray." In *Standards and Public Policy*, edited by Shane Greenstein and Victor Stango, 260–95. Cambridge: Cambridge University Press.

Wiggins, Richard. 2000. "Al Gore and the Creation of the Internet." *First Monday*, October 2. http://firstmonday.org/htbin/cgiwrap/bin/ojs/index. php/fm/article/view/799/708, accessed October 2012.

Wilder, Clinton. 1995. "Deal with Spry Give Online Service Provider Access to Internet Software." InformationWeek. http://www.informationweek.com

/520/20iucom.htm; jsessionid=VXM1INNH25RMSQSNDLRSKH0CJUN N2JVN, accessed August 2009.

Wladawsky-Berger, Irving. 2005. "The IBM Internet Division." http://blog .irvingwb.com/blog/2005/11/the_ibm_interne.html, accessed October 2012.

Woolley, Scott. 2001. "Digital Hubris." *Forbes*, May 28.

Woroch, Glenn. 2001. "Local Network Competition." In *Handbook of Telecommunications Economics*, edited by Martin Cave, Sumit Majumdar, and Ingo Vogelsang, 642–715. Boston: Elsevier Publishing.

Zittrain, Jonathan. 2009. *The Future of the Internet—And How to Stop It*. New Haven, CT: Yale University Press.

Zook, Matthew. 2005. *The Geography of the Internet Industry*. Malden, MA: Blackwell Publishing.

Index

Note: Page numbers followed by "f" or "t" denote figures and tables, respectively